PATERNOSTER THEOLOGICAL MONOGRAPHS

Providence Made Flesh

Divine Presence as a Framework for a Theology of Providence

PATERNOSTER THEOLOGICAL MONOGRAPHS

A full listing of all titles in this series and Paternoster Biblical Monographs appears at the close of this book.

PATERNOSTER THEOLOGICAL MONOGRAPHS

Providence Made Flesh

Divine Presence as a Framework for a Theology of Providence

Terry J. Wright

Foreword by Nigel G. Wright

WIPF & STOCK · Eugene, Oregon

Wipf and Stock Publishers
199 W 8th Ave, Suite 3
Eugene, OR 97401

Providence Made Flesh
Divine Presence as a Framework for a Theology of Providence
By Wright, Terry J.
Copyright©2009 Paternoster
ISBN 13: 978-1-60899-160-0
Publication date 10/29/2009
Previously published by Paternoster, 2009

"This Edition published by Wipf and Stock Publishers
by arrangement with Paternoster"

PATERNOSTER THEOLOGICAL MONOGRAPHS

Series Preface

In the West the churches may be declining, but theology—serious, academic (mostly doctoral level) and mainstream orthodox in evaluative commitment—shows no sign of withering on the vine. This series of *Paternoster Theological Monographs* extends the expertise of the Press especially to first-time authors whose work stands broadly within the parameters created by fidelity to Scripture and has satisfied the critical scrutiny of respected assessors in the academy. Such theology may come in several distinct intellectual disciplines—historical, dogmatic, pastoral, apologetic, missional, aesthetic and no doubt others also. The series will be particularly hospitable to promising constructive theology within an evangelical frame, for it is of this that the church's need seems to be greatest. Quality writing will be published across the confessions—Anabaptist, Episcopalian, Reformed, Arminian and Orthodox—across the ages—patristic, medieval, reformation, modern and counter-modern—and across the continents. The aim of the series is theology written in the twofold conviction that the church needs theology and theology needs the church—which in reality means theology done for the glory of God.

Series Editors

† David F. Wright, Emeritus Professor of Patristic and Reformed Christianity, University of Edinburgh, Scotland, UK

Trevor A. Hart, Head of School and Principal of St Mary's College School of Divinity, University of St Andrews, Scotland, UK

Anthony N.S. Lane, Professor of Historical Theology and Director of Research, London School of Theology, UK

Anthony C. Thiselton, Emeritus Professor of Christian Theology, University of Nottingham, Research Professor in Christian Theology, University College Chester, and Canon Theologian of Leicester Cathedral and Southwell Minster, UK

Kevin J. Vanhoozer, Research Professor of Systematic Theology, Trinity Evangelical Divinity School, Deerfield, Illinois, USA

To Ruth and Isaac

Contents

Foreword by Nigel G. Wright	xiii
Preface	xv
Abbreviations	xvii

Chapter 1: Secondary Causation in the Doctrine of Providence — 1
§ 1.1 Introduction — 1
§ 1.2 The Doctrine of Providence in Reformed Doctrinal Statements — 2
§ 1.3 The Threefold Scheme of Providence — 6
§ 1.4 Primary and Secondary Causation — 8
§ 1.5 The Question of Mediation — 13
§ 1.6 The Aim and Structure of this Study — 16

Chapter 2: The 'Proper Place' of Secondary Causation in the Theology of John Calvin — 23
§ 2.1 Introduction — 23
§ 2.2 God's Fundamental Relation to the World — 26
§ 2.3 God's Providence and the Fall of Creation — 33
§ 2.4 God's Providence and the Restoration of Creation — 42
§ 2.5 Conclusion — 49

Chapter 3: Secondary Causation and the Displacement of God — 55
§ 3.1 Introduction — 55
§ 3.2 From Geneva to England — 57
§ 3.3 Resisting the Reformed — 61
§ 3.4 Secondary Causation or Natural Occurrence? — 67
§ 3.5 Locating the Problem — 72
§ 3.6 Conclusion — 78

Chapter 4: Secondary Causation and the Action of the Triune God — 79
§ 4.1 Introduction — 79
§ 4.2 Causal Distinctions — 80
§ 4.3 The Ordering of Creation — 85
§ 4.4 Causation and Analogy — 91
§ 4.5 Searching for a Place to Act — 96
§ 4.6 Changing Conceptual Frameworks — 105
§ 4.7 Conclusion — 109

Chapter 5: Mediating the Presence of God — 113
§ 5.1 Introduction — 113
§ 5.2 Extending the Garden — 115
§ 5.3 God's Presence in Christ — 123
§ 5.4 Christ, the Holy Spirit and the Church — 131
§ 5.5 Conclusion — 135

Chapter 6: Providence and the Faithfulness of God — 137
§ 6.1 Introduction — 137
§ 6.2 The Calling of Israel: Presence, Covenant and Law — 138
§ 6.3 The Law Opposed: Galatians 3:1-18 — 145
§ 6.4 The Law Ousted: Galatians 3:19-29 — 156
§ 6.5 A Faithfulness Embodied — 163
§ 6.6 Conclusion — 165

Chapter 7: Providence and the Faithfulness of Jesus Christ — 167
§ 7.1 Introduction — 167
§ 7.2 The *ḥaṭṭā't* Offering: Leviticus 4 — 168
§ 7.3 The Day of Atonement: Leviticus 16 — 175
§ 7.4 Jesus, Our High Priest: Hebrews 1–7 — 179
§ 7.5 Jesus, Our Sacrifice: Hebrews 8–10 — 184
§ 7.6 A Faithfulness Emulated — 188
§ 7.7 Conclusion — 191

Chapter 8: Providence and the Faithfulness of the Holy Spirit — 193
§ 8.1 Introduction — 193
§ 8.2 The Person of the Mediator in the Theology of John Calvin — 195
§ 8.3 The Divided Mediator — 203
§ 8.4 The Spirit and Christ's Obedience: Matthew's Gospel — 208
§ 8.5 A Faithfulness Empowered — 215
§ 8.6 Conclusion — 218

Chapter 9: Shaping a Theology of Providence — 221
§ 9.1 Introduction — 221
§ 9.2 Summary of the Argument — 221
§ 9.3 Potential Objections — 223
§ 9.4 Clearing the Ground for a Theology of Providence — 225
§ 9.5 Providence and the Intensity of God's Presence — 229

Bibliography — 233

Index — 261

Foreword

In this fine and beautifully written book, Dr Terry Wright offers us a new framework within which to address the Christian doctrine of divine providence. In doing so, he demonstrates a clear understanding of the theology of significant Christian figures who have shaped this doctrine in times past, and indicates why and how their accounts fall short, in his analysis, of a fully biblical and Trinitarian approach to the subject. The argument he puts forward is a coherent contribution towards re-imagining and re-expressing this doctrine.

Dr Wright's intention is simultaneously modest and far-reaching. It is modest in that it claims only to be offering a framework for a new construction of the doctrine rather than a fully worked out doctrine itself. Despite this, there are a number of indications here of where such a doctrine might lead, and we are entitled to look forward to further development of the author's theme. It is far-reaching in that if his proposal finds acceptance it suggests distinctive ways for approaching an old and important doctrine in such a way as to safeguard the integrity of creation and its human inhabitants whilst in no way losing sight of the faithfulness of creation's God to the things that have been made.

Theologians must continually take into account how our forms of speaking of divine realities perpetually obscure as well as clarify truthful expression. It may be that speaking of divine agency, the ways God acts within the world, is a particularly difficult instance of this general problem. God is not one agent among others but the foundation and ground of all agency. The danger constantly to hand in speaking of the Living God is that of trivialising the One who is inscrutable and ineffable. At the same time there is that which needs to be said and which to leave unsaid would lead to profound impoverishment. By re-focusing the discussion about the ways in which God governs and accompanies the projects both of creation and redemption, Terry Wright allows us to find a way in which we may speak of God's providential action in a way that does not trivialise the language of divine action. This is a contribution to be welcomed and it gives promise of writing yet to come by this able theologian. I am very pleased to commend both the book and the author to their readership.

Nigel G. Wright
Spurgeon's College, London
April 2009

PREFACE

This volume began its life as a Ph.D thesis at Spurgeon's College in south London, submitted for examination in October 2007. I am grateful to Nigel Wright, the College's Principal, for his impeccable supervision; to John Colwell for continually challenging me; and to Judy Powles for always providing fine service when I sought obscure journal articles.

During my doctoral registration, I was also employed by the Methodist Church of Great Britain. My former colleagues were extremely supportive of my research, and I wish especially to mention Jane Bates, Peter Relf, Margaret Jones, Joy Barrow, David Rudiger and Peter Heath.

Completing a Ph.D thesis is quite the character- and stamina-building exercise. I would not have fared quite so well without continuous encouragement, support and advice from my friends: David Southall, Chris Walker, Jon Horne, Lincoln Harvey, Lindsey Hall, David McIlroy, Tim Keene, and Ben and Kelly Sargent.

There are others – many others! – whom I wish to thank. My doctoral examination was conducted by Trevor Hart and Peter Stevenson, and I still recall how enjoyable (yes, that is the right adjective) they made the occasion for me. Stephen Wright and Tom Smail provided insightful comments on early drafts of chapters six and eight respectively. John Coffey read an early draft of chapter three. Allan Coppedge allowed me to see an electronic version of his (at the time of writing) forthcoming book, *The God Who is Triune: Revisioning the Christian Doctrine of God*. Paul Cumin provided me with an electronic copy of the relevant parts of his own Ph.D thesis, *Christ at the Crux: The Mediation of Creator and Creation in Systematic Christological Perspective*. I have also benefited from brief e-mail conversations with Paul Helm (on John Calvin and causation), Stephen Holmes and Anthony Lane (on Gottschalk and Calvin), and David Pailin and Peter Byrne (on deism). Robin Parry and Anthony R. Cross from Paternoster have patiently responded to my queries regarding the publication process.

Finally, I cannot neglect to mention Ruth, who has never ceased to accommodate my enthusiasm for academic study and the perplexing diffidence that seems always to accompany it. Just over a month after my doctoral examination, Isaac was born, and has proved to be a delight – and a handful – ever since. It is to Ruth and Isaac, my family, that I dedicate this work.

Terry J. Wright
Associate Research Fellow,
Spurgeon's College, London
April 2009

ABBREVIATIONS

The following abbreviations for edited book series appear in the footnotes of the main text and in the bibliography. Abbreviations of journals titles are not used.

ABC	Anchor Bible Commentary
ASHPT	Ashgate Studies in the History of Philosophical Theology
BIS	Biblical Interpretation Series
BNTC	Black's New Testament Commentaries
BRS	The Biblical Resource Series
BST	The Bible Speaks Today
BTCL	Biblical and Theological Classics Library
CCT	Contours of Christian Theology
CIT	Current Issues in Theology
CPEL	The Christian Practice of Everyday Life Series
CSCD	Cambridge Studies in Christian Doctrine
CTHP	Cambridge Texts in the History of Philosophy
CTS	Calvin Translation Society
ESCT	Edinburgh Studies in Constructive Theology
HBM	Hebrew Bible Monographs
HCT	The History of Christian Theology
ILP	International Library of Philosophy
JPTS	Journal for Pentecostal Theology Supplement Series
JSNTS	Journal for the Study of the New Testament Supplement Series
JSOTS	Journal for the Study of the Old Testament Supplement Series
LCC	Library of Christian Classics
LPT	Library of Philosophy and Theology
NIB	New Interpreter's Bible
NICNT	New International Commentary on the New Testament
NIGTC	New International Greek Testament Commentary
NSBT	New Studies in Biblical Theology
NTC	New Testament Commentary
NTG	New Testament Guides
NTT	New Testament Theology

OBS	The Oxford Bible Series
OCT	Outstanding Christian Thinkers
ORP	Oxford Readings in Philosophy
OSHT	Oxford Studies in Historical Theology
OTG	Old Testament Guides
OTL	The Old Testament Library
OHM	Oxford Historical Monographs
OTM	Oxford Theological Monographs
PBM	Paternoster Biblical Monographs
PBTM	Paternoster Biblical and Theological Monographs
PHC	The Penguin History of the Church
RANBC	Readings: A New Biblical Commentary
RILP	Roehampton Institute London Papers
RP	Religious Perspectives
RRS	Reason and Religion Series
RRSS	Routledge Religious Studies Series
SCHT	Studies in Christian History and Thought
SEHT	Studies in Evangelical History and Thought
SHCT	Studies in the History of Christian Traditions
SHS	Scripture and Hermeneutic Series
SHT	Studies in Historical Theology
SJT / CIT	*Scottish Journal of Theology* Current Issues in Theology
SNTSMS	Society for New Testament Studies Monograph Series
TBS	The Biblical Seminar
TOTC	Tyndale Old Testament Commentaries
TNTC	Tyndale New Testament Commentaries
UNDSPR	University of Notre Dame Studies in the Philosophy of Religion
WBC	Word Biblical Commentary

CHAPTER 1

Secondary Causation in the Doctrine of Providence

§ 1.1 Introduction

God provides. These two words, which constitute the heart of the Christian doctrine of providence, immediately present us with two questions: *What* does God provide and *how* does he provide it?

One prevalent and important response to these questions posits the existence of secondary causes. This term refers to 'the causal powers of created things', that is, to use Paul Helm's examples, 'the power of the seed to germinate, of a person to be angry or to walk down the street, and so on';[1] but because this type of causation is labelled *secondary*, there is presupposed the existence also of *primary* causation, most commonly identified with the sovereign will of God.[2] Accordingly, the response to our second question of *how* God provides simply points to the divine will to act through secondary causes; but as each and every creaturely action or event constitutes secondary causation, it appears that *what* God provides is in fact *everything*.

This contention may prove comforting. Certainly, the notion that nothing happens without God's direct involvement means that we can be sure that whatever good happens to us is by God's provision. It also means, of course, that we must be willing to accept the converse, that God wills that we be afflicted, harmed, tormented. Commenting on Psalm 88:6, John Calvin notes that the Psalmist 'acknowledges more distinctly, that whatever adversities he endured proceeded from the Divine hand'; indeed, the Psalmist can only seek relief from God because he is first persuaded that 'it is the Divine hand which smites him, and that nothing happens by chance.'[3] Perhaps strangely, the accuracy of Calvin's conviction is not our main concern. There is always a danger that providence will be interpreted using categories appropriate to theodicy, with the concomitant danger that the doctrine itself is reduced simply to a justification of God's involvement in (negative) creaturely affairs. Instead, our immediate concern is the possibility that the claim that God *blesses*, that God *afflicts*, that God *acts* in fact reduces creaturely activity merely to instrumentality and negates any causal efficacy that might be attributed to it. Is

---

[1] P. Helm, *The Providence of God* (CCT; Leicester: IVP, 1993), 86.
[2] See § 1.5.
[3] J. Calvin, *Commentary on the Book of Psalms, Vol. 3* in *Calvin's Commentaries* V (CTS; Grand Rapids: Baker Books, 2003), 411.

such an undesirable possibility truly a corollary of the more positive statement that God provides?

§ 1.2 The Doctrine of Providence in Reformed Doctrinal Statements

Apart from one exception, the term 'providence' (in Greek, πρόνοια; in Latin, *providentia*) is not found in Scripture; but it is certainly a biblical concept.[4] Indeed, 'ideas of divine provision and government are implicit' throughout the Old and New Testaments.[5] This emphasis on active provision and government suggests that God's providence is not merely the divine foreseeing of the future; as Karl Barth, referring to Genesis 22, notes, providence is 'an active and selective predetermining', a 'to see about' but not a 'to see'.[6] For Barth, 'providence' means 'the superior dealings of the Creator with His creation, the wisdom, omnipotence and goodness with which He maintains and governs in time this distinct reality according to the counsel of His own will.'[7] Barth's concise definition remains true to his roots in the Reformed tradition,[8] alluding to certain important emphases of many of its doctrinal statements. The Belgic Confession, for example, affirms that God has

> given all creatures their being, form, and appearance, and their various functions for serving their Creator. Even now he also sustains and governs them all, according to his eternal providence, and by his infinite power, that they may serve man, in order that man may serve God.[9]

---

[4] M.J. Langford, *Providence* (London: SCM Press, 1981), 39–42. The one instance of πρόνοια in the Protestant canon is found in Acts 24:2, where it refers to human foresight. Outside the Protestant canon, references are found, for example, in Wisdom of Solomon 14:3; 17:2; 3 Maccabees 4:21; 5:30; 4 Maccabees 9:24; 13:19; 17:22.

[5] Langford, *Providence*, 39, 41; quote from 39.

[6] K. Barth, *Church Dogmatics* (13 vols.), edited by G.W. Bromiley and T.F. Torrance (Edinburgh: T&T Clark, 1957–1975), III/3, 3.

[7] Barth, *Church Dogmatics*, III/3, 3.

[8] 'The historic identity of Reformed theology has always been expressed through public confessional documents such as the First and Second Helvetic Confessions, the *Consensus Tigurinus*, the Heidelberg Catechism, the Belgic Confession, the Canons of Dordt and the Westminster Standards. These were the production of committees and of historical circumstances and thus embody a certain theological catholicity; they certainly did not represent either the work or the thought of any one individual.' (C.R. Trueman, 'Calvin and Calvinism', in D.K. McKim [ed.], *The Cambridge Companion to John Calvin* [Cambridge: Cambridge University Press, 2004], 225–244 [225; emphasis original]). See also § 3.3, n. 49. Explicit mention of the Reformed tradition at this point should indicate the intellectual context in which this study is situated, however far from its established formulations it departs.

[9] 'Article 12: The Creation of All Things', *The Belgic Confession, 1561*, in J. Pelikan and V. Hotchkiss (eds.), *Creeds and Confessions of Faith in the Christian Tradition,*

Secondary Causation in the Doctrine of Providence 3

This inspires confidence that

> this good God, after he created all things, did not abandon them to chance or fortune but leads and governs them according to his holy will, in such a way that nothing happens in this world without his orderly arrangement.[10]

Turning to the Heidelberg Catechism, we see a declaration that 'the eternal Father of our Lord Jesus Christ ... upholds and sustains [all things] by his eternal counsel and providence'.[11] Here, providence is understood to mean

> The almighty and ever-present power of God whereby he still upholds, as it were by his own hand, heaven and earth together with all creatures, and rules in such a way that leaves and grass, rain and drought, fruitful and unfruitful years, food and drink, health and sickness, riches and poverty, and everything else, come to us not by chance but by his fatherly hand.[12]

Finally, the Westminster Confession of Faith asserts that

> God the great Creator of all things doth uphold, direct, dispose, and govern all creatures, actions, and things, from the greatest even to the least, by his most wise and holy providence, according to his infallible foreknowledge, and the free and immutable counsel of his own will, to the praise of the glory of his wisdom, power, justice, goodness, and mercy.[13]

Each of these three doctrinal statements, though devised in different circumstances, times and places during the course of almost a century, shares with one another certain features that Barth himself assimilated into his own theology of providence. There is a common emphasis that God's upholding and sustaining of the world is an act of divine power, unrivalled by anything that can be done by creatures. This power is qualified by God's wisdom, by his goodness, by his justice; God's rule is not tyrannical but benevolent, as he orchestrates all things in a particular but not haphazard way. The priority of God's will to arrange the world's affairs accordingly is absolutely crucial to the

---

Volume 2. Part Four: Creeds and Confessions of the Reformation Era (New Haven: Yale University Press, 2003), 411.

[10] 'Article 13: The Doctrine of God's Providence', *The Belgic Confession, 1561*, in Pelikan and Hotchkiss, *Creeds and Confessions of Faith in the Christian Tradition, Volume 2*, 412.

[11] 'Question 26', *The Heidelberg Catechism, 1563*, in Pelikan and Hotchkiss, *Creeds and Confessions of Faith in the Christian Tradition, Volume 2*, 433.

[12] 'Question 27', *The Heidelberg Catechism, 1563*, in Pelikan and Hotchkiss, *Creeds and Confessions of Faith in the Christian Tradition, Volume 2*, 434.

[13] 'Chapter 5: Of Providence, Article 1', *The Westminster Confession of Faith, 1647*, in Pelikan and Hotchkiss, *Creeds and Confessions of Faith in the Christian Tradition, Volume 2*, 612.

Reformed teaching on providence: it is only because God has willed the existence of something distinct from himself and wills not to abandon it that there can even be such a declaration of God's unceasing involvement in creaturely activity.

Barth's theology of providence draws from these earlier statements, but they themselves echo in various ways the theology of Calvin, who himself believed that God the Creator is also God the Governor and Preserver who 'sustains, nourishes, and cares for, everything he has made, even to the least sparrow.'[14] As such, 'God's providence ... is opposed to fortune and fortuitous happenings';[15] instead, 'all events are governed by God's secret plan.'[16] Tied in with this is Calvin's teaching on predestination:

> We call predestination God's eternal decree, by which he compacted with himself what he willed to become of each man. For all are not created in equal condition; rather, eternal life is foreordained for some, eternal damnation for others. Therefore, as any man has been created to one or the other of these ends, we speak of him as predestined to life or to death.[17]

As such, providence is the execution of God's eternal decree in created time and space. The Westminster Confession, for example, captures something of this in its declaration that 'God from all eternity did, by the most wise and holy counsel of his own will, freely, and unchangeably ordain whatsoever comes to pass',[18] including the foreordination of each person either to everlasting life or everlasting death.[19] Such a link between providence and predestination, though not unique or exclusive to it, pervades the Reformed tradition.[20] Providence

---

[14] J. Calvin, *Institutes of the Christian Religion* (2 vols.), translated by F.L. Battles (LCC XX / XXI; Philadelphia: The Westminster Press, 1960), 1:16:1, 197–198.

[15] Calvin, *Institutes*, 1:16:2, 198.

[16] Calvin, *Institutes*, 1:16:2, 199.

[17] Calvin, *Institutes*, 3:21:5, 926. We will explore Calvin's teaching on providence and predestination throughout § 2 and § 3.

[18] 'Chapter 3: Of God's Eternal Decree, Article 1', *The Westminster Confession of Faith, 1647*, in Pelikan and Hotchkiss, *Creeds and Confessions of Faith in the Christian Tradition, Volume 2*, 610.

[19] 'Chapter 3: Of God's Eternal Decree, Article 3, *The Westminster Confession of Faith, 1647*, in Pelikan and Hotchkiss, *Creeds and Confessions of Faith in the Christian Tradition, Volume 2*, 610.

[20] Neither a pancausal conception of providence nor a notion of 'double predestination', whereby God predestines people either to salvation or damnation, is unique to John Calvin or, more widely, the Reformed tradition, though the exposition of the doctrines found therein arguably is the most orderly and cogent. A full analysis is impossible to attempt, but we see that comparable ideas about providence were advocated at least as far back as the Stoics and as recently (to Calvin) as Huldrych Zwingli. Thomas Aquinas and Martin Luther each held that God determined all things, including the eternal fate of individual men and women. Gottschalk of Orbais,

first presupposes the existence of a world for which God will provide; and this world exists because, in the words of the Westminster Confession,

> It pleased God the Father, Son, and Holy Ghost, for the manifestation of the glory of his eternal power, wisdom, and goodness, in the beginning, to create, or make of nothing, the world, and all things therein whether visible or invisible, in the space of six days – and all very good.[21]

However, providence is not predestination, and predestination is not providence; Barth writes,

> Predestination is ... the presupposition, and its fulfilment in history the constitutive centre, of God's overruling, and the basis and goal of its realisation. In predestination we certainly have to do with the creature under God's lordship, but with the creature, i.e., man, as the object of the original, central and personal intention of God, with man as the partner in the covenant of grace made by God in and with creation. In providence, on the contrary, we have to do with the creature as such and in general; with God's active relation to the reality created by and therefore distinct from Himself.[22]

Thus for Barth, providence 'is the execution of the eternal decree of God's eternal election of grace.'[23] We can agree, then, with Helm that '[a]ll predestination is providential, and all exercises of providence are predestinarian.'[24] Given that, according to at least the Reformed tradition, God exercises his providence over creation continually, we can agree also with

---

a ninth century monk of whom Calvin appears to have no knowledge, and who was likely inspired by the teaching of Augustine, similarly believed that God does not will the salvation of all people and so predestines not only to life but also to death. It is possible even to detect early notions of double predestination outside Christian thought in the Dead Sea Scrolls. For summaries and comment, see, for example, P.H. Reardon, 'Calvin on Providence: The Development of an Insight', *Scottish Journal of Theology* 28 (1975), 517–533 (on Stoicism); A.E. McGrath, *Reformation Thought: An Introduction*, 3rd ed. (Oxford: Blackwell; 1999), 132–133, and T. George, *Theology of the Reformers* (Nashville: Broadman Press, 1988), 122–126 (on Zwingli); G.W. Bromiley, *Historical Theology: An Introduction* (Edinburgh: T&T Clark, 1978), 110–111, 115–116, 165–170, 242–245 (on Augustine, Gottschalk and Luther); and E.P. Sanders, *Paul and Palestinian Judaism: A Comparison of Patterns of Religion* (London: SCM Press, 1977), 257–270 (on the Dead Sea Scrolls). See also § 4.3 (on Aquinas).

[21] 'Chapter 4: Of Creation, Article 1', *The Westminster Confession of Faith, 1647*, in Pelikan and Hotchkiss, *Creeds and Confessions of Faith in the Christian Tradition, Volume 2*, 611.
[22] Barth, *Church Dogmatics*, III/3, 4.
[23] Barth, *Church Dogmatics*, III/3, 6.
[24] Helm, *The Providence of God*, 20.

Helm's view that, essentially, providence is *'God's activity now'*[25] and that 'God's activity *now* links with the past (with the plan of God), and with the future (with where the activity of God is leading).'[26]

§ 1.3 The Threefold Scheme of Providence

Very often, Protestant theologians, particularly those in the Lutheran and the Reformed traditions, have articulated the doctrine of providence by constructing what we might call its threefold scheme. We may understand providence in terms of *conservatio* (God's preservation or sustaining of creation), *concursus* (his concurrence, cooperation or accompaniment of creation in its activity) and *gubernatio* (his governing of it to a particular end).[27] The Lutheran Johann Andreas Quenstedt understood the terms thus:

> Providence is the external action of the entire trinity whereby 1. God most efficaciously upholds the things created, both as an entirety and singly, both in species and in individuals; 2. concurs in their actions and results; and 3. freely and wisely governs all things to his own glory and the welfare and safety of the universe, and especially of the godly.[28]

---

[25] Helm, *The Providence of God*, 17, emphasis original.

[26] Helm, *The Providence of God*, 17, emphasis mine.

[27] Some theologians articulate a scheme that is twofold rather than threefold, with providence understood solely in terms of *conservatio* and *gubernatio*. It is a mistake, however, to see the twofold scheme as excluding *concursus*, as it is already included in *conservatio* and *gubernatio*. (L. Berkhof, *Systematic Theology* [London: Banner of Truth, 1958], 166). For example, Herman Hoeksema writes, 'Preservation and government are the two elements in divine providence. Frequently a third element is mentioned, that of cooperation. But this is, strictly speaking, not necessary: for what is meant by cooperation is after all nothing else than the preservation and government of God with regard to the moral life and deeds of the rational creature.' (H. Hoeksema, *Reformed Dogmatics* [Grand Rapids: Reformed Free Publishing Association, 1966], 233–234). The introduction specifically of a threefold scheme to the doctrine of providence appears primarily to be a Reformation initiative. Wolfhart Pannenberg notes that the 'older Protestant dogmatics ... subdivided providence into preservation, concursus, and overruling' onwards from Abraham Calovius, a seventeenth-century Lutheran. (W. Pannenberg, *Systematic Theology* [3 vols.], translated by G.W. Bromiley [Edinburgh: T&T Clark, 1991–1998], Vol. 2, 36–37). Charles Wood sees the threefold scheme becoming standard, at least in Lutheran dogmatics, with the theology of Calovius's contemporary, Johann Andreas Quenstedt. (C.M. Wood, 'How Does God Act?', *International Journal of Systematic Theology* 1 [1999], 138–152 [142, n. 11]).

[28] Johann Andreas Quenstedt, *Theologia Didactico–Polemica*, quoted in Wood, 'How Does God Act?', 142, n. 11.

Theologians within the Reformed tradition made similar distinctions. Johannes Braun, for example, writes,

> The acts of providence are three: (1) He preserves all things in their being and duration; (2) He moves all things to their action by concurrence, in fact by precurrence; (3) He steers and guides all things to the desired end to which they were appointed from eternity.[29]

Herman Bavinck contends,

> Preservation tells us that nothing exists, not only no substance, but also no power, no activity, no idea, unless it exists totally from, through, and to God. Concurrence makes known to us the same preservation as an activity such that, far from suspending the existence of creatures, it above all affirms and maintains it. And government describes the other two as guiding all things in such a way that the final goal determined by God will be reached. And always, from beginning to end, providence is one simple, almighty, and omnipresent power.[30]

Barth and G.C. Berkouwer organise their discussions of providence largely around the threefold scheme;[31] and more recently, Wayne Grudem offers the following definition of providence:

> God is continually involved with all created things in such a way that he (1) keeps them existing and maintaining the properties with which he created them; (2) cooperates with created things in every action, directing their distinctive properties to cause them to act as they do; and (3) directs them to fulfill his purposes.[32]

It seems, then, that the threefold scheme is an appropriate way to understand God's providential activity. That said, we should not assume that preservation, concurrence and government are three separate divine actions; instead, they are three aspects of the one divine action.[33] Louis Berkhof explains,

---

[29] Johannes Braun, *Doctrina Foederum sive Systema Theologiae didacticae et elencticae*, quoted in H. Heppe, *Reformed Dogmatics: A Compendium of Reformed Theology*, revised and edited by E. Bizer; translated by G.T. Thomson (London: Wakeman Great Reprints, 1950), 256.

[30] H. Bavinck, *Reformed Dogmatics, Volume 2: God and Creation*, translated by J. Vriend (Grand Rapids: Baker Academic, 2004), 605.

[31] Barth, *Church Dogmatics*, III/3, 58–238; G.C. Berkouwer, *The Providence of God*, translated by L.B. Smedes (Grand Rapids: Eerdmans, 1952), 50–160.

[32] W. Grudem, *Systematic Theology: An Introduction to Biblical Doctrine* (Leicester: IVP, 1994), 315, original emphasis removed.

[33] Cf. Wood, 'How Does God Act?', 143.

> While preservation has reference to the *being*, concurrence to the *activity*, and government to the *guidance* of all things, this should never be understood in an exclusive sense. In preservation there is also an element of government, in government an element of concursus, and in concursus an element of preservation.[34]

Accordingly, as Charles Wood observes,

> God's providing ... is a matter of God's sustaining creation in its own activity; cooperating with or concurring in that activity; and directing the outcomes of that activity for the well-being of creation and for God's own glory.[35]

Essentially, then, God founds, upholds and empowers each and every creature in its activity, assuming that activity as his own so that he is active alongside the creature as it acts, and this for a specific reason. At this point, however, we encounter again the problems we noted earlier concerning the potential conflict between God's action and creaturely action, between divine causal efficacy and creaturely causal efficacy. We may illustrate the dilemma by using as mundane and everyday an example as my morning shave. According to the threefold conception of providence, God so upholds the act of my shaving that it is something that really happens (*conservatio*). He concurs with the act of my shaving, somehow assuming my action as his own action (*concursus*), and does so for a particular end, or perhaps on the way to a particular end (*gubernatio*). This understanding ought to be applied to *every* creaturely action, *every* creaturely occurrence; and thus God works not only in this manner in the ordinary events of life, but also in those rather extraordinary, unexpected things as well. Just as God upholds, concurs with and directs my shaving, so he must uphold, concur with and direct every lottery win, every birth, every theft, every rape – and so on. Ignoring matters of theodicy, the crucial issue for us is whether or not God's action here negates the causal efficacy of the creature's action, or, to use our earlier illustration, in what sense my act of shaving may be said to be *my* act of shaving.

§ 1.4 Primary and Secondary Causation

This issue particularly concerns God's concurrence with creaturely action, and the Reformed tradition generally has developed its stance on the matter from

---

[34] Berkhof, *Systematic Theology*, 167, emphasis original; cf. Bavinck, *Reformed Dogmatics, Volume 2*, 605: 'From the very beginning preservation is also government, and government is concurrence, and concurrence is preservation.'
[35] Wood, 'How Does God Act?', 142.

within the conceptual framework of primary and secondary causation.[36] At least since Plato,[37] this 'long and honourable tradition'[38] has sought to safeguard both divine and creaturely causal efficacy in relation to one another. God founds, upholds and empowers the creature's action; creaturely secondary causation presupposes divine primary causation. We see this distinction, for example, in Calvin's teaching on providence:

> Therefore the Christian heart, since it has been thoroughly persuaded that all things happen by God's plan, and that nothing takes place by chance, will ever look to him as the principal cause of things, yet will give attention to the secondary causes in their proper place.[39]

Importantly, secondary causes, although God concurs with them as they act, are affirmed as genuinely efficacious. Heinrich Heppe, in his anthology of Reformed texts, clarifies that divine concurrence 'is an activity of God such that by it God directly and predeterminedly grasps the powers of the creatures and so arouses them to activity in their natural way that the activity of the creature is God's own action.'[40] Thus the Reformed tradition generally has adopted the stance of the Second Helvetic Confession that

> we do not spurn as useless the means by which divine providence works, but we teach that we are to adapt ourselves to them in so far as they are recommended to us in the word of God. Wherefore we disapprove of the rash statements of those who say that if all things are managed by the providence of God, then our efforts and endeavours are in vain.[41]

The Westminster Confession consolidates this position on secondary causation: although God's decree is the First Cause by which

---

[36] By 'conceptual framework', we mean no more than a series of ideas organised around a particular concept or theme, in this case, the concept of primary and secondary causes.

[37] See, for example, Plato, *Timaeus*, translated by D.J. Zeyl, in *Plato: Complete Works*, edited, with introduction and notes, by J.M. Cooper (Indianapolis: Hackett Publishing, 1997), 1224–1291 (46cd; 68e, 1249, 1270).

[38] Helm, *The Providence of God*, 86.

[39] Calvin, *Institutes*, 1:17:6, 218.

[40] Heppe, *Reformed Dogmatics*, 259.

[41] 'Chapter 6: Of the Providence of God, Article 4', *The Second Helvetic Confession, 1566*, in Pelikan and Hotchkiss, *Creeds and Confessions of Faith in the Christian Tradition, Volume 2*, 467.

all things come to pass immutably, and infallibly, yet, by the same providence, he ordereth them to fall out, according to the nature of second causes, either necessarily, freely, or contingently.[42]

Individual Reformed theologians also make positive claims for the genuine causal efficacy of secondary causes. Berkhof states that it is 'only on condition that second causes are real, that we can properly speak of a concurrence or co-operation of the First Cause with secondary causes.'[43] Charles Hodge contends that secondary causes 'are real causes' and that the 'agency of God neither supersedes, nor in any way interferes with the efficiency of second causes.'[44] Bavinck asserts,

> Concurrence is precisely the reason for the self-activity of the secondary causes, and these causes, sustained from beginning to end by God's power, work with a strength that is appropriate and natural to them. So little does the activity of God nullify the activity of the creature that the latter is all the more vigorous to the degree that the former reveals itself the more richly and fully. Hence, the primary cause and the secondary cause remain distinct. The former does not destroy the latter but on the contrary confers reality on it, and the second exists solely as a result of the first. Neither are the secondary causes merely instruments, organs, inanimate automata, but they are genuine causes with a nature, vitality, spontaneity, manner of working, and law of their own.[45]

The majority position, then, of Reformed theology is that divine primary causation works through creaturely secondary causation in such a way that the divine will is fulfilled even as the integrity of creaturely causal efficacy is maintained. Here, though, some tensions begin to emerge. Bavinck argues that as primary causation works through secondary causation, 'the effect that proceeds from the two is one and the product is one.' Accordingly,

> There is no division of labour between God and his creature, but the same effect is totally the effect of the primary cause as well as totally the effect of the proximate cause. The product is also in the same sense totally the product of the primary as well as totally the product of the secondary cause.[46]

---

[42] 'Chapter 5: Of Providence, Article 2', *The Westminster Confession of Faith, 1647*, in Pelikan and Hotchkiss, *Creeds and Confessions of Faith in the Christian Tradition, Volume 2*, 612.
[43] Berkhof, *Systematic Theology*, 172.
[44] C. Hodge, *Systematic Theology* (3 vols.), Vol. 1 (London: James Clarke, 1960), 600.
[45] Bavinck, *Reformed Dogmatics, Volume 2*, 614.
[46] Bavinck, *Reformed Dogmatics, Volume 2*, 614–615.

Each cause may be said to be *the* cause of any given action;[47] but Bavinck modifies his claim:

> But because the primary cause and the secondary cause are not identical and differ essentially, the effect and product are *in reality* totally the effect and product of the two causes, to be sure, but *formally* they are only the effect and product of the secondary cause. Wood burns and it is God alone who makes it burn, yet the burning process may not be formally attributed to God but must be attributed to the wood as subject.[48]

Is this coherent? Bavinck affirms the causal integrity of both God and the creature; but to say that God *alone* makes the wood burn at least suggests that the secondary cause, that is, the flame that sets the piece of wood alight, does *not* have genuine causal efficacy. Its integrity to incinerate the wood is negated by God, who instead causes the wood to burn. All that appears to be ascribed to the flame itself, then, is the *effect* that it sets fire to the wood; but if this is so, and if this were to apply to each and every creaturely action, then the possibility arises that primary causation alone is causally efficacious and that God is the sole causal agent, using creatures as his instruments.[49]

Does an understanding of providence in terms of primary and secondary causation entail necessarily either divine determinism (that God ordains all that happens) or occasionalism (that God is the sole causal agent)?[50] It appears so;[51] primary causation is said to do that which properly belongs to secondary

---

[47] Cf. V. Brümmer, *Speaking of a Personal God: An Essay in Philosophical Theology* (Cambridge: Cambridge University Press, 1992), 116. See also § 4.2, n. 19.

[48] Bavinck, *Reformed Dogmatics, Volume 2*, 615, emphasis original.

[49] Bavinck appears to recognise this implication. (Bavinck, *Reformed Dogmatics, Volume 2*, 614).

[50] Determinism is 'the view that every event or state of affairs is brought about by antecedent events or states of affairs in accordance with universal causal laws that govern the world.' (B. Berofsky, 'Determinism', in *The Cambridge Dictionary of Philosophy*, 2nd ed. [Cambridge: Cambridge University Press, 1999], 228–229 [228]). We may understand this so-called scientific determinism to mean that from some first or initial cause, the history of the world unfolds in a predetermined path that cannot be altered: whatever happens cannot *not* happen. The Reformed tradition offers a determinism that issues from God's willing of all things according to his secret plan (which itself corresponds somewhat to the idea of an initial cause in scientific determinism). Although creaturely history is the temporal unfolding of this plan, the emphasis is on God's *constant* effecting of things as the guarantee of this unfolding. God is the first cause of *each* instance, without deviation from what he has willed to do from eternity. For a summary of occasionalism, see S. Nadler, 'Occasionalism', in *The Cambridge Dictionary of Philosophy*, 2nd ed. (Cambridge: Cambridge University Press, 1999), 626–627.

[51] Cf. D. Fergusson, 'Divine Providence and Action', in M. Volf and M. Welker (eds.), *God's Life in Trinity* (Minneapolis: Fortress Press, 2006), 153–165 (162–163).

causes. However, many seek to avoid the tensions here by depicting primary and secondary causation operating from different causal levels. On this account, primary causation *transcends* secondary causation; God's action *cannot* be compared to that of the creature. The very fact that primary causation founds, upholds and empowers secondary causation points to the incomparability of the two types of causation. Kathryn Tanner argues that we must adhere to certain rules to ensure the coherence of Christian discourse on this matter:

> First, a rule for speaking of God as transcendent vis-à-vis the world: avoid both a simple univocal attribution of predicates to God and world and a simple contrast of divine and non-divine predicates. In the case of univocity, God is not really transcendent at all. In the case of a simple contrast, God's transcendence is not radical enough.... The second rule is as follows: avoid in talk about God's creative agency all suggestions of limitation in scope or manner. The second rule prescribes talk of God's creative agency as immediate and universally extensive.[52]

Comparison between God and any created thing risks reducing the former to the level of the latter and thus sets them in opposition.[53] 'God becomes one being among others within a single order.'[54] That said, it is difficult to speak of one thing as *totally* unlike another without making some kind of comparison that shows *how* the two are unlike. This is clear even when applied to primary and secondary causation. So whilst Tanner agrees that 'it is proper to say that God is directly affected or determined by what the creature does,' this is 'only so long as the creature's effect on God is part of the complex creative intention by which God determines himself.'[55] However, surely the very idea that somehow God accommodates the creature's effect within his own agency at least implies that a comparison is made between divine and creaturely action. Indeed, God's action is shown to be superior to that of the creature, with the further connotation that they each inhabit the same causal order. From this, we may suggest that it is impossible to speak of God's action in a way entirely different from how we would speak of a creature's action; but talk of distinct causal orders can only function on the presupposition that it is not impossible. At the heart of the distinction between primary and secondary causation, then, is the ambiguity of how each type of causation relates to the other.[56]

---

[52] K. Tanner, *God and Creation in Christian Theology: Tyranny or Empowerment?* (Minneapolis: Fortress Press, 1988), 47.
[53] Tanner, *God and Creation*, 45–46.
[54] Tanner, *God and Creation*, 45.
[55] Tanner, *God and Creation*, 97.
[56] Cf. P.S. Fiddes, *Participating in God: A Pastoral Doctrine of the Trinity* (London: DLT, 2000), 117. We will explore the matter of the relation between primary and secondary causation more fully in § 4.4 (with reference to Aquinas's notion of analogical predication) and § 4.6.

§ 1.5 The Question of Mediation

The distinction between primary and secondary causation presupposes what we shall refer to as the fundamental ontological distinction between God and the world. God is God and the creature is not. Given this distinction, how should we say that God acts in a world that is totally unlike him? A simple positing of two causal orders, primary and secondary, does little to explain how they relate and, indeed, cannot be maintained consistently without reducing one to the level of the other; as Berkouwer notes, even 'the use of the terms first and second causes implies that God is only the most important cause among equal causes'.[57] We see, then, that the problem of the relation between primary and secondary causation effectively is a question of mediation. Colin Gunton explains,

> Mediation denotes the way we understand one form of action – God's action – to take shape in and in relation to that which is not God; the way, that is, by which the actions of one who is creator take form in a world that is of an entirely different order from God because he made it to be so.[58]

The conceptual framework of primary and secondary causation depicts God's action as mediated through creaturely action; but we have suggested that it cannot do so without at least jeopardising the integrity of creaturely causal efficacy. This is because primary causation is shaped within a voluntaristic notion of divine action: God *wills* to act through secondary causation. Calvin, for example, argues that 'the will of God is the great cause of all things that are done in the whole world';[59] indeed, 'everything in nature depends upon the will of God, and ... the whole course of nature is only the prompt carrying into effect of his orders.'[60] Accordingly, we may observe that God's will to act through secondary causation appears to reduce it merely to instrumentality, with the consequence that it becomes simply the means by which the divine will acts in a world totally unlike itself.[61] Why, though, is the identification of primary causation as God's will to act so problematic? Gunton argues that

> although will is an essentially personal concept because it is personal agents who will, it is also one that easily collapses into impersonalism. This is because it can

---

[57] Berkouwer, *The Providence of God*, 155.
[58] C.E. Gunton, *The Christian Faith: An Introduction to Christian Doctrine* (Oxford: Blackwell, 2002), 5.
[59] J. Calvin, *A Defence of the Secret Providence of God*, in *Calvin's Calvinism: Treatises on the Eternal Predestination of God and the Secret Providence of God*, translated by H. Cole (Grand Rapids: Reformed Free Publishing Association, 1987), 223–350 (233).
[60] J. Calvin, *Commentary on the Book of Psalms, Vol. 5* in *Calvin's Commentaries* VI (CTS; Grand Rapids: Baker Books, 2003), 301.
[61] Cf. Tanner, *God and Creation*, 86; Fergusson, 'Divine Providence and Action', 163.

encourage the kind of conception of unmediated divine omnicausality that ultimately undermines rather than establishes the being of that which is willed. God can be conceived to will everything in such a way that the reality of the other is in some way or other imperilled – it becomes his 'creature' in the pejorative sense of that term.[62]

The identification of primary causation as God's will to act also avoids the need to speak of the action of the *triune* God, whom the Christian Church – including the Reformed tradition – confesses is present and active within the world. Paul Fiddes observes that

> the 'two-cause' theory operates with the concept of God as a single acting subject. All discussions of it within the philosophy of religion, from Aquinas onwards, simply refer to the primary or sovereign cause as 'God'. In this case, the persons of the Trinity appear to be not only inseparable in their operations outwardly in the world, but indistinguishable from each other, since 'primary causation' can hardly be appropriated or assigned as a characteristic to any particular person. Reflection on the Trinity with regard to the 'causative power' of God seems to be at best an unnecessary complication, and at worst irrelevant.[63]

The tensions between primary and secondary causation stem from a misconceived notion of mediation, that is, God's will to act through secondary causation displaces the action of the Son and the Holy Spirit within the world. Against this, we should recognise that the Church's confession of faith in God's providence ultimately is its confession of faith *in Jesus Christ* and therefore in God's superior dealings with the world as it is drawn to the Father through him by the Spirit.[64] It is entirely inappropriate and insufficient to portray divine providence predominantly in terms of God's will to act: the trinitarian focus is lost and the particularity of God's action in Christ diluted. Often this happens when our preconceived notions cloud our understanding of how God acts in the world and the type of relationship he has with us. There is no denying that we have these preconceived notions; the key thing is to prevent any inaccurate or inadequate notions we might hold from blurring our discernment of God's activity in this world. Biblically speaking, this activity is in Christ and by the Spirit, very specific activity. However, once we lose sight of God's specific action in Christ, the temptation to generalise divine action within the world becomes overwhelming. Though acknowledging God's action in Christ, instead we emphasise those biblical texts that refer to God's sovereign power over all

---

[62] C.E. Gunton, 'The End of Causality? The Reformers and their Predecessors', in C.E. Gunton (ed.), *The Doctrine of Creation: Essays in Dogmatics, History and Philosophy* (Edinburgh: T&T Clark, 1997), 63–82 (65).
[63] Fiddes, *Participating in God*, 123–124.
[64] Cf. Barth, *Church Dogmatics*, III/3, 26–27.

and so diminish how that power was and is manifest specifically in the life and death of the now risen and ascended Christ.⁶⁵

Through this generalising, something interesting happens: God's particular action, once understood to be focussed in Christ, then becomes manifest in creation as a whole. The whole of creation is understood to be an instance of God's specific action so that everything that happens is said to be the result of God's activity, caused or determined by his hand; even the life of Christ becomes just another divinely determined event. God's action in Christ remains the way in which he has chosen to act to reconcile the world to himself, but the particularity of this sovereign action is muted somewhat because of the overemphasis on God's pancausality.

Yet the New Testament is not shy to focus on the particularity of God's action in Christ. Central to the New Testament is the conviction that in the man Jesus of Nazareth, called the Christ (Mt 1:16; Acts 5:42), God was acting within creation: 'in Christ God was reconciling the world to himself' (2 Cor 5:19); 'we have peace with God through our Lord Jesus Christ, through whom we have obtained access to this grace in which we stand' (Rom 5:1-2); 'God sent his only Son into the world so that we might live through him' (1 Jn 4:9). Furthermore, God not only enters into relationship with us through Christ, but he even ensures our very existence by him. Christ is

> the image of the invisible God, the firstborn of all creation; for in him all things in heaven and on earth were created, things visible and invisible, whether thrones or dominions or rulers or powers – all things have been created through him and for him. He himself is before all things, and in him all things hold together. (Col 1:15-17)

For the New Testament writers, all that is derives its existence from Christ and from him alone. This specificity, this particularity, arises again and again: in *Christ*, in *him*, through *him*. If we wish to understand God's providential activity within creation, we ought to follow the New Testament's lead and grasp the particularity of Christ as the only one through whom this activity is mediated. In the life of Christ, we see God's providence made flesh. Consequently, the crucial task for a doctrine of providence is to elucidate the way in which God relates to his creation by emphasising the doctrine's christological and therefore trinitarian aspects.

---

⁶⁵ 'The orthodox Lutheran and Reformed teachers are rather at one in teaching the divine lordship over all occurrence both as a whole and in detail without attempting to say what is the meaning and purpose of this lordship. They understand it as the act of a superior and absolutely omniscient, omnipotent and omnioperative being whose nature and work do of course display such moral qualities as wisdom, righteousness and goodness, etc. But this is all. According to the agreed doctrine of orthodoxy, this empty shell is the object of the Christian belief in providence.' (Barth, *Church Dogmatics*, III/3, 31).

Given this, any doctrine of providence first explicated from within the conceptual framework of primary and secondary causation will likely deny to the creature the integrity of its causal efficacy. Such accounts of providence tend excessively to focus upon God's power in abstraction from the way that he acts in creation through his Son and by his Spirit. The conviction so emphasised by the Reformed tradition that God's will is the cause of all things effectively displaces the roles that the Son and the Spirit have in mediating God's presence and action within the world. Although a specifically Christian doctrine of providence must take into account both God's sovereign action within creation and the integrity of creaturely causal efficacy, we have reason to doubt that any such account developed using the terms of primary and secondary causation successfully testifies to the activity of the triune God, which alone makes providence a specifically Christian doctrine.

§ 1.6 The Aim and Structure of this Study

My thesis is that the conceptual framework of God's active presence in the world embodied in Jesus Christ and mediated by the Holy Spirit is a corrective to the conceptual framework of primary and secondary causation favoured by common and traditional doctrines of providence.[66] Although the question of

---

[66] This does not mean that other conceptual frameworks cannot be employed to elucidate divine providence. Kevin Vanhoozer, for example, affirms the providential action of the triune God but sets it within a conceptual framework of divine communicative action: '[T]he Father makes provision for the world through the Word in the power of the Spirit. Framing the doctrine in terms of Word and Spirit means contrasting a merely mechanical or causal view of providence with a richer and more personal communicative notion.' (K.J. Vanhoozer, 'Providence', in *Dictionary for Theological Interpretation of the Bible* [Grand Rapids: Baker Academic, 2005], 641–645 [644]; cf. 'Effectual Call or Causal Effect? Summons, Sovereignty and Supervenient Grace', *Tyndale Bulletin* 49 [1998], 213–251). According to Vanhoozer, speech is 'a form of action, but not the sort of action that can by itself deprive another of his freedom. God's infinite freedom meets finite human freedom not primarily in terms of causal action and reaction (the latter is too impersonal), but rather in a communicative interaction that respects the integrity of the creature in addressing itself specifically to its rational and spiritual nature.' (Vanhoozer, 'Providence', 645).

Similarly, F. LeRon Shults's insistence that divine agency is conditioned by the fact that 'God is love' (1 Jn 4:8) means that divine causation qualified by divine love frees the former from connotations of determinism. (F.L. Shults, *Reforming the Doctrine of God* [Grand Rapids: Eerdmans, 2005], 235, 241). 'Love,' Shults argues, 'is a force that does not simply push; it also pulls, draws, unites, enlivens, engages, reorders, and evokes'; and the reliance of seventeenth-century theologians 'on the concept of God as a single subject [simply] complicated their task of articulating the role of the Son (and the Spirit) in divine agency.' (Shults, *Reforming the Doctrine of God*, 241). The conceptual framework of divine presence, I submit, most

how God acts in the world is not resolved simply by an appeal to christology,[67] removing the discussion from one conceptual framework and placing it within another changes the conditions under which the issues are explored. Consequently, our contention is that the conceptual framework of divine presence challenges the traditional Reformed theology by demonstrating that God's providence is not first and foremost about divine willing or causation but about his activity within the whole of creation by his Son and Spirit. Furthermore, an examination of the concept of divine presence as it appears in Scripture shows that providence has an eschatological orientation whereby God indeed works out his sovereign purposes but not as the pancausal execution of an eternal decree fixed by God's will prior to creation. At its heart, then, providence concerns the gracious provision of a loving God as in Christ he calls people to himself for the rest of creation; it does not concern God's meticulous control of all things.

To demonstrate this, we will endeavour to describe more fully the problems with the conceptual framework of primary and secondary causation and then seek to demonstrate the legitimacy of the conceptual framework of God's presence as the most appropriate foundation and context for the Christian doctrine of providence. We shall move from considering the more traditional (pan)causal depictions of providence to an outline of the contours of a doctrine of providence based upon the conceptual framework of God's presence. It is

---

appropriately accounts for the scriptural presentation of divine providence, but the directions proposed by Vanhoozer and Shults certainly complement it.

[67] William Placher accepts that because Jesus 'represents the culmination of God's self-revelation ... many of the usual problems about "God's action" disappear.' (W.C. Placher, *The Domestication of Transcendence: How Modern Thinking About God Went Wrong* [Louisville: Westminster John Knox Press, 1996], 193). The point is that God was acting in Jesus Christ to reconcile the world, 'and Jesus had a voice and a body. We can understand what it means to say that he "acted."' Indeed, we can 'point to the pattern of enacted intentions that make up this particular human life and say: "He is the image of the invisible God": (Col. 1:15).' (Placher, *The Domestication of Transcendence*, 193). However, Placher is less certain that this makes as much of a difference as some might claim: 'Appealing to Christology does not,' he argues, 'provide a way of dodging the questions [about the action of a transcendent God] I have just been discussing. The Gospels identify Jesus as the self-revelation of the God Israel had already come to know in its history. And they offer the fact that God raised Jesus from the dead as the decisive evidence that Jesus is the one they proclaim him to be. So we cannot simply point to the actions of the human Jesus to identify the activity of the God revealed in Christ and avoid *all* problems about divine action in history.' (Placher, *The Domestication of Transcendence*, 193–194, emphasis mine). Placher is right; the issues that primary and secondary causation were developed and employed to address are not resolved simply by pointing to God's action in Christ. Our contention, however, is that the way in which we understand those issues *must be conditioned by* God's action in Christ and *not* by the conceptual framework of primary and secondary causation. See also § 4.6.

important to note, therefore, that there will be no attempt to construct a doctrine of providence in this study beyond indicating the shape that a theology of providence could take on account of its conceptual framework. The main concern, as noted already, will be to demonstrate the legitimacy of developing a doctrine of providence along these lines.

Given this, first we will consider the concept of secondary causation as it appears in Calvin's theology (§ 2), identifying both negative and positive aspects of his thought on the matter.[68] We will explore Calvin's views of God's fundamental relation to the world he has made, of how the fall affects such a relation, particularly with regard to Adam's freedom before God, and of how God reconciles the fallen world to himself through Christ. Our concern is not to offer a fully developed account of Calvin's theology; our focus instead is the integrity of creaturely causal efficacy in his teaching on providence. Essentially, we will argue that although he aims to safeguard the integrity of the causal efficacy of both God and the creature, Calvin's assertion that God wills to mediate his presence and action through secondary causation means in fact that God accommodates himself to it, with the implication that this commandeers the activity of the creature and negates the causal integrity that he wishes to affirm. Following this, we intend further to demonstrate the ambiguity of Calvin's stance on secondary causation by showing how, coupled with his teaching on predestination, it both influenced the burgeoning natural science of the day and prepared the way for the rejection of God's presence and action in the world altogether (§ 3).

All this prompts the question of whether the conceptual framework of primary and secondary causation is the most adequate for conceiving God's providence (§ 4). Although different sorts of causes do not necessarily compete against one another, there seems always to exist a tension with primary and secondary causation because each is said somehow to be *the* cause of an effect. We will explore the teaching of Thomas Aquinas on providence and how his notion of analogical predication might be used to ascertain the legitimacy of an appeal to different causal orders to help elucidate the matter. Such illumination might also come from the concept of a so-called 'causal joint' or by employing the panentheistic analogy. Our contention will be that each of these attempts to account for God's providential activity in the world in fact displaces the action

---

[68] Why Calvin? To an extent, my decision to choose Calvin as the foil for our discussion is arbitrary: Aquinas instead could have been selected (though we do consider his thought in § 4.3–§ 4.4), as could any of the Reformed theologians that have been mentioned. However, Calvin stands arguably as the most recognised theologian within his tradition; his theological influence makes him a significant contributor to discussions of providence. Furthermore, Calvin's insistence on the goodness of creation and the integrity of secondary causation despite God's pancausal relation to the world shows well the ambiguities that I wish to expose. That Calvin writes, for the most part, clearly and accessibly is a welcome bonus.

of the triune God mediated there by his Son and Holy Spirit, a displacement that entails the negation of the integrity of creaturely causal efficacy.

Against this, we will argue that the conceptual framework of God's presence is a corrective to that of primary and secondary causation (§ 5). All too often, accounts of providence have been devised from selecting and connecting a variety of apposite scriptural texts but which have been removed inappropriately from their immediate context;[69] there appears little concern to explicate divine providence from within the scriptural context of God's continuous relationship with the world shaped through his dealings with his elected covenant people. Accordingly, texts such as Genesis 45:7, Proverbs 21:1, Isaiah 45:1-7 and Acts 2:23 are stripped of context, reduced merely to propositions about how God acts in the world rather than affirmed as the faithful witness to the reasons for and goal of his action. This scriptural context is what the conceptual framework of God's presence aims to preserve. The central idea here is that of God's intention to mediate his active presence from the garden of Eden across the world eschatologically to transform it entirely into the place of his presence. To elucidate this, we will consider first the Old Testament conviction that God dwells amongst his people Israel initially in the tabernacle and then in the temple; secondly, the New Testament's account of the embodiment of this presence in Christ; and finally, the Spirit's enabling of the body of Christ, that is, the Church, to participate in the divine presence. We will contend that God's active presence is mediated throughout the world by the Church's faithful obedience.

The remaining chapters will seek to defend the claim that divine providence may be understood from within the conceptual framework of God's presence. Importantly, we must note once more that it is not our intention to counter as such the problems identified in the conceptual framework of primary and secondary causation; that would mean in practice developing an alternative doctrine of providence, which is beyond the scope of this study. Although it should be possible to attend to tradition and continue to explicate providence in terms of God's preservation, concurrence and government of all things from within the conceptual framework of divine presence,[70] our immediate purpose is to assess the *foundation* of the Christian doctrine of providence and so to demonstrate the legitimacy of understanding that doctrine in terms of the christological – and so trinitarian – orientation of the mediation of God's presence throughout the world. On this account, providence is God's sovereign

---

[69] Throughout his discussion of providence, Wayne Grudem, for example, cites or alludes to more than fifty scriptural texts, seemingly only to demonstrate that providence may be understood as God's preservation, concurrence and government. (Grudem, *Systematic Theology*, 315–351). There is little attention to what we might describe as the scriptural *pattern* of divine providence.

[70] We shall offer some tentative suggestions for the continued use of these terms in § 9.4.

action within creation to remain faithful to the promise he made to it, the promise not to abandon the world but to lead it to the good end that he desires for it in relationship with himself – namely, that the world in its entirety shall be the place of his presence. This sovereign action ultimately is defined by Christ, who, by the power of the Holy Spirit, remains faithful to the will of his Father. We see that this action first takes shape only from within the context of God's relationship with Israel; this is indicated by God's promise to Abram that 'in [him] all the families of the earth shall be blessed' (Gen 12:3). God calls Israel, the children of Abram, to be his 'treasured possession', 'a priestly kingdom and a holy nation' (Ex 19:5-6), and so to mediate his presence to the surrounding nations (§ 6). Our argument will consider God's giving of the *tôrāh* or law to Israel, her willing acceptance of the law but inability to keep it, and Paul's argument in his letter to the Galatians that the law was a temporary institution 'until Christ came' (Gal 3:24). Such an insight, we will suggest, indicates that the law plays a crucial role in God's dealings with the world but does not determine them. It does not prevent God from remaining faithful to the promises he made originally to Abram before the law was given, promises that are fulfilled in Christ and by his faithfulness to his Father's commands.

This leads us to consider what Christ does in faithful response to God (§ 7). The letter to the Hebrews links Christ's faithfulness with his crucifixion and does so using imagery derived from the law's sacrificial system. As part of the divinely given law, the sacrificial system facilitated the Israelite's celebration of their relationship with God and with one another; it also provided the means by which inevitable estrangement between various parties would be resolved. In particular, the accumulation of Israel's sins each year would be said eventually to penetrate the holy of holies, the place of God's presence, and pollute it; and each year, the Day of Atonement rituals would be performed to decontaminate the holy of holies from Israel's sin so that God would remain present amongst his people. Hebrews builds upon this imagery and presents Jesus as a faithful high priest who willingly offers himself to God as a sacrifice to make atonement on behalf and in place of those whom he represents. Jesus enters the holy of holies by his death, thus maintaining the relation between God and the world; he opens the whole of creation to the place of God's presence.

Hebrews makes it clear that Jesus's willing self-offering to God is 'through the eternal Spirit' (Heb 9:14). We will offer an account of the role of the Holy Spirit in the life of the incarnate Son (§ 8), and will do so first by returning to Calvin's theology. Once more, we will discern tensions that at least suggest that Calvin reduces the Son's humanity merely to an instrument through which God wills to act. To counter this, we will examine the presentation of the relation between Christ and the Spirit in Matthew's Gospel to show that Jesus was empowered by the Spirit to remain faithful to his Father, even though this would mean his death. Our discussion will also consider precisely what it means to say that Jesus was *empowered* by the Spirit so that the integrity of his faithfulness to God remains undoubted. Finally, we will anticipate potential objections to our treatment of providence, clear the ground for a theology of providence and indicate the shape that such a theology could take from within the conceptual framework of God's presence (§ 9).

Overall, then, our aim is to defend the claim that divine providence is God's sovereign action within creation to remain faithful to the promise he made to it. God remains faithful to his promise for creation, that he will extend his presence across the entire world; and Jesus Christ, by the power of the Holy Spirit, demonstrates his own faithfulness to his Father and in doing so reveals the Father's faithfulness to the world. The triune God mediates his active presence to the world not through creaturely secondary causation but through creaturely faithfulness made possible and guaranteed by his own, faithful action. Insofar as Christ's faithfulness reveals the fidelity of both the Father and the Spirit, we may say that God's sovereign action is providence made flesh.

CHAPTER 2

The 'Proper Place' of Secondary Causation in the Theology of John Calvin

§ 2.1 Introduction

Positively, John Calvin's teaching on providence affirms the closest possible relation between God and his creation without conflating the two; negatively, Calvin's depiction of this relation is vulnerable to charges of determinism or even occasionalism.[1] Convictions that 'nothing takes place by chance'[2] and that all events and creatures 'are governed by God's secret plan in such a way that nothing happens except what is knowingly and willingly decreed by him'[3] certainly suggest that such charges are not without reason. However, Calvin insists that God's providence has a dynamism that cannot be overshadowed by the implied determinism of his position. God governs all that he has made, he preserves it, he drives its celestial frame and all its parts; he sustains, nourishes and cares for it;[4] and the omnipotence by which he governs creation is not empty or idle but of 'a watchful, effective, active sort, engaged in ceaseless activity.'[5] His is 'not an unconcerned sitting ... in heaven, from which He merely observes the things that are done in the world; but that all-active and all-concerned seatedness on His throne above, by which He governs the world which He Himself hath made.'[6] The world does not, therefore, persist

---

[1] Though it is surely beyond doubt that John Calvin's basic position on divine providence is deterministic, we should not assume that he supposes God to be the first uncaused cause in a chain of causes and their effects. Paul Helm is right not to ask whether Calvin is a determinist but rather, if his views 'tend towards determinism, what kind of determinism would this be?' (P. Helm, *John Calvin's Ideas* [Oxford: Oxford University Press, 2004], 123). Calvin's understanding of secondary causation, as we shall see, prevents his theology from lapsing into Stoicism. For a summary of occasionalism, the notion that causal efficacy truly belongs to God alone, see S. Nadler, 'Occasionalism', in *The Cambridge Dictionary of Philosophy*, 2nd ed. (Cambridge: Cambridge University Press, 1999), 626–627.
[2] J. Calvin, *Institutes of the Christian Religion* (2 vols.), translated by F.L. Battles (LCC XX / XXI; Philadelphia: The Westminster Press, 1960), 1:16:4, 203.
[3] Calvin, *Institutes*, 1:16:2, 199; 1:16:3, 201; quote from 201.
[4] Calvin, *Institutes*, 1:16:1, 197–198.
[5] Calvin, *Institutes*, 1:16:3, 200.
[6] J. Calvin, *A Defence of the Secret Providence of God*, in *Calvin's Calvinism: Treatises on the Eternal Predestination of God and the Secret Providence of God*,

according to its own nature but rather God 'so regulates all things that nothing takes place without his deliberation.'[7] Thus God rules 'not only because he watches over the order of nature set by himself, but because he exercises especial care over *each* of his works.'[8] Calvin's emphasis, then, is that God is involved intimately with every single thing that happens and with every individual creature that constitutes creation.

Accordingly, God is *causa prima* or first cause, but not in the sense that he is the first in a series of many *causae secundae* or secondary causes;[9] instead, he is *causa prima* because of the ontologically prior causal relation in which he stands to *each* and *every* individual *causa secunda*. The introduction of the conceptuality of secondary causation means that although 'the Christian heart ... has been thoroughly persuaded that all things happen by God's plan', and that it should 'ever look to him as the principal cause of things', yet it will 'give attention to the secondary causes in their proper place.'[10] Despite affirming God's pancausal relation to creation, nonetheless Calvin retains a place – a 'proper place' – for genuine creaturely causation. By recognising the existence and thus the reality of secondary causes, Calvin hopes to distinguish his view from a flat, mechanistic causation whereby God is the only acting or causal agent irresistibly influencing all things.[11] Yet Calvin's teaching on providence is not without its difficulties. Precisely what is the relation between primary and secondary causation? How do we say that God causes all things *and* that creaturely agents also have true causal efficacy? Surely the relation between God as primary cause and creaturely agents as secondary causes is not illuminated by a simple insistence that they are not opposed or contradictory. An explanation is required as to how or why creaturely secondary causation is genuine when ostensibly divine primary causation must surely negate the efficacy of that secondary causation. Is Calvin inconsistent here or is his conception of providence more nuanced than is commonly noted?

Our intention in this chapter is to assess Calvin's conception of secondary causation – which functions effectively as a technical term for creaturely

---

translated by H. Cole (Grand Rapids: Reformed Free Publishing Association, 1987), 223–350 (224).

[7] Calvin, *Institutes*, 1:16:3, 200.

[8] Calvin, *Institutes*, 1:16:4, 203, emphasis mine.

[9] Cf. C. van der Kooi, *As in a Mirror: John Calvin and Karl Barth on Knowing God. A Diptych*, translated by D. Mader (SHCT 120; Leiden: Brill, 2005), 127.

[10] Calvin, *Institutes*, 1:17:6, 218.

[11] '[Calvin's] clear commitment to secondary or "inferior" causation implies that he does not think that God is the only causal agent. The activities of secondary causal agents may be *due to* the activity of God, their causal powers may be endowed and upheld by God, but that's a different matter.' (Helm, *John Calvin's Ideas*, 124, emphasis original; cf. van der Kooi, *As in a Mirror*, 127).

causation, agency or action – and its relation to divine primary causation.[12] We will divide our account into three sections. First, we will consider Calvin's view of God's fundamental relation to the world he has made. Secondary causation is employed here conceptually both to accommodate God within creation and to distinguish him from it. Calvin articulates his position not only by making positive statements about God's providence that he draws from Scripture, but also negative statements as he distances himself from what he perceives as the errors of Libertinism, Epicureanism and Stoicism.

Secondly, we will examine Calvin's stance on the fall of creation, particularly as it concerns Adam's disobedience to God and the notion that God actually determined the fall to happen. Here, secondary causation appears to conflict with primary causation insofar as God's will that the fall should happen

---

[12] At this point we should confess that we cannot do justice to the entirety of Calvin's writings in what is, after all, a single chapter of a discussion of the doctrine of providence and not specifically of Calvin's theology. That said, our discussion will not be restricted to his chapters on providence in the 1559 edition of *Institutes of the Christian Religion* (1:16–18) – the *locus classicus* – but will draw also from his commentaries and other related writings. Certainly, it is important not to see Calvin's writings as unrelated to one another: the circumstances that led Calvin to compose his occasional pieces contributed to the final shape of the *Institutes*. (Cf. R.A. Muller, *The Unaccommodated Calvin: Studies in the Foundation of a Theological Tradition* [OSHT; Oxford: Oxford University Press, 2000], 16; M.-C. Ong, *John Calvin on Providence: The Locus Classicus in Context* [unpublished Ph.D thesis, King's College London, 2003], 30–31). Calvin himself says that his purpose in writing the *Institutes* is 'to prepare and instruct candidates in sacred theology for the reading of the divine Word'; it is so ordered 'that if anyone rightly grasps it, it will not be difficult for him to determine what he ought especially to seek in Scripture, and to what end he ought to relate its contents.' (Calvin, *Institutes*, 'John Calvin to the Reader', 4).

The *Institutes* is not, therefore, a systematic theology or even a system of theology; it is, if anything, pedagogical, and so is 'best categorised as a work of dialectical, rhetorical, and contemplative theology, written for the purpose of clarifying the doctrine and strengthening the piety of the future pastors and teachers of the church.' (R.C. Zachman, *John Calvin as Teacher, Pastor, and Theologian: The Shape of His Writings and Thought* [Grand Rapids: Baker Academic, 2006], 102; cf. R.A. Muller, 'The Placement of Predestination in Reformed Theology: Issue or Non-Issue?', *Calvin Theological Journal* 40 [2005], 184–210 [194–195]; F. Wendel, *Calvin: The Origins and Development of his Religious Thought*, translated by P. Mairet [London: Collins, 1963], 357; M. de Kroon, *The Honour of God and Human Salvation: A Contribution to an Understanding of Calvin's Theology According to his Institutes*, translated by J. Vriend and L.D. Bierma [Edinburgh: T&T Clark, 2001], xiii). Nonetheless, the *Institutes* does indicate, at least in principle, how Calvin himself related various issues to each other. For a decent summary of the whole of the *Institutes*, see Zachman, *John Calvin as Teacher, Pastor, and Theologian*, 101–102.

seems to preclude the possibility that Adam might choose *not* to fall. The implication is that the integrity of Adam's will is jeopardised, with the concomitant suggestion that God's will can and does overwhelm secondary causation.

Following this, thirdly, we look at Calvin's account of the restoration of fallen creation to God through Jesus Christ, whose willing submission to God's will reversed the effects of Adam's own disobedience. The problem here is Calvin's emphasis on the divine will as the cause of human salvation: Is it possible that God's will renders Christ's obedience irrelevant? This questions the efficacy and integrity of secondary causation and, from this, the love and justice of God.

To conclude, we will make four observations about Calvin's teaching on providence and his conception of secondary causation. This chapter, then, serves both as an interpretation of Calvin's understanding of God's providence and as an introduction to the issues surrounding the conceptuality of secondary causation. Whilst Calvin introduces no novelty to the matter, his theological influence throughout the world – and certainly the Western world – makes him a significant contributor to discussions of divine providence.[13] We turn, then, first to Calvin's view of God's fundamental relation to the world.

§ 2.2 God's Fundamental Relation to the World

Providence is the idea that 'the presence of divine power [is] shining as much in the continuing state of the universe as in its inception.'[14] In speaking generally of it, Calvin suggests that God's relation to the world is always characterised and shaped by his sovereignty over it. Even in its pre-fallen state, creation is unstable and so designed to exist in total dependence upon God.[15] This should not be interpreted negatively: before God 'perfected the world it was an indigested mass'; if he 'should but withdraw his hand a little, all things would immediately perish and dissolve into nothing'.[16] Thus for Calvin, the total involvement of God in creation – and so creation's total dependence upon God – is thoroughly positive: God is 'constantly at work'[17] to prevent creation from dissolving into chaos.[18] Calvin is concerned especially to show that

---

[13] We will assess the influence of Calvin's teaching on providence and predestination in § 3.
[14] Calvin, *Institutes*, 1:16:1, 197.
[15] S.E. Schreiner, *The Theater of His Glory: Nature and the Natural Order in the Thought of John Calvin* (Grand Rapids: Baker Academic, 1995), 22.
[16] J. Calvin, *Commentaries on the Book of Genesis, Vol. 1* in *Calvin's Commentaries* I (CTS; Grand Rapids: Baker Books, 2003), 73, 103.
[17] Calvin, *Comm. Gen. 1*, 103.
[18] Calvin, *Comm. Gen. 1*, 73–74.

providence is not simply God knowing the future in advance,[19] as though 'bare prescience was the cause of things',[20] for this would imply that God only watches creaturely events unfold. However, providence 'pertains as much to [God's] operating hands as to His observing eyes', and he not only 'maintains and preserves' the order of nature but 'holds and continues a peculiar care of every single creature that He has created.'[21] Neither is providence limited to those extraordinary events of life termed miracles;[22] it extends to everything, even to something as commonplace as the passing of one day or one season into the next:

> That the sun rises upon us day by day; that in a course so rapid his rays should be so tempered and his degrees so adjusted; that the order of the stars, so wonderfully arranged, should never be disturbed; that the vicissitudes of the seasons should recur so continuously; that the earth should open her bowels with such annual regularity for the nourishment of man; that the elements and their separate particles should not cease to perform their appointed functions; in a word, that the fecundity of nature should never be worn out nor fail – all this marvellous operation, co-operation and continuance, can surely never be thought to proceed from any other cause than from the directing hand of God![23]

Providence, then, is essentially benevolent, maintaining the existence of that which is not God in relationship with God. Calvin's exposition of Psalm 104 in particular captures his sense of awe at the unlimited goodness of God in managing creation, whether that is to be seen in something as mundane as the formation of daily weather conditions, in the provision of dry land for living space, or in supplying wine to drink and not just water.[24] God shows himself to be 'the best of fathers' by not excluding any creature from his providential care; he is 'the master of a household, and a foster-father towards all sorts of living

---

[19] Calvin, *Institutes*, 1:16:4, 202; cf. 3:23:6, 954–955; J. Calvin, *Commentary Upon the Acts of the Apostles, Vol. 2* in *Calvin's Commentaries* XIX (CTS; Grand Rapids: Baker Books, 2003), 165.

[20] J. Calvin, *Commentaries on the Book of Genesis, Vol. 2* in *Calvin's Commentaries* I (CTS; Grand Rapids: Baker Books, 2003), 325.

[21] Calvin, *Secret Providence*, 224.

[22] '[God's] works which flow in the usual course have the name of nature; and they are miracles and retain not the name of nature, when God changes their wonted course; but yet they all proceed from God as their author.' (J. Calvin, *Commentaries on the Twelve Minor Prophets, Vol. 3* in *Calvin's Commentaries* XIV [CTS; Grand Rapids: Baker Books, 2003], 138).

[23] Calvin, *Secret Providence*, 224.

[24] J. Calvin, *Commentary on the Book of Psalms, Vol. 4* in *Calvin's Commentaries* VI (CTS; Grand Rapids: Baker Books, 2003) 146–147, 151, 155. Calvin marvels rather excessively at the fact that God providentially prevents the waters from submerging the world; see, for example, Calvin, *Comm. Gen. 1*, 80–81; cf. Schreiner, *The Theater of His Glory*, 22–28; van der Kooi, *As in a Mirror*, 134–136.

creatures, by providing liberally for them.'[25] Such provision demonstrates that it is absurd even to suppose that God created only to abandon that which he has made to its own course:[26] 'the earth does not possess such fruitfulness and riches of itself, but solely by the blessing of God'.[27] Indeed, 'nothing in the world is stable except in as far as it is sustained by the hand of God. The world did not originate from itself, consequently, the whole order of nature depends on nothing else than his appointment, by which each element has its own peculiar property.'[28]

The work of preservation by which the world is rendered stable is ascribed to the Holy Spirit. Citing the opening verses of Genesis, Calvin notes that 'the beauty of the universe (which we now perceive) owes its strength and preservation to the power of the Spirit'; this is entirely appropriate, for 'it is the Spirit who, everywhere diffused, sustains all things, causes them to grow, and quickens them in heaven and earth.'[29] Providence, then, has an explicitly pneumatological component: the life of the world is a gift of God, imparted to it by the Spirit. Importantly, the Spirit does not act independently; he effects that which the Father plans by conforming it to the pattern established by the Son, in whom alone is found 'the ordered disposition of all things'.[30] Although the Spirit gives life to the world, it is the Son who first shapes and orders that world, conditioning the manner in which the world relates to its triune creator: 'The Father has given all power to the Son that he may by the Son's hand govern, nourish, and sustain us, keep us in his care, and help us.'[31] This christological mediation, itself enabled and effected by the Spirit's work,[32] is essential to the relation between God and creation. Calvin goes so far even to say that had humanity 'remained free from all stain, his condition would have been too lowly for him to reach God without a Mediator.'[33] In making this point, Calvin does not wish to belittle humanity but seeks to stress that some form of mediation is necessary to relate divinity and humanity; the fallenness or otherwise of the created order does not affect this fundamental condition.

For Calvin, then, creation and providence are the work of the triune God, who supplies all that is necessary for its existence. Providence reveals God's gracious stance towards creation: by caring for his world, God shows his

---

[25] Calvin, *Comm. Psa. 4*, 160, 166.
[26] J. Calvin, *Commentary on the Book of Psalms, Vol. 3* in *Calvin's Commentaries* V (CTS; Grand Rapids: Baker Books, 2003), 427; cf. *Institutes*, 1:16:1, 197.
[27] Calvin, *Comm. Psa. 4*, 164–165.
[28] Calvin, *Comm. Psa. 4*, 149.
[29] Calvin, *Institutes*, 1:13:14, 138; cf. Calvin, *Comm. Acts 2*, 168.
[30] Calvin, *Institutes*, 1:13:18, 142–143; quote from 143.
[31] Calvin, *Institutes*, 2:15:5, 500; cf. P.W. Butin, *Revelation, Redemption, and Response: Calvin's Trinitarian Understanding of the Divine–Human Relationship* (Oxford: Oxford University Press, 1995), 52.
[32] Cf. Calvin, *Institutes*, 1:13:18, 143; 3:1:1, 537–538.
[33] Calvin, *Institutes*, 2:12:1, 465.

commitment to it and demonstrates that he does not begrudge the existence of something other to him, as though he were required somehow to nurse that which he had not willed. The Genesis refrain concerning the goodness of creation (Gen 1:4, 10, 12, 18, 21, 25, 31) suggests to Calvin that although God derives pleasure from his work, the main thrust of the observation is to move people 'to apply all [their] senses to the admiring contemplation of the works of God'.[34] That said, creation has a fundamentally anthropological orientation: 'God himself has shown by the order of Creation that he created all things for man's sake.'[35] Indeed, 'before he fashioned man, [God] prepared everything he foresaw would be useful and salutary for him.'[36] God's providence is 'concerned principally in the care and government of the human race.'[37] Sounded here is a muted note intimating that the non-human creation is diminished to mere utility; but we do not hear in this a discord advocating the concomitant exploitation of that creation,[38] nor do we suspect that Calvin had no time for less 'spiritual' matters in general. Activities such as astronomy for Calvin are entirely appropriate:

> To be sure, there is need of art and of more exacting toil in order to investigate the motion of the stars, to determine their assigned stations, to measure their intervals, to note their properties. As God's providence shows itself more explicitly when one observes these, so the mind must rise to a somewhat higher level to look upon his glory. Even the common folk and the most untutored, who have been taught only with the aid of the eyes, cannot be unaware of the excellence of divine art, for it reveals itself in this innumerable and yet distinct and well-ordered variety of the heavenly host. It is, accordingly, clear that there is no one to whom the Lord does not abundantly show his wisdom.[39]

This exploration and appreciation of the world should prompt people to look beyond the creaturely and towards God himself. So although Calvin allows that we should 'not be ashamed to take pious delight in the works of God open and manifest in this most beautiful theatre',[40] that God 'by the power of his Word and Spirit ... has so wonderfully adorned heaven and earth with as unlimited abundance, variety, and beauty of all things as could possibly be',[41] the contemplation of his works should enable us 'to feel [God's] power and grace in ourselves and in the great benefits he has conferred upon us, and so bestir

---

[34] Calvin, *Comm. Gen. 1*, 77.
[35] Calvin, *Institutes*, 1:14:22, 181–182.
[36] Calvin, *Institutes*, 1:14:22, 182.
[37] Calvin, *Secret Providence*, 225.
[38] Cf. Zachman, *John Calvin as Teacher, Pastor, and Theologian*, 231–242.
[39] Calvin, *Institutes*, 1:5:2, 53.
[40] Calvin, *Institutes*, 1:14:20, 179.
[41] Calvin, *Institutes*, 1:14:20, 179–180.

ourselves to trust, invoke, praise, and love him.'[42] Here the concept of secondary causation emerges as Calvin recognises the efficacy of creaturely actions even whilst affirming God's active presence within those actions. God remains at all times the 'first cause and author', working through creaturely secondary causes, whether human or non-human, to provide good things for his creation.[43] When the sun rises daily, it is really God who enlightens the earth. As the earth produces its fruits, it is really God who gives bread and the strength that comes from it. 'In a word,' Calvin writes, 'as all inferior and secondary causes, viewed in themselves, veil like so many curtains the glorious God from our sight (which they too frequently do), the eye of faith must be cast up far higher, that it may behold the hand of God working by all these His instruments.'[44] Ultimately, secondary causation demonstrates that God's involvement is not remote as the first cause in a chain of events but near as the first cause of every individual event.

Calvin developed his general teaching on providence by distinguishing his position from that of the so-called Libertines[45] and the resurgence of the philosophies of Epicureanism and Stoicism.[46] Each of these conceived of the relation between God (or the gods) and the world wrongly.[47] The Libertines, says Calvin, were pantheists who thought that nature is constituted from a

---

[42] Calvin, *Institutes*, 1:14:22, 181. We will look further at Calvin's appreciation of the world in § 3.1 and § 3.4.

[43] Calvin, *Secret Providence*, 230–231; quote from 230.

[44] Calvin, *Secret Providence*, 231.

[45] The Libertines were 'a group of speculative spiritualists whose pantheistic view of the divine Spirit and deterministic view of divine omnipotence had theological and ethical consequences which threatened the faith and life of French-speaking Reformed communities from within.' (A. Verhey, 'Calvin's Treatise "Against the Libertines"', *Calvin Theological Journal* 15 [1980], 190–219 [197]).

[46] Both Stoic and Epicurean thought had sixteenth-century advocates whose views Calvin opposed as he formulated his own teaching on providence. (Schreiner, *The Theater of His Glory*, 16–21). Epicurean doctrine stressed that the gods are not at all concerned with human activities and that their very distance frees humanity to order its own affairs in a world subject to chance. Conversely, the Stoics affirmed a providence that reduced everything to a system of causes, so much so that true freedom lies in acknowledging that all is fated to happen and living in accordance with that knowledge. (W.J.T. Kirby, 'Stoic *and* Epicurean? Calvin's Dialectical Account of Providence in the *Institute*', *International Journal of Systematic Theology* 5 [2003], 309–322 [314–315]; C. Partee, *Calvin and Classical Philosophy* [Louisville: Westminster John Knox Press, 2005], 67, 77, 95). Effectively, Epicureanism celebrates the absence of divinity while Stoicism reduces it to the level of nature. See also P.H. Reardon, 'Calvin on Providence: The Development of an Insight', *Scottish Journal of Theology* 28 (1975), 517–533 (525).

[47] Meng-Chai Ong argues further that Calvin's rejection of these positions is because they also conceived of God wrongly, that is, God was not understood to be the triune God of Scripture. (Ong, *John Calvin on Providence*, 35–38).

single, pervasive divine spirit, and who thus affirmed that 'everything in the world must be seen directly as His doing.'[48] Accordingly, God and the world are conflated. There is no ontological distinction between the two, and what is said of one necessarily must be said of the other. To counter this pantheism, Calvin once more emphasises that 'whatever comes to pass does so by the will of God',[49] but he adds that this providential ordering has three steps to it. First, 'there is a universal operation by which [God] guides all creatures according to the condition and propriety which He had given each when he made them. This guidance,' Calvin continues, 'is nothing other than what we call "the order of nature."'[50] Secondary causation has, therefore, its proper place. Indeed, by saying that all creatures are guided in a manner appropriate to them, Calvin strongly suggests that God accommodates his action to them so that, in some sense, his action is conditioned by them. God does not use secondary causes in a way that forces them out of their natural capacities. So although we are 'to think of creatures as instruments in [God's] hand', nonetheless 'this universal operation of God's does not prevent each creature ... from having and retaining its own quality and nature and from following its own inclination.'[51] However God acts through secondary causation, Calvin is sure that his action does not negatively affect creaturely action.

This leads Calvin to say that, secondly, God causes his creatures 'to serve His goodness, righteousness, and judgement according to His present will to help His servants, to punish the wicked, and to test the patience of His faithful, or to chastise them in His fatherly kindness.'[52] God's use of secondary causation is purposive. There is no place for fortune, no opportunity for chance to raise its head, for all that happens is due to God's 'special ordinance by which He guides all things'.[53] Calvin concludes,

> Therefore, let us adopt this resolution: that prosperity and adversity alike, rain, wind, sleet, hail, good weather, abundance, famine, war, and peace are all works of God's hand; and that creatures who constitute secondary causes are only means by which He fulfils His will; and consequently He commands and uses them as it pleases Him in order to bring them to that end which He has ordained should come to pass.[54]

---

[48] J. Calvin, *Against the Fantastic and Furious Sect of the Libertines who are Called 'Spirituals'*, in *Treatises Against the Anabaptists and Against the Libertines*, translated and edited by B.W. Farley (Grand Rapids: Baker Books, 1982), 187–326 (238).
[49] Calvin, *Against the Libertines*, 242.
[50] Calvin, *Against the Libertines*, 242–243.
[51] Calvin, *Against the Libertines*, 243.
[52] Calvin, *Against the Libertines*, 243–244.
[53] Calvin, *Against the Libertines*, 244; cf. *Institutes*, 1:16:9, 208–209.
[54] Calvin, *Against the Libertines*, 244–245.

Calvin's third comment about God's providence is that 'God governs His faithful, living and reigning in them by His Holy Spirit.'[55] It is God alone who 'illumines us that we might come to His knowledge' and he alone who 'creates new hearts in us, softening our hardness.'[56] For Calvin, then, the formation and establishment of the Church is a specific goal to which God directs all things, no matter how apparently insignificant or irrelevant these seem.

Essentially, Calvin dismisses Libertinism because it is pantheistic. It makes no ontological distinction between God and the world and therefore is easily refuted by the introduction of the conceptuality of secondary causation. When writing against Epicureanism and Stoicism, however, Calvin is aware that a simple affirmation of secondary causation is not enough to counter them; his employment of this notion must demonstrate that God is neither distant from nor confined within creation, as these philosophies respectively would suppose. Calvin wastes little effort in dismissing the Epicurean belief that God is not involved in the world's affairs. 'What good is it,' he asks, 'to profess with Epicurus some sort of God who has cast aside the care of the world only to amuse himself in idleness?'[57] Indeed, God is the very opposite of idle: his power 'is not inactive' but is a 'constantly operating power' by which he governs the world 'in righteousness and equity'.[58] Epicurus may believe that God reclines on a couch, but Calvin is certain that God sits alert on his throne, attending to 'the [created] order which he himself at first established.'[59] Stoicism, however, is harder to resist, and Calvin repeatedly identifies the differences between Stoic fate and Christian providence to demonstrate that he himself does not advocate a belief in the former.[60] The problem with the Stoic view that all things happen necessarily is that God is made subject to secondary causation.[61] 'We do not,' Calvin says, 'with the Stoics, contrive a necessity out of the perpetual connection and intimately related series of causes, which is contained in nature'; rather, 'we make God the ruler and governor of all

---

[55] Calvin, *Against the Libertines*, 247.
[56] Calvin, *Against the Libertines*, 248.
[57] Calvin, *Institutes*, 1:2:2, 41.
[58] J. Calvin, *Commentary on the Book of Psalms, Vol. 1* in *Calvin's Commentaries* IV (CTS; Grand Rapids: Baker Books, 2003), 117.
[59] Calvin, *Comm. Psa. 1*, 164–165; quote from 165.
[60] Despite the fact that his first published work was a commentary on Seneca's *De Clementia*, there is no suggestion that Calvin was influenced by the Stoic's philosophy in connection with providence. P.H. Reardon claims that if providence was a major theme in Calvin's thought at this earliest point in his writing career, he would surely have commented instead on Seneca's *De Providentia*. (Reardon, 'Calvin on Providence', 522–523). Calvin's distancing of himself from Stoic fatalism should not be considered a turning away from previously held convictions but is, given the *prima facie* similarities between his teaching on providence and the Stoic doctrine, an attempt to say why Christian providence is *not* fatalism.
[61] Calvin, *Secret Providence*, 234, 261.

things.'[62] There is a significant difference between the belief that all things form part of 'a complicated chain of causes' and that 'the world, and every part of it, is directed by the will of God.'[63] By distinguishing his position from Epicurean and Stoic conceptions of God's relation to the world, Calvin affirms that God is both intimately involved in creation's affairs and not imprisoned by them.[64] Secondary causation functions conceptually to mediate between God and the world without either conflating them or making it impossible for them to interact.[65] Thus against Epicureanism, God is present and active within creation precisely because he accommodates his action to creaturely action; and against the Stoics and, to an extent, the Libertines, God cannot be confused with creaturely action precisely because he cannot be confined to that action. Accordingly, the conceptuality of secondary causation is vital to Calvin's understanding of God's relation to the world because without it, he would lapse either into a strict dualism where God and creation do not and cannot relate (as in Epicureanism), or into pantheism, where God and creation are indistinguishable (as in Libertinism or Stoicism). For Calvin, the conceptuality of secondary causation demonstrates that God is present to the world without him being the world.

§ 2.3 God's Providence and the Fall of Creation

The catastrophic event of the fall does not affect the fundamental relation between God and the world.[66] Whether uncorrupted or fallen, creatures continue to rely on God's provision of everything they need to exist, including life itself. What does change with the entrance of sin into the world is humanity's ability to recognise God acting in the world through secondary

---

[62] Calvin, *Institutes*, 1:16:8, 207.

[63] J. Calvin, *Commentary on a Harmony of the Evangelists, Vol. 1* in *Calvin's Commentaries* XVI (CTS; Grand Rapids: Baker Books, 2003), 464–465; quote from 465.

[64] W.J. Torrance Kirby encapsulates Calvin's position when he writes that 'Calvin's account of providence presents us with a God who is simultaneously *more* remote in his transcendence than the gods of Epicurus, and *more* intimately involved in cosmic governance through his special providence than the Stoics ever dreamed possible.' (Kirby, 'Stoic *and* Epicurean?', 321, emphasis original).

[65] Calvin seems to prioritise the mediation of secondary causation over the christological mediation mentioned earlier. Secondary causation for Calvin surely has a wider application, relating God and the whole of creation to one another, whereas, apart from nods at appropriate times to his role in providence, the Son's mediation appears to be mainly soteriological. This is not necessarily a problem – we will argue something similar to this latter point in § 7 – but to avoid an unnecessary ambiguity, Calvin needs more carefully to articulate how the Son's sustaining of all things is understood within the general framework of secondary causation.

[66] Cf. Schreiner, *The Theater of His Glory*, 32, 36.

causes. Calvin exhorts the godly to consider secondary causes with gratitude but also to praise God as the principal author who provides through them.[67] In doing so, he implies strongly that, before the fall, this would have been a person's natural response to the action of his or her fellow creatures, human and non-human. Secondary causation would have been acknowledged with God, as primary cause, working through those causes. Post-fall, however, people see only nature, that is, secondary causation alone and so, effectively, only natural occurrence.[68] So although the essential relation between God and the world does not change because of the fall, for Calvin our perception of God's presence within the world has changed. Sinners do not see – or do not *want* to see – God at work in the world.

Here arises the question of how sin could enter an unblemished world governed by God to diminish human awareness of his presence in the world. Calvin's response is to argue that people were created to respond freely to God's provision in an appropriate manner. Through exercising their minds, people are guided by reason 'to distinguish good from evil, right from wrong'.[69] Subsequently, they have the choice to do what they have discerned either to be good or evil; but the power to choose itself is controlled by the will, which translates whatever choice is made into action and so from possibility into actuality. For pre-fallen humanity, then, sound reason would guide it into distinguishing between good and evil aright, enabling it to choose what is good so that the will ensures that action's implementation.[70] However, Adam, the first man, did not submit his will to reason. Although God denied to him the tree of the knowledge of good and evil 'to test his obedience and prove that he was willingly under God's command',[71] Adam 'fell solely by his own will',[72] that is, he recognised what was required by the divine command but chose the opposite and so enslaved his will to sin, which could no longer ensure the execution of right actions. Adam thus introduced sin into the world by his disobedience and subjected the whole of creation – including his descendants – to sin's curse:

> [A]fter the heavenly image was obliterated in [Adam], he was not the only one to suffer this punishment – that, in place of wisdom, virtue, holiness, truth, and justice, with which adornments he had been clad, there came forth the most filthy

---

[67] Cf. Calvin, *Institutes*, 1:17:9, 221.
[68] Cf. Calvin, *Comm. Psa. 1*, 479; J. Calvin, *Commentary on the Book of Psalms, Vol. 5* in *Calvin's Commentaries* VI (CTS; Grand Rapids: Baker Books, 2003) 300-301.
[69] Calvin, *Institutes*, 1:15:8, 195.
[70] Calvin, *Institutes*, 1:15:8, 195.
[71] Calvin, *Institutes*, 2:1:4, 245.
[72] Calvin, *Institutes*, 1:15:8, 195.

plagues, blindness, impotence, impurity, vanity, and injustice – but he also entangled and immersed his offspring in the same miseries.[73]

This so-called 'inherited corruption' or 'original sin'[74] for Calvin is 'a hereditary depravity and corruption of our nature' that 'first makes us liable to God's wrath, then also brings forth in us those works which Scripture calls "works of the flesh".'[75] Fallen humanity is so saturated with sin that it 'stand[s] justly condemned and convicted before God, to whom nothing is acceptable but righteousness, innocence, and purity.'[76] Such a judgement is warranted because of the perpetuation of sin: it is not merely a single act of transgression but continuous wrongdoing, like 'water ceaselessly bubbl[ing] up from a spring.'[77] From this, Calvin argues that sinful humanity can do nothing good.[78] A person's will is so inclined towards evil that even if good is distinguished from evil aright, nonetheless it is the evil that is chosen and implemented.[79] Humanity is so thoroughly corrupted that it is 'surely subject to the necessity of sinning.'[80] Calvin elucidates,

> [M]an is evil not to nature nor to the origin of the first man, but only to his wrongdoing, by which he brought this wretchedness on himself. For we do not deny that man was created with free choice, endowed as he was with sound intelligence of mind and uprightness of will. We do declare that our choice is now held captive under bondage to sin, but how did this come about except by Adam's misuse of free choice when he had it?[81]

At this point, Calvin claims that whilst a person sins and does so necessarily, that sin nonetheless is committed willingly.[82] Ordinarily, to say that an act is performed willingly is to say that it is performed freely and without coercion. However, freedom for Calvin is not the unrestricted ability to choose one option from a variety: this matters little, for a person 'confined in a nail-studded wine cask' may well be able freely to exercise his or her will, but of what use is

---

[73] Calvin, *Institutes*, 2:1:5, 246; cf. J. Calvin, *The Bondage and Liberation of the Will: A Defence of the Orthodox Doctrine of Human Choice Against Pighius*, edited by A.N.S. Lane and translated by G.I. Davies (Grand Rapids: Baker Books, 1996), 2.263, 46–47.
[74] Calvin, *Institutes*, 2:1:5, 246.
[75] Calvin, *Institutes*, 2:1:8, 251.
[76] Calvin, *Institutes*, 2:1:8, 251.
[77] Calvin, *Institutes*, 2:1:8, 251.
[78] Cf. Calvin, *Institutes*, 2:2:1, 255.
[79] Calvin, *Institutes*, 2:2:26, 286–287.
[80] Calvin, *Institutes*, 2:3:5, 296.
[81] Calvin, *Bondage and Liberation*, 2.263, 47.
[82] For a clarification of Calvin's teaching here, see Helm, *John Calvin's Ideas*, 172–177.

it?[83] In fact, the idea of 'free will' is misleading because of itself, fallen humanity wills only to sin;[84] the possibility of not sinning is not an option. To elucidate his understanding of the will, Calvin argues that initially it may be said either to be free, bound, self-determined or coerced. 'People generally understand a free will to be one which has it in its power to choose good or evil'. The two ideas contained within the concept of a coerced will are essentially contradictory, says Calvin, but he does use them to explain more clearly that a coerced will is directionless and so 'forcibly driven by an external impulse'. A self-determined will 'of itself ... directs itself in the direction in which it is led, when it is not taken by force or dragged unwillingly.' Finally, Calvin argues that the corruption inherent in a bound will is taken hostage by evil desires so that it chooses nothing but evil, 'even if it does so of its own accord and gladly, without being driven by any external impulse.'[85] This means that humanity has self-determined choice, that is, a person chooses willingly and without being forced to make that choice by an external agent. Nonetheless, that choice is not free – it is conditioned by the will, which itself is bound by the necessity of sinning.[86] For Calvin,

> [M]an is [not] dragged unwillingly into sinning, but that because his will is corrupt he is held captive under the yoke of sin and therefore of necessity wills in an evil way. For where there is bondage, there is necessity. But it makes a great difference whether the bondage is voluntary or coerced. We locate the necessity to sin precisely in corruption of the will, from which it follows that it is self-determined.[87]

---

[83] Calvin, *Institutes*, 2:4:8, 316.

[84] Calvin is extremely wary of the term 'free will' and thinks it will 'be a great boon for the church if it be abolished.' (Calvin, *Institutes*, 2:2:8, 266). He does accept that 'free will' may be used if its sense is that of choice exercised without external pressure: 'If, I say, [choice is] called free in the sense of not being coerced or forcibly moved by an external impulse, but moving of its own accord, I have no objection. The reason I find this epithet unsatisfactory,' he continues, 'is that people commonly think of something quite different when they hear or read it being applied to the human will. Since in fact they take it to imply ability and power, one cannot prevent from entering the minds of most people, as soon as the will is called free, the illusion that it therefore has both good and evil within its power, so that it can by its own strength choose either one of them.' (Calvin, *Bondage and Liberation*, 2.279, 68; cf. de Kroon, *The Honour of God and Human Salvation*, 54; Helm, *John Calvin's Ideas*, 160).

[85] Calvin, *Bondage and Liberation*, 2.280, 69.

[86] It would seem that Calvin means that choice is 'free' insofar as it is not coerced but that it desires only to choose that which is sinful; see also Helm, *John Calvin's Ideas*, 151.

[87] Calvin, *Bondage and Liberation*, 2.280, 69–70.

There is nothing that sinful humanity can do to extract itself from the sin by which it is bound because that very sinfulness is what keeps it from doing what is necessary to be free to do good. It is not in a person's power 'to abandon ... wickedness and turn to the good.'[88] This must come, can only come from God, who himself is free from sin. Accordingly, any movement of the bound will towards good is itself a turn towards God, which is the result of divine grace:

> But all that we say amounts to this. First, that what a person is or has or is capable of is entirely empty and useless for the spiritual righteousness which God requires, unless one is directed to the good by the grace of God. Secondly, that the human is of itself evil and therefore needs transformation and renewal so that it may begin to be good, but that grace itself is not merely a tool which can help someone if he is pleased to stretch out his hand to [take] it. That is, [God] does not merely offer it, leaving [to man] the choice between receiving it and rejecting it, but he steers the mind to choose what is right, he moves the will also effectively to obedience, he arouses and advances the endeavour until the actual completion of the work is attained. Then again, that [grace] is not sufficient if it is just once conferred upon someone, unless it accompanies him without interruption.[89]

Human sinfulness is such a radical anomaly in creation that it takes something equally radical – and more powerful – to address the matter. There is nothing that humanity can do to extract itself from its proclivity to sin. Sinners require divine action on their behalf if their situation is to improve. Calvin is certain, therefore, that before his fall, Adam could exercise a truly free will in the sense that he could choose to do good;[90] but this means that when he chose evil, that too was a free choice. He need not have fallen and when he did, he did so willingly. Here, though, we must return to Calvin's contention that all things 'proceed from [God's] set plan, that nothing takes place by chance.'[91] So although Adam willed to choose what was evil, nonetheless his fall was orchestrated by God's decision: Adam's will, Calvin claims, was 'capable of being bent to one side or the other, and was not given the constancy to persevere, that he fell easily.'[92] This was by Adam's free choice; but Calvin also says that it was God's will that Adam so fell – otherwise he would have ensured the first man's perseverance. 'Adam fell, not only by the permission of God, but by His very secret counsel and decree'.[93] Similarly, it must also be God's will that Adam's descendants are implicated in his fall: the contagion of

---

[88] Calvin, *Bondage and Liberation*, 4.335, 149.
[89] Calvin, *Bondage and Liberation*, 3.311, 114; cf. *Institutes*, 2:3:5, 294.
[90] Cf. Helm, *John Calvin's Ideas*, 161.
[91] Calvin, *Institutes*, 1:16:4, 203.
[92] Calvin, *Institutes*, 1:15:8, 195.
[93] Calvin, *Secret Providence*, 267; cf. 280; J. Calvin, *Concerning the Eternal Predestination of God*, translated with an introduction by J.K.S. Reid (Cambridge: James Clarke, 1982), 101–102, 121, 122; *Institutes*, 3:23:4, 951.

original sin comes not from Adam himself but through the ordination of God so that 'the first man should at one and the same time have and lose, both for himself and for his descendants, the gifts that God had bestowed upon him.'[94] Why should God so will? The reason for this lies hidden in God's plan,[95] a stance that Calvin adopts repeatedly when he seeks to defend God's will from accusations of wrongdoing or injustice. Whatever it means to say that God ordains the fall, Calvin is clear that it is Adam and not God who is responsible for it:

> Adam fell, though not without God's knowledge and ordination, and destroyed himself and his posterity; yet this neither mitigates his guilt nor involves God in any blame.... For the proper and genuine cause of sin is not God's hidden counsel but the evident will of man.[96]

God's proximate causation effectively is suspended for this event[97] – the fall cannot be 'one of the works of God'; but Calvin has to confess that he does not know 'how it was ordained by the foreknowledge and decree of God ... without God being implicated as associate in the fault as the author or approver of transgression'. It is a secret that 'excel[s] the insight of the human mind'.[98]

At this point, a tension emerges from Calvin's conception of the relation between primary and secondary causation. Throughout his teaching on providence, Calvin strives to maintain a cautious balance between the two types of causation. He is concerned to recognise and affirm secondary causation even whilst positing primary causation as that from which the former draws its efficacy. Positively, this means that God provides good things such as food and drink through secondary causes; negatively, it suggests that God provides bad things through secondary causes, and clearly we see this in Calvin's understanding of the fall. Certainly, Adam has the ability to obey God's command not to eat from the tree; but he does not have the inclination to do so *unless he is so motivated by God*. Does this mean that the integrity of Adam's ability to discern, to choose and then to will what is good into actuality is somewhat overwhelmed by God's primary causation to ensure instead that the divine will – which here is the rather inexplicable intention to subject creation to the effects of sin – is executed?[99] Granted, the concept of secondary

---

[94] Calvin, *Institutes*, 2:1:7, 250; *Secret Providence*, 267.
[95] Calvin, *Institutes*, 1:15:8, 196.
[96] Calvin, *Eternal Predestination*, 121–122.
[97] Calvin, *Eternal Predestination*, 123–124.
[98] Calvin, *Eternal Predestination*, 124.
[99] We should stress that it is the *integrity* of Calvin's *ability* to discern, choose and will that is jeopardised. If Adam cannot choose what is good apart from God's action in his decision, that is not a problem. It remains Adam's decision, even if the power by which he makes and then executes it is not his own. However, if Adam *cannot* exercise his ability to choose what is good because of a prior decision by God that he

causation requires God to be present in all creaturely events, actions and even decisions, but we are now discerning a genuine friction between God working *through* secondary causation and his working *despite* or *against* secondary causation. This is seen particularly in Calvin's distancing of God's direct causation from Adam's disobedience, even though in some sense the latter is made possible by the divine ordination.[100]

Perhaps the most contentious aspect of Calvin's teaching on providence, then, concerns the relation of God's will to evil or sinful actions. Calvin is not hesitant to say that 'the will of God is the great cause of all things that are done in the whole world';[101] indeed, God's will is '(so to speak) the *cause of causes.*'[102] Here we see an explicit acknowledgement that there is some kind of relation between God's causation and creaturely causation: '[T]he world stands through no other power than that of God's word, and that therefore inferior or secondary causes derive from him their power; and produce different effects as they are directed.'[103] There is no problem in this basic conceptuality: secondary causation depends upon God for its efficacy inasmuch as he provides the means for creaturely action to take place. The conditions for creaturely action cannot be provided by the creature itself; it must presuppose that prior, divine action to prepare the way for its action. However, the matter is complicated somewhat when Calvin suggests that the creature *must* act in the way that God has prepared. Does God's providence, then, make creaturely activity possible or inevitable? Certainly, Calvin depicts the fall as unavoidable. Adam could choose either to obey or to disobey God's command; but because it was God's intention for Adam to fall, effectively he had to choose to disobey God even though ostensibly he retained the integrity of his action not to fall. God's will demonstrates its superiority over Adam's will but in doing so surely negates the integrity of the latter to choose either good or evil.

Nonetheless, although the divine will causes all things that are done, Calvin denies that God is therefore the author of evil.[104] God as *causa prima* is distinct from creaturely *causae secundae*: there is sufficient conceptual distance

---

should not do so, then we may suspect that God has denied the integrity of that ability.

[100] Cf. Calvin, *Comm. Gen.* 2, 378: 'Meanwhile, it is right to maintain, what is declared by the clear testimonies of Scripture, that whatever men may contrive, yet, amidst all their tumult, God from heaven overrules their counsels and attempts; and, in short, does, by their hands, what he has himself decreed.' To be sure, Calvin here speaks of human evil that God uses to bring about a good end; but the process by which God does this is similar if not identical to that by which he condemns Adam to fall.

[101] Calvin, *Secret Providence*, 233; cf. Calvin, *Institutes*, 1:17:1, 211.

[102] Calvin, *Comm. Gen.* 2, 51, emphasis original.

[103] J. Calvin, *Commentaries on the Catholic Epistles* in *Calvin's Commentaries* XXII (CTS; Grand Rapids: Baker Books, 2003), 416. We should note that Calvin does not actually explain the relation between the two types of causation.

[104] Calvin, *Secret Providence*, 233.

between God and his creation for him to employ secondary causation without being identified with it. Thus God is able to use a person's evil actions for his own good purposes without being blamed for those actions, in the same way that the sun's heat causes an exposed corpse to stink without itself smelling.[105] Calvin implies, therefore, that intention plays a significant role in action, both divine and human. Although the action that a sinful person does is so governed by God that they 'cannot move even one of their fingers without accomplishing the work of God much more than their own',[106] it is important to know that what they do 'vainly or unrighteously', God himself does 'rightly and righteously'.[107] So whilst some sin willingly in disobedience to the divine command, nonetheless what they do 'proves that they were only fulfilling all the while that which had been ordained by God, and that, too, against their own will, while they knew nothing about it!'[108]

Is Calvin here suggesting that there exists a strong distinction between what God wills and what he commands? Can God both will a person's murder and command that murder should not happen? Calvin says that we are to obey what God commands, for he does not command us to do evil – and yet Calvin surely claims that somehow God wills our disobedience.[109] The problem is not that God has 'two contrary wills' but that we cannot understand how God's will both 'wills and does not will something to take place.'[110] Regardless, we again see here the importance that Calvin places upon the intention behind an action. Those who commit evil do not render service to God in the same way as the faithful,[111] but he is able to use that evil to do good. To illustrate his point, Calvin examines the story of Job. Although Job was attacked by the Chaldeans, ostensibly it stemmed from Satan in accordance with God's will.[112] This one event may be said to issue from the actions of three agents, the Chaldeans, Satan and God; but the Chaldeans and Satan are not excused from their deeds, and God himself is not tainted by their evil.[113] Calvin sees three different intentions or purposes at play. First, God wishes 'to exercise the patience of His servant by calamity'; next, 'Satan endeavours to drive him to desperation'; and

---

[105] Calvin, *Institutes*, 1:17:5, 217; *Against the Libertines*, 247.

[106] Calvin, *Secret Providence*, 238.

[107] Calvin, *Secret Providence*, 233.

[108] Calvin, *Secret Providence*, 239.

[109] Calvin, *Institutes*, 1:17:5, 217.

[110] Calvin, *Institutes*, 1:18:3, 233–234; cf. P. Helm, 'Calvin (and Zwingli) on Divine Providence', *Calvin Theological Journal* 29 (1994), 388–405 (398): 'There may be a hidden counsel and a revealed voice, but the end of each is the same, hence there is one will in God.'

[111] Calvin, *Institutes*, 1:17:5, 216–217; *Secret Providence*, 238.

[112] Calvin, *Institutes*, 1:18:1, 230. Satan himself 'cannot undertake anything unless God so wills.' (Calvin, *Institutes*, 1:18:1, 229; cf. 1:18:2, 232; 2:4:5, 313).

[113] Calvin, *Institutes*, 2:4:2, 310.

finally, 'the Chaldeans strive to acquire gain from another's property contrary to law and right.'[114] From this, we see that

> The Lord permits Satan to afflict His servant; He hands the Chaldeans over to be impelled by Satan, having chosen them as His ministers for this task. Satan with his poison darts arouses the wicked minds of the Chaldeans to execute that evil deed. They dash madly into injustice, and they render all their members guilty and befoul them by the crime.[115]

Calvin concludes that there is 'no inconsistency in assigning the same deed to God, Satan and man; but the distinction in purpose and manner causes God's righteousness to shine forth blameless there, while the wickedness of Satan and of man betrays itself by its own disgrace.'[116] Satan and the Chaldeans each desire to persecute Job and so clash with God's own intent: God wishes to see Job develop patience, whereas Satan and the Chaldeans, in their own ways, seek to ruin him. Here, though, is our problem: whilst Calvin shows that the three distinct purposes may be compatible with each other, it is uncertain to what extent he ascribes causal efficacy to the actions presumably initiated by these purposes. God's will for Job certainly is the dominant *causa* to which the *causae* of Satan and the Chaldeans are subordinate; but does this dominance overrule the creaturely *causae*, and what is the connection between them and the various intentions? Certainly, Calvin makes no attempt here to clarify the relation between primary and secondary causation, nor does he think one is needed. He appears instead to assume a hierarchy of causes in which the creaturely *causae* can only serve the purposes of the *causa prima*.[117] Accordingly, the actions of Satan and the Chaldeans, though sinful in and of themselves and liable to the judgement of God, somehow are rendered permissible if God himself uses them. We see, then, the surfacing of the distinction between God's willing and his commanding: God must will that sin happens in order to test Job's patience, even though he does not command or condone such action. This means that the Chaldeans' attack on Job is willed by God, empowered by him but apparently justified on the grounds that God's reasons are nobler than those of the Chaldeans. Although the Chaldeans do wish to plunder Job and cannot be excused for their sin, God's primary causation is so determinative that it is uncertain that they can do other than what his divine plan orchestrates. Does this deny to the Chaldeans the integrity of their actions? It must at least jeopardise it, not because it is God's primary causation that makes it possible for them to carry out their desires, but because

---

[114] Calvin, *Institutes*, 2:4:2, 310.
[115] Calvin, *Institutes*, 2:4:2, 310–311.
[116] Calvin, *Institutes*, 2:4:2, 311. See also Calvin's discussion of Acts 2:23 in J. Calvin, *Commentary Upon the Acts of the Apostles, Vol. I* in *Calvin's Commentaries* XVIII (CTS; Grand Rapids: Baker Books, 2003), 95–99.
[117] Helm, *John Calvin's Ideas*, 125.

God's primary causation is accommodated to secondary causation, the action of the Chaldeans, in order himself to act. The crucial issue is whether this action nullifies the secondary causation it adopts.

§ 2.4 God's Providence and the Restoration of Creation

We see, then, that the disorder that always threatened creation before the fall is now an actuality through Adam's disobedience;[118] but Calvin's conviction that the fall was decreed by God to happen finally is unsurprising, given creation's inherent instability that necessitates its total dependence upon God even for its very existence. Any form of chaos that enters God's world can do so only by his design and under his conditions. This state of fallenness, however, is not final: humanity is the 'most excellent example of [God's] works',[119] and so, despite its sin, God 'wills not to lose what is his in us'.[120] In establishing this, however, Calvin affirms two seemingly contradictory divine attitudes towards humanity in its fallenness: first, 'God is, so to speak, hostile to us, and his hand is armed for our destruction';[121] but God's love, secondly, motivates him to draw humanity back to himself once more.[122] There seems to be a genuine tension here: God both hates and loves his fallen creation. It is important, however, to understand that for Calvin, God has loved people in Christ from before the creation of the world;[123] God's abhorrence of humanity is due ultimately to its contamination by sin.[124] So although God cannot tolerate

---

[118] Cf. Schreiner, *The Theater of His Glory*, 28.

[119] Calvin, *Institutes*, 1:14:20, 180.

[120] Calvin, *Institutes*, 2:16:3, 505.

[121] Calvin, *Institutes*, 2:16:2, 505.

[122] Calvin, *Institutes*, 2:16:3, 506; cf. S. Edmondson, *Calvin's Christology* (Cambridge: Cambridge University Press, 2004), 94.

[123] Cf. J. Calvin, *Commentary on the Epistles of Paul the Apostle to the Corinthians, Vol. 2* in *Calvin's Commentaries* XX (CTS; Grand Rapids: Baker Books, 2003), 237, emphasis original: 'For so long as God imputes to us our sins, He must of necessity regard us with abhorrence; for he cannot be friendly or propitious to sinners. But this statement may seem to be at variance with what is said elsewhere – that we were loved by Him before the creation of the world, (Eph. i. 4,) and still more with what he says, (John iii. 16,) that the love, which he exercised towards us was the reason, why He expiated our sins by Christ, for the cause always goes before its effect. I answer, that we were loved before the creation of the world, but it was only *in Christ*. In the mean time, however, I confess, that the love of God was first in point of time, and of order, too, as to God, but with respect to us, the commencement of his love has its foundation in the sacrifice of Christ. For when we contemplate God without a Mediator, we cannot conceive of Him otherwise than as angry with us: a Mediator interposed between us, makes us feel, that He is pacified towards us.' See also Calvin, *Institutes*, 2:16:4, 506, and Helm, *John Calvin's Ideas*, 395.

[124] Calvin, *Institutes*, 2:6:1, 340–341.

humanity's sinfulness, because of his love for sinners he eradicates their sinfulness by the expiatory death of Christ.[125] Indeed, this christological emphasis demonstrates that 'God is pleased and kindly disposed toward us', for it is through Christ alone that 'we escape the imputation of our sins to us – an imputation bringing with it the wrath of God.'[126]

The divine work of salvation focuses, therefore, on Christ. Calvin contends that 'man, who by his disobedience had become lost, should by way of remedy counter it with obedience, satisfy God's judgement, and pay the penalties for sin.'[127] However, this is something that a fallen person can never do: since the fall, each person's nature is so 'depraved ... that he can be moved or impelled only to evil.'[128] It is into this grim situation that Christ, the Son of God steps as Mediator, '[u]ngrudgingly [taking] our nature upon himself to impart to us what was his, and to become both Son of God and son of man in common with us.'[129] Only by being a man himself could the sanctified Son of God reverse the effects of the fall through his own willing obedience:

> [O]ur Lord came forth as true man and took the person and the name of Adam in order to take Adam's place in obeying the Father, to present our flesh as the price of satisfaction to God's righteous judgement, and, in the same flesh, to pay the penalty that we deserved. In short, since neither as God alone could he feel death, nor as man alone could he overcome it, he coupled human nature with divine that to atone for sin he might submit the weakness of the one to death; and that, wrestling with death by the power of the other nature, he might win victory for us.[130]

Christ's obedience is crucial to Calvin's understanding of the divine work of salvation, for it is through his obedience that Christ recreates fallen humanity and enables it to stand once more before God.[131] Importantly, Christ's obedience is not simply a matter of his movement towards his death on the cross. 'From the time when [Christ] took on the form of a servant, he began to pay the price of liberation in order to redeem us.'[132] All that he did as a man contributed to the work of salvation that he achieved. Nonetheless, Calvin does emphasise the obedience that led Christ to the cross, where he demonstrated his

---

[125] Calvin, *Institutes*, 2:16:3, 506.
[126] Calvin, *Institutes*, 2:16:3, 506.
[127] Calvin, *Institutes*, 2:12:3, 466.
[128] Calvin, *Institutes*, 2:3:5, 296.
[129] Calvin, *Institutes*, 2:12:2, 465.
[130] Calvin, *Institutes*, 2:12:3, 466. We will look at the constitution of the person of Christ in § 8.
[131] Cf. T. Hart, 'Humankind in Christ and Christ in Humankind: Salvation as Participation in our Substitute in the Theology of John Calvin', *Scottish Journal of Theology* 42 (1989), 67-84 (76).
[132] Calvin, *Institutes*, 2:16:5, 507.

total submission to his Father's will.¹³³ '[E]ven in death itself his willing obedience is the important thing because a sacrifice not offered voluntarily would not have furthered righteousness.'¹³⁴ Furthermore, the particular course of Christ's death demonstrates that God has somehow 'burdened [him] with another's sin rather than his own.'¹³⁵ Calvin writes,

> [Christ] therefore suffered under Pontius Pilate, and by the governor's official sentence was reckoned among criminals. Yet not so – for he was declared righteous by his judge at the same time, when Pilate affirmed that he 'found no cause for complaint in him' [John 18:38]. This is our acquittal: the guilt that held us liable for punishment has been transferred to the head of the Son of God [Isa. 53:12]. We must, above all, remember this substitution, lest we tremble and remain anxious throughout life – as if God's righteous vengeance, which the Son of God has taken upon himself, still hung over us.¹³⁶

Thus, for Calvin, '[t]he Son of God, utterly clean of all fault, nevertheless took upon himself the shame and reproach of our iniquities, and in return clothed us with his purity.' In taking upon himself the curse of sin, Christ offered himself as 'an expiatory sacrifice' by which 'he discharged all satisfaction', ensuring that 'we might cease to be afraid of God's wrath.'¹³⁷ Calvin makes the point that in order for Christ truly and fully to achieve salvation, he has to suffer both physically and, we might say, spiritually:

> The point is that the Creed sets forth what Christ suffered in the sight of men, and then appositely speaks of that invisible and incomprehensible judgement which he underwent in the sight of God in order that we might know not only that Christ's body was given as the price of our redemption, but that he paid a greater and more excellent price in suffering in his soul the terrible torments of a condemned and forsaken man.¹³⁸

It is obvious enough to understand what Calvin means by Christ's bodily suffering; but it is through his spiritual suffering that he bore 'the severity of God's vengeance, to appease his wrath and satisfy his just judgement. For this reason,' Calvin continues, 'he must also grapple hand to hand with the armies of hell and the dread of everlasting death.'¹³⁹ This was not because he simply feared death; rather, he feared the divine judgement that would be a significant factor in that death:

---

¹³³ Calvin, *Institutes*, 2:16:5, 507–508.
¹³⁴ Calvin, *Institutes*, 2:16:5, 508; cf. *Comm. Acts 1*, 95–96.
¹³⁵ Calvin, *Institutes*, 2:16:5, 509.
¹³⁶ Calvin, *Institutes*, 2:16:5, 509–510.
¹³⁷ Calvin, *Institutes*, 2:16:6, 510.
¹³⁸ Calvin, *Institutes*, 2:16:10, 516.
¹³⁹ Calvin, *Institutes*, 2:16:10, 515; cf. Edmondson, *Calvin's Christology*, 104.

He had no horror at death, therefore, simply as a passage out of the world, but because he had before his eyes the dreadful tribunal of God, and the Judge himself armed with inconceivable vengeance; and because of our sins, the load of which was laid upon him, pressed him down with their enormous weight. There is no reason to wonder, therefore, if the dreadful abyss of destruction tormented him grievously with fear and anguish.[140]

This suffering is how Calvin interprets the creedal affirmation of Christ's descent into hell, but it is also a way in which he confirms Christ's humanity, because, in facing death, Christ 'had, therefore, to conquer, that fear which by nature continually torments and oppresses all mortals.'[141] Calvin concludes, 'No wonder, then, if he is said to have descended into hell, for he suffered the death that God in his wrath had inflicted upon the wicked!'[142] Thus the death of Christ for Calvin is 'the complete fulfilment of salvation, for through it we are reconciled to God, his righteous judgement is satisfied, the curse is removed, and the penalty paid in full.'[143] That said, there must be a place for Christ's subsequent resurrection, by which he is shown to have triumphed over death. Sin is 'wiped out and death extinguished' by Christ's death, true; but it is through his resurrection that righteousness is 'restored and life raised up, so that – thanks to his resurrection – his death manifested its power and efficacy in us.'[144] Indeed, it is through his righteousness that our sins are overwhelmed, it is his salvation that rescinds our condemnation and his worthiness that compels God to overlook our unworthiness.[145] All this is meaningless, however, if there is no communication of Christ's work to sinners to enable them to participate in his life of obedience. Accordingly, the Holy Spirit forges this link to Christ, joining sinners to him so that they may benefit from the salvation he secured for them.[146] By the Spirit's power, Christ 'engrafts us into his body' so that we may 'become partakers of every good'[147] and 'receive a double grace: namely, that being reconciled to God through Christ's blamelessness, we may have in heaven instead of a Judge a gracious Father; and secondly, that sanctified by Christ's spirit we may cultivate blamelessness and purity of life.'[148] Those united to Christ are both justified by his imputed purity and sanctified by the

---

[140] J. Calvin, *Commentary on a Harmony of the Evangelists, Vol. 3* in *Calvin's Commentaries* XVII (CTS; Grand Rapids: Baker Books, 2003), 228; cf. J. Calvin, *Commentaries on the Epistle of Paul the Apostle to the Hebrews* in *Calvin's Commentaries* XXII (CTS; Grand Rapids: Baker Books, 2003), 122–123.
[141] Calvin, *Institutes*, 2:16:11, 517.
[142] Calvin, *Institutes*, 2:16:10, 516.
[143] Calvin, *Institutes*, 2:16:13, 520.
[144] Calvin, *Institutes*, 2:16:13, 521.
[145] Calvin, *Institutes*, 3:2:24, 570; cf. *Comm. Ep. Cor. 2*, 242.
[146] Calvin, *Institutes*, 3:1:1, 537.
[147] Calvin, *Institutes*, 3:2:35, 583.
[148] Calvin, *Institutes*, 3:11:1, 725.

Spirit, who takes imputed purity and makes it actual,[149] recapitulating in their lives the events that Christ himself experienced as he submitted himself to his Father.[150] The divine work of salvation, then, is thoroughly trinitarian in shape as God reconciles his fallen creation to himself.[151]

Nonetheless, there is a dark side to Calvin's soteriology: the Spirit draws only certain individuals to the Father through Christ: 'only those predestined to salvation receive the light of faith and truly feel the power of the gospel'.[152] This contributes to a further tension between primary and secondary causation in Calvin's theology. As sinful people can do nothing to extract themselves from bondage to sin, God himself must liberate them through the Spirit's uniting of them to Christ. We see no problem here: it makes sense for an agent who is personally unaffected by a negative situation to act on behalf of and for the one who is imprisoned in that situation. The emerging problem is that God's will seems to be the predominant cause in all things in such a way that it makes secondary causation irrelevant. First, humanity is enslaved to sin by God's will; we have already suggested that God's primary causation works against rather than through secondary causation here, insofar as the integrity of Adam's ability to exercise his will is jeopardised by God's will. Following this, secondly, Christ's obedient life by which he achieves salvation for fallen humanity is effective primarily, it seems, because *God wills it to be effective.* Human salvation ultimately rests upon God's *decision* that Christ's action as Mediator be effective rather than upon the efficacy of that particular action itself.[153] There is an insinuation, therefore, that, similarly to Adam, there is no integrity of Christ's action, though rather than his will, it is the integrity of his obedience that is jeopardised. Christ's obedience is simply the clothing in which the divine will is dressed, with no power of its own.[154] Is the Son's incarnate life therefore tangential to the divine purpose? Does Calvin set primary causation – that is, God's will – against secondary causation? Calvin's emphasis on the divine will certainly suggests that the actual accomplishment of salvation through Christ's cross and resurrection is somewhat unnecessary;

---

[149] Cf. J.R. Beeke, 'Calvin on Piety', in D.K. McKim (ed.), *The Cambridge Companion to John Calvin* (Cambridge: Cambridge University Press, 2004), 125–152 (130).

[150] Cf. Edmondson, *Calvin's Christology*, 142–143.

[151] Cf. Butin, *Revelation, Redemption, and Response*, 24, 52.

[152] Calvin, *Institutes*, 3:2:11, 555; cf. *Eternal Predestination*, 149.

[153] Calvin, *Institutes*, 2:12:1, 464; 2:17:1, 529; cf. J. Calvin, *Commentary on the Gospel According to John, Vol. 2* in *Calvin's Commentaries* XVIII (CTS; Grand Rapids: Baker Books, 2003), 105–106; *Comm. Acts 1*, 95–96. See also Wendel, *Calvin*, 228–229. Helm argues that Calvin's point is that by God's will, Christ's death is effective *for us*. (Helm, *John Calvin's Ideas*, 337). However, the basic criticism remains: Is there a genuine *creaturely* connection between Christ's work and humanity's salvation, or is everything effected at the level of divine volition?

[154] We will return to this point in § 8.3.

they are almost historical accidents of God's decision to predestine a certain number of people to salvation:

> We call predestination God's eternal decree, by which he compacted with himself what he willed to become of each man. For all are not created in equal condition; rather, eternal life is foreordained for some, eternal damnation for others. Therefore, as any man has been created to one or the other of these ends, we speak of him as predestined to life or to death.[155]

All creaturely history in some sense is the result or effect of this decree.[156] Providence may be seen, then, at least in part, as God's governing of his creation so that those who have been predestined to life are enabled to respond positively to the message of salvation preached by the Church, and for those facing eternal damnation to respond negatively.[157] Accordingly, people find themselves directed by God's will: as the human will is bound to sin, salvation comes only through God's sovereign action on humanity's behalf, an action to which no person can contribute. For the person predestined to life, this is undoubtedly good news; but for the person condemned to eternal damnation, the fact that his or her fate is sealed by a mere decision is surely something of an indignity. Calvin is emphatic that people are either condemned by their own sin[158] or saved by nothing other than the grace of God.[159] Individuals cannot

---

[155] Calvin, *Institutes*, 3:21:5, 926.

[156] 'The world is a contingent order dependent in its every moment, its every bit of matter, its every activity, on the divine will. If, then, God did not ordain "whatsoever comes to pass," *nothing would come to pass. The eternal decree does not, therefore, abolish history – it makes history possible.*' (R.A. Muller, 'The Myth of "Decretal Theology"', *Calvin Theological Journal* 30 [1995], 159–167 [165, emphasis original]).

[157] That Calvin places his discussion of predestination in a soteriological context in Book III of the *Institutes* should not detract from the fact that Calvin describes the eternal decree starkly. (Cf. Muller, 'The Myth of "Decretal Theology"', 163). Calvin's separation of providence and predestination in the *Institutes* is not because he makes no connection between them, but because God's decree of predestination ultimately is concerned with the salvation of certain individuals, whereas providence is a more general statement about God's relation to the world. (Cf. R.A. Muller, *Christ and the Decree: Christology and Predestination in Reformed Theology from Calvin to Perkins* [SHT 2; Durham, North Carolina: The Labyrinth Press, 1986], 19; Partee, *Calvin and Classical Philosophy*, 140). Accordingly, predestination surely assumes priority in God's dealings with the world because it is the divine plan to bring some people to salvation and to pass over the rest; providence ensures that that plan is executed.

[158] Calvin, *Institutes*, 3:23:1, 948; 3:23:8, 957; *Eternal Predestination*, 116; cf. *Institutes* 3:21:7, 931; 1:18:4, 235.

[159] Calvin, *Institutes*, 3:21:1, 921; 3:24:1, 966; 3:24:2, 967; cf. *Eternal Predestination*, 82–83.

influence God's decision, as though by foreknowledge he sees who is deserving of life and who warrants destruction.[160] Should God choose to pass over and condemn some, 'he does [this] for no other reason than that he wills to exclude them from the inheritance which he predestines for his own children.'[161] God's will is absolutely pivotal in matters of human salvation: 'For when it is said that God hardens or shows mercy to whom he wills, men are warned by this to seek no cause outside his will.'[162]

Although he is convinced that it is the teaching of Scripture and requires appropriate exposition,[163] nonetheless Calvin is aware that his position is controversial. This is clear in the way he defends himself against accusations that he depicts God as capricious and a tyrant. Certainly, this seems to be the case: Calvin comments that God's will is 'the cause of all things that are', so much so that 'whatever he wills, by the very fact that he wills it, must be considered righteous.'[164] Does this mean that God himself does not distinguish between good and evil, because, in determining all things in accordance with his secret plan, all things must ultimately be good, whether that means suitable employment for one person or the rape and dismemberment of another?[165] No; though it is true that God has a purpose in all that he does,[166] it does not mean that he acts arbitrarily or without reason. God's will is 'the sole rule of righteousness, and the truly just cause of all things.'[167] The will of God is 'not only free of all fault but is the highest rule of perfection, and even the law of all laws.'[168] What God decrees, he does so 'in accordance with his wisdom'.[169] For

---

[160] Calvin, *Institutes*, 3:22:4, 936.
[161] Calvin, *Institutes*, 3:23:1, 947.
[162] Calvin, *Institutes*, 3:22:11, 947.
[163] Calvin, *Institutes*, 3:21:3, 924.
[164] Calvin, *Institutes*, 3:23:2, 949.
[165] John Sanders lists a provocative array of examples to demonstrate what it means *prima facie* to say that God determines everything: '[I]f Susan has a job with excellent benefits, it is because God specifically wanted that to happen and it serves a specific good purpose in God's plan, even if Susan does not know it. If Susan is raped and dismembered, it is because God specifically wanted that to happen and it serves a specific good purpose in God's plan, even if Susan does not know it.... If Jones is afflicted with a debilitating mental illness in which he loses touch with reality, or if a three-year-old child contracts an incurable and intractably painful bone cancer, or if a number of kindergartners are murdered in a school gymnasium in Scotland, or if Christian women and children are raped and sold into slavery in Sudan, such experiences were specifically selected by God to happen to these individuals.' (J. Sanders, *The God Who Risks: A Theology of Providence* (Downers Grove: IVP, 1998), 212, 253).
[166] Calvin, *Eternal Predestination*, 119.
[167] Calvin, *Institutes*, 1:17:2, 214.
[168] Calvin, *Institutes*, 3:23:2, 950.
[169] Calvin, *Institutes*, 1:16:8, 207.

Calvin, God's decree has a sapiential element that prevents his will from ordering things simply according to an unrestricted whim;[170] God's power 'cannot be rightly separated from his wisdom and justice',[171] and, indeed, it is wrong to do so.[172] Accordingly, when God predestines some to life and the remainder to death, we can be assured that he does so for the very best of reasons, even if those reasons remain hidden to us. Calvin summarises his stance as follows:

> For the Scriptures furnish an abundance of testimonies concerning the secret and hidden will of God. What I have from them learned, I fearlessly assert and speak of as a thing sure and certain. But as my human intellect cannot soar to a height so stupendous, I adore with reverence, fear and trembling, that mystery which is too high and too deep for the angels themselves to penetrate.[173]

God's decree is not unfair: it only seems so because we do not know why the decree takes the form it does. It is a mystery that commands faithful submission. In matters of providence and predestination, then, Calvin concludes that 'our wisdom ought to be nothing else than to embrace with humble teachableness, and at least without finding fault, whatever is taught in Sacred Scripture.'[174]

§ 2.5 Conclusion

To conclude, we shall make four observations about Calvin's teaching on providence and his understanding and use of the conceptual framework of primary and secondary causation. These observations are based upon the preceding analysis of Calvin's theology.

Our first comment is that Calvin's conception of the fundamental relationship between God and creation has dualistic leanings, suggesting

---

[170] Implied here is the late medieval distinction between the *potentia Dei absoluta* and the *potentia Dei ordinata*, that is, between God's unrestricted power to do anything and that power as it is expressed and realised in actuality. God could have created *any* world but he willed to create *this* world. By stressing the connection between God's will and his wisdom and justice, Calvin makes no attempt to understand this will in terms of the *potentia Dei absoluta*. (Cf. van der Kooi, *As in a Mirror*, 183). Nonetheless, Calvin's teaching on providence and predestination does assume the priority of the causal efficacy of God's will, even if this is *de potentia ordinata*.

[171] J. Calvin, *Brief Reply in Refutation of the Calumnies of a Certain Worthless Person in which he Attempted to Pollute the Doctrine of the Eternal Predestination of God*, in *Calvin: Theological Treatises*, translated with introductions and notes by J.K.S. Reid (LCC XXII; Philadelphia: The Westminster Press, 1954), 333–343 (335).

[172] Cf. Calvin, *Bondage and Liberation*, 4.334, 148.

[173] Calvin, *Secret Providence*, 311–312.

[174] Calvin, *Institutes*, 1:18:4, 237.

perhaps that the two do not easily relate. This is no platonic dualism: there is no significant hint that the materiality of the world affects God's dealings with it. Instead, Calvin magnifies the proper ontological distinction between God and the world – that God is God and the creature is not – to such a degree that whatever mediates between the two to relate them must do so strictly by accommodating the one to the other; and Calvin finds such mediation in the conceptual framework of primary and secondary causation. Indeed, God appears to take secondary causation to himself in similar fashion to the eternal Son's taking flesh to himself in the incarnation. Accordingly, secondary causation bridges the ontological distance between God and the world and so is the means by which God is present and active within creation; but we may also suggest that given the ontological distinction, God must employ secondary causation *necessarily* to be present. The matter is complicated further by creation's fallenness: the holy God cannot truly interact with the world and in fact hates it until somehow it is purged of its sin. Does this mean, then, that God is faced with the dilemma of how to relate to a world whose contamination by sin prohibits an interaction to some extent already conditioned by the fact that he is God and the world is not? Calvin does not believe this to be the case: we have seen that it is only our perception that the Father hates us and that in going willingly to the cross, Christ successfully restores humanity to the loving Father whose wrath is now appeased. Nonetheless, there lingers a suspicion that for Calvin, divinity and humanity cannot easily relate: the ontological distinction between God and the world is almost a strict dualism, intensified by the existence of sin. So although secondary causation functions to affirm God's presence and action within the world, its employment cannot completely assuage the anxiety that God in fact may be absent and impotent.

From this, secondly, we see that this near-dualism fuels Calvin's excessive stress on the will of God, which strongly implies that it alone has causal efficacy. God maintains his ontological distance from the world by *willing* that his action *should be* accommodated to secondary causation; indeed, God's *decision* to mediate his presence to the world through secondary causation takes precedence over the *actuality* of that mediated presence. Creation exists, therefore, ultimately for the sake of fulfilling the eternal decree of predestination rather than as the result of its implementation. Accordingly, the world is the effect of divine volition rather than something exhibiting its own causal efficacy and integrity that God affirms through his triune action within it. This is not to say that Calvin fails to understand providence as the action of the triune God but that it is difficult to see how he reconciles this conception with his emphasis on the divine will. Such a voluntaristic notion of divine action suggests that God's self-accommodation to secondary causation displaces the mediation of the incarnate Son or the Holy Spirit. If this is so, then God's action would either be equated with creaturely action or, if the latter truly retains some genuine and distinct form of causal efficacy, be placed in direct relation to it and so raise the possibility that the two types of agency do in fact compete against one another for supremacy – something that Calvin denies emphatically. In this case, the causal efficacy of the sovereign will of God can only overwhelm the integrity of the creature's own action, demonstrated, for example, in God's suppression of Adam's ability to choose not to sin. On this account, then, God does not so much work *through* or *by means of* secondary causation but by *commandeering* it to the point where creaturely causal efficacy is rendered negligible or even void. We see this tension arise perhaps paradigmatically in Calvin's soteriology: Is salvation attained for the elect through Christ's obedience, death and resurrection or through God's *decision* that Christ's obedience, death and resurrection *should be that* which attains such salvation? Granted, it should be possible to affirm that God decides to save through Christ's obedience, death and resurrection; but the fact that such questions may be asked at least suggests that the spectre of occasionalism looms far nearer to Calvin's teaching on providence than his acknowledgement of secondary causation should allow.

Certainly, Calvin's emphasis on the divine will and the ambiguity about its relation to the world of creatures means, thirdly, that the place of secondary causation in his teaching on providence similarly is ambiguous.[175] Secondary causation affirms genuine creaturely causal efficacy, which remains subject at all times to possible negation by the divine will. It is no surprise, therefore, to know that Calvin had to defend himself from accusations that his teaching reduced human activity in particular to an irrelevance or that he championed some form of fate.[176] That he always reacted to such allegations somewhat angrily suggests that however he saw God's primary causation operating in the world, he did not think that it freed humanity from the responsibility of its own actions.[177] The Libertines, for example, could not truly distinguish between good and evil because they conflated primary and secondary causation; if they are correct, then, says Calvin, 'we must either attribute sin to God or dissolve the world of sin, inasmuch as God does everything.'[178] For Calvin, a pancausal doctrine of providence neither absolves people of responsibility for their actions, particularly their sinful actions, nor makes God the author of sin. However, although he could affirm secondary causation as having its own causal efficacy, Calvin was never able to explain how it related to primary causation.[179] He did make it quite clear that God was no *remote* first cause: God's primary causation is ontologically but not sequentially prior to creaturely secondary causation, and, in this sense, it is very much a positive notion,

---

[175] Cf. Schreiner, *The Theater of His Glory*, 30.
[176] Calvin's occasional writings, such as *Bondage and Liberation*, *Eternal Predestination* and *Secret Providence*, were all written, at least in part, against various criticisms in defence of his position stated in earlier editions of the *Institutes*.
[177] Cf. van der Kooi, *As in a Mirror*, 149.
[178] Calvin, *Against the Libertines*, 239.
[179] Helm, *John Calvin's Ideas*, 121–122.

ensuring that God plays a role personally in everything that happens (though this personal action effectively is God's *willing* of each and every thing that happens). Nonetheless, Calvin's stance on the relation of primary causation to secondary causation is little more than a simple assertion that the two types of causation are not in competition; but this leads us to ask why we should see creaturely events and actions in terms of primary and secondary causation. Is it not far simpler to affirm without qualification that God either determines all things or that he allows the world to act without his pancausal involvement? There remains, then, an ambiguity about the relation between God and his creation, and so between primary and secondary causation. Although Calvin's desire to avoid the extremes of occasionalism and divine inaction is laudable, he seems not entirely to have avoided confusion with the first.

Finally, we may wonder if Calvin's teaching on providence is formulated too much in response to the controversies in which he found himself. This is not to say that Calvin could have written more clearly without engaging his opponents: it is almost a cliché that theology is not done in a vacuum. That said, Calvin's concern to distinguish his teaching on providence from that of, say, the sixteenth-century Stoics and Epicureans means that it takes its shape from its conceptual distance from these philosophies rather than from a more positive grounding in Scripture. Accordingly, if it is true to say that Calvin 'out-Stoicises the Stoics' by asserting God's radical immanence to creation and 'exceeds Epicurus' in maintaining God's transcendence over creation,[180] then we may be uncertain of the extent to which Calvin intends his teaching on providence to be a positive doctrine in and of itself in faithfulness to Scripture, rather than a teaching that derives its significance from how it is *not* Stoicism and *not* Epicureanism. My contention, therefore, is that Calvin's teaching on providence, certainly as it is found in Book I of his *Institutes of the Christian Religion*, is not actually a full reflection of his views on the matter, which instead are found throughout the exegetical framework that the *Institutes* adopts. Although Calvin's explicit teaching on providence is articulated in opposition to Libertinism, Stoicism and the rest, its content arguably is shaped more subtly and significantly by his reading of the scriptural narrative that itself 'reads' creaturely history. Consequently, Calvin's teaching on providence adopts a notably different form that we will discuss elsewhere.[181]

We have claimed that Calvin assumes that the ontological distinction between God and the world conditions their interaction with one another; that this distinction accounts for why so much emphasis is placed on the causal efficacy of the divine will; that Calvin never saw this as problematic; and that his explicit teaching on providence takes its overall shape from its distinction from rival stances on the relation between God and the world. Positively, Calvin affirms that God is present and active within creation; negatively, his

---

[180] Kirby, 'Stoic *and* Epicurean?', 318.
[181] See § 4.6.

use of the conceptuality of secondary causation makes it difficult to see how God's presence does not overwhelm creation and jeopardise the integrity of its action. Nonetheless, as we shall see in the next chapter, Calvin's teaching on providence essentially aims to affirm the goodness of creation, and this in part influenced the burgeoning natural science of the day; but it could not do so without giving those whose piety was somewhat less than Calvin's own the opportunity to distance God from the world forever.

CHAPTER 3

Secondary Causation and the Displacement of God

§ 3.1 Introduction

According to John Calvin, God is 'the principal cause of things';[1] this means that 'he so regulates all things that nothing takes place without his deliberation' or 'by chance.'[2] Despite emphasising the priority of God's action, Calvin does not wish to deny causal efficacy to creatures themselves: he notes that 'the Christian heart ... will give attention to the secondary causes in their proper place.'[3] Actions and events within the world presuppose God's primary causation; secondary causation witnesses to God's unceasing involvement in creaturely affairs. Essentially, then, Calvin's teaching on providence is an affirmation of God's continuing presence and action within the world.

This means that Calvin can both encourage the formal exploration of the world and insist that this study should also point away from that world and towards its Creator. We should 'contemplate in all creatures, as in mirrors, those immense riches of [the Lord's] wisdom, justice, goodness, and power' and so 'not merely run over them cursorily'; rather, 'we should ponder them at length, turn them over in our minds seriously and faithfully, and recollect them repeatedly.'[4] The scientific enterprises gathering momentum during the Reformation era were not, therefore, to be dismissed, even if in many instances they were steered by those whose piety did not match Calvin's standards: '[I]f the Lord has willed that we be helped in physics, dialectic, mathematics, and other like disciplines, by the work and ministry of the ungodly, let us use this assistance.'[5] Clearly, Calvin approves the scientific investigation of the world, but this is possible only because the Spirit of God first empowers the human mind to comprehend its secrets.[6]

Calvin's stance here complements his teaching on providence. It is because God rules all things by his providence that anyone who examines 'the most beautiful structure and order of the universe' should also remember the Creator and not 'sit idly in contemplation of his works'.[7] Here, though, is a further

---

[1] J. Calvin, *Institutes of the Christian Religion* (2 vols.), translated by Battles, F.L. (LCC XX / XXI; Philadelphia: The Westminster Press, 1960), 1:17:6, 218.
[2] Calvin, *Institutes*, 1:16:3, 200; 1:16:4, 203.
[3] Calvin, *Institutes*, 1:17:6, 218.
[4] Calvin, *Institutes*, 1:14:21, 180.
[5] Calvin, *Institutes*, 2:2:16, 275.
[6] Calvin, *Institutes*, 2:2:16, 275.
[7] Calvin, *Institutes*, 1:5:11, 63.

indication of the ambiguity that marks the place of secondary causation in Calvin's theology. Secondary causation presupposes primary causation; but primary causation cannot be known apart from secondary causation. The concept of secondary causation accounts, therefore, for God's involvement in the world's affairs but does so by referring ultimately to itself, to creaturely causation, whilst maintaining that somehow divine causation also is present and, indeed, paramount. Science must always point beyond the object of its study to the one who governs and preserves the world – and yet in doing so, we are immediately brought back to focus on the secondary causation by which we know by faith that God is present and active within the world.[8]

All this prompts the question of whether the conceptual framework of primary and secondary causation is the most adequate way of conceiving God's providence. That is the concern of our next chapter; for now, we must demonstrate more clearly the potential dangers of understanding providence in these terms. Our concern, then, is to explore how Calvin's teaching on providence, particularly understood as the execution of God's will in creaturely time and space, in part supported the development of natural science and, through that support, made it possible for God's presence and activity within the world eventually to be denied.[9] A combination of two intellectual trends engendered this possibility: first, those who reacted against Calvin's teaching on predestination, certainly as it had been received and propounded in sixteenth-century England, found its claims morally abhorrent and therefore false when judged against the 'reasonableness' of a more natural religion; and secondly, basic assumptions about divine providence and the passivity of matter freed the new science to analyse the world without any necessary reference to the Creator. To elucidate this contention, we must first provide an account of the dissemination of Calvin's thought throughout Tudor England.[10]

---

[8] Cf. J. Calvin, *A Defence of the Secret Providence of God*, in *Calvin's Calvinism: Treatises on the Eternal Predestination of God and the Secret Providence of God*, translated by H. Cole (Grand Rapids: Reformed Free Publishing Association, 1987), 223–350 (231).

[9] We have already suggested that providence for Calvin, at least in part, is the execution of God's eternal decree; see § 2.4. This means that the reception of Calvin's teaching on providence entailed receipt of his teaching on predestination and vice versa. The two are distinguishable – predestination concerns soteriology whereas providence refers more generally to God's pancausal relation to the world – but inseparable.

[10] To clarify, the aim of this chapter is not to produce a comprehensive analysis of the theological, historical and scientific context of the sixteenth and seventeenth centuries, but to trace only a single thread of this rich tapestry. Our concern is to identify certain intellectual trends of this period and we do not need, therefore, to exhaust the details. The sketches offered are sufficient for our purposes, but further details about the influence of Calvin's theology in England may be found in, for example, J.T. McNeill, *The History and Character of Calvinism* (Oxford: Oxford

§ 3.2 From Geneva to England

That providence was no abstract concept for Calvin is suggested at least by his account of his arrival at Geneva in 1536.[11] Although he sought 'some secluded corner where [he] might be withdrawn from the public view',[12] Calvin recalls that Guillaume Farel, who first introduced Protestant ideas to Geneva,[13] 'detained me ... not so much by counsel and exhortation, as by a dreadful imprecation, which I felt to be as if God had from heaven laid his mighty hand upon me to arrest me.'[14] Knowing that Calvin wished to devote himself to private studies, Farel persuaded the would-be Reformer to stay and serve the Genevan church by announcing that God would curse Calvin's retirement and studies if he should decide to leave. 'By this imprecation,' Calvin writes, 'I was so stricken with terror, that I desisted from the journey which I had undertaken'.[15] Despite a rather tempestuous relationship with the city officials, Geneva would prove to be the base where Calvin prepared and delivered his teaching and from where his ideas would spread across Europe and into England.

Calvin was not the first of the continental Reformers to find an audience in England. During the reign of Edward VI (1547–53), for example, Martin Bucer

---

University Press, 1967), 309–330; P. Benedict, *Christ's Churches Purely Reformed: A Social History of Calvinism* (New Haven: Yale University Press, 2002), 230–254; P.E. Hughes, 'Calvin and the Church of England', in W.S. Reid (ed.), *John Calvin: His Influence in the Western World* (Grand Rapids: Zondervan, 1982), 173–196; and R.T. Kendall, 'The Puritan Modification of Calvin's Theology', in W.S. Reid (ed.), *John Calvin: His Influence in the Western World* (Grand Rapids: Zondervan, 1982), 199–214.

For accounts of the relation between Protestant theology and the scientific developments of the day, see, for example, C.B. Kaiser, *Creation and the History of Science* (HCT 3; London: Marshall Pickering, 1991); G.R. Cragg, *The Church and the Age of Reason 1648–1789* (PHC 4; London: Penguin Books, 1970); J.H. Brooke, *Science and Religion: Some Historical Perspectives* (Cambridge: Cambridge University Press, 1991); D. Alexander, *Rebuilding the Matrix: Science and Faith in the 21st Century* (Oxford: Lion Publishing, 2002); C. Brown, *Philosophy and the Christian Faith: A Historical Sketch from the Middle Ages to the Present Day* (London: Tyndale Press, 1969) and *Christianity and Western Thought: A History of Philosophers, Ideas and Movements, Volume One: From the Ancient World to the Age of Enlightenment* (Leicester: Apollos, 1990); and P. Gay, *The Enlightenment, An Interpretation: The Science of Freedom* (London: Norton Library, 1977).

[11] McNeill, *The History and Character of Calvinism*, 136; Benedict, *Christ's Churches Purely Reformed*, 81–82.

[12] J. Calvin, J., *Commentary on the Book of Psalms, Vol. 1* in *Calvin's Commentaries* IV (CTS; Grand Rapids: Baker Books, 2003), xli.

[13] R.C. Gamble, 'Switzerland: Triumph and Decline', in W.S. Reid (ed.), *John Calvin: His Influence in the Western World* (Grand Rapids: Zondervan, 1982), 55–71 (55).

[14] Calvin, *Comm. Psa. 1*, xlii.

[15] Calvin, *Comm. Psa. 1*, xliii.

and Peter Martyr Vermigli each served as professor of divinity at the universities of Cambridge and Oxford respectively.[16] Through Bucer's influence in particular, the English were already primed to receive continental Reformed teachings;[17] and Calvin himself seemed particularly keen to forge links personally with those across the Channel. He corresponded both with Protector Somerset, the Regent of England, and Edward himself, at one point encouraging the latter to imitate the example of 'the good king Josiah' by overthrowing 'impieties which are clearly repugnant to the honour and service of God' and abolishing 'whatsoever serve[s] merely to nourish superstition.'[18] Certainly, Edward furthered Protestant ideals in his nation: his reign saw the production of the Book of Common Prayer (1552) and the development of the Forty-Two Articles of Religion (1553).[19] Before further policies could be implemented, however, Edward died suddenly, and eventually his Catholic half-sister Mary was established as Queen of England (1553–1558). In her desire to reinstate Catholicism as the official religion of the English people, Mary directed the persecution and execution of numerous Protestants; but many others fled into Europe, approximately a quarter of whom found appropriate sanctuary in Geneva and developed further appreciation there for the aims of the Reformation.[20] Somewhat unwittingly, then, Mary's actions stoked the fires of the Protestantism she sought to destroy.

Once Elizabeth acceded to the throne in November 1558, the English Protestant exiles returned to their homeland with the teaching of Calvin and his followers entrenched firmly in their minds. Although the extent to which they were influenced by Calvin himself is impossible to judge, it is very likely that living in a climate such as that of Geneva helped them in turn to exercise a deep

---

[16] C.R. Trueman, 'The Theology of the English Reformers', in D. Bagchi and D.C. Steinmetz (eds.), *The Cambridge Companion to Reformation Theology* (Cambridge: Cambridge University Press, 2004), 161–173 (162); P. White, *Predestination, Policy and Polemic: Conflict and Consensus in the English Church from the Reformation to the Civil War* (Cambridge: Cambridge University Press, 1992), 44–52.

[17] R.W. Holder, 'Calvin's Heritage', in D.K. McKim (ed.), *The Cambridge Companion to John Calvin* (Cambridge: Cambridge University Press, 2004), 245–273 (247); cf. McNeill, *The History and Character of Calvinism*, 309–310.

[18] J. Calvin, 'Letter to the King of England, January 1551' in *Letters of John Calvin Selected from the Bonnet Edition with an Introductory Biographical Sketch* (Edinburgh: Banner of Truth, 1980), 120, 121.

[19] G. Bray (ed.), *Documents of the English Reformation* (Cambridge: James Clarke, 1994), 272–276, 284–311. The Forty-Two Articles eventually became the Thirty-Nine Articles and passed into use in 1571.

[20] McNeill, *The History and Character of Calvinism*, 310–311; Trueman, 'The Theology of the English Reformers', 163. Approximately 800 Englishmen – of which 233 went to Geneva – chose exile over the reinstatement of Catholic worship. (Benedict, *Christ's Churches Purely Reformed*, 242; Kendall, 'The Puritan Modification of Calvin's Theology', 200).

influence of his ideas on the Church of England.[21] In early 1559, to try further to ingratiate himself to the new monarch, Calvin wrote to William Cecil, Elizabeth's secretary of state, disclosing his conviction that the Queen had been 'raised to the throne in a wonderful manner by the hand of God' and that Cecil himself similarly enjoyed a 'rank of dignity and favour' due to divine providence.[22] On another occasion, Calvin transcribed some of his sermons and sent them to Elizabeth; this action demonstrated the seriousness with which he took the progress of the Reformation across Europe, for usually he did not preserve his sermons in writing.[23] Indeed, he seemed concerned to show the Queen that he could assist the English Protestants. Elizabeth herself, however, seemed quite indifferent to Calvin;[24] but gradually, through the sway of the returned Protestant exiles, the acceptance and popularising of the Geneva Bible and its marginal notes (for which Calvin himself had no direct responsibility),[25] and the increasing availability of Calvin's writings in English,[26] the Elizabethan church not only adopted Reformed theology as its own but 'with time ... grew distinctly Calvinist.'[27]

---

[21] Kendall, 'The Puritan Modification of Calvin's Theology', 200–201; Trueman, 'The Theology of the English Reformers', 163; R.A. Muller, 'John Calvin and Later Calvinism: The Identity of the Reformed Tradition', in D. Bagchi and D.C. Steinmetz (eds.), *The Cambridge Companion to Reformation Theology* (Cambridge: Cambridge University Press, 2004), 130–149 (137).

[22] J. Calvin, 'Letter to William Cecil, 29th January 1559' in *Letters of John Calvin Selected from the Bonnet Edition with an Introductory Biographical Sketch* (Edinburgh: Banner of Truth, 1980), 207, 208; cf. Hughes, 'Calvin and the Church of England', 192–193.

[23] W.S. Reid, 'The Transmission of Calvinism in the Sixteenth Century', in W.S. Reid (ed.), *John Calvin: His Influence in the Western World* (Grand Rapids: Zondervan, 1982), 33–52 (44).

[24] Hughes, 'Calvin and the Church of England', 192–194.

[25] The Geneva Bible (1560) was an annotated edition of Scripture popular amongst many people and not just the Genevan Reformed. Though available in England during the 1560s, the Geneva Bible was not printed there until 1576. (White, *Predestination, Policy and Polemic*, 91–92; Kendall, 'The Puritan Modification of Calvin's Theology', 200–201; Muller, 'John Calvin and Later Calvinism', 137–138).

[26] Calvin's writings – including his *Institutes of the Christian Religion* and commentaries – proved extremely popular in England, especially so during the 1580s. They were available both in English translation and in the original languages. See, for example, A. Pettegree, 'The Spread of Calvin's Thought', in D.K. McKim (ed.), *The Cambridge Companion to John Calvin* (Cambridge: Cambridge University Press, 2004), 207–224 (210–211); McNeill, *The History and Character of Calvinism*, 313; Kendall, 'The Puritan Modification of Calvin's Theology', 202; and Benedict, *Christ's Churches Purely Reformed*, 245.

[27] Benedict, *Christ's Churches Purely Reformed*, 245. See also Kendall, 'The Puritan Modification of Calvin's Theology', 200–201; N. Tyacke, *Anti-Calvinists: The Rise of English Arminianism c. 1590–1640* (OHM; Oxford: Oxford University Press,

This is seen clearly in the English church's handling of the Reformed teaching on predestination. The church's Thirty-Nine Articles of Religion, implemented in 1571, affirmed that God 'hath constantly decreed by his divine counsel secret to us, to deliver from curse and damnation those whom he hath chosen in Christ out of mankind, and to bring them by Christ to everlasting salvation, as vessels made to honour.'[28] Such a position was consistent with Calvin's own teaching on predestination and perhaps especially that of Bucer, who emphasised predestination as election to life.[29] During the mid-1580s, however, there was growing expectation that predestination to damnation should be made explicit in the Thirty-Nine Articles.[30] Though this failed to happen, the sentiment eventually found unambiguous expression in the Lambeth Articles of 1595, drafted by William Whitaker, Regius Professor of Divinity at Cambridge University.[31] These stated that '[f]rom eternity God has predestined some men to life and condemned others to death'; that '[t]he moving or efficient cause of predestination to life is ... only the will of God's good pleasure'; that '[t]here is a predetermined and fixed number of predestinate which cannot be increased or diminished'; and that '[i]t is not placed in the will or power of any and every man to be saved.'[32] By the time the Lambeth Articles were devised, Calvin himself had long since died; but here was evidence – if evidence was needed – that his spirit continued to animate those whom he had inspired to walk his doctrinal path.

One such person was Theodore Beza, who succeeded Calvin as the head of the Genevan church. Calvin's works proved popular in England, but so too did Beza's, perhaps more so, and strongly reflected the way in which Reformed doctrine was taking root and flourishing in the country.[33] Beza's most famous – some would say notorious – achievement was his *Tabula praedestinationis* of 1555, made available in English by 1576 in *The Treasure of Truth*, and found in William Perkins's *Armilla Aurea*, first published in 1590 and translated into English as *A Golden Chaine* the following year.[34] The *Tabula*'s opening line

---

1990), 3; McNeill, *The History and Character of Calvinism*, 313. Owen Chadwick points out that initially, people 'were drawn by the Calvinist discipline and thereby led to Calvinist orthodoxy.' (O. Chadwick, *The Reformation* [PHC 3; London: Penguin Books, 1972], 96).

[28] 'Article 17: Of Predestination and Election', *The Thirty-Nine Articles, 1571*, in Bray, *Documents of the English Reformation*, 294.

[29] White, *Predestination, Policy and Polemic*, 45.

[30] Benedict, *Christ's Churches Purely Reformed*, 303.

[31] White, *Predestination, Policy and Polemic*, 101–117; McNeill, *The History and Character of Calvinism*, 314; P. Harrison, *'Religion' and the Religions in the English Enlightenment* (Cambridge: Cambridge University Press, 1990), 21–22.

[32] 'Articles 1, 2, 3 and 9', *The Lambeth Articles, 1595*, in Bray, *Documents of the English Reformation*, 399–400.

[33] Benedict, *Christ's Churches Purely Reformed*, 245.

[34] Tyacke, *Anti-Calvinists*, 29.

indicates that God, 'whose wayes are unsearchable', is understood to be the one who determines the fate of individual persons by his 'everlasting and unchangeable purpose, going also in order before all causes, whereby he hath decreed from everlasting in him selfe, to choose certaine men for his owne purpose', that is, either to be 'saved in Christ' or to 'refuse certaine through theyr owne faulte to bee dampned'.[35] That Beza's *Tabula* is reprinted approvingly in Perkins's *A Golden Chaine*, albeit with embellishments, indicates not only that Calvin's theological heir genuinely and successfully impacted the English Reformers, but also that there was significant and welcome reception of Genevan Reformed theology in England generally and of Calvin's influence in particular.[36]

Between them, then, Beza and Perkins drew more attention than ever to matters of predestination; but this was not because it was a unique teaching expressing an undeniable truth.[37] The enthusiasm with which many of the English embraced the Reformed formulation of the doctrine was perhaps an extension of the common belief that everyday life is subject to forces outside a person's control. There was a providential element already strong in England:

> Providentialism was not a marginal feature of the religious culture of early modern England, but part of the mainstream, a cluster of presuppositions which enjoyed near universal acceptance. It was a set of ideological spectacles through which individuals of all social levels and from all positions on the confessional spectrum were apt to view their universe, an invisible prism which helped them to focus the refractory meanings of both petty and perplexing events. Central to the political, medical, and philosophical thought and the literary and historical discourse of the period, it was also an ingrained parochial response to chaos and crisis, a practical source of consolation in a hazardous and inhospitable environment, and an idea which exercised practical, emotional, and imaginative influence upon those who subscribed to it.[38]

The achievement of the Reformed influence was to strip this providentialism of superstition and give it a scripturally informed framework.

§ 3.3 Resisting the Reformed

Despite its strength and appeal, the Reformed stance on predestination did not exercise a total sway over the minds of the English masses. It peaked, under

---

[35] Benedict, *Christ's Churches Purely Reformed*, 106; White, *Predestination, Policy and Polemic*, 14.
[36] Kendall, 'The Puritan Modification of Calvin's Theology', 204; Benedict, *Christ's Churches Purely Reformed*, 302.
[37] See also § 1.2, n. 20.
[38] A. Walsham, *Providence in Early Modern England* (Oxford: Oxford University Press, 1999), 2–3.

Perkins's influence, around the turn of the seventeenth century. Certainly, the Reformed viewpoint always had its critics, even during the height of its dominance in England. One public demonstration of this defiance was a sermon preached by Samuel Harsnett, Bishop of Norwich, at Paul's Cross in 1585. 'Paul's Cross was the most public pulpit in the land, the preachers selected by the Bishop of London, and those sermons which ended up in print normally did so with the blessing of authority.'[39] Harsnett's sermon opposed the Calvinist teaching on predestination by suggesting that it was a Goliath needing to be slain. Indeed, the very idea that God had created a vast number of people simply to condemn them to eternal damnation was contrary to reason and made little of Christ, through whom grace is offered to all. Referring to 1 Timothy 2:4, Harsnett believed that according to the Calvinist interpretation of this verse,

> God would have all to be saved, that is God would have a few to be saved: God would not have any to perish, that is, God would that almost all should perish: so God loved the world, that is, so God loved a small number of the world ...[40]

Harsnett's sermon was but a quiet voice almost inaudible among the vivacious singing of the Reformed; but it proved not to be merely a single voice. Indeed, the Lambeth Articles, for example, were drafted amidst a controversy at Cambridge, where Peter Baro, the Lady Margaret Professor of Divinity, held a proto-Arminian understanding of divine predestination, according to which, Baro argued, God had not predestined anyone to eternal death, even if some are so condemned by their sin and lack of repentance. Crucially for Baro, God elects or condemns people by foreknowing how they would respond to the grace offered to them in Christ.[41] The composition of the Lambeth Articles, which asserted that '[t]he moving or efficient cause of predestination to life is not the foresight of faith or of perseverance, or of good works, or of anything inherent in the persons predestined, but only the will of God's good pleasure',[42] in part was a response to Baro, or, if not to him

---

[39] Tyacke, *Anti-Calvinists*, 248.

[40] Samuel Harsnett, *A Sermon Preached at Paul's Cross*, quoted in White, *Predestination, Policy and Polemic*, 99–100. Of 1 Timothy 2:4, Calvin claims that 'the Apostle simply means, that there is no people and no rank in the world that is excluded from salvation; because God wishes that the gospel should be proclaimed to all without exception.' (J. Calvin, *Commentaries on the Epistles to Timothy, Titus, and Philemon* in *Calvin's Commentaries* XXI (CTS; Grand Rapids: Baker Books, 2003), 54–55).

[41] Tyacke, *Anti-Calvinists*, 30; White, *Predestination, Policy and Polemic*, 112; Muller, 'John Calvin and Later Calvinism', 138.

[42] 'Article 2', *The Lambeth Articles, 1595*, in Bray, *Documents of the English Reformation*, 399.

specifically, then at least to the theology that Baro espoused.[43] Reformed theology, then, dominated the late sixteenth century. From the 1620s onwards, however, the number of critics increased sharply,[44] and by the 1630s, the balance had shifted, indicated strongly by the increasing number of sermons preached against the Reformed teaching on predestination at Paul's Cross.[45] Such a swift transformation in people's attitudes to predestination was one indication amongst many that the intellectual atmosphere of the early seventeenth century, religious or otherwise, was changing,[46] and changing rapidly.

To many minds, the Reformed teaching that some were predestined to eternal life and others to eternal damnation had been dealt a crippling blow by the apparent ignorance of the Christian story shown by the indigenous peoples of far-flung lands with whom European explorers were now engaging. Whilst these peoples certainly were not Christians, they had moral, even religious, codes of their own.[47] Confronted by the enormous variety of religious belief in the world, certain free-thinkers began to doubt whether the Christian understanding of the world was as true as it had been claimed; there was the rising suspicion that Christian belief essentially was made of those doctrines the priests in charge favoured. Much of the new knowledge obtained from around the world provided the critics of the Church with enough ammunition to attack many of its beliefs[48] – and it did not take long for the Reformed teaching on predestination to become a target. The thought that God had condemned certain persons to damnation was simply abhorrent, especially now there seemed to be much evidence that the damned would be the majority of the world's population. It was the unreasonableness of the idea that struck a dissonant chord, that people who had never heard about the love of God revealed in Christ would be eternally tormented for a decision they were denied even the opportunity of making. According to the Reformed, predestination was a truth revealed by God to assure the elect of their salvation;[49] but to those who did

---

[43] Though the Lambeth Articles were not written to attack Peter Baro, they were used to threaten him. Baro's position as Lady Margaret Professor of Divinity came to an end in late 1596. (White, *Predestination, Policy and Polemic*, 111, 117).

[44] Benedict, *Christ's Churches Purely Reformed*, 329.

[45] Tyacke, *Anti-Calvinists*, 265. Appendix I in Tyacke's volume provides a useful account of the Paul's Cross sermons and of how the balance of sermon content shifted from Reformed convictions to those of its critics.

[46] Chadwick, *The Reformation*, 219.

[47] Cragg, *The Church and the Age of Reason 1648–1789*, 46.

[48] Cf. Cragg, *The Church and the Age of Reason 1648–1789*, 47.

[49] Calvin was clear that 'Christ ... is the mirror wherein we must, and without self-deception may, contemplate our own election.' Indeed, 'we have a sufficiently clear and firm testimony that we have been inscribed in the book of life [cf. Rev. 21:27] if we are in communion with Christ.' (Calvin, *Institutes*, 3:24:5, 970). According to R.T. Kendall, however, Calvin's successors did not share the same conviction; Beza,

not, it smacked of a self-assured elitism that in the light of new discoveries across the globe was unjustified. Certainly, it was for this reason that Edward, Lord Herbert of Cherbury opposed the teaching of Beza and Perkins on predestination.[50] He writes,

> How could I believe that a just God would take pleasure in the eternal reprobation of those to whom he never afforded any means of salvation ... and whom he

---

argues Kendall, held that Christ died only for the elect (the doctrine of limited atonement) and, consequently, assurance is not a matter solely of trusting in Christ for there is no guarantee that the person seeking assurance is one of the elect for whom Christ died. Instead, that person must perform good works to demonstrate the reality of his or her election. (R.T. Kendall, *Calvin and English Calvinism to 1649* [OTM; Oxford: Oxford University Press, 1981], 29–33). Kendall's aim was 'in part to reassess the assumption that Calvin's soteriology was faithfully upheld by the venerable divines who drew up the Westminster Confession and the Shorter and Larger catechisms.' (Kendall, *Calvin and English Calvinism to 1649*, 2).

Such a thesis proved controversial and led to a number of rebuttals. (S.D. Wright, *Our Sovereign Refuge: The Pastoral Theology of Theodore Beza* [SCHT; Carlisle: Paternoster, 2004], 41–46, 71–81). Our concern, however, is not the correctness or otherwise of Kendall's interpretation of Beza's theological continuity with Calvin; it is enough for us here to say that the truth of predestination assures the elect of their salvation, regardless of whether that assurance is sought in Christ alone or through human introspection. That said, Kendall's thesis does raise the issue of theological continuity within the Reformed tradition. Did Calvin's immediate successor and followers so depart from his teaching that Reformed theology cannot truly be called 'Calvinist' in a formal sense of the term?

Part of the solution surely is found in clarifying the meaning of 'Reformed theology'. Carl Trueman points out that '[t]he historic identity of Reformed theology has always been expressed through public confessional documents such as the First and Second Helvetic Confessions, the *Consensus Tigurinus*, the Heidelberg Catechism, the Belgic Confession, the Canons of Dordt and the Westminster Standards.' This means that Calvin's theology cannot be equated with Reformed teaching *per se* or be the determining factor for what counts as Reformed theology. (C.R. Trueman, 'Calvin and Calvinism', in D.K. McKim [ed.], *The Cambridge Companion to John Calvin* [Cambridge: Cambridge University Press, 2004], 225–244 [225, emphasis original]; cf. Muller, 'John Calvin and Later Calvinism', 130, 148–149; P. Helm, *Calvin and the Calvinists* [Edinburgh: Banner of Truth, 1982], 3). Reformed theology and Calvin's theology may be said to share certain family resemblances (Cf. S.R. Holmes, 'Calvin Against the Calvinists?', in *Listening to the Past: The Place of Tradition in Theology* [Carlisle: Paternoster, 2002], 68–85 [84]); but if this is so, then the matter of Beza's apparent divergence from Calvin's teaching on assurance as claimed by Kendall should not be quite so controversial as it proved.

[50] R.D. Bedford, *The Defence of Truth: Herbert of Cherbury and the Seventeenth Century* (Manchester: Manchester University Press, 1979), 145.

foresaw must be damned of absolute necessity, without the least hopes of escaping it?[51]

'There was a universalism in [Herbert's] sympathies that made him deeply unhappy with suggestions that God's providence and salvation are not fully available to a large portion of humanity through no fault of its own.'[52] Instead, he identified five 'Common Notions',[53] truths or elements of truth found in all religions: there is a supreme God; this deity should be worshipped; a life of virtue and piety is the most important element in religious practice; there should be repentance for wickedness; and there is reward or punishment after this life.[54] The fourth of these, repentance for wickedness, was particularly important, given the Reformed teaching of predestination. Any repentance that issued from the work of Christ on the cross for Herbert was too particular. Rather, '[g]eneral agreement among religions, the nature of divine goodness, and above all conscience, tell us that our crimes may be washed away by true penitence, and that we can be restored to new union with God.'[55] Herbert saw no need, therefore, to accept the traditional concept of original sin, and in rejecting it he also rejected the need for redemption and therefore the need for a redeemer.[56] Consequently, the thought that God could predestine a minority to salvation was ridiculous:

> [U]nless wickedness can be abolished by penitence and faith in God, and unless the Divine goodness can satisfy the Divine justice (and no further appeal can be invoked), then there does not exist, nor ever has existed any universal source to which the wretched mass of men, crushed beneath the burden of sin, can turn to obtain grace and inward peace. If this were the case, God has created and condemned certain men, in fact the larger part of the human race, not only without their desire, but without their knowledge. This idea is so dreadful and consorts so ill with the providence and goodness, and even the justice of God, that it is more charitable to suppose that the whole human race has always possessed in repentance the opportunity of becoming reconciled with God. And as long as men did not cut themselves off from it their damnation would not have been due to the

---

[51] Herbert, *The Ancient Religion of the Gentiles*, quoted in P. Byrne, *Natural Religion and the Nature of Religion: The Legacy of Deism* (RRSS; London: Routledge, 1989), 25.
[52] D.A. Pailin, 'Should Herbert of Cherbury be Regarded as a Deist?', *Journal of Theological Studies*, NS 51 (2000), 113–149 (132).
[53] See, for example, Edward, Lord Herbert of Cherbury, *De Veritate*, translated by M.H. Carré (Bristol: J.W. Arrowsmith, 1937), 289.
[54] Herbert, *De Veritate*, 291, 293, 296, 298, 300.
[55] Herbert, *De Veritate*, 298.
[56] Byrne, *Natural Religion and the Nature of Religion*, 25–26; Harrison, *'Religion' and the Religions in the English Enlightenment*, 69.

benevolent will of God, but to their own sins, nor could God have been charged with blame if they failed to find salvation.[57]

Rather, says Herbert, as God's providence intends to bring good to all people, it would be against the divine nature to exclude certain people from the possibility of knowing him. '[T]o declare that God has cut us off from the means by which we can return to Him, provided that we play our part to the utmost of our ability, is a blasphemy so great that those who indulge in it [the Reformed] seek to destroy not merely human goodness, but also the goodness of God.'[58] Thus God gives to each person the means by which to become acceptable to him; there is no elite class of people predestined to have privileged access to him.[59] Such universalistic thinking was beginning to characterise the time, as many people sought to free themselves from the shackles of organised, priestly religion. For Herbert, God was present to all via the Common Notions; he saw, therefore, no need for a pack of mostly corrupt men to mediate between the masses and the divine. There is no 'stricter or purer religion' than what is contained in the Common Notions.[60]

Herbert was no lone voice in the wilderness.[61] He was but one of many whose thought essentially lessened the importance of the role of revelation without necessarily denying its existence. Other thinkers towards the end of the seventeenth century echoed Herbert's sentiments and began increasingly to stress the reasonableness of a general, natural religion. The Cambridge Platonists,[62] for example, maintained that because God is rational, the God of

---

[57] Herbert, *De Veritate*, 299.

[58] Herbert, *De Veritate*, 299–300; cf. Byrne, *Natural Religion and the Nature of Religion*, 25.

[59] Cf. Harrison, *'Religion' and the Religions in the English Enlightenment*, 69.

[60] Cf. Herbert, *De Veritate*, 306.

[61] That said, neither did everybody think that the Common Notions were as universal as Herbert claimed. John Locke, for example, argued against any idea of innate principles on the grounds that 'there are none to which all mankind give an universal assent.' The very fact 'that all *children* and *idiots*, have not the least apprehension or thought of them ... is enough to destroy that universal assent'. (J. Locke, *An Essay Concerning Human Understanding*, edited by R. Woolhouse [London: Penguin, 1997], 1:2:4; 1:2:5, 60, emphasis original).

[62] 'The Cambridge Platonists were a group of seventeenth-century English theologians and philosophers who were distinguished by their veneration of Plato and Plotinus, their opposition to religious fanaticism, and their preaching of a reasonable religion of holiness. The major figures in the school were Benjamin Whichcote, Ralph Cudworth, Henry More, Nathaniel Culverwel, Peter Sterry, and John Smith.' Essentially concerned with the issue of the certainty of religious knowledge, the Cambridge Platonists prized ideas such as 'common notions'. (Harrison, *'Religion' and the Religions in the English Enlightenment*, 28–29, quote from 28).

the Reformed is too arbitrary.⁶³ Instead, they believed that 'God's activity must be as lawful and universal in the religious realm as in the physical world'; that reason was not tied to institutional or biblical authority in the matter of religious pluralism; that the religion of nature was therefore valid; and that such things as common notions could be verified historically.⁶⁴ In denying the primacy of or even the need for revelation whilst at the same time elevating what could be known of the divine in the natural world, the Cambridge Platonists 'inadvertently paved the way for the evacuation of supernatural elements from the concept "religion".'⁶⁵ Similarly, the so-called deists,⁶⁶ influenced in large part by the emergent view of the universe as an orderly system,⁶⁷ were keen to show that the teachings of Christianity did not – or should not! – contradict the findings of the natural scientists. Thus John Toland argued, *'That nothing can be said to be a Mystery, because we have not an adequate Idea of it, or a distinct View of all its Properties at once; for then every thing would be a Mystery.'* Accordingly, *'no Christian Doctrine, no more than any ordinary Piece of Nature, can be reputed a Mystery.'*⁶⁸ Though Toland's concern was to judge by reason the validity of Christian revelation without necessarily denying it,⁶⁹ later deists were more ready to 'drop from the Church's teaching everything that [did not] immediately and easily fit in [with the new knowledge and methods].'⁷⁰ With their questions and assumptions about the place of revelation and particularity in an ever more reason-centred and universalist world, such figures as Herbert, the Cambridge Platonists and the deists beat a wider path through the seventeenth century to a more general truth than the Reformed would allow – and there was no shortage of people quick to follow in their footsteps.

§ 3.4 Secondary Causation or Natural Occurrence?

Although Calvin's teaching on predestination gained a warm reception amongst many of the English, nonetheless there was also a significant reaction against it

---

[63] Brown, *Philosophy and the Christian Faith*, 75; J. Byrne, *Glory, Jest and Riddle: Religious Thought in the Enlightenment* (London: SCM Press, 1996), 103.
[64] Harrison, *'Religion' and the Religions in the English Enlightenment*, 59–60.
[65] Harrison, *'Religion' and the Religions in the English Enlightenment*, 28.
[66] David Pailin argues that describing someone as a deist 'conveys in practice little more than that the person making the charge considers that the accused is deficient in some unspecified beliefs which the accuser deems essential to authentic religious understanding.' (D.A. Pailin, 'Herbert of Cherbury and the Deists', *The Expository Times* 94 [1983], 196–200 [197]; cf. Byrne, *Glory, Jest and Riddle*, 100).
[67] Cragg, *The Church and the Age of Reason 1648–1789*, 157. See also § 3.4.
[68] J. Toland, *Christianity Not Mysterious* (London: Garland Publishing, 1978), 75, 80, emphasis original.
[69] D.A. Brown, 'Christianity and Mystery', *Theology* 72 (1969), 347–352 (348).
[70] Brown, 'Christianity and Mystery', 350.

from those who would not accept this as an accurate depiction of the relation between God and humanity. That there was such a reaction indicates the extent of Calvin's influence upon English theology; but this influence extended not only to the debates about predestination in the sixteenth and seventeenth centuries, but also to matters of less doctrinal importance. Calvin's recognition of secondary causes, for example, led him to celebrate the fundamental goodness of the world God had created. He writes,

> And the natural qualities themselves of things demonstrate sufficiently to what end and extent we may enjoy them. Has the Lord clothed the flowers with the great beauty that greets our eyes, the sweetness of smell that is wafted upon our nostrils, and yet will it be unlawful for our eyes to be affected by that beauty, or our sense of smell by the sweetness of that odour? What? Did he not so distinguish colours as to make some more lovely than others? What? Did he not endow gold and silver, ivory and marble, with a loveliness that renders them more precious than other metals or stones? Did he not, in short, render many things attractive to us, apart from their necessary use?[71]

God's creation for Calvin is a 'beauteous theatre' filled with a 'variety of good things';[72] heaven and earth are 'quite like a spacious and splendid house, provided and filled with the most exquisite and at the same time most abundant furnishings.'[73] Furthermore, Calvin encourages scientific investigation of the world because such study can only disclose further evidence of God's wisdom by which he provides for his creation:[74]

> [A]stronomers investigate with great labour whatever the sagacity of the human mind can comprehend. Nevertheless, this study is not to be reprobated, nor this science to be condemned, because some frantic persons are wont boldly to reject whatever is unknown to them. For astronomy is not only pleasant, but also very useful to be known: it cannot be denied that this art unfolds the admirable wisdom of God. Wherefore, as ingenious men are to be honoured who have expended useful labour on this subject, so they who have leisure and capacity ought not to neglect this kind of exercise.[75]

Although Calvin's attitude here is entirely positive, nonetheless he is careful to insist that such explorations should lead the mind beyond the world itself to reflection upon God. 'It is a diabolical science ... which fixes our

---

[71] Calvin, *Institutes*, 3:10:2, 721

[72] J. Calvin, *Commentary on the Book of Psalms, Vol. 4* in *Calvin's Commentaries* VI (CTS; Grand Rapids: Baker Books, 2003), 169.

[73] Calvin, *Institutes*, 1:14:20, 180.

[74] Cf. A.E. McGrath, *Reformation Thought: An Introduction*, 3rd ed. (Oxford: Blackwell, 1999), 273–274.

[75] J. Calvin, *Commentaries on the Book of Genesis, Vol. 1* in *Calvin's Commentaries* I (CTS; Grand Rapids: Baker Books, 2003), 86–87.

contemplations on the works of nature, and turns them away from God.'[76] Calvin here seems to acknowledge that consideration of secondary causes need not point towards the primary cause, however nonsensical a stance.[77] 'If, then, we would avoid a senseless natural philosophy,' he warns, 'we must always start with this principle, that everything in nature depends upon the will of God, and that the whole course of nature is only the prompt carrying into effect of his orders.'[78] Assuming that scientific investigation of the world is conducted with ready acknowledgement of God's wisdom, there is no reason why such activity should be discouraged or forbidden.

Calvin's attitude towards the scientific enterprises of his day was by no means unusual. The Reformers generally were convinced that God had created a world so ordered and comprehensible that it would yield its secrets when probed.[79] Human reason was a gift from God that enabled people accurately to discern the movements of the stars or to make judgements about the various causal interactions within nature.[80] In seventeenth-century Holland and England in particular, many scientists were encouraged by the positive Reformed stance towards creation and began to study it on its own terms;[81] but as the study of the natural world increased, so the minds of the natural scientists began to broaden, toying with ideas that people in the previous century would have deemed scandalous or absurd. Consequently, 'the impact of new knowledge on old patterns of thought was raising questions that religious thinkers would have to face. A new class was beginning to emerge: men of sceptical outlook, impatient of all restraint.'[82] Nonetheless, the development of the natural sciences could not shake its indebtedness to its formative past. Fundamental to the new science was the notion that matter is passive: the material order has no inherent power of its own and has to be acted upon from without in order to move.[83] This understanding of the world shared certain affinities with the

---

[76] J. Calvin, *Commentary on the Book of Psalms, Vol. 1* in *Calvin's Commentaries* IV (CTS; Grand Rapids: Baker Books, 2003), 479.

[77] Calvin criticises Aristotle for showing 'such ingenuity upon the subject of meteors, that he discusses their natural causes most exactly, while he omits the main point of all', that is, knowing that 'all things concur to carry [God's will] into effect.' (J. Calvin, *Commentary on the Book of Psalms, Vol. 5* in *Calvin's Commentaries* VI [CTS; Grand Rapids: Baker Books, 2003], 301).

[78] Calvin, *Comm. Psa.* 5, 301.

[79] Cf. T.F. Torrance, *Divine and Contingent Order* (Edinburgh: T&T Clark, 1998), vii; Kaiser, *Creation and the History of Science*, 121.

[80] Kaiser, *Creation and the History of Science*, 121.

[81] Cragg, *The Church and the Age of Reason 1648–1789*, 45; Kaiser, *Creation and the History of Science*, 122; McGrath, *Reformation Thought*, 274; Brooke, *Science and Religion*, 111.

[82] Cragg, *The Church and the Age of Reason 1648–1789*, 45.

[83] G.B. Deason, 'Reformation Theology and the Mechanistic Conception of Nature', in D.C. Lindberg and R.L. Numbers (eds.), *God and Nature: Historical Essays on the*

Reformed teaching on providence, that nothing could happen in the world without God himself acting through secondary causes. Both the Reformed concept of divine action and the natural scientific understanding of the passivity of matter depended on there being something not subject to or even outside the material order to set it in motion. Accordingly, belief in God's providence as his sovereign determination of all things confirmed the intuitions of many Protestant scientists that the structure of the world was something rational that could be investigated and in turn supported their conviction that such work was good and pleasing to God.[84]

Protestant scientists generally assigned to the world a relative autonomy that reflected its status as God's creation and so contingent upon his continuous act of preservation that enabled the divine direction of all things.[85] There was, however, a subtle but significant shift from the way Calvin portrayed God's relation to the world. Although in Elizabethan England there was a growing number of people who expressed their thought and findings about the world in ways that echoed the determinism of the Reformed teachings spread throughout the country, there was also much more of a focus upon the role of secondary causes in the world. Accordingly, there was 'a growing marginalisation of any discussion of God as the first cause', for these scientists believed that the world 'could explain its properties with reference to itself, rather than require the invocation of God.'[86] Three brief examples will suffice to outline the initial stages of this shift. Thomas Cooper, Bishop of Lincoln, affirmed that there is no such thing as chance but only divine providence; but by this he meant little more than that God works through secondary causes. For Cooper, there was no sense that God could act extraordinarily. Similarly, Richard Hooker, Master of the London Temple, held that God's works are restricted by the laws of nature he established at creation and therefore are regular rather than unpredictable or chaotic. Walter Bailey, Elizabeth's physician, asserted that God did not work in any new way after the sixth day of creation and that any acts of God now are by natural means alone; to suggest otherwise would undermine the integrity of that which he had established.[87] In an age where debate continued over the technicalities of his teaching on predestination, Calvin's thoughts on providence had been assimilated with few reservations and then reshaped to fit the emerging science of the day. Cooper, Hooker and Bailey, whilst all keen to

---

Encounter Between Christianity and Science (Berkeley: University of California Press, 1986), 167–191 (168).

[84] Deason, 'Reformation Theology and the Mechanistic Conception of Nature', 170; Alexander, *Rebuilding the Matrix*, 81–83.

[85] Cf. Deason, 'Reformation Theology and the Mechanistic Conception of Nature', 170; Kaiser, *Creation and the History of Science*, 131.

[86] A.E. McGrath, *A Scientific Theology, Volume One: Nature* (Edinburgh: T&T Clark, 2001), 100.

[87] Kaiser, *Creation and the History of Science*, 136.

affirm God's presence and activity within the world, effectively reduced secondary causation to natural occurrence and neglected to acknowledge a more positive teaching of how God continues to act in the world.[88]

The assumption that matter is passive, then, consolidated by the pancausal relation of God to the world, led to a new portrayal of that world as a machine, where each part of nature was seen to interrelate in a grand system of cause and effect. Phenomena such as colours and tastes, for example, were no longer seen as fundamental to reality but merely as the effect of certain particles impacting upon the human senses.[89] Although Calvin's teaching on providence could be described as deterministic, it was never a rigid, mechanical determinism such as that now presupposed by the scientists. Whereas for Calvin, God remained sovereign over his creation, the new science suggested that nature was 'an inert, reliable and ordained mechanism, which could be controlled and regulated.'[90] According to the new conception of reality, there was no need for God to exercise providential control over the world for he had made it to run according to its own inner workings. Few natural scientists sought actively to remove God from his office;[91] but the more they observed a world governed by its own natural laws, the more they began unconsciously to sever the ropes of providence that tied God to his creation. This reached its pinnacle towards the end of the seventeenth century with the thought of Isaac Newton. Despite regarding the universe as a product of 'the design and dominion of an intelligent and powerful being',[92] Newton conceived far more explicitly than his predecessors of God as holding the universe together by its natural laws rather than through any other means.[93] In itself, this posed no real threat to a

---

[88] Cf. Kaiser, *Creation and the History of Science*, 136.

[89] Brooke, *Science and Religion*, 118. Locke makes a similar distinction. He argued that primary qualities refer to solidity, extension, figure and mobility, and that secondary qualities are colours, sounds, tastes, and so on. A snowball, for example, has the qualities of 'white', 'cold' and 'round', and these produce the ideas, or sensations, of 'whiteness', 'coldness' and 'roundness'. (Locke, *An Essay Concerning Human Understanding*, 2:8:8–10, 134–135). The point is that for Locke, some conception of the passivity of matter seems to be a given: secondary qualities are produced by the 'impulse' or impact of primary qualities upon the human senses. (Locke, *An Essay Concerning Human Understanding*, 2:8:11, 135).

[90] McGrath, *A Scientific Theology, Volume One: Nature*, 107.

[91] Cf. Alexander, *Rebuilding the Matrix*, 134; Cragg, *The Church and the Age of Reason 1648–1789*, 74–75.

[92] I. Newton, *The Principia: Mathematical Principles of Natural Philosophy*, translated by I.B. Cohen and A. Whitman, assisted by J. Budenz (Berkeley: University of California Press, 1999), 940.

[93] McGrath, *A Scientific Theology, Volume One: Nature*, 107, 226; R.S. Westfall, 'The Rise of Science and the Decline of Orthodox Christianity: A Study of Kepler, Descartes and Newton', in D.C. Lindberg and R.L. Numbers (eds.), *God and Nature: Historical Essays on the Encounter Between Christianity and Science* (Berkeley:

providential understanding of creaturely reality; indeed, Newton saw the natural laws as proof that God continued to be present to the world.[94] Nonetheless, his system gave the so-inclined the opportunity to ignore God's presence within creation and then to exclude him altogether. During a century in which free-thinkers such as Herbert, the Cambridge Platonists and the deists voiced their incredulity at certain religious teachings, the new, mechanistic view of the world propounded by the natural scientists only supplied them with further ammunition to target the Christian God and force him to leave the world. For these people, then, natural occurrence ceased masquerading as secondary causation; there was need no more to refer to a primary cause.

§ 3.5 Locating the Problem

Our broad brushstrokes have covered only the smallest area of an impossibly large canvas. Essentially, we have sketched how Calvin's teaching on providence and predestination spread throughout England, and in turn how it was welcomed by some and rejected by others. The picture painted is that of the growth of human knowledge of the way in which the natural world works and of the variety of life within it, a growth that Calvin himself influenced in part. We need now to look more closely at the pattern that appears.

Essentially, we have suggested that Calvin's teaching somehow contributed to the emergence of deism, that God is no longer concerned about the world he created.[95] To paint broadly again, the Reformers' concept of the sovereignty of God strengthened the natural scientists' own beliefs in the passivity of matter, that in order for something to move it has to be impacted from without. Those emphasising the mechanistic view of the world particularly were free to draw from this idea and employ the Reformed teaching on providence to support their findings: effectively, God sets all things in motion and they unfold according to the laws of nature he established. However, this led eventually to the possibility that God could be displaced from his providential role within creation, that as the ability of natural science to explain away the puzzles of the world increased, the need for God to be invoked as the one who exercises his sovereign providence receded dramatically. Whereas for Calvin, each individual occurrence is planned by and depends upon the very activity of God, the natural scientists unwittingly shifted him to the beginning of a causal chain of events that he had no need to interrupt. Accordingly, the new knowledge of the natural world seemed to push God further and further away from it, and the

---

University of California Press, 1986), 233; Gay, *The Enlightenment, An Interpretation*, 141.

[94] Brooke, *Science and Religion*, 118.

[95] The issue of deism should remain distinct from that of atheism; for the development of this latter trend, see M.J. Buckley, *At the Origins of Modern Atheism* (New Haven: Yale University Press, 1987).

less God was perceived to do in the world, the less people thought he needed to be involved. If there was a role for God in this brave, new world, then it was as a *deus ex machina* 'invoked to make the system work';[96] and as the natural scientists further explained things previously accounted for by mystery, miracles or Scripture, they 'paved the way for the drastic revisions' to religious belief required by the burgeoning intellectual regime.[97] Our contention, then, is that this happened in part due to the negative reaction to the Reformed teaching of predestination in England as the new science was developing. Even as Calvin's thought, passed through Beza to Perkins, was received favourably by many of the English, there was a significant number who in turn rejected aspects of it on the basis of the fresh knowledge of the world coming to light. Thus during the seventeenth century, characters such as Herbert of Cherbury, and later, the Cambridge Platonists and the deists, were able to affirm a general providence where human knowledge of the divine was available to all through the exercise of reason in consideration of the natural world. There was therefore little reason for God to be involved as 'the balance shifted from what God has revealed to what man has discovered.'[98] The natural laws were thought to preserve the world from dissolution without any need of the divine power.

Is such a picture free from disproportion? Certainly, it is hard absolutely to claim without hesitation that a particular sixteenth-century intellectual trend led inexorably to another a century or two later. Although it is something against which surely few would argue,[99] it is impossible to say definitively that the Protestant emphasis on the goodness of creation *caused* the scientific revolution. John Hedley Brooke is quite correct to note that '[t]o establish a correlation is not necessarily to establish a connection.'[100] Admittedly, it is 'difficult to discount the evidence that Protestant theology provided important resources for those who saw in experimental science the key to human progress';[101] but, Brooke continues, even if it were established incontestably that the majority of scientists were Protestants, this does not mean that 'it was their religious convictions that supplied the motivation for their science.'[102] This would suggest that Calvin's positive stance towards science and the arts did not motivate the beginning of such practices but supported them as already existing enterprises and legitimised them from the Reformed perspective.

---

[96] Brown, *Philosophy and the Christian Faith*, 57.
[97] Cragg, *The Church and the Age of Reason 1648–1789*, 75.
[98] Cragg, *The Church and the Age of Reason 1648–1789*, 13.
[99] McGrath, *A Scientific Theology, Volume One: Nature*, 273–274; Kaiser, *Creation and the History of Science*, 122, 135, 174; Deason, 'Reformation Theology and the Mechanistic Conception of Nature', 170, 172; Alexander, *Rebuilding the Matrix*, 138.
[100] Brooke, *Science and Religion*, 113.
[101] Brooke, *Science and Religion*, 111.
[102] Brooke, *Science and Religion*, 112.

However, even once these methodological observations have been taken into consideration, it remains possible to detect certain elements that suggest more than a coincidental association between Calvin's teaching on providence and predestination and the intellectual displacement of God from the world.

Perhaps the first point to note is that for Calvin, the identification of creaturely actions and events as secondary causation is a matter of faith. Calvin accepts, for example, that '[t]he earth brings forth her fruits; but,' he continues, 'it is God that giveth bread, and it is God that giveth strength by the nourishment of that bread.' Accordingly, 'as all inferior and secondary causes, viewed in themselves, veil like so many curtains the glorious God from our sight (which they too frequently do), the eye of faith must be cast up far higher, that it may behold the hand of God working by all these His instruments.'[103] Here we see a suggestion that secondary causes do not necessarily witness – at least, not efficaciously – to divine primary causation; rather, it is a person's *faith* that recognises in secondary causation the presence and activity of God. Though there is no problem with Calvin's stance here, neither is there any reason why someone less pious should confess the same. If there is no 'eye of faith', or if that 'eye' fails to look past secondary causation in the manner Calvin suggests, there is nothing whatsoever to indicate that there is anything beyond the creaturely action or event itself. The notion of primary causation is irrelevant and secondary causation is reduced to simple, natural occurrence. Certainly, Calvin concedes this possibility: where believers see God governing and moderating all things, 'unbelievers only recognise in the arrangement of the world what their eyes see and thus view nature as a design or essence that rules over all'.[104] Nonetheless, the responsibility that Calvin placed upon the human agent to value creaturely activity as secondary causation means that it is unsurprising that eventually the latter was not distinguished as such, particularly when those unsympathetic to Reformed teachings took the developments of natural science to support their own arguments for a more 'reasonable' religion.

That said, it was the ambivalence of the concept of secondary causation that made it possible to speak of creaturely actions and events as simple, natural occurrence. For Calvin, secondary causation functions conceptually both to prevent the conflation of God and creation and to assert his presence therein.[105] This is, however, a conviction that cannot be supported phenomenologically. Primary causation cannot be seen apart from observing creaturely actions and events and by faith interpreting them as God's activity. This means, however,

---

[103] Calvin, *Secret Providence*, 231.

[104] J. Calvin, *Against the Fantastic and Furious Sect of the Libertines who are Called 'Spirituals'*, in *Treatises Against the Anabaptists and Against the Libertines*, translated and edited by B.W. Farley (Grand Rapids: Baker Books, 1982), 187–326 (243).

[105] See § 2.2.

that the dangers of conflation or strict dualism that the concept of secondary causation is employed to overcome are in fact fostered by it: either the freedom and integrity of creaturely causation is overwhelmed by divine primary causation, or there is no meaningful relation between the two. If there is no faith to recognise God present in and through creaturely causation, the Reformed teaching on providence and predestination becomes indistinguishable from fate or mechanical determinism and so lends itself to an ordered world but without any particular religious metaphysic. Again, it is unsurprising that something like deist thought could arise within this intellectual context.

The problem stems from the conceptual framework presupposed by primary and secondary causation. Effectively, this posits two agents, God and the creature, in relation to one another; but the precise formulation of this relation is difficult to elucidate. It is not enough simply to suggest that divine primary causation and creaturely secondary causation are in relation but not in competition:[106] the location of the problem of the relation between primary and secondary causation is found not in any perceived opposition between the two but ultimately in the description of the agents themselves. Secondary causation entails a plurality of creaturely agents, that is, secondary *causes*; but primary causation is the action of the one God, the primary *cause* or *causa prima*, who effects by his will almost to the exclusion of his triune identity.[107] This in turn suggests that the status of the proper ontological distinction entailed here – that God is God and the creature is not – assumes undue priority over the actuality of their relation. Calvin's tendency, then, to speak of God's providence in terms of the divine will lessened the impact of the more overtly trinitarian elements of his thoughts on the matter, making it difficult for later theologians to conceive of providence trinitarianly and possible to reduce God to the supreme agent amongst many, lesser agents.[108] Without the mediation of the incarnate Son and

---

[106] We will make this claim more fully in § 4.6.

[107] Cf. P.S. Fiddes, *Participating in God: A Pastoral Doctrine of the Trinity* (London: DLT, 2000), 123–124.

[108] To be fair, the problem of conceiving God's trinitarian action unitarianly is not limited to Calvin's thought but stands within Western theological thought as a whole. Referring specifically to Lutheran and Reformed dogmatics, Charles Wood writes, '[F]ollowing the ancient principle that whatever God does *ad extra* is done by the entire Trinity, it typically asserted that providence, like creation, is the "work of the entire Trinity", the "activity of the triune God". However, it has been justly observed that the principle followed here has usually led to an implicit denial that the doctrine of the Trinity has any bearing on our understanding of God's works in the world. Because the works of God *ad extra* are not to be divided up among the persons of the Trinity, theologians have tended to ignore the Trinity when it comes to understanding God's works, and have, in effect, produced "unitarian" accounts of God's involvement with the world. By a strange irony, then, rather than leading to an understanding of how God acts "triunely", the principle that all of God's works *ad extra* are the work of the entire Trinity seems to have encouraged theologians to think

the Holy Spirit to traverse the ontological distinction between God and the world, there is either the possibility that God stands isolated from the world he created or that his agency is conflated with or placed in opposition to creaturely agency. Furthermore, the priority given to the divine will in matters of providence denies to God's action its specificity or particularity as mediated by the Son and the Spirit. Once we lose sight of God's specific action in Christ, we focus instead on the abstract efficacy of God's will rather than on how his action is shaped in Christ and brought to fulfilment by the Spirit. Consequently, there is a generalising of God's action in Calvin's thought that relegates everything that happens simply to the effect of the divine will. Although Calvin understood providence as the action of the triune God,[109] it is difficult to see how this positively affected his notion of God as *causa prima*.

The overshadowing of an explicit trinitarian dimension by an emphasis on the divine will deprived Calvin's teaching on providence and predestination of the means, therefore, to safeguard itself from influencing the eventual intellectual displacement of God from descriptions of the natural order. Newton, writing more than a century after Calvin died, spoke of God as the one who 'rules all things, not as the world soul but as the lord of all', for 'a god without dominion, providence, and final causes is nothing other than fate and nature.'[110] Such language would not be out of place in Calvin's treatment of providence, yet Newton believed that the Christian doctrine of the Trinity was a

---

of God's action as if God were *not* triune. In consequence, they have tended to stress the notion of God's acting *upon* the world'. (C.M. Wood, 'How Does God Act?', *International Journal of Systematic Theology* 1 [1999], 138–152 [141–142, emphasis original]; cf. C.E. Gunton, 'The Holy Spirit who with the Father and the Son together is Worshipped and Glorified', in *Father, Son and Holy Spirit: Essays Toward a Fully Trinitarian Theology* [London: T&T Clark, 2003], 75–90 [79]).

Is this account reasonable? Certainly; but William Placher surely is right to note that the essential difference between Thomas Aquinas, Martin Luther and Calvin and the theology of the seventeenth century is that the former knew that their language about God was necessarily imprecise, whereas the latter sought increasingly greater levels of clarity in its articulation. For the later theologians, precision and concision led to a more reasonable understanding of God's relation to the world, a very important task in an intellectual climate that demanded rigour in theoretical discourse; but the price paid was a loss of God's transcendence and the concomitant reduction of divine agency to the level of the creaturely. (W.C. Placher, *The Domestication of Transcendence: How Modern Thinking About God Went Wrong* [Louisville: Westminster John Knox Press, 1996], 71, 76, 87, 111, 126–127, 181–182). It remains feasible, however, that certain language and concepts used by Aquinas, Luther and Calvin nonetheless made it possible for the seventeenth-century quest for theological precision to lapse into non-trinitarian forms of expression.

[109] See § 2.2.
[110] Newton, *Principia*, 940, 942.

superstition to be rejected.[111] Though the Reformers had assumed their determining God to be trinitarian, they did not work through the implications of this for his relationship with creation; the unitarian expression of their theologies meant that those who for whatever reason did not accept trinitarian theology found it easier to assign to God the role of Newton's cosmic legislator or reject his interaction altogether.[112]

Would this problem and situation have been avoided if Calvin tempered his stance on the divine will with an explicitly trinitarian conception of providence? It is hard to say; an affirmation of God's triunity does not guarantee the adequate expression of his triune action within the world.[113] Underlying the problem of Calvin's teaching on providence and predestination is not simply the compromised trinitarian exposition but his dualistic leanings suggesting that divinity and creation cannot easily relate.[114] This is resolved somewhat by understanding the triune God to be at work within creation mediately through the Son and the Spirit and not through the abstract causation of the divine will, which wills to mediate God's action through secondary causation. 'The point of stressing a trinitarian way of construing the relation of Creator and creation is that it enables us to understand both the past and the continuing creative divine agency toward the world without closing the space between God and the created order.'[115] What is required, then, is some kind of mediation between God and the world so that God can work within the world

---

[111] Brooke, *Science and Religion*, 136; Westfall, 'The Rise of Science and the Decline of Orthodox Christianity', 231.

[112] Cf. Deason, 'Reformation Theology and the Mechanistic Conception of Nature', 186–187.

[113] J. Augustine Di Noia writes, 'A properly trinitarian account of divine causality in creation understands that as universal transcendent personal agent the Triune God, in his Word and Wisdom, is not only the cause of existence but also the cause of causes.' Despite using the language of causation, Di Noia insists that because divine causality ought not to be understood in a way similar to created causality, 'God's action does not displace or supplant the ·activity of creaturely causes; rather he enables creaturely causes to act according to their natures and, nonetheless, to bring about the ends he intends.' The Triune God, as primary cause, does this through creaturely secondary causes. (J.A. Di Noia, 'By Whom All Things were Made: Trinitarian Theology of Creation as the Basis for a Person-Friendly Cosmology', in C.R. Seitz [ed.], *Nicene Christianity: The Future for a New Ecumenism* [Grand Rapids: Brazos Press, 2001], 63–73 [70]). In what way, however, does Di Noia's affirmation of God's triunity impact upon his understanding of God's action within the world? Despite the continuous references to 'the Triune God', the swift return to depicting God as 'the cause of causes' surely suggests how little the notion of God's triune action has affected Di Noia's thought.

[114] See § 2.5 and § 8.3.

[115] C.E. Gunton, 'The End of Causality? The Reformers and their Predecessors', in C.E. Gunton (ed.), *The Doctrine of Creation: Essays in Dogmatics, History and Philosophy* (Edinburgh: T&T Clark, 1997), 63–82 (81).

without overwhelming and depersonalising its created, space-time structures;[116] this is why a trinitarianly-informed doctrine of the incarnation should play a prominent role in any doctrine of providence, for it is in the incarnation and by his Spirit that God acts within the world and not against it. Unfortunately, Calvin's failure to incorporate this into his teaching on providence sufficiently means that he has to employ instead the concept of secondary causation to mediate, a turn that led eventually to the intellectual displacement of God from the world.

§ 3.6 Conclusion

We have argued that the ambiguity of the concept of secondary causation in Calvin's teaching on providence not only supported the development of natural science but also contributed in part to the emergence of intellectual trends such as deism. The reason for this stems ultimately from the conceptual framework of primary and secondary causation that Calvin employs to depict God's pancausal relation to the world. There always exist two dangers: first, that divine primary and creaturely secondary causation will be so conflated that the former overwhelms the latter and renders it impotent (as in Calvin's teaching on providence); and secondly, that no positive or meaningful relation between the two can be conceived, that God and the world exist in parallel and never interact (as in deism). Both dangers arise because the actuality of God's action in the world as his *triune* action is not fully appropriated. All this prompts the question, as we said earlier, of whether the conceptual framework of primary and secondary causation is the most adequate way of conceiving of God's providence. Given the problems we have identified with the concept, our task now is to see whether it can or should be rehabilitated.

---

[116] Gunton, 'The Holy Spirit ... is Worshipped and Glorified', 80.

CHAPTER 4

Secondary Causation and the Action of the Triune God

§ 4.1 Introduction

By assigning a 'proper place' to secondary causation,[1] John Calvin aims to safeguard both the integrity of creaturely causal efficacy and the certainty that 'the will of God is the great cause of all things that are done in the whole world'.[2] Accordingly, human enterprises such as the arts and the natural sciences are quite legitimate pursuits, but always on the proviso that those engaging in these activities look beyond the secondary causes themselves and towards God, who provides all things through them. Creaturely secondary causation presupposes divine primary causation, and so the person with faith may discern that God has not abandoned his creation to follow its own course but is present and active within it at all times. Indeed, Calvin enthuses, 'when [the] light of divine providence has once shone upon a godly man, he is then relieved and set free not only from the extreme anxiety and fear that were pressing him before, but from every care.'[3] The heart of Calvin's teaching on providence, then, is thoroughly positive.

This encouraging sentiment is tempered somewhat by the tension that remains in Calvin's defence of the integrity of creaturely causal efficacy, a tension that emerges from the ambiguity that lies at the centre of his employment of the concept of secondary causation. Calvin's emphasis on the divine will means that to act in the world, God must accommodate his action to secondary causes; but Calvin seems unable to articulate his thought here without also laying himself open to charges that his teaching on providence makes God the sole causal agent to the detriment of the world of creatures. The priority of the divine will here mediated not through the Son and the Holy Spirit but through secondary causation engenders confusion about the relation of God to the world. It is never entirely clear how Calvin can suggest that the divine presence is mediated to the world by God's self-accommodation to

---

[1] J. Calvin, *Institutes of the Christian Religion* (2 vols.), translated by F.L. Battles (LCC XX / XXI; Philadelphia: The Westminster Press, 1960), 1:17:6, 218.
[2] J. Calvin, *A Defence of the Secret Providence of God*, in *Calvin's Calvinism: Treatises on the Eternal Predestination of God and the Secret Providence of God*, translated by H. Cole (Grand Rapids: Reformed Free Publishing Association, 1987), 223–350 (233).
[3] Calvin, *Institutes*, 1:17:11, 224.

secondary causation without either conflating the two or setting them in opposition on the same level of agency. Certainly, neither of these alternatives would have been taught by Calvin; but his dependency on the conceptual framework of primary and secondary causation to formulate his teaching on providence exposes the tendency of that conceptuality eventually to undermine what it tries to uphold.

All this prompts the question of whether the conceptual framework of primary and secondary causation is the most adequate way of conceiving God's providence. Our concern in this chapter, then, simply is to probe more fully the relation between primary and secondary causation.[4] Calvin is not the only person to have employed this terminology, and so we will explore a number of these alternative accounts to see if they avoid the traps into which Calvin himself fell. We will argue that providence explicated in terms of primary and secondary causation displaces the action of the triune God and that a more appropriate way of illuminating the matter is that of the conceptual framework of divine presence. To begin, however, we must first consider whether it is inherently difficult or even impossible to reconcile different sorts of causes.

§ 4.2 Causal Distinctions

Causal distinctions first find systematic presentation in the philosophy of Aristotle,[5] who distinguished between four different senses of the word 'cause' (αἰτία), standardised in Latin as the *causa materialis* ('material cause'), the *causa formalis* ('formal cause'), the *causa efficiens* ('efficient cause') and the *causa finalis* ('final cause').[6] The material cause is 'that out of which a thing

---

[4] Our intention is not to offer any account of causation, that is, of how things actually affect or effect one another, but rather to assume that things genuinely have causal efficacy, however this might be understood. For accounts of causation, see J. Kim, 'Causation', in *The Cambridge Dictionary of Philosophy*, 2nd ed. (Cambridge: Cambridge University Press, 1999), 125–127; P.J. Mackie, 'Causality', in T. Honderich (ed.), *The Oxford Companion to Philosophy*, 2nd ed. (Oxford: Oxford University Press, 2005), 131–133; E. Sosa and M. Tooley (eds.), *Causation* (ORP; Oxford: Oxford University Press, 1993); and D.H. Mellor, *The Facts of Causation* (ILP; London: Routledge, 1995).

[5] E. Sosa and M. Tooley, 'Introduction', in E. Sosa and M. Tooley (eds.), *Causation* (ORP; Oxford: Oxford University Press, 1993), 1–32 (30).

[6] Aristotle, *Physics*, translated by R.P. Hardie and R.K. Gaye, in *The Basic Works of Aristotle*, edited by R. McKeon (New York: Modern Library, 2001), 213–394 (2.3.194^{b}24–2.3.195^{b}30, 240–242); *Metaphysics*, translated by W.D. Ross, in *The Basic Works of Aristotle*, 681–926 (5.2.1013^{a}24–5.2.1014^{a}25, 752–754). For a summary of the Latin variations of *causa*, see R.A. Muller, *Dictionary of Latin and Greek Theological Terms Drawn Principally from Protestant Scholastic Theology* (Grand Rapids: Baker Book House, 1985), 61–64.

comes to be and which persists', such as 'the bronze of the statue'.[7] This complements the formal cause, that is, 'the form or the archetype' of a particular object,[8] for example, the shape of the statue sculpted from bronze.[9] Aristotle defined efficient causation as 'the primary source of the change or coming to rest'; this source could be human – 'the man who gave advice is a cause, the father is cause of the child' – or non-human, insofar as anything that produces change may be described as an efficient cause.[10] Finally, Aristotle argued that all activity is done for a particular end – 'health is the cause of walking about' – and so the end at which activity aims is termed the final cause.[11]

Importantly, Aristotle's four causes do not conflict with one another. '[T]here are several causes of the same thing,' he notes; for example, 'both the art of the sculptor and the bronze are causes of the statue.'[12] Each is a cause but they do not cause in the same way: the bronze is the material cause, the sculptor the efficient cause. 'Some things,' he continues, 'cause each other reciprocally, e.g. hard work causes fitness and *vice versa*, but again not in the same way, but the one as end, the other as the origin of change.'[13] It is possible also that one particular thing may be said to cause different effects, such as when the absence of a ship's pilot wrecks the vessel but the pilot's presence ensures its safety.[14] Aristotle's examples suffice to demonstrate, then, that different causes do not of necessity compete against one another.

These distinctions are helpful if made appropriately. Calvin himself makes use of Aristotle's four causes in commentating on Paul's letter to the Ephesians. In his interpretation of Ephesians 1:5, Calvin first detects three causes of salvation: '[t]he efficient cause is *the good pleasure of the will* of God, the material cause is, *Jesus Christ*, and the final cause is, *the praise of the glory of his grace*.'[15] The formal cause eventually is identified by Calvin as 'the

---

[7] Aristotle, *Physics*, 2.3.194^{b}24, 240.

[8] Aristotle, *Physics*, 2.3.194^{b}26, 240.

[9] C. Brown, *Christianity and Western Thought: A History of Philosophers, Ideas and Movements, Volume One: From the Ancient World to the Age of Enlightenment* (Leicester: Apollos, 1990), 43. Aristotle's own example is rather more cryptic: 'e.g. the ratio 2:1 and number in general are causes of the octave'. (Aristotle, *Metaphysics*, 5.2.1013^{a}28–29, 752).

[10] Aristotle, *Physics*, 2.3.194^{b}29–31, 241.

[11] Aristotle, *Physics*, 2.3.194^{b}32–33, 241.

[12] Aristotle, *Physics*, 2.3.195^{a}4–5, 241.

[13] Aristotle, *Physics*, 2.3.195^{a}9–11, 241, emphasis original.

[14] Aristotle, *Physics*, 2.3.195^{a}12–14, 241.

[15] J. Calvin, *Commentaries on the Epistles of Paul to the Galatians and Ephesians* in *Calvin's Commentaries* XXI (CTS; Grand Rapids: Baker Books, 2003), 200, emphasis original.

preaching of the gospel, by which the goodness of God *overflows upon us*.'[16] Again, there is no suggestion that this basic fourfold distinction admits of internal contradiction. There is no inconsistency in a person's salvation being caused by God's will, by the death of Jesus Christ, by the preaching of the gospel message and for the glory of God. Each *causa* is a genuine cause but works its effect differently. Thus a strength of Aristotle's four causes is its conceptual flexibility that allows for elaboration; but such elaboration risks confusion. By making the good pleasure of the will of God the efficient cause of salvation, Calvin is clear that '[t]he cause of our salvation did not proceed from us, but from God alone.'[17] Prior to this assertion, however, Calvin refers to God's eternal election as '[t]he foundation and first cause, both of our calling and of all the benefits we receive from God'.[18] Assuming that he does not wish to distinguish too sharply – if at all – between the good pleasure of God's will and his eternal election, Calvin surely equates God's will as the *first* cause (*causa prima*) of human salvation *and so* the *efficient* cause of human salvation. It is also possible that the final cause is not to be separated from this efficient causation, for God wills salvation for the end of the praise of his glory. If so, then there is the implication that the remaining material and formal causes of salvation – Christ and the preaching of the gospel respectively – in some way serve the efficient and final causes as secondary causation. This does not entail necessarily that the saving work of Christ as *causa materialis* must be reduced to a mere instrument of God's will; but crucially, Calvin does not here suggest that Christ's death is in any way an example of efficient causation, creaturely or divine. Christ's death instead is the embodied instantiation of the divine will to save, which alone is the efficient cause of salvation. No doubt Calvin would have wished to affirm the 'efficiency' of Christ's action, but again it seems that he is bound by the causal categories he uses and prone, therefore, to the ambiguity that comes through assigning a 'proper place' to secondary causation whilst insisting upon God's pancausal relation to the world. Such an equation of divine efficient causation with divine primary causation demonstrates once more that it is difficult to avoid suggestions that for Calvin, it is the divine will alone that truly acts in the world of creatures; and the causal distinctions he borrows from Aristotle do little to persuade us otherwise.

The problem lies in Calvin's employment of Aristotle's four causes within an existing conceptual framework of primary and secondary causation, whereas

---

[16] Calvin, *Comm. Eph.*, 203, emphasis original. Elsewhere, John Calvin identifies 'the efficient cause of our obtaining eternal life' as 'the mercy of the Heavenly Father and his freely given love towards us'; the material cause as Christ, 'with his obedience'; the 'formal or instrumental cause' as 'faith'; and the final cause as both 'the proof of divine justice' and 'the praise of God's goodness'. (Calvin, *Institutes*, 3:14:17, 783–784; cf. *Institutes*, 3:14:21, 787).

[17] Calvin, *Comm. Eph.*, 200.

[18] Calvin, *Comm. Eph.*, 197.

the philosopher himself operated with no such system; and whilst material, formal, efficient and final causes do not of necessity contradict each other, divine primary causation and creaturely secondary causation are not material, formal, efficient or final causes – at least, not so carefully defined. There are three points to note. First, primary causation and secondary causation appear to function on different causal levels or orders, with the former ontologically prior to the latter and so setting the conditions within which secondary causes operate; but Aristotle's four causes do not warrant admission of different causal orders as such. Primary causation, secondly, is efficient causation; but secondary causation, if it is not to be seen purely as instrumental, also is efficient. God acts; the creature acts. Finally, the underlying assumption is that in acting, God and the creature each has the power to effect something. Both God and the creature are said to be *the* cause of a particular action or event,[19] which we may designate the effective cause – and certainly, Calvin intends to affirm both the efficiency and the efficacy of secondary causation. Accordingly, we see that primary causation is efficient and effective; but secondary causation equally is efficient and effective. What, then, is the difference between primary causation and secondary causation?

Paul Helm observes this same tension, but frames it in the language of necessary and sufficient conditions. The 'primary cause is an enabling and sustaining cause, making possible secondary causes and setting bounds to them.' Furthermore, the primary cause is 'an eternal cause which has the whole of creation as its effect', whereas secondary causes are 'event[s] in time'.[20] However, Helm identifies a problem:

> Precisely what is the primary causal power from which my action issues? 'Issue' in what sense? Clearly it is not adequate to understand such issuing in terms merely of God's provision of *necessary* conditions for my action. For while the provision of necessary conditions would permit or make possible my action, such conditions would not ensure that it took place. In order to ensure that the action took place, the divine conditions, conditions in the primary order, would have to be both necessary *and sufficient.*[21]

---

[19] '[F]or example we sometimes ask for *the* cause of an event from curiosity as to why it occurred at that specific time and place and in that specific way. In that case *the* cause will be the factor which is most peculiar to the effect and not those factors like the negative and standing conditions which would also apply if the effect were to take on another form or occur at another time and place. Thus *the* cause of the match igniting now is my striking it rather than the oxygen in the atmosphere'. (V. Brümmer, *Speaking of a Personal God: An Essay in Philosophical Theology* [Cambridge: Cambridge University Press, 1992], 116, emphasis original).

[20] P. Helm, *The Providence of God* (CCT; Leicester: IVP, 1993), 86.

[21] Helm, *The Providence of God*, 181, emphasis original.

The presence of both necessary and sufficient conditions 'ensure[s] that the action takes place.'[22] Yet if God provides these conditions for creaturely action to occur, precisely 'what part do a person's own desires and reasons (and whatever else we ordinarily think our actions issue from) play'?[23] If my action – such as typing a sentence – issues from me as the secondary agent, 'then my desires and motives and other such factors ... ensure that the action will take place.'[24] Given this, Helm then asks,

> So what, in these circumstances, does the first order, the divine cause, play? For if my desires are sufficient to produce the action in question, why are the first-order causes necessary, let alone sufficient, for producing it?[25]

Helm implies that there would be no problem if all that God provides is the creature's existence and causal potency. On this account, God would provide the necessary but not the sufficient conditions for the creature to act – and yet primary causation is said to provide both necessary and sufficient conditions, enabling the creature to perform *specific* actions. In short, then, Helm finds it 'hard to see that there can be two separate sets of necessary and sufficient conditions for the same action'. He concludes, 'Calling certain conditions "primary" and others "secondary", does not by itself solve anything.'[26]

Any attempt, then, to elucidate the relation between primary and secondary causation either in terms of efficiency and efficacy or by referring to necessary and sufficient conditions does not adequately address the matter. Should we aim, therefore, to qualify secondary causation somehow, perhaps by saying not only that it is efficient and effective but that it is also instrumental, whereas primary causation simply is efficient and effective? An instrumental cause (*causa instrumentalis*) can certainly be an efficient cause – a hammer driving a nail into a plank is an instrument in the hands of the carpenter, but is itself efficient compared to the nail[27] – but there always exists the possibility that an efficient cause conceived as an instrumental cause will have its 'efficiency' stripped from it, for the notion of instrumentality lends itself to being used by another, efficient agent.[28] This conceptual flexibility – or better, instability – exposes the potential for ambiguity at the heart of these causal distinctions.

---

[22] Helm, *The Providence of God*, 181.
[23] Helm, *The Providence of God*, 181–182; quote from 182.
[24] Helm, *The Providence of God*, 182.
[25] Helm, *The Providence of God*, 182.
[26] Helm, *The Providence of God*, 182.
[27] We disagree, then, with David Burrell's claim that it is only the carpenter who may be said to drive the nails. (D.B. Burrell, *Freedom and Creation in Three Traditions* [Notre Dame: University of Notre Dame Press, 1993], 97).
[28] Cf. S.L. Brock, *Action and Conduct: Thomas Aquinas and the Theory of Action* (Edinburgh: T&T Clark, 1998), 110: '[A]n instrumental agent is an agent only in a rather weak sense. It would be more correct to say that insofar as it is a cause of what

How, then, should we clarify the relation between primary and secondary causation? Perhaps a way forward may be drawn still from Aristotle, given that each of his four causes is said to cause in a particular way without restricting the efficacy of the others. May we suggest that primary causation effects an action or event differently from the way a secondary cause effects that same action or event?

§ 4.3 The Ordering of Creation

Calvin depicts divine primary causation as ontologically prior to creaturely secondary causation; this means that the two types of causation function on different ontological levels and must be said to cause in different ways. However, Calvin's acceptance of two causal orders is little more than a restatement of the fundamental ontological distinction between God and the world, that God is God and the creature is not. This ontological distance is bridged by God's will to accommodate his action to individual, particular secondary causes: primary causation thus establishes the actuality and integrity of secondary causation. There is always the danger, however, that Calvin's account of the relation between these two causal orders conflates rather than confirms them in the distinctiveness of their causal agencies. God's will to accommodate his action to secondary causation effectively is a decision to commandeer that particular order and so to risk the integrity of its causal efficacy. So whilst Calvin affirms both primary and secondary causation, his failure sufficiently to clarify the relation between the two leaves that relation ambiguous.

Calvin was not the first person, of course, to distinguish between primary and secondary causation. Thomas Aquinas earlier made the distinction; indeed, he anticipated Calvin's concerns for the integrity of creaturely causal efficacy and the priority of the divine will,[29] although he did not subject all things explicitly to God's eternal decree of predestination in the way that Calvin himself construed. For Aquinas, the 'direction of a rational creature towards the end of life eternal is called predestination'; and 'predestination, as regards its objects, is a part of providence.'[30] Aquinas, like Calvin after him, also held to

---

the principal agent intends, it is not wholly distinct from the principal agent. It is such a cause insofar as it is in the power of the principal agent or is appropriated by him.'

[29] Anthony Lane suggests that similarities between Thomas Aquinas and John Calvin may be attributed either to earlier writings from which they both drew, for example, from the works of Peter Lombard; or that Calvin was influenced by followers of Aquinas rather than by Aquinas himself. Lane argues that it is most likely that Calvin knew Aquinas only through intermediate sources. (A.N.S. Lane, *John Calvin: Student of the Church Fathers* [Edinburgh: T&T Clark, 1999], 15–16, 45).

[30] T. Aquinas, *Summa Theologica*, translated by Fathers of the English Dominican Province (Notre Dame: Christian Classics, 1981), 1a.23.1, 126.

the reality of reprobation;[31] some are permitted to fall away from the end of eternal life,[32] and this permission is based upon God's will 'not [to] wish every good' to 'all men and all creatures'.[33] There seems, however, to be no mention of a divine decree specifically to foreordain some to eternal life and the remainder to everlasting damnation.[34] The difference is between Calvin's protological orientation of providence and Aquinas's influence by the Aristotelian *causa finalis*. Whereas for Calvin, providence is the implementation of the eternal decree by which the end is already set in advance, the subordination of predestination to providence in Aquinas's theology means that God's providence is an *ordering* of all things towards a particular end, which is God himself.[35]

Providence for Aquinas refers specifically to 'the type of the order of things foreordained towards an end' or 'the design of government',[36] and 'the

---

[31] Aquinas, *Sum. Theol.*, 1a.23.3, 127.
[32] Aquinas, *Sum. Theol.*, 1a.23.3, 127.
[33] Aquinas, *Sum. Theol.*, 1a.23.3, *reply objection* 1, 127.
[34] That said, Aquinas does write, '[P]redestination, in its proper sense, is a certain Divine preordination from eternity of those things which are to be done in time by the grace of God.' (Aquinas, *Sum. Theol.*, 3a.24.1, 2144). The point remains, however, that for Aquinas, reprobation is a matter of God's permission, whereas for Calvin, it concerns a specific decree of God. Calvin's stance is arguably more consistent than that of Aquinas: the distinction between God's permission and God's will is meaningless, because 'why shall we say "permission" unless it is because God so wills?' (Calvin, *Institutes*, 3:23:8, 956).
[35] See, for example, T. Aquinas, *Summa Contra Gentiles, Book Three: Providence* (2 vols.), translated, with an introduction and notes, by V.J. Bourke (Notre Dame: University of Nature Dame Press, 1975), 3(1).17.7, 73. Charles Partee's illustration admirably summarises the differences between Aquinas and Calvin on predestination, although it perhaps makes Aquinas's conception of grace rather static: 'The resulting situation is something like this. God has made a wonderful house with a heavenly attic and a hellish cellar. Man is placed in the living room. According to Thomas, some men are given a floor plan and these, with the plan *and* through their own efforts, ascend the stairs. Those without the plan can only, but through their own efforts, descend the other stairs. According to Calvin, God is the real estate agent who leads some upward and others downward. The proper attitude for those on the upward way is praise and gratitude to God and hope for the others. In both Thomas and Calvin, God is ultimately responsible for all men, but in different ways. For Thomas, God is directly involved in giving or withholding the floor plan which man is said to be free to follow if he has it, and yet bound to get lost if he does not. For Calvin, God directs the entire tour. Thus it seems that in terms of salvation the freedom of man in Thomas is basically illusory and in Calvin essentially non-existent.' (C. Partee, 'Predestination in Aquinas and Calvin', *Reformed Review* 32 [1978], 14–22 [21], emphasis original).
[36] Aquinas, *Sum. Theol.*, 1a.22.3, 124; 1a.103.6, 509.

execution of this order ... is called government.'[37] This enables Aquinas to discuss the matter within two different contexts in his *Summa Theologica*. He locates providence as the ordering of creation (*Summa Theologica* 1a.22) within his consideration of the divine essence (1a.2–26) and then the government of all things (1a.103–119) within the chapters on the creation (1a.44–119).[38] Aquinas portrays God's ordering of creation as a hierarchy in which God is the first cause managing an extensive number of secondary causes that derive their efficacy from him.[39] Accordingly, God structures his creation so that secondary causes have the power they require to complete the effects assigned to them;[40] indeed, this is entirely appropriate, as it is God's will that his action be mediated through 'the action of secondary causes; which are the executors of His order'.[41] Importantly, God is not compelled to act through intermediaries but rather through his goodness desires to impart 'the dignity of causality ... even to creatures.'[42] Such a statement, with its suggestion that the creature has only but genuinely what God gives to it, aims to affirm both the integrity and sovereignty of divine causal efficacy and the integrity of creaturely causal efficacy, as creatures participate in God's own governance of the world by means of their own action.[43] The reason Aquinas divides his discussion of providence, then, according to Michael Hoonhout, points to what we have called the fundamental ontological distinction between God and the world, which entails this dissimilarity of causal operations. Hoonhout observes,

> There is no doubt that [Aquinas] considers both God and creatures actively responsible for how the mysterious ways of divine providence take shape in our world. But because he knows that the manner in which God acts is not the manner

---

[37] Aquinas, *Sum. Theol.*, 1a.22.3, 124; 1a.103.6, 509; cf. 1a.22.1 *rep. obj.* 2, 121.

[38] M.A. Hoonhout, 'Grounding Providence in the Theology of the Creator: The Exemplarity of Thomas Aquinas', *The Heythrop Journal* 43 (2002), 1–19 (4–5). Leo Scheffczyk argues that this division 'leads to a divorce between Providence and Creation that is detrimental to any vital conception of the latter. For when Providence is derived from God's prudence ... and is thus conceived of as essentially an attribute of God, as the strict purposefulness of his knowledge and will, then the necessity of Providence is no longer derived from Creation as such and is no longer sought there.' (L. Scheffczyk, *Creation and Providence*, translated by R. Strachan [London: Burns & Oates, 1970], 149).

[39] H. Davies, *The Vigilant God: Providence in the Thought of Augustine, Aquinas, Calvin and Barth* (New York: Peter Lang, 1992), 65–66; cf. C.E. Gunton, *The Triune Creator: A Historical and Systematic Study* (ESCT; Edinburgh: Edinburgh University Press, 1998), 99. Elsewhere, Aquinas compares God's role within this causal hierarchy to 'a master, who not only imparts knowledge to his pupils, but gives also the faculty of teaching others.' (Aquinas, *Sum. Theol.*, 1a.103.6, 509).

[40] Aquinas, *Sum. Theol.*, 1a.22.3, 124.

[41] Aquinas, *Sum. Theol.*, 1a.22.3, *rep. obj.* 2, 124.

[42] Aquinas, *Sum. Theol.*, 1a.22.3, 124; cf. 1a.23.8, *rep. obj.* 2, 133.

[43] Hoonhout, 'Grounding Providence', 5.

in which creatures act, he cannot explain the contributions of both kinds of agency in one context. For the conditions under which either operate – and hence the intelligibility of their acting – are not the same. The only 'condition' under which God acts is his own transcendent mystery, a perfect wisdom, goodness and freedom which are the equal of him.... Yet creatures are not so unconditioned – their manner of acting is in accordance with the actual conditions of our universe, conditions freely created by God so that he may accomplish his providential designs or purposes in and through the conditioned causality of creatures themselves.[44]

Aquinas posits the existence of two different causal orders, both efficacious in the manner most appropriate to each. At this point, he seems even to allow more scope for the integrity and *freedom* of creaturely causal efficacy than does Calvin: the apparent rigidity and determinism of the Reformer's eternal decree of predestination appears to be for Aquinas no more than the sovereign shepherding of all things towards an appointed end. Crucial for Aquinas, however, is precisely the *comprehensiveness* of the divine guidance: God's will 'is the universal cause of all things' that cannot fail to produce its effect.[45] The intermediate or particular causes that stand under God's universal causation 'have power to produce certain effects'[46] and even effect in ways that God has not specifically ordained but merely permitted. Accordingly, Aquinas contends that 'to some effects [God] has attached necessary causes, which cannot fail; but to others defectible and contingent causes, from which arise contingent effects.'[47] Certain effects are ordained, therefore, to 'happen from contingency' and others 'infallibly and of necessity'.[48] It seems, then, that Aquinas not only allows for the integrity of creaturely causal efficacy but ostensibly for the freedom of creaturely action. God's universal causation allows for variations in creaturely activities, and even chance; but the creature is not abandoned, for God does not allow those variations to multiply beyond the boundaries he sets them.[49] Considered generally, Aquinas declares, 'nothing can resist the order of the Divine government.'[50]

As later with Calvin, Aquinas very much emphasises the priority of the divine will that ordains things to happen either from contingency or of necessity. Here, though, is a suspicion that God is depicted as the only

---

[44] Hoonhout, 'Grounding Providence', 5–6.
[45] Aquinas, *Sum. Theol.*, 1a.19.6, 108.
[46] Aquinas, *Sum. Theol.*, 1a.19.7, *rep. obj.* 2, 109.
[47] Aquinas, *Sum. Theol.*, 1a.19.8, 110; cf. T. Aquinas, *Summa Contra Gentiles, Book One: God*, translated, with an introduction and notes, by A.C. Pegis (Notre Dame: University of Nature Dame Press, 1975), 1.85.4, 267; 3(2).94.11, 56.
[48] Aquinas, *Sum. Theol.*, 1a.22.4, *rep. obj.* 1, 124–125.
[49] Aquinas, *Sum. Theol.*, 1a.22.2, *rep. obj.* 1, 122–123; cf. B. Davies, *The Thought of Thomas Aquinas* (Oxford: Clarendon Press, 1992), 161.
[50] Aquinas, *Sum. Theol.*, 1a.103.8, 510.

genuinely causal agent: in his right ordering of the universe, God arranges for some effects to have necessary causes and others to have contingent causes. However, Aquinas qualifies this by saying that 'it is not because the proximate causes are contingent that the effects willed by God happen contingently, but because God has prepared contingent causes for them, it being His will that they should happen contingently.'[51] Is there a suggestion here that rather than ascribing causal efficacy to creaturely action, Aquinas in fact disconnects creaturely causation from its effects, insofar as God orders to creaturely causation the effect that is most appropriate for the occasion? If so, then the integrity of creaturely causal efficacy surely is jeopardised, if not ruined. Yet Aquinas consistently maintains that the creature does produce certain effects appropriate to its causal ability, even if that causal ability is given to it by God. We should be clear that there is no problem in saying that a creature depends at all times upon God in order to act; a creature's action is that creature's action, even if it could not be performed without divine primary causation enabling it to happen. Aquinas seems to go beyond this, however; in the *Summa Contra Gentiles*, he argues,

> Now, in the order of agent causes, God is the first cause.... And so, all lower agent causes act through His power. But the cause of an action is the one by whose power the action is done rather than the one who acts: the principal agent, for instance, rather than the instrument. Therefore, God is *more especially* the cause of every action than are the secondary agent causes.[52]

That said,

> we do not take away their proper actions from created things, though we attribute all the effects of created things to God, as an agent working in all things.[53]

According to Aquinas, an agent consists of two things: the thing that acts and the power by which it acts. God's enabling of a creature to cause certain effects means that any effect is said to be produced both by the creature and by God.[54] Aquinas later qualifies this further by explaining that God 'is the cause of every operation as its end', that 'the second [agent] always acts in virtue of the first', and that God 'gives created agents their forms and preserves them in being.'[55] It is in this sense that God may be said to be 'more especially' the cause of an action. This leads Aquinas to conclude that 'nothing hinders the

---

[51] Aquinas, *Sum. Theol.*, 1a.19.8, 110.
[52] Aquinas, *Sum. Con. Gent.*, 3(1).67.5, 222, emphasis mine; cf. 3(1).17.4: 'Besides, in any kind of causes, the first cause is more a cause than is the secondary cause, for a secondary cause is only a cause through the primary cause.'
[53] Aquinas, *Sum. Con. Gent.*, 3(1).69.29, 235.
[54] Aquinas, *Sum. Con. Gent.*, 3(1).70.5, 236.
[55] Aquinas, *Sum. Theol.*, 1a.105.5, 518–519.

same action from proceeding from a primary and a secondary agent.'[56] The fundamental ontological distinction between God and the world means that the causality of one differs from that of the other. Each level of causality effects a particular action in a way distinct from the other.

For Aquinas, then, divine primary causation posits and supports the reality and integrity of creaturely secondary causation; and his equation of primary causation with universal causation and secondary causation with particular causes allows creatures some measure of autonomy, even as God orders them towards the end that is himself. That said, Aquinas's emphasis on the divine will as the first and universal cause of all things means ultimately that he struggles consistently to maintain that the creature does have genuine causal efficacy. Although we discern no problem in the claim that the creature acts from the power given it by God, nonetheless a number of difficulties arise. Even if Aquinas is correct to say that God also operates in all things as the end towards which they act and by giving created agents their form and being, as well as the power by which they act – and we see no reason to disagree at least with the latter two claims – why, then, must we interpret this as meaning that God is 'more especially the cause of every action'? Are we compelled also to accept that God grants to the creature the power only to act in a *specific* way, as when Aquinas speaks of the divine attachment of certain effects to necessary causes? Indeed, how do we distinguish between what we do 'infallibly and of necessity' or simply contingently? Does God's impartation of power to creatures in fact reduce them to the level of mere instrumentality? Raising such questions implies that far from functioning on different causal levels, primary and secondary causation effectively operate on the same level; and if the distinctiveness and integrity of the two causal orders are maintained, then it makes little sense to describe God as 'more especially' a cause. The most that should be said is that God's causation differs from and causes something different from creaturely causation.

All this points to an ambiguity in Aquinas's thought concerning the relation between primary and secondary causation. For Aquinas, as with Calvin, the emphasis on the divine will as the cause of all things effectively suppresses creaturely causal efficacy even as it intends to uphold it. The subtle difference between Calvin and Aquinas lies within their accounts of how God's will is effected. According to Calvin, God determines the action of each and every secondary cause by mediating his active presence through that cause; God *accommodates* his action, then, to secondary causation, and this to such a degree that we may raise the possibility that primary and secondary causation in fact are conflated. Conversely, for Aquinas, God *delegates* his action to secondary causation; the suggestion here is that God is distanced from certain creaturely actions because of the hierarchy of causes of which he is the first, though we should not understand this to mean that God is dissociated from the

---

[56] Aquinas, *Sum. Theol.*, 1a.105.5, *rep. obj.* 2, 519.

world as in later deism.⁵⁷ In each case, though, for both Aquinas and Calvin, God wills that his action be mediated through secondary causation. Our earlier discussion of Calvin argued that his conception of secondary causation as that which mediates between God and the world displaces the mediation of the Son and the Holy Spirit;⁵⁸ to be consistent, we should say the same about Aquinas's teaching on providence.⁵⁹

§ 4.4 Causation and Analogy

Despite the questions that we have asked of Aquinas's portrayal of the relation between primary and secondary causation, it remains possible that we have failed to grasp the significance of the distinctiveness of each causal order from the other. Hoonhout argues that we should go so far as to expect inconsistencies in Aquinas's thought here, as he is trying to do justice to the particular causal integrity of both orders. Indeed, Hoonhout contends, 'there can be no real contradiction when the terms are of entirely different orders of intelligibility; attributes proper to one are improper to the other because "God" and "world" are not in some common genus, called "reality as we know it".' Conflation of the two causal orders is avoided 'only when the theologian recognises the radical non-equivalency of the terms "God" and "world" that is the core implication of the Christian doctrine of God as Creator.'⁶⁰ The two causal orders reflect the fundamental ontological distinction between God and the world, and what is said of the latter cannot be said of the former because God is not a creature or even like a creature.

How, then, should we speak of God's relation to the world? It is not enough simply to say *that* God differs from the world; we must also understand *why* this is the case. For Aquinas, this difference lies primarily in the fact that God is Creator: 'It must be said that every being in any way existing is from God.... Therefore all beings apart from God are not their own being, but are beings by participation.' All things that participate in being 'are caused by one First

---

⁵⁷ Cf. W.C. Placher, *The Domestication of Transcendence: How Modern Thinking About God Went Wrong* (Louisville: Westminster John Knox Press, 1996), 111.

⁵⁸ See § 2.5 and § 3.5.

⁵⁹ Colin Gunton argues that although 'personal or trinitarianly conceived agency in creation is [not] completely lacking from [Aquinas's] thought' here, there is still the problem that God's 'act of willing is rather monistically conceived. The Trinity plays little or no constitutive part in [Aquinas's] treatment of the divine realisation of creation'. (C.E. Gunton, 'The End of Causality? The Reformers and their Predecessors', in Gunton, C.E. [ed.], *The Doctrine of Creation: Essays in Dogmatics, History and Philosophy* [Edinburgh: T&T Clark, 1997], 63–82 [67]). For Gunton, what emerges from Aquinas's understanding of God's relation to the world 'is a fairly strong conception of unitary divine activity, at the expense of mediation through the Son and Spirit.' (Gunton, *The Triune Creator*, 100).

⁶⁰ Hoonhout, 'Grounding Providence', 7.

Being, Who possesses being most perfectly.'[61] As the source of all that is, then, God transcends the order of things that are said to exist.[62] Indeed, God's essence and his existence cannot be separated, whereas creatures *are* only by virtue of their participation in God.[63] This means that 'it may be admitted that creatures are in some sort like God';[64] as each effect resembles its cause to some degree, so too does the creature, the effect of God's creative causation, resemble its cause.[65] Such an admission does not, however, mean the converse, that God is like creatures.[66] The concept of being is not a generic property that they *share* with one another. Rudi te Velde explains,

> Both are being, God as well as the creature, but each in a radically different way: God is 'being through its essence' (*ens per essentiam*) and the creature is 'being through participation' (*ens per participationem*). The creature is the same as God but differently. While God *is* his being, the creature only participates in being, and thus possesses being in a particular manner according to a specific nature.[67]

Given the total dissimilarity between God and the creature that the fundamental ontological distinction entails, terms ('names') cannot be applied to God *univocally*, that is, in the same way as they would apply to creatures. If we are to say that God is wise and that a particular human person is wise, the term 'wise' is not being used identically. Aquinas argues that this is because for a human person, 'wise' signifies a perfection that is distinct from or accidental to the essence of that person; when applied to God, however, 'we do not mean to signify anything distinct from His essence, or power, or existence.'[68] There is no intimation that the ontological distinction between God and the world means subsequently that we must speak of God *equivocally*; the term 'wise' applied first to God and then to a human person does not mean a completely different thing in each case. If univocity mirrors a conflation of God and the world, then

---

[61] Aquinas, *Sum. Theol.*, 1a.44.1, 229.
[62] Aquinas, *Sum. Theol.*, 1a.4.3, *rep. obj.* 2, 23.
[63] Aquinas, *Sum. Theol.*, 1a.3.4, 17; 1a.4.3, *rep. obj.* 3, 23.
[64] Aquinas, *Sum. Theol.*, 1a.4.3, *rep. obj.* 4, 23.
[65] Aquinas contends that effects resemble their causes in three ways. First, there is a likeness of form between creatures of the same species; this is seen in human reproduction. Secondly, there is a likeness that oversteps the boundary between different species, such as when 'things generated by the sun's heat may be in some sort spoken of as like the sun'. Finally, there is a likeness between that which causes from outside any species altogether and that which it causes. (Aquinas, *Sum. Theol.*, 1a.4.3, 22–23; quote from 22).
[66] Aquinas, *Sum. Theol.*, 1a.4.3, *rep. obj.* 4, 23.
[67] R.A. te Velde, *Aquinas on God: The 'Divine Science' of the Summa Theologiae* (ASHPT; Aldershot: Ashgate, 2006), 114, emphasis original.
[68] Aquinas, *Sum. Theol.*, 1a.13.5, 64.

equivocity resembles a complete dissociation, a dualism, between them. Here, Aquinas's reasoning is simple:

> if names are said of God and creatures in a purely equivocal way, we understand nothing of God through those names; for the meanings of those names are known to us solely to the extent that they are said of creatures. In vain, therefore, would it be said or proved of God that He is a being, good, or the like.[69]

For Aquinas, then, the proper way to speak of God is not univocally or equivocally, but *analogically*. Analogical predication itself may be understood in two ways, 'either according as many things are proportionate to one ... or according as one thing is proportionate to another'.[70] The first form of analogy, the so-called analogy of attribution, 'links two analogous entities which are different in many respects. One of these entities possesses the characteristic attributed to both in the "proper" or ordinary sense, while the other possesses this characteristic in a derived sense.'[71] Aquinas illustrates this form of analogy using the example of health: the term '*healthy* is predicated of medicine and urine in relation and in proportion to health of a body'.[72] Medicine or urine are said to be 'healthy' because they are understood in connection with the health of a particular body.

The second form of analogy is that of proportionality, where 'the attribution which is ascribed in two different statements is the same, but must be seen in relation to the nature of the different entities to which it is ascribed.'[73] Accordingly, 'healthy' may apply both to medicine and to the creature, but medicine is not 'healthy' in the same way that a creature is 'healthy';[74] or, to use the term 'wise' again, God is wise in the way that God is wise and a human person is wise in the way that a human person is wise.[75] There can be no direct comparison between divine and human wisdom without reducing the former to the level of the latter.[76] Aquinas argues that it is according to the analogy of proportionality that things are said of God analogically;[77] the analogy of attribution alone is insufficient to speak of God because 'we should then have to posit something prior to God'.[78] If the term 'wise' is applied to God solely by means of this form of analogy, God and the creature somehow might be classified under a generic concept of 'wise', or, indeed, some universal or

---

[69] Aquinas, *Sum. Con. Gent.*, 1.33.6, 146–147.
[70] Aquinas, *Sum. Theol.*, 1a.13.5, 64.
[71] Brümmer, *Speaking of a Personal God*, 44–45.
[72] Aquinas, *Sum. Theol.*, 1a.13.5, 64, emphasis original.
[73] Brümmer, *Speaking of a Personal God*, 45.
[74] Aquinas, *Sum. Theol.*, 1a.13.5, 64.
[75] Cf. Brümmer, *Speaking of a Personal God*, 46.
[76] Cf. Placher, *The Domestication of Transcendence*, 29.
[77] Aquinas, *Sum. Theol.*, 1a.13.5, 64; *Sum. Con. Gent.*, 1.34.4, 147.
[78] Aquinas, *Sum. Con. Gent.*, 1.34.4, 147.

Platonic form of 'wisdom' in which each participates. Although the analogy of attribution shows how terms may be applied both to God and the creature, it does so adequately only when qualified by the analogy of proportionality. Predicating 'wise' of God, for example, is based first upon our understanding of human wisdom; but as we know that God himself is the cause of all things, we recognise that the term 'wise' applies properly to him in a way appropriate to him, and to creatures only by derivation.[79] Analogical predication, then, 'underlines the fact that creatures and God do not fall under the same genus',[80] whilst establishing rules for how we may speak of their relation.

Here, though, some tensions emerge. The analogy of attribution supports the idea that creatures are wise because somehow they resemble their cause, God, who *essentially* is wise; in this sense, though, the term 'wise' is used *univocally*, because both God and the creature are said to be wise. Indeed, 'analogous predication ... demands and presupposes a univocal basis'.[81] This raises the possibility that God's wisdom is the same sort of wisdom as possessed by a human person, elevated to the ultimate degree, inviting comparison. Conversely, the analogy of proportionality assigns the term 'wise' both to God and the creature in ways appropriate to them. Again, 'wise' is used univocally, but it seems also to reveal a more basic distinction, that is, it suggests that God's wisdom somehow is different from creaturely wisdom. God is wise in a way that a human person is *not* wise, that is, God is wise essentially and not accidentally; but surely this means that the term 'wise' is used *equivocally*. We cannot know what it means to possess a perfection essentially; the divine wisdom is completely unlike human wisdom. However, if this is so, if we cannot understand what it means to say that God is wise on the basis that a human person is wise, precisely *what* can we say? Do Aquinas's two forms of analogy ultimately qualify or militate against each other? They appear to tell us very little indeed about how a term such as 'wise' applies truly to God because the term itself fluctuates from univocity to equivocity with no sense that we may say anything positive about God and his relation to the creature.[82] Even if the analogy of proportionality qualifies the analogy of attribution by suggesting that a creature is wise by participation in God, this does not negate the fact that God's wisdom is entirely different from that of the creature, with the suspicion of equivocation that this entails.

---

[79] Aquinas, *Sum. Con. Gent.*, 1.34.5–6, 148.
[80] te Velde, *Aquinas on God*, 112.
[81] W. Pannenberg, *Systematic Theology* (3 vols.), translated by G.W. Bromiley (Edinburgh: T&T Clark, 1991–1998), Vol. 1, 344, n. 14; cf. 'Analogy and Doxology', in *Basic Questions in Theology, Volume One* (LPT; London: SCM Press, 1970), 211–238 (224–226); R.W. Jenson, *Systematic Theology, Volume 2: The Works of God* (Oxford: Oxford University Press, 2001), 38; C.E. Gunton, *Act and Being: Towards a Theology of the Divine Attributes* (London: SCM Press, 2002), 69–70.
[82] Cf. Brümmer, *Speaking of a Personal God*, 46.

The confusion is exacerbated when we turn to the term 'cause'. Initially, we might suggest that 'cause' is exempt from these concerns of clarity when applied to God's action. Divine primary causation founds, upholds and empowers creaturely secondary causation; they are two different sorts of action, one appropriate to God and the other to the creature. Already, though, we have modified primary causation by stating what God *does* – he *founds*, he *upholds*, he *empowers*. Causation is an elastic concept that is understood through our use of other words – words such as 'produce', 'bring about', 'issue', 'generate', and so on – to explain precisely what is being caused and in what way.[83] Elucidation of what we mean by primary causation, then, opens it to the possibility of comparison with creaturely action as we predicate terms analogously to God: to say, for example, that God *sustains* the universe (Heb 1:3) might evoke images similar to that of Atlas holding the world on his shoulders. So what do we mean, then, when we say that God *causes* something and that in doing so, he causes *differently* from the creature? If we say that a creature *causes* a piano to roll down a hill, we might clarify that description by saying that the creature *pushes* the piano down the hill; but are we compelled equally to say that *God* pushes the piano? Confusion arises from the analogical application of the word 'pushes' to primary causation. Do we state that God *pushes* even though the word cannot be used in the sense that it applies to the creature's own act of pushing? Is the effect of a piano rolling down the hill caused by divine pushing and creaturely pushing concurrently? Or should we contend that God wills this particular effect to issue from the creature's act of pushing, even though this dissociates a creature's causal efficacy from its causal potency? Certainly, it is not impossible to ascribe two causes to one effect; Aquinas's earlier statement that 'the cause of an action is the one by whose power the action is done rather than the one who acts'[84] seems compatible with an Aristotelian notion of causal complementarity, for here God is *causa efficiens* and the creature is *causa instrumentalis*. However, as both primary and secondary causation are efficient and effective, that is, each cause, primary and secondary, is said to be *the* cause of the action, a major tension emerges that Aquinas appears to resolve simply by claiming that although the creature pushes the piano down the hill, it is God who is 'more especially' the cause of that action.[85] Such a contention contrasts creaturely causal efficacy with divine causal efficacy and so reduces the creature *merely* to instrumentality by denying it causal integrity.

Analogy, then, is of little help here to Aquinas; all that he can affirm is that God's causation is appropriate to him and that the creature also has its own, proper causal powers. What analogy does is to complement and reinforce the notion that it is secondary causation, and not the Son and the Spirit of God, that

---

[83] Kim, 'Causation', 125; cf. Gunton, 'The End of Causality?', 63.
[84] Aquinas, *Sum. Cont. Gent.*, 3(1).67.5, 222.
[85] Aquinas, *Sum. Cont. Gent.*, 3(1).67.5, 222.

mediates between God and the world: the distinction between the two is bridged ontologically by God's will to delegate his causal action through creaturely causal efficacy, and linguistically by accounting for how we may speak of God's causation in relation to creaturely causation. The problem with each form of mediation is that there is always a possibility that the attempt to maintain the distinction between God and the world in fact collapses it. God wills to delegate his action through secondary causation and so renders the creature merely instrumental; the analogical predication that is employed to preserve the distinction between God and the world means that we must say either that God does the same thing as the creatures or that he does completely the opposite of what can be said of creatures. It is impossible to speak of God's action in ways entirely different from how we would speak of a creature's action. Accordingly, the use of analogy to explain how we do speak of God's action suffers from the same ambiguity as does the concept of secondary causation: either it conflates God and the world, or it imposes a dualism and negates the relation between them.

§ 4.5 Searching for a Place to Act

We have argued that for both Aquinas and Calvin, divine primary causation founds, upholds and empowers creaturely secondary causation; but their accounts of God's providence do not finally avoid the strong suggestion either that primary and secondary causation are conflated or that they are set in opposition. As neither theologian intends these implications, we must conclude that the relation between the two different causal orders is ambiguous. The problem of the relation between primary and secondary causation effectively is that of mediation: Given the fundamental ontological distinction between them, how does God act in a world that is totally unlike him?[86] Our contention is that Aquinas and Calvin each depicts, albeit in subtly different ways, God willing to mediate his action through secondary causation; but here we find the source of the problem. Mediation enables true relation between two or more parties; but if God *identifies* his action with secondary causation, whether by delegation or accommodation, it is difficult to discern what ontological distance exists between him and the world to enable true mediation – and hence the possibility arises that God is the only agent with genuine causal efficacy.

Perhaps a way to overcome this problem is to posit the existence of a place within the created order where God interacts with and influences the world, a

---

[86] It is worth quoting again Colin Gunton's understanding of mediation: 'Mediation denotes the way we understand one form of action – God's action – to take shape in and in relation to that which is not God; the way, that is, by which the actions of one who is creator take form in a world that is of an entirely different order from God because he made it to be so.' (C.E. Gunton, *The Christian Faith: An Introduction to Christian Doctrine* [Oxford: Blackwell, 2002], 5; cf. § 1.5).

so-called 'causal joint'.[87] Austin Farrer denounced the possibility. God's agency cannot be compared in any way to the agency of the creature, and 'as soon as we try to conceive it in action, we degrade it to the creaturely level and place it in the field of interacting causalities. The result can only be (if we take it literally) monstrosity and confusion.'[88] Farrer warns against attempting clarification of the relation between divine and creaturely agency: 'the direct relating of finite causal agency to divine action is a task which, in our living concern with the divine, we never attempt, and have no means of placing in a practical light.'[89] This notion of 'double agency'[90] means that we may speak of God and creatures as active in the world but in such a way that we can never hope to explain the former's agency by means of creaturely action. Paul Fiddes summarises Farrer's position memorably:

> The two causes, it might also be said, are not related in the 'two-storey' way proposed by Aquinas ... but are 'two stories', two completely different kinds of language about reality which should not be confused. Talk about what God does, and what the world and its inhabitants do, are two quite separate language-games.[91]

Fiddes is not impressed by Farrer's stance. He argues that '[w]e are left with no connections between the world-view of faith and the world-view of science. The two worlds fail to meet as faith and science are allotted to two totally separate compartments.'[92] John Polkinghorne is more scathing: Farrer's notion of double agency is 'an unintelligible kind of theological doublespeak.'[93] Indeed, Polkinghorne admits that he 'cannot give up the search for a causal joint', though he acknowledges that any 'actual attainments in that quest will necessarily be tentative and provisional.'[94] For Polkinghorne and others, such a

---

[87] A. Farrer, *Faith and Speculation: An Essay in Philosophical Theology* (London: Adam & Charles Black, 1967), 65. Although the terminology of 'causal joint' appears to originate with Austin Farrer, the conceptuality goes back at least to René Descartes and his attempt to find a location for the interaction of mind and body in 'a certain very small gland' in the brain. (R. Descartes, 'The Passions of the Soul, Part 1 [Selections]', in M.D. Wilson [ed.], *The Essential Descartes* [New York: Meridian, 1983], 353–368 [362]).

[88] Farrer, *Faith and Speculation*, 62.

[89] Farrer, *Faith and Speculation*, 63.

[90] Farrer, *Faith and Speculation*, v.

[91] P.S. Fiddes, *Participating in God: A Pastoral Doctrine of the Trinity* (London: DLT, 2000), 120.

[92] Fiddes, *Participating in God*, 120.

[93] J. Polkinghorne, *Science and Christian Belief: Theological Reflections of a Bottom-Up Thinker* (London: SPCK, 1994), 81–82.

[94] J. Polkinghorne, *Belief in God in an Age of Science* (New Haven: Yale University Press, 1998), 58–59.

causal joint is found at the quantum level of the world, 'since the indeterminacies of measurement [there] seem to provide a natural gap in which God can act';[95] and chaos theory particularly seems fruitful for advancing discussions about divine action at the quantum level. According to its advocates,

> chaos theory allows divine action to take place without interference in the laws of the natural order. Because chaos allows very small perturbations to have very large effects, imperceptible input by God can have profound impact on the order of things that we perceive.[96]

Philip Clayton adds,

> Given the billions and billions of such minute interventions – the potential number would be limited neither by science nor by inability on the part of God – God *might* be able to effect significant changes on the macroscopic level.[97]

The popular image used to explain chaos theory is that a butterfly flapping its wings on one side of the world affects weather on the other. If God acts upon or works within the world at the quantum level, the impact he has there will multiply and so have extremely far-reaching effects and consequences. Polkinghorne argues that the unpredictability of chaotic systems points to 'an ontological openness' in the world that allows for God's providential input.[98] Humans act in the world 'both energetically and informationally',[99] that is, by physical interaction and by influencing and setting limits to the way that future possibilities develop.[100] God, however, acts 'solely through information input',[101] influencing all that happens in a way that preserves the integrity of creaturely causal action. This means, for example, that although God himself may not have caused y to happen at t_4, we could say that at the quantum level,

---

[95] G.R. Peterson, 'God, Determinism, and Action: Perspectives from Physics', *Zygon* 35 (2000), 881–890 (882). Alister McGrath warns that as there is no uniformity of approach in the field of quantum theory, it is 'unwise to speak of "the metaphysics of quantum theory"' as though the field is unified. (A.E. McGrath, *A Scientific Theology, Volume Three: Theory* [Edinburgh: T&T Clark, 2003], 270–271). We need only to keep this in mind, as we do not intend to explore quantum theory or chaos theory in any significant detail.

[96] Petersen, 'God, Determinism, and Action', 882.

[97] P.D. Clayton, *God and Contemporary Science* (ESCT; Edinburgh: Edinburgh University Press, 1997), 194, emphasis original.

[98] Polkinghorne, *Belief in God in an Age of Science*, 62–63.

[99] Polkinghorne, *Belief in God in an Age of Science*, 63.

[100] Polkinghorne, *Belief in God in an Age of Science*, 62, 66; cf. Fiddes, *Participating in God*, 145–146.

[101] Polkinghorne, *Belief in God in an Age of Science*, 63.

God influenced x at t_1 with the specific intention that x at t_1, along with p at t_2 and q at t_3, would be amplified chaotically and eventually produce y at t_4 at the macro level. That God is wise, all-powerful and all-knowing ensures that x at t_1 is sufficient for y at t_4.

Does this mean, then, that chaos theory supports notions of God's pancausal relation to the world, such as those offered by Aquinas and Calvin? Such a presentation does appear to suggest that events at the quantum level happen deterministically, echoing in particular Aquinas's view that God delegates his action to secondary causation. Yet surely the theory is called *chaos* theory because it deals with all things unpredictable and random. The very fact that a butterfly's movements might affect the course of a storm three thousand miles away demonstrates a certain level of unpredictability at the quantum level 'because of the inexactitude of our knowledge of initial conditions, combined with [chaotic] systems' exquisite sensitivity to the precise character of those conditions.'[102] Taede Smedes notes that scientific experimentation requires a steady reality in order to work; it assumes 'the intimate and stable connection between cause and effect: If I do this, that will be the effect, and if I repeat this experiment in exactly the same way tomorrow, the same effect will be the result.'[103] However, chaos theory would indicate that the same experiment conducted tomorrow would not be *exactly* the same experiment, if only by virtue of it being conducted tomorrow rather than today.

Chaos theory's insight, then, is that we can never have full knowledge of all things, that tomorrow there might be tiny but quite significant differences from today in the way that the experiment is conducted that would possibly affect the results. Thus it seems that the created order is deterministic in principle; but because '[w]e can never know the precise initial conditions nor oversee and predict ... the way in which causal chains intersect', there is room for indeterminism and chance.[104] John Byl notes that, effectively, 'chance' is the label we attribute to things if we cannot pinpoint their cause; however, we ought not to conclude that the absence of a *physical* cause is indicative of there being *no* cause.[105] Byl considers a roulette wheel: the outcome of each spin of the wheel 'seems to be due to chance', but it remains that 'any individual outcome is precisely fixed by the initial conditions. That the outcome of the roulette wheel has the appearance of chance is due only to our ignorance of the initial conditions and our inability to deduce the end result from the initial

---

[102] J. Polkinghorne, 'The Nature of Physical Reality', *Zygon* 35 (2000), 927–940 (931–932).

[103] T.A. Smedes, 'Is Our Universe Deterministic? Some Philosophical and Theological Reflections on an Elusive Topic', *Zygon* 38 (2003), 955–979 (960).

[104] Smedes, 'Is Our Universe Deterministic?', 967.

[105] J. Byl, 'Indeterminacy, Divine Action and Human Freedom', *Science and Christian Belief* 15 (2003), 101–116 (103).

conditions.'[106] Certainly, chaos theory appears to depict a deterministic universe with a vibrant structure, similarly to Aquinas, and on this basis we may think it quite reasonable to say that the sovereign God influences reality at its quantum level through some unspecified causal joint.

There are three difficulties that arise. Gregory Peterson argues that the need to posit a causal joint effectively assumes the validity of the deist presumption that the natural laws that govern the world's behaviour are inviolable. As 'it is inconceivable that God would choose to violate the laws of nature, some causal joint is deemed necessary.'[107] Against this, Peterson argues that natural laws may not be rational accounts of fixed certainties but could rather be statistical in character insofar as a law may describe either the regularity with which a phenomenon occurs in the world or the ways in which particular phenomena must occur.[108] Consequently, the status of natural laws as fixed is an assumption that needs challenging, certainly in discussions of divine action.[109] Peterson's insight is quite crucial: How can we *demonstrate* whether a natural law is a prescription for all natural events or a description of the way in which natural events have occurred? Furthermore, if it is shown that the natural laws are not inviolable, if these laws, whether of quantum mechanics or chaos theory, 'are statistical in character or are limit cases ... the notion of "violation" disappears.'[110] The search for a causal joint is therefore unnecessary.

Secondly, we said earlier that God might influence x to happen at t_1 at the quantum level with the specific intention that x at t_1, along with p at t_2 and q at t_3, would eventually produce y at t_4 at the macro level. However, there will always be a possibility that God's influence may not be enough to ensure the occurrence of a particular event. Chaos theory holds that the amplification of events from the quantum level impacts the whole world; but amplification is by no means a fast process. This may not be a problem in many situations, but, as Timothy Sansbury notes, there are times when God's action at the quantum level may not happen quickly enough to be useful, such as when human prayers seek a swift response.[111] Furthermore, if God acts at the quantum level, his action is subject also to potential interference; Sansbury argues that '[t]he very indeterminacy that makes divine action possible also makes it possible that it could be naturally thwarted or become unnecessary.'[112] The way to avoid these problems is to state that God determines all that happens, but this is not something that chaos theory itself can ascertain. According to Alister McGrath,

---

[106] Byl, 'Indeterminacy, Divine Action and Human Freedom', 104.
[107] Petersen, 'God, Determinism, and Action', 883.
[108] Petersen, 'God, Determinism, and Action', 884.
[109] Petersen, 'God, Determinism, and Action', 884–885.
[110] Petersen, 'God, Determinism, and Action', 885.
[111] T. Sansbury, 'The False Promise of Quantum Mechanics', *Zygon* 42 (2007), 111–121 (117).
[112] Sansbury, 'The False Promise of Quantum Mechanics', 117.

'it is empirically impossible to determine whether the world is deterministic or indeterministic; the matter simply cannot be settled on the basis of observation'.[113]

Finally, and most importantly, the notion of a causal joint fails to show *how* God and the world interact or even *that* they interact.[114] Were God to move a mountain on the macroscopic level or a photon at the quantum level, the problem of how God and the world interact remains. Identifying a causal joint is not the same as explaining this interaction.

Is it possible, however, to affirm God's action in the world not at the quantum level but more generally, that is, by contending that God has granted to the world the ability to develop according to its own internal workings? Howard Van Till, for example, argues that the world is

> gifted by God from the outset with all of the form-producing capacities necessary for the actualisation of the multitude of physical structures and life forms that have appeared in the course of Creation's formative history, and a world whose formational fecundity can be understood only as a manifestation of the Creator's continuous blessing for fruitfulness.[115]

Furthermore, following Augustine,

> the universe was brought into being in a less than fully formed state but gifted with the capacities to transform itself, in conformity with God's will, from unformed matter into a truly marvellous array of physical structures and life forms.[116]

As God has given his creation the ability to evolve and change, we may say that it has 'functional integrity' and behaves truly according to the way it has been created. This appears to suggest that God has no continuing involvement with the world. Van Till counters this potential deism by affirming that natural phenomena are explained 'only by appeal to a higher level of causation', that is, to God's will.[117] Does this mean, however, that the world's functional integrity is little more than a variation of the concept of secondary causation? It is

---

[113] McGrath, *A Scientific Theology, Volume Three: Theory*, 269; cf. N. Saunders, *Divine Action and Modern Science* (Cambridge: Cambridge University Press, 2002), 83; Smedes, 'Is Our Universe Deterministic?', 973.

[114] 'The physical sciences are not, in fact, any help in the attempt to describe *how* God engages with his world.' (T.J. Gorringe, *God's Theatre: A Theology of Providence* [London: SCM Press, 1991], 26, emphasis original).

[115] H.J. Van Till, 'Basil, Augustine, and the Doctrine of Creation's Functional Integrity', *Science and Christian Belief* 8 (1996), 21–38 (23).

[116] Van Till, 'Basil, Augustine, and the Doctrine of Creation's Functional Integrity', 32, original emphasis removed.

[117] Van Till, 'Basil, Augustine, and the Doctrine of Creation's Functional Integrity', 33.

difficult to discern what advantage functional integrity has that the concept of secondary causation does not already entail.

Similarly, in Niels Henrik Gregersen's concept of 'autopoiesis', meaning 'self-creation' or 'self-production', 'God is creative by supporting and stimulating autopoietic processes'; the world behaves in the way it does because that is the way God has made it.[118] God's act of creation 'is a context-constitutive action' that enables creation to develop in an appropriate manner,[119] and he continues to uphold it in its developmental, self-productive activity.[120] Therefore, God 'continually supports autopoietic processes ... [and] stimulate[s] them in particular directions'.[121] The scriptural basis for this idea is taken from Genesis 1, where God not only creates but also 'invite[s] the created to produce future creations on their own'.[122] Following Fred Dretske, Gregersen goes on to distinguish between triggering causes (for example, typing a letter on a keyboard brings up the letter on the monitor screen) and structuring causes (the hardware and electrical connections in the computer that allow the letter to be produced): '[s]tructuring causes ... configure the circumstances under which future triggering causes can work'. Thus God is the 'underlying causality that enables the creatures to trigger themselves forth in their given setting.'[123] Scientifically speaking, then, God does very little in a world where everything seems to run itself; but, Gregersen argues, he continues to make a difference by 'stimulat[ing] the powers of nature to follow new pathways for their use of energy.'[124] This means, however, that autopoiesis still requires a causal joint wherein God physically interacts with the world – and Gregersen acknowledges that we can never hope to find one.[125] Consequently, we may suggest that the 'structuring cause' and 'triggering causes' are no more than a restatement of primary and secondary causation.

Although both Van Till and Gregersen are pleased to affirm that the created order develops according to a divinely given ability, they cannot do so apart from the conceptual framework of primary and secondary causation and the concomitant problem of the relation between the two causal orders. Yet if the notion that God interacts with the world at the quantum level is problematic, and if it is not enough simply to say that God gives creation the means to develop according to its own internal workings, should we turn instead to panentheism, the idea that somehow the world acts within God? Such a turn

---

[118] N.H. Gregersen, 'The Idea of Creation and the Theory of Autopoietic Processes', *Zygon* 33 (1998), 333–367 (334).
[119] Gregersen, 'The Idea of Creation', 351.
[120] Gregersen, 'The Idea of Creation', 355.
[121] Gregersen, 'The Idea of Creation', 335.
[122] Gregersen, 'The Idea of Creation', 348, following Genesis 1:1-4, 11.
[123] Gregersen, 'The Idea of Creation', 359.
[124] Gregersen, 'The Idea of Creation', 362.
[125] Gregersen, 'The Idea of Creation', 359.

may prove advantageous, as panentheism is explicated apart from categories derived from the conceptual framework of primary and secondary causation. Philip Clayton writes,

> God is fully immanent in the world; in him we live and move and have our being – and this in the strictest sense: to the extent that we have being at all, we are 'composed' out of him who is Being itself. To use a spatial metaphor, we are 'in' God, although he also extends above and beyond what is this (finite) body.[126]

Elsewhere,

> Indeed, that the 'in' is used metaphorically should be obvious from the fact that panentheists use it in two different directions – the world is in God, and God is in the world – whereas in mundane spatial relations this is impossible: the pie can't be in the cupboard and the cupboard in the pie at the same time![127]

Thus God's divine space both transcends and encompasses creaturely, physical space;[128] it is his absolute space that 'makes it possible to think of God as coextensive with the world'. However, though 'the world is contained within God', it is 'not identical to God.'[129] To say that the world is contained within God requires a partial rejection of any notion that God stands outside creation; more properly, panentheism has God enveloping creaturely space within his space, so much so that it is pointless to distinguish between them. This does not mean that panentheism is really a sophisticated pantheism, though, because in asserting that the world is not identical to God, the distinction is made on the basis that 'we are different *in our fundamental nature* from God.'[130] Clayton concludes that 'it does not matter where we are located: within the overarching divine presence, and even (in one sense) within the divine being itself, we remain God's created product, the work of his hands.'[131] What Clayton stresses is that God and the world are *inter*dependent. He writes,

> The world depends on God because God is its necessary and eternal source; without God's creative act it would neither have come into existence nor exist at

---

[126] Clayton, *God and Contemporary Science*, 47.

[127] P. Clayton, 'Panentheism in Metaphysical and Scientific Perspective', in P. Clayton and A. Peacocke (eds.), *In Whom We Live and Move and Have Our Being: Panentheistic Reflections on God's Presence in a Scientific World* (Grand Rapids: Eerdmans, 2004), 73–91 (83).

[128] Clayton, *God and Contemporary Science*, 89.

[129] Clayton, *God and Contemporary Science*, 90.

[130] Clayton, *God and Contemporary Science*, 90, emphasis original; cf. J. Moltmann, *God in Creation: An Ecological Doctrine of Creation*, translated by M. Kohl (London: SCM Press, 1985), 156.

[131] Clayton, *God and Contemporary Science*, 90.

this moment. And God depends on the world because the nature of God's actual experience depends on interactions with finite creatures like ourselves.[132]

Thus the best way to imagine the world's relationship to God is to understand it to be 'analogous to the body's relationship to the mind or soul.'[133] This is the so-called panentheistic analogy: '[a]s mental activity supervenes on the physical processes, so divine action supervenes on the processes of nature.'[134] Clayton presses it further by comparing natural regularities to the 'automatic responses within an individual's body', such as breathing.[135] An apparent advantage to the analogy is the way it allows the notion of mental causation to correspond to God's action: just as we might move our arm by *thinking* it to move, so might God influence physical processes. That mental causation 'is more than physical causation and yet still a part of the natural world' means that no natural laws are broken, just as no laws are broken when mind and body interact.[136] However, although the panentheistic analogy 'offers the possibility of conceiving divine actions that express divine intentions and agency without breaking natural law',[137] nonetheless it leaves us dissatisfied. As an analogy based upon the relation between mind and body, it raises the possibility that it requires a causal joint or some other explanation to account for God's interaction with the world. It also assumes in common with causal joint theories that natural laws should not be violated, a presupposition that we have already suggested is deist in structure. Furthermore, the analogy is employed to affirm God's interaction with the world but ultimately, it can do little else. There is no reason to suppose that this interaction is similar to that of the mind and body –

---

[132] Clayton, 'Panentheism in Metaphysical and Scientific Perspective', 83.

[133] Clayton, *God and Contemporary Science*, 101; 'Panentheism in Metaphysical and Scientific Perspective', 83.

[134] K.J. Vanhoozer, 'Effectual Call or Causal Effect? Summons, Sovereignty and Supervenient Grace', *Tyndale Bulletin* 49 (1998), 213–251 (229). Within the philosophy of mind, the concept of supervenience portrays certain properties arising or, more properly, emerging from other properties so that what has emerged may be said to supervene on that from which it emerged. Thus '[m]ental properties such as consciousness supervene on physical properties such as brain states. Thoughts *depend* on neural firings and other subvenient physical events but they are not *identical* to these physical events nor can they be explained in terms of the brain states alone. Supervenient properties, that is, cannot be explained in terms of lower level, subvenient properties.' (Vanhoozer, 'Effectual Call or Causal Effect?', 228, emphasis original). Further discussion of supervenience is found in N. Murphy, *Beyond Liberalism and Fundamentalism: How Modern and Postmodern Philosophy Set the Theological Agenda* (Pennsylvania: Trinity Press International, 1996), 141–144.

[135] Clayton, *God and Contemporary Science*, 101.

[136] Clayton, 'Panentheism in Metaphysical and Scientific Perspective', 83.

[137] Clayton, 'Panentheism in Metaphysical and Scientific Perspective', 84.

and even if the analogy proves helpful in explaining the relation between God and the world, it may not accurately represent the truth of the matter. Finally, the panentheistic analogy is yet another way of explaining God's action in the world without the mediation of the Son and the Holy Spirit. So although panentheism appears not to require an understanding of God's providential action from within the conceptual framework of primary and secondary causation, it is not a satisfactory corrective because it still has no explicit place for the action of the *triune* God.

§ 4.6 Changing Conceptual Frameworks

The doctrine of providence affirms that God is present and active within the world, guiding it towards a particular end; but what does it mean to say that God is present and active within that world? Essentially, the matter centres upon the fundamental ontological distinction between God and the world, that is, the conviction that God is God and the world is not. This distinction portrays God's activity as divine primary causation that founds, upholds and empowers creaturely secondary causation. These two causal orders must remain distinct to avoid conflating God and the world but somehow must also relate if the proper distinction is not to become a sharp dualism.

However, although primary causation is said to found, uphold and empower secondary causation, often advocates of the distinction go further and say that primary causation is also as much a cause of the creature's action as is the creature itself. Primary and secondary causation are both said to be *the* cause of an effect. The ambiguity that emerges from this assertion understandably concerns how each can be said to cause without negating the integrity of the causal efficacy of either God or the creature. Aquinas and Calvin both affirm God's will to work through secondary causes, in subtly different ways: for Aquinas, God delegates his action to secondary causation, whereas God for Calvin accommodates his action to it. This raises the possibility that the two causal orders are conflated as God's will to use secondary causation risks reducing the latter merely to instrumentality. We see, then, that God's employment of secondary causation to mediate between the two causal orders does not resolve but rather intensifies the problem of how they relate. Simply stating that the two causal orders are not in competition does not resolve the tensions that we have identified,[138] for the question of how they relate to one another remains.

---

[138] Kathryn Tanner writes, 'Unlike the case of creatures bringing about effects through the workings of others, God's creative activity extends directly to everything and not indirectly to some things by way only of their causes. Created causes are not the means by which God brings into existence the effects of those causes, since the whole of those causes, their workings, and effects are the result of God's creative activity. Picture the whole world, in all its complexity of causal process, as a

More recent accounts of divine action seek a causal joint between God and the world, a place where God interacts with and influences the world; but causal joint theories also presuppose the validity of understanding divine action from within the conceptual framework of primary and secondary causation. The main difference between Calvin's teaching on providence and, for example, that of John Polkinghorne is that for the latter, primary causation does appear to effect something different from secondary causation: God sovereignly influences creaturely action at the quantum level rather than determining it according to a set plan. Precisely *how* God interacts with the world, whether through causal joints or autopoietic processes, remains unspecified, in turn raising the suspicion that all we have done is to offer illustrative aids or models of divine action that may or may not approximate to the reality of the matter. In this respect, the panentheistic analogy also falls short, even though it seems not to require deliberate allusion to primary and secondary causation.

As we said earlier, the problem of the relation between primary and secondary causation effectively is that of mediation: Given the fundamental ontological distinction between them, how does God act in a world that is totally unlike him? The problem is not solved by asserting that God wills either to accommodate his action to secondary causation or to delegate his action through it; such statements persistently raise the possibility either that God alone is the sole causal agent or that his action competes with creaturely action for causal supremacy.[139] Yet we do not resolve these tensions by positing the existence of a causal joint or developing an analogy or model to account for divine action in the world, for any of these do little more than to state *that* God acts in the world. Perhaps this is appropriate; perhaps, as Austin Farrer believed, we should not try to clarify the relation between primary and secondary causation. However, the very terminology of the conceptual framework of primary and secondary causation – that such action may be explained in terms of *primary* and *secondary* causation – will seldom stray far,

---

horizontal plane, suspended into existence, at each and every point, by the vertical threads (infinite and infinitesimal) of God's own working, and you will begin to see the sense this all makes.' (K. Tanner, 'Is God in Charge? Creation and Providence', in W.C. Placher [ed.], *Essentials of Christian Theology* [Louisville: Westminster John Knox Press, 2003], 116–131 [129]).

Appealing though it is, Tanner's position does not avoid the problems we have encountered. Is the question of the relation between primary and secondary causation adequately addressed simply by picturing each causal order operating either vertically or horizontally? Are we not tempted to enquire about a place or places where they intersect? How do we avoid the lingering suggestion that there is no creaturely causal efficacy?

[139] Even though Aquinas and Calvin each affirmed creaturely causal efficacy, nonetheless they had to defend themselves against charges that they in fact denied it. This suggests that the simple assertion of two different causal orders is not as free from confusion as might be claimed.

if at all, from the question of their relation and of how God acts in a world that is totally unlike him. A 'two-stories' account of divine and creaturely action is insufficient for the content of divine providence, unless we accept that there may be no causal connection between them at all.[140]

Our consistent objection, our *main* objection, has been that primary and secondary causation does not require explicit reference to the mediation of the Son and the Holy Spirit, which, for any specifically Christian account of divine providence, is essential. In all the cases we have considered, God's will to act through secondary causation effectively displaces whatever the Son and the Spirit are said to do within the world, making possible the recurrent problems that we have identified. Given this, we may suggest that, essentially, the difference between primary and secondary causation is that primary causation is the action of the *triune* God and so cannot be discussed without 'express reference to the doctrine of the Trinity'.[141] Karl Barth's advice is sound; but his attempt to preserve the complete unlikeness of God as *causa* compared to the creature as *causa* by replacing *causa prima* and *causae secundae* with *causa divina* or *creatrix* and *causa non divina* or *creata* is little more than a recasting of the more traditional terminology.[142] The point is that once we begin to speak about God's action in the world by the Son and the Spirit, there is little reason to refer to divine action as primary causation and so little reason to describe creaturely action as secondary causation.[143] God relates to the world not because he wills to act through secondary causation but because he has chosen to relate to creation through the Son and the Spirit. Colin Gunton writes, 'God comes into relation with that which is not himself through his Son, the mediator between himself and the creation'; and 'by his Spirit God enables the creation to be open to him.'[144] Through the Son, God holds the world together; by the Spirit, all those held things are related to one another in their particularity. Gunton explains that it is

> the Son who is the unifier of creation, the one in whom all things hold together. By contrast but not in contradiction, we can understand the Spirit's distinctive

---

[140] Fiddes, *Participating in God*, 120.

[141] K. Barth, *Church Dogmatics* (13 vols.), edited by G.W. Bromiley and T.F. Torrance (Edinburgh: T&T Clark, 1957–1975), III/3, 104.

[142] Barth, *Church Dogmatics*, III/3, 104. It is regrettable that space precludes further discussion of Karl Barth's account of providence; but we may suggest that as the terms *causa divina* and *causa non divina* do not sufficiently supersede the *concepts* denoted by *causa prima* and *causae secundae*, he is open to the same charges that we have levelled at Aquinas and Calvin. See also Fiddes, *Participating in God*, 117.

[143] We may suggest further that the concept of secondary causation is little more than an attempt to conceive of God's action in a world that seems not to require it. See also Gunton, 'The End of Causality?', 74, n. 36.

[144] C.E. Gunton, *The One, the Three and the Many: God, Creation and the Culture of Modernity* (Cambridge: Cambridge University Press, 1993), 178–179, 181–182.

mode of action as the one who maintains the particularity, distinctiveness, uniqueness, through the Son, of each within the unity.[145]

All things, all particulars, are 'formed by their relationship to God the creator and redeemer and to each other. Their particular being is a being in relation, each distinct and unique and yet each inseparably bound up with other, and ultimately all, particulars.'[146]

Given this, my contention is that the conceptual framework of God's active presence in the world embodied in Jesus Christ and mediated by the Holy Spirit is a corrective to the conceptual framework of primary and secondary causation favoured by common and traditional doctrines of providence. This does not resolve the tensions that we have identified. Even within a conceptual framework of God's presence, we would still have questions about *how* God interacts with the world. William Placher is right, therefore, to observe that an appeal to christology does not avoid the issue of *how*, for example, God raises Jesus from the dead,[147] even if we have no doubt that he did so by his Spirit. However, the conceptual framework of God's presence is, I submit, the most appropriate place to discuss the matter of God's providence[148] because it accompanies the scriptural presentation of divine action in a way that notions of primary and secondary causation neglect.

As we have suggested, the problem with Aquinas, Calvin and the more recent accounts of divine action that we have explored is that they explicate divine providence from within the conceptual framework of primary and secondary causation, or at least assume the validity of positing two sorts of causation. Accordingly, they prioritise the actuality of the fundamental ontological *distinction* between God and the world rather than the *distinctiveness* of the triune God's action *in relation to* creaturely action as testified to in the scriptural narrative. Indeed, to return to Calvin, we may suggest that he would still have a solid theology of providence even if his *locus classicus* on providence in the *Institutes of the Christian Religion* were absent.[149] Calvin's chapters on providence (*Institutes* 1:16–18) stand between an affirmation of the predestined nature of Adam's fall (1:15:8) and an account of what it means to say that Adam fell and how it implicates the whole of humanity (2:1-3). Apart from a number of pastoral exhortations, by which Calvin grants to the doctrine of providence undeniably positive content, we may observe that at times his *locus classicus* is little more than a justification of

---

[145] Gunton, *The One, the Three and the Many*, 206.

[146] Gunton, *The One, the Three and the Many*, 207.

[147] W.C. Placher, *The Domestication of Transcendence: How Modern Thinking About God Went Wrong* (Louisville: Westminster John Knox Press, 1996), 193–194; cf. § 1.6, n. 67.

[148] I am grateful to Lincoln Harvey for this way of expressing the point.

[149] See § 2.1, n. 12; § 2.5.

God's entitlement to ordain the fall, insofar as 'all events are governed by God's secret plan.'[150] Against this, we may say that Calvin offers an alternative account of providence throughout the *Institutes*. He explains that the knowledge of God, the triune Creator, and of ourselves is interconnected but impossible to discern aright due to humanity's sinful condition; that humanity can do nothing to extract itself from its sinful condition; that God works in creaturely history, providing first the Mosaic Law to point to Christ's coming and then Christ himself to reconcile people to God; and that God sends his Spirit to incorporate people into the body of the risen Christ. Our conviction is that this pattern captures exactly the essence of divine providence,[151] which declares not that God wills to work through secondary causation but that God is faithful to that which he has created and his purposes for it – a conviction that is informed by the conceptual framework of God's presence.

§ 4.7 Conclusion

Aquinas and Calvin offer accounts of God's providence that depend upon the conceptual framework of primary and secondary causation; more recent descriptions of divine action, such as those that express the relation between the

---

[150] Calvin, *Institutes*, 1:16:2, 199.

[151] Allan Coppedge identifies this pattern as *historical* providence, in distinction from *special* or *personal* providence. (A. Coppedge, *The God Who is Triune: Revisioning the Christian Doctrine of God* [Downers Grove: IVP, 2007], 300–301). Interestingly, the pattern we have sketched here need draw upon neither an acceptance of God's pancausal relation to the world, nor an eternal decree. The focus instead is upon the action of the triune God in relation to his fallen creation, and all other doctrines – soteriology, election, providence, pneumatology, ecclesiology, and so on – are shaped by this trinitarian foundation. We may suggest further that when Calvin himself concentrates on the action of the triune God and on what God does for us in Christ, it becomes unnecessary even to allude to the notion of an eternal decree. For Calvin, of course, the possibility of such a willful omission is an impious absurdity; but our point stands. It *is* possible to speak of the triune God's action in the world without assuming the existence of an eternal decree or that creaturely events and actions are caused by God's pancausal execution of this decree.

Is Trevor Hart intimating something similar when he observes 'that when grace is interpreted from a christological perspective, being seen not as some *tertium quid* of an external divine decree or an infused substance, but rather as the self-giving of God himself for us and to us in the person of Christ, the dilemma which has so long plagued Western Christianity [that is, the 'objectivity' or 'subjectivity' of divine grace] is disposed of'? (T. Hart, 'Humankind in Christ and Christ in Humankind: Salvation as Participation in our Substitute in the Theology of John Calvin', *Scottish Journal of Theology* 42 [1989], 67–84 [84, emphasis original]). Hart's 'but rather' certainly complements our own contention, contrasting as it does Calvin's idea of salvation by Spirit-participation in Christ with his claim that the salvation of individuals is by God's decree.

two causal orders in terms of causal joints, presuppose the validity of the framework. Such accounts, however, cannot avoid the problem that God's will to mediate his action through secondary causation in fact displaces the action of God's Son and Holy Spirit and leads to the suspicion either that divine causal efficacy suppresses creaturely causal efficacy or that they are set in opposition within the same causal order. Instead, we have suggested that the conceptual framework of primary and secondary causation is corrected by the conceptual framework of God's presence, which, as we shall see, prioritises the scriptural presentation of the actuality of the triune God guiding creation providentially to its divinely ordained end over the more philosophical issues that, inevitably, cannot be avoided but which ought not to determine the shape or content of the doctrine of providence; and although this framework does not ease the tensions we have encountered, it does offer a more suitable place to attempt their resolution.

Fundamentally, then, we see that the very essence of divine providence, that God has resolved not to abandon that which he has made and is faithful to his purposes for it, is obscured by its explication from within the conceptual framework of primary and secondary causation. Our intention in the following chapters is to elucidate our claim – to this point, *merely* a claim – that the conceptual framework of God's presence is the most appropriate foundation and context for the doctrine of providence. We will do this not by developing an alternative doctrine of providence to counter that which takes its shape from concepts of (pan)causality, but by demonstrating the legitimacy of understanding the doctrine in terms of the mediation of God's presence throughout the world. This means that, perhaps unexpectedly, we shall not consider the threefold scheme of providence – that is, preservation, concurrence and government – as it might take shape from within the conceptual framework of divine presence;[152] neither shall we offer any interpretations of those scriptural texts – such as Genesis 45:7, Proverbs 21:1, Isaiah 45:1-7 and Acts 2:23 – cited by the more conventional accounts of providence. Indeed, we may suggest that it is inappropriate to discuss texts such as these in abstraction from the total scriptural witness to God's relationship with the world through his elected covenant people, Israel and the Church.

We must examine, then, the scriptural portrayal of this relationship between God and the world as it is illuminated by the Old Testament notion of divine presence and, from this, the New Testament conviction that this presence is now embodied in Jesus Christ, the eternal Son of God made flesh. Such an examination, though, must lead eventually to a surprising series of texts for discussing providence, to certain passages from the Pentateuch, and to Galatians, Hebrews, and Matthew's Gospel; but we shall see that far from obscuring the scriptural content of divine providence, these texts witness

---

[152] We shall offer some tentative suggestions for the continued use of these terms in § 9.4.

faithfully to the activity of the triune God and so reveal especially the proper foundation and context for the doctrine of providence.

CHAPTER 5[1]

Mediating the Presence of God

§ 5.1 Introduction

The doctrine of providence affirms that God is present and active within the world. God has not abandoned that which he created but is guiding it towards the particular end that he desires for it. This conviction has often been explicated from within the conceptual framework of primary and secondary causation, but we have argued that this does not account sufficiently for the scriptural presentation of the providential activity of the triune God. Furthermore, such a conceptuality does little to safeguard the integrity of creaturely causal efficacy in relation to the causal efficacy of the sovereign God. Against this, we have suggested that the conceptual framework of God's active presence is the most appropriate foundation and context for the Christian doctrine of providence.

We must be clear from the start that this notion of divine presence cannot be determined by anything other than Scripture. It is too easy to imagine a vague sense of presence, in which we can be sure that God is *with* us, accompanying us through our varied experiences, both joyous and painful – but doing little else.[2] The scriptural presentation of divine presence points us to an elusive

---

[1] An earlier version of this chapter is published as T.J. Wright, 'How is Christ Present to the World?', *International Journal of Systematic Theology* 7 (2005), 300–315.

[2] Surely Ruth Page's so-called pansyntheism, that God is *with* everything, cannot affirm God's *action* in any meaningful sense. The idea also appears to take shape without any positive influence from a specifically Christian notion of divine presence, which, as we shall see, is focussed in Jesus Christ. Page chooses not to include Christ in her discussion of divine presence as 'any proper discussion of his role would involve too many extra areas of argument in what is already a broad enough field. Without proper discussion,' she continues, 'references to Jesus Christ may be clouded by undisclosed assumptions. In one sense, therefore, christology is bracketed out of the ... theology which concentrates on the relationship between God and the world.' (R. Page, *Ambiguity and the Presence of God* [London: SCM Press, 1985], 7). This is not to say that Page has no place for Christ; she admits that God is known only in and through Christ. Yet this fact plays no formative role in the construction of her theology. See also R. Page, 'Panentheism and Pansyntheism: God in Relation', in Clayton, P. and Peacocke, A. (eds.), *In Whom We Live and Move and Have Our Being: Panentheistic Reflections on God's Presence in a Scientific World* (Grand Rapids: Eerdmans, 2004), 222–232.

presence, impossible to capture and tame.³ God's presence is his *active* presence, indeed, his *sovereign* presence; but notions of primary and secondary causation cannot avoid transforming this divine sovereign presence into the pancausal execution of a fixed eternal decree. What the scriptural presentation reveals instead is that God is present and active within the world to fulfil the purposes he has for it; indeed, the doctrine of providence concerns God's *faithfulness* to fulfil those purposes.⁴

It is this faithfulness that the conceptual framework of divine presence entails. God mediates his active presence not through secondary causation but through creaturely faithfulness made possible and guaranteed by his own, faithful action. This is surely the heart of the scriptural presentation of divine providence, that God provides for his wayward creation ultimately by providing *himself*. The scriptural narrative is not subordinate to the issues of primary and secondary causation but rather gathers them within itself and reorientates them. Though the issues remain, they now serve as witnesses to the providential activity of the triune God who desires to be present and active within the world he has created.

Our task in this chapter, then, is to summarise the scriptural notion of divine presence and explain more fully its appropriateness for the context in which the doctrine of providence is situated. We will consider first the idea of God's presence amongst his people initially in the tabernacle and then in the temple; secondly, the conviction that Jesus Christ himself is the embodiment of this presence; and finally, how the Church, the body of Christ, mediates the presence of God to the world through the action of the Holy Spirit.⁵ The intention is not to develop an exhaustive account of the conceptual framework of divine presence but to draw attention to its central themes. It is important to note, therefore, that we will not be doing this in order subsequently to develop a doctrine of providence in this study. Instead, we seek to outline the contours of a doctrine of providence based upon the conceptual framework of God's presence and then to demonstrate the legitimacy of this move.

---

³ S. Terrien, *The Elusive Presence: The Heart of Biblical Theology* (RP 26; San Francisco: Harper & Row, 1978), 43; cf. W. Brueggemann, 'The Crisis and Promise of Presence in Israel', in *Old Testament Theology: Essays on Structure, Theme, and Text*, edited by P.D. Miller (Minneapolis: Fortress Press, 1992), 150–182 (150–151).

⁴ 'God fulfils promises, not predictions, and is free to fulfil them in unexpected ways; he has purposes, not blueprints for his world.' (P.S. Fiddes, *Past Event and Present Salvation: The Christian Idea of Atonement* [London: DLT, 1989], 32).

⁵ We should recognise immediately that we cannot hope to offer even a near-exhaustive account of the scriptural presentation of God's presence. For a masterly overview of God's presence in relation to the temple traditions, see G.K. Beale, *The Temple and the Church's Mission: A Biblical Theology of the Dwelling Place of God* (NSBT 17; Leicester: Apollos, 2004); cf. N.G. Wright, *God on the Inside: The Holy Spirit in Holy Scripture* (Oxford: BRF, 2006), 125–130.

§ 5.2 Extending the Garden

The concept of God's presence is inseparable from the conviction that God is pleased to dwell amongst his people, Israel. This sentiment finds rich expression in Leviticus 26:11-12, where he declares, 'I will place my dwelling in your midst, and I shall not abhor you. And I will walk among you, and will be your God, and you shall be my people.' God's 'going' or 'walking' (*hālak*) is echoed throughout the Pentateuchal account of his action within the world. Genesis 3:8, for instance, mentions that 'the LORD God [was] walking in the garden at the time of the evening breeze'.[6] Exodus 13:21 and 33:14 both refer to God's 'going' with his people Israel, leading and accompanying her as she

---

[6] The image of God's 'walking' to depict his active presence within creation is, of course, anthropomorphic. Consequently, we might be tempted to conclude that as God has no physical body, he did not *really* walk in the garden or amongst Israel; the anthropomorphic imagery of walking must be, therefore, the language of accommodation. John Calvin suggests that 'as nurses commonly do with infants, God is wont in a measure to "lisp" in speaking to us ... [S]uch forms of speaking do not so much express clearly what God is like as accommodate the knowledge of him to our slight capacity.' (J. Calvin, *Institutes of the Christian Religion* [2 vols.], translated by F.L. Battles [LCC XX / XXI; Philadelphia: The Westminster Press, 1960], 1:13:1, 121).

It seems, then, that a point of some importance is intended by portraying God as walking. However, we must resist the temptation to consider anthropomorphism *merely* as accommodation, as though we can skin the imagery to reveal a demythologised skeleton underneath. Scripture's frequent references to God assuming a physical body – of which Genesis 3:8 is but one – is surely the basic but valuable theological insight that God is not hostile to that which he has created. He has no qualms about participating in created reality. His space is not incompatible with creaturely space. As J. Andrew Dearman argues, 'using or possessing form is not alien to God's divine being as spirit'. This is God's metacorporeality, which 'means that God's "appearance" in visible form is consistent with a definition of God as spirit, and not antithetical to it.' Rather than Scripture accommodating lofty ideas to our limited comprehension, Old Testament anthropomorphism is a means by which God deliberately chose to reveal himself in anticipation of the incarnation. (J.A. Dearman, 'Theophany, Anthropomorphism, and the *Imago Dei*: Some Observations in the Light of the Old Testament', in S.T. Davis, D. Kendall and G. O'Collins [eds.], *The Incarnation: An Interdisciplinary Symposium on the Incarnation of the Son of God* [Oxford: Oxford University Press, 2002], 31–46 [43–45; quotes from 43, n. 38 and 45, n. 44]; cf. M. Barker, *Temple Theology: An Introduction* [London: SPCK, 2004], 53–54).

We may suggest further, with John Sanders, that Jesus himself, as God incarnate, is 'the consummate anthropomorphism'; and if this is so, then 'it does not seem that God is especially concerned about having human characteristics predicated of him.' Indeed, as humans are created in the image of God, 'so the human must be seen as a theomorphism.' (J. Sanders, *The God Who Risks: A Theology of Providence* [Downers Grove: IVP, 1998], 21).

travels to the promised land. Furthermore, the imagery of divine movement found in these passages and elsewhere in the Old Testament relates to God's command that the Israelites should build for him a sanctuary in which he would be present within their community (Ex 25:8); indeed, this is the very purpose for which he liberated them from Egypt (Ex 29:46).[7] Upon completion, God filled the tabernacle with his glory (Ex 40:34) and 'continuously manifested his guiding and protecting presence to all the people in the form of a cloud by day with fire in it by night over the tabernacle' (Ex 40:34-38; cf. Num 9:15-23; 10:11-12, 33-34).[8] Once in the Promised Land, the temple became the seat of God's presence and the centre of Israel's cultic life (see, for example, 1 Kings 5:2-5; 8:2-11; 1 Chr 28:2-8; 2 Chr 7:1-3); both the temple and the tabernacle before it were 'points of access to God's continuous manifest presence in the midst of his people'.[9] That said, we must note that though present, God is not confined or domesticated. Texts such as 1 Kings 8:27 (see also 2 Chr 2:6; 6:18) indicate the elusiveness of God's presence: God dwells in the midst of the Israelites not only because he is pleased to so reside but because he has called them specifically to be his 'treasured possession', indeed, 'a priestly kingdom and a holy nation' (Ex 19:5-6). Israel is *his*, called to mediate the divine presence amongst her to the surrounding nations.[10]

The occurrence of this imagery within the context of God's provision of the Israelite cult and in the opening chapters of Genesis suggests something very important for our understanding of creation as a whole and the way in which we perceive both God's relation to it and humanity's place within it. Genesis, as we have seen, describes God as 'walking in the garden' (Gen 3:8); the same language is used in Leviticus 26 to portray God's presence amongst his liberated people Israel. This shared imagery and terminology indicates the closest possible connection between the idea of God's presence in the garden and that of his presence within the Israelite community, a connection that is strengthened by certain similarities between the accounts of the construction of the tabernacle (Ex 25:1-31:17) and the seven days of creation (Gen 1:1-2:3). Each of God's 'seven speeches' to Moses (Ex 25:1-30:10; 30:11-16; 17-21; 22-33; 34-38; 31:1-11; 12-27), for example, 'contains the cultic equivalent of the seven days of creation';[11] language employed to portray God's act of creation

---

[7] Cf. J. Palmer, 'Exodus and the Biblical Theology of the Tabernacle', in T.D. Alexander and S. Gathercole (eds.), *Heaven on Earth: The Temple in Biblical Theology* (Carlisle: Paternoster, 2004), 11–22 (13).

[8] R.E. Averbeck, 'Tabernacle', in *Dictionary of the Old Testament: Pentateuch* (Leicester: IVP, 2003), 807–827 (807).

[9] Averbeck, 'Tabernacle', 825.

[10] We will explore further God's calling of Israel in § 6.2.

[11] C.H.T. Fletcher-Louis, 'God's Image, his Cosmic Temple and the High Priest: Towards an Historical and Theological Account of the Incarnation', in T.D. Alexander and S. Gathercole (eds.), *Heaven on Earth: The Temple in Biblical Theology* (Carlisle: Paternoster, 2004), 81–99 (89); Beale, *The Temple and the*

(Gen 1:31; 2:1; 2:2; 2:3) is paralleled by that used to describe the completion of the tabernacle (Ex 39:43; 39:42; 40:33; 39:43);[12] and the infrequently occurring phrase *rûaḥ 'ĕlōhîm* (spirit of God) appears in Genesis (1:2) and Exodus (31:3; 35:31) to enable the formation of both the world and the tabernacle.[13] According to Israel's cultic tradition, then, not only was the tabernacle constructed to mirror and represent creation but creation itself *is* God's tabernacle, his temple, the place of his presence.[14] Psalm 78:69 memorably expresses this conviction: God 'built his sanctuary like the high heavens, like the earth, which he has founded for ever.'[15]

That the temple was built to mirror creation suggests that the outer court represented the world; the holy place, the heavens and heavenly bodies; and the holy of holies, the place where God himself dwelt with his heavenly hosts.[16] In the outer court, for example, the bronze basin used by the priests for washing (Ex 30:17-21; 38:8) was called 'the cast sea' and stood upon 'twelve oxen' facing north, east, south and west (1 Kings 7:23-26; 2 Chr 4:2-5). Such imagery of sea and earth connects the outer court with the world in general.[17] Furthermore, the seven lights (*mĕ'ōrōt*) of the lampstand in the holy place (Ex 25:31-32; 37:17-18) could connote anything from the tree of life (Gen 2:9) to the burning bush (Ex 3:2-6),[18] but are just as likely to point to the seven visible lights (*mĕ'ōrōt*), that is, the sun, moon and five planets (cf. Gen 1:14-18).[19] If

---

Church's Mission, 61; J.R. Middleton, *The Liberating Image: The* Imago Dei *in Genesis 1* (Grand Rapids: Brazos Press, 2005), 84–85.

[12] Beale, *The Temple and the Church's Mission*, 60–61.

[13] Middleton, *The Liberating Image*, 85–86.

[14] Averbeck, 'Tabernacle', 822; Palmer, 'Exodus and the ... Tabernacle', 15; Barker, *Temple Theology*, 17; Middleton, *The Liberating Image*, 81; S.W. Hahn, 'Canon, Cult and Covenant: The Promise of Liturgical Hermeneutics'; in C. Bartholomew, S. Hahn, R. Parry, C. Seitz and A. Wolters (eds.), *Canon and Biblical Interpretation* (SHS 7; Milton Keynes: Paternoster, 2006), 207–235 (213). This is not to say that *only* Israel's temple was designed to mimic the universe. G.K. Beale notes that 'Ancient Near Eastern archaeology and texts portray ancient temples as microcosms of heavenly temples or of the universe in a manner similar to that of the Old Testament.' (Beale, *The Temple and the Church's Mission*, 51). There were, however, significant differences between the theology of Israel's tabernacle and temple and that of her neighbours. Israel, for example, came to realise that she could not manipulate God through rituals, something that other nations sought to do; and although Israel was called to serve her deity, she, unlike her neighbours, was not required to care for and feed him. (Beale, *The Temple and the Church's Mission*, 59–60).

[15] Cf. Beale, *The Temple and the Church's Mission*, 31–32.

[16] Beale, *The Temple and the Church's Mission*, 32–33.

[17] Cf. Beale, *The Temple and the Church's Mission*, 33.

[18] J.I. Durham, *Exodus* (WBC 3; Nashville: Thomas Nelson, 1987), 364–365.

[19] Beale observes that *mĕ'ōrōt* (lights) appears five times in Genesis 1:14-18 to describe the sun and moon and only ten times thereafter in the Pentateuch, and always to

so, the association of the holy place with the heavens and heavenly bodies is quite apposite. Finally, the identification of the holy of holies with the place of God's presence is indicated by the presence of the cherubim at each end of the atonement slate (*kappōret*; Ex 25:31-32; 37:17-18; cf. 2 Sam 6:2; 2 Kings 19:15; 1 Chr 13:6; Ps 80:1; 99:1),[20] and the common portrayal of the ark of the covenant (Ex 25:10; 37:1) as God's throne or footstool (1 Chr 28:2; Ps 99:5; 132:7-8; Isa 66:1; Lam 2:1).[21] Temple rituals and the priests who enacted them were seen, therefore, as 'the visible manifestation of the heavenly reality'; indeed, the temple itself was 'the centre, the key point of both space and time; it was the holiest place on earth.'[22] To see the temple's contents was to gaze into the heavenly realm of God himself;[23] and the high priest on the Day of Atonement passed from earth to heaven as he entered the very presence of God.[24] Accordingly, we may say that for the Israelite, 'the cult ... is a microcosm of the whole of creation. Tabernacle and [t]emple are organised to reflect Israel's understanding of the structure of the cosmos, and the worship and rituals of the cult actualise and guarantee the God-intended order and stability of creation.'[25]

G.K. Beale is right, therefore, to suggest that 'the Old Testament tabernacle and temples were symbolically designed to point to the cosmic eschatological reality that God's tabernacling [or cultic] presence, formerly limited to the holy

---

denote the lights on the lampstand; see *The Temple and the Church's Mission*, 34; cf. G.J. Wenham, *Genesis 1–15* (WBC 1; Nashville: Thomas Nelson, 1987), 22; Barker, *Temple Theology*, 17.

[20] Here we follow John Hartley's translation of *kappōret*; see J.E. Hartley, *Leviticus* (WBC 4; Dallas: Word Books, 1992), 235; cf. § 7.3, n. 37.

[21] Margaret Barker argues that some traditions saw the ark of the covenant as the throne of God, others as the throne's footstool. (M. Barker, *The Gate of Heaven: The History and Symbolism of the Temple in Jerusalem* [London: SPCK, 1991], 138).

[22] Barker, *The Gate of Heaven*, 17, 62.

[23] Cf. G.A. Anderson, 'Mary in the Old Testament', *Pro Ecclesia* 16 (2007), 33–55 (43).

[24] Although the high priest enters the divine presence, 'the cloud of the incense' (Lev 16:13) shields him directly from seeing God. We will examine the Day of Atonement rituals in § 7.3.

[25] Fletcher-Louis, 'God's Image ... and the High Priest', 82; cf. Beale, *The Temple and the Church's Mission*, 26. Barker probes further the connections between temple and creation. She identifies Day One of God's act of creation with the holy of holies, the throne of God and the source of life; Day Two with the veil that separates the holy of holies from the holy place (Ex 26:33), symbolising the divide between the created realm and the heavenly; Day Three with the table on which the bread of the Presence is set (Ex 25:23, 30), indicating the earth's vegetation, wine and incense; Day Four with the lampstand (Ex 25:31-32), representing the sun, moon and five known planets; Day Five with the altar of the burnt offering (Ex 27:1-8), signifying the non-human creation; and Day Six with the high priest (Ex 28:1), that is, the human as the high priest of creation. (Barker, *Temple Theology*, 16–19).

of holies, was to be extended throughout the whole earth.'[26] We must draw from Beale's insight a further, crucial point: *God promises that the world in its entirety shall be the place of his presence.* This promise that God will extend his presence across the world is the teleological – or better, *eschatological* – foundation of the doctrine of providence and the basis for creaturely causal integrity. According to Genesis, God gives to the world its own causal integrity: it is the *earth*, for example, that produces vegetation and the *great lights* that rule the day (Gen 1:11, 14-18). Crucially, however, we see that the integrity of creaturely causal efficacy is the gracious provision of God, who secures it by his own presence within the world. Certainly this is the thrust of the claim that God rested on the seventh day (Gen 2:2-3): God does not depart from the world but, as Neil MacDonald expresses it, 'determines *himself* – posits himself – to be part of, belong to, coexist with, his own creation.'[27] It is God's continuous presence in the world that prevents it from collapsing into chaos; and the sentiment that God's cultic presence is to extend from the Edenic holy of holies across the entire world is the promise that God will never abandon that which he has created. God is faithful, acting within the world to bring it to the end he desires for it. Creation, then, in Colin Gunton's words,

> is a project – that is to say, it is made to go somewhere ... Creation is that which God enables to exist in time, and is in and through time to bring it to its completion, rather like an artist completing a work of art.[28]

Creation has 'a temporality and directedness to an end which is greater than its beginnings';[29] it is not 'a timelessly perfect whole, but ... an order of things that is planned to go somewhere; to be completed or perfected, and so *projected* into time.'[30] All this is what gives creation its 'eschatological orientation'; the act of creation was 'not simply the making of a world out of nothing, not even that world continually upheld by the providence of God, but the making of a world destined for perfection.'[31] Gunton notes from Genesis 1:28 that even

---

[26] Beale, *The Temple and the Church's Mission*, 25; G. Beale, 'The Final Vision of the Apocalypse and its Implications for a Biblical Theology of the Temple', in T.D. Alexander and S. Gathercole (eds.), *Heaven on Earth: The Temple in Biblical Theology* (Carlisle: Paternoster, 2004), 191–209 (191).

[27] N.B. MacDonald, *Metaphysics and the God of Israel: Systematic Theology of the Old and New Testaments* (Milton Keynes: Paternoster, 2006), 75, emphasis original.

[28] C.E. Gunton, *The Triune Creator: A Historical and Systematic Study* (ESCT; Edinburgh: Edinburgh University Press, 1998), 12.

[29] C.E. Gunton, 'Atonement and the Project of Creation: An Interpretation of Colossians 1.15-23', in *The Promise of Trinitarian Theology*, 2nd ed. (Edinburgh: T&T Clark, 1997), 178–192 (180–181).

[30] Gunton, 'Atonement and the Project of Creation', 181, emphasis original.

[31] C.E. Gunton, *Christ and Creation* (Carlisle: Paternoster Press, 1992), 45.

prelapsarian creation needed to be subdued if it was to reach its destiny. We must recognise

> that creation is not yet completely as God would have it be; that in eschatological perspective there is something still to do, and that this involves at least the overcoming of a measure of continuing disorder or at least absence of what we can call eschatological order and freedom.[32]

For Gunton, this is no problem, for the

> world is of such a kind that it requires obedient human activity to enable the achievement of that for which it was created. Creation is perfect – 'very good' – but remains to be perfected, in part by faithful human action.[33]

There is an important role for humanity, then, in the extension of the garden of God's presence across the entire world, a role shaped fundamentally by the conviction that humanity is made, male and female, in the image of God (Gen 1:27). This, notes Crispin Fletcher-Louis, is 'language otherwise reserved for idols', and it is either 'dangerously obtuse or deliberately subversive' to describe humanity in this way.[34] In the ancient Near East, an idol typically represented a deity; as a temple was the god's house on earth, its residence would be indicated through 'a cult object, which could either be an anthropomorphic or theriomorphic statue'.[35] Though these temples found their Israelite equivalent in the tabernacle and the temple of Solomon,[36] Israel herself was forbidden from making an idol to represent Yahweh (Ex 20:4).[37] Francis Watson observes that

> the person who contemplates making a surrogate image of the divine in the shape of one of the creatures of air, land and sea is himself or herself already the only

---

[32] C. Gunton, 'The Spirit Moved Over the Face of the Waters: The Holy Spirit and the Created Order', *International Journal of Systematic Theology* 4 (2002), 190–204 (192); cf. *The Christian Faith: An Introduction to Christian Doctrine* (Oxford: Blackwell, 2002), 29.

[33] Gunton, 'The Spirit Moved', 192.

[34] C.H.T. Fletcher-Louis, 'The Image of God and the Biblical Roots of Christian Sacramentality', in G. Rowell and C. Hall (eds.), *The Gestures of God: Explorations in Sacramentality* (London: Continuum, 2004), 73–89 (75).

[35] P. Pitkänen, 'From Tent of Meeting to Temple: Presence, Rejection and Renewal of Divine Favour', in T.D. Alexander and S. Gathercole (eds.), *Heaven on Earth: The Temple in Biblical Theology* (Carlisle: Paternoster, 2004), 23–34 (23).

[36] Pitkänen, 'From Tent of Meeting to Temple', 26.

[37] This is another distinction between Israel's temples and those of her neighbours (see n. 14).

authorised divine image. Humans are not to create an image of God because they are already that image, created by God.[38]

Given the idol language used in Genesis 1, then, Fletcher-Louis suggests that 'the Israelite view of the cosmos has at its apex the human being ... as the particular concrete physical form and manifestation of the one creator god.'[39] Consequently, humanity 'is to function in relation to the one and only creator god as do pagan statues and idols in relation to their gods.'[40] As humanity 'has the peculiar responsibility for bearing divine presence and carrying out the divine will',[41] it 'is to be the eyes, ears, mouth, being and action of the creator god within his creation.'[42] Those made in God's image both represent his presence on earth and are intended obediently to serve in his garden-temple; in doing so, they are to extend his presence throughout the whole earth.[43]

Humanity's role in this intended expansion is therefore quite crucial. According to Genesis 1:28, humanity is to 'fill the earth and subdue it', an action that mimics, though in reverse order, God's own creative activity in taming the primordial chaos and populating the earth with living creatures.[44] Richard Middleton contends that

> humans are called to imitate or continue God's own twofold creative activity by populating and organising (in a manner appropriate to humans) the unformed and unfilled earth ... God has, in other words, started the process of forming and filling, which humans, as God's earthly delegates, are to continue. Even the reverse order of this twofold activity makes sense since humans must first reproduce before they can engage in the task of organising/subduing the earth.[45]

More specifically, the man Adam is called to serve (*'ābad*) in the garden and keep (*šāmar*) it (Gen 2:15). These two words in particular are another connection between garden and tabernacle, for they are used also of Israel's

---

[38] F. Watson, *Text and Truth: Redefining Biblical Theology* (Edinburgh: T&T Clark, 1997), 289; cf. Fletcher-Louis, 'The Image of God', 76; T.E. Fretheim, *God and World in the Old Testament: A Relational Theology of Creation* (Nashville: Abingdon Press, 2005), 18.
[39] Fletcher-Louis, 'The Image of God', 75.
[40] Fletcher-Louis, 'The Image of God', 76; 'God's Image ... and the High Priest', 83.
[41] Fletcher-Louis, 'The Image of God', 77.
[42] Fletcher-Louis, 'The Image of God', 76; cf. T.J. Gorringe, *The Education of Desire: Towards a Theology of the Senses* (London: SCM Press, 2001), 10–11, emphasis original: 'The senses are the means through which we explore materiality, or rather, I am suggesting, *the means by which God chooses to explore materiality through us*, just as the Spirit prays through us, according to Paul'.
[43] Beale, 'The Final Vision of the Apocalypse', 201; Middleton, *The Liberating Image*, 87.
[44] Middleton, *The Liberating Image*, 89.
[45] Middleton, *The Liberating Image*, 89.

service in the tabernacle (see, for example, Num 3:7-8; 8:25-26; 18:5-6; 1 Chr 23:32; Ezek 44:14).[46] Beale argues that it is likely that 'the writer of Genesis 2 was portraying Adam ... [as] the archetypal priest who served in and guarded (or "took care of") God's first temple.'[47] Adam was to tend the garden 'by maintaining its order and keeping out uncleanness. This includes "gardening" but likely went beyond it to managing the affairs of the sacred space where God's presence dwelt and maintaining its orderliness in contrast to the disordered space outside.'[48] Thus Adam was to 'guard' the garden from 'the threat of unclean things entering into it and corrupting it'[49] through faithful observance of his divinely given responsibility to mediate God's presence to the entire world.[50]

The irony is that humanity *did* fill the earth – but with violence (Gen 6:11). Humanity was called to emulate God's creative activity but instead parodied it.[51] This is seen clearly in the account of the construction of the tower of Babel (Gen 11:1-9), a story that Middleton believes tells of humanity's decision not to fulfil its vocation to 'fill the earth' but to 'settle in one place ... and to build a city with a tower that reaches heaven.'[52] Behind the narrative lies a warning about the homogenising principle that imposes uniformity on all that it encounters – in this case, the attempt to collapse all languages into one (Gen 11:1).[53] Babel is the story of humanity's refusal faithfully to meet its responsibilities as the priest of God's creation. It is the story of humanity's resistance to God, of human action in opposition to divine action. Against this,

---

[46] Beale, *The Temple and the Church's Mission*, 66–67; Hahn, 'Canon, Cult and Covenant', 213.

[47] Beale, *The Temple and the Church's Mission*, 68; cf. M. Barker, *The Hidden Tradition of the Kingdom of God* (London: SPCK, 2007), 19; A. Schmemann, *The World as Sacrament* (London: DLT, 1966), 16.

[48] Beale, *The Temple and the Church's Mission*, 85; cf. Middleton, *The Liberating Image*, 89: 'Besides the definitive human task represented in [Genesis] 2:15 by the agricultural metaphor (to "till" and "keep" the garden), which is a paradigmatic form of organising and transforming the environment into a habitable world for humans, we may note the pervasive interest throughout the primeval history in human cultural achievements and technological innovations such as city-building (4:17; 11:1-9) and nomadic livestock-herding, music, and metallurgy (4:20-22). The human task thus reflects in significant ways the divine artisan portrayed in Genesis 1 as artfully constructing a world.'

[49] Beale, *The Temple and the Church's Mission*, 85.

[50] Middleton, *The Liberating Image*, 89–90.

[51] Cf. Middleton, *The Liberating Image*, 220.

[52] Middleton, *The Liberating Image*, 221.

[53] Middleton, *The Liberating Image*, 224–225. Following David Smith, Middleton argues that 'the story does not portray an idyllic world unified with a single primal language, but reflects the Neo-Assyrian imperial practice of imposing the single language of the conqueror on subjugated peoples.' (Middleton, *The Liberating Image*, 223).

God's scattering (Gen 11:8) must be seen as his sovereign action to frustrate the plans of humanity and to ensure the fulfilment of his original promise to extend his presence across the entire world.

Certainly, the scriptural narrative indicates that God's presence *will* one day fill the earth (see, for example, Ezek 48:35; Hab 2:14; Rev 21-22). It is for this reason, then, that the story of the calling of Abram (Gen 12:1-3) follows that of the tower of Babel.[54] Although Adam had failed to prevent disorder and sin from entering the garden-temple,[55] God's promise to Abram that 'all the families of the earth shall be blessed' in him (Gen 12:3) is the first step towards the fulfilment of his wider promise to extend the divine presence throughout the world. God's promise to Abram is realised by the calling of Israel to be God's 'treasured possession' (Ex 19:5) and, from her number, the coming of 'the one who is righteous' (ὁ δίκαιος) who lives 'by faith' (ἐκ πίστεως; Gal 3:11, quoting Hab 2:4) and makes possible the inclusion of all people in God's purposes.[56] This universal scope means that although the temple was the intersection of heaven and earth,[57] any temple structure built in Israel could never do justice to its eschatological dimension, that is, to the notion that God would be present throughout the world and not limited to a single building. Beale argues that the Old Testament 'restoration' texts, such as Jeremiah 3 or Haggai 2, point not to a future temple building conventionally understood, but to a way in which God will dwell in his creation in the fullest way imaginable.[58] The first temple commissioned by Solomon and the second temple eventually destroyed in 70 CE can be seen only as temporary constructions in the light of God's overall promise to dwell within the whole of his creation, a promise confirmed by John's vision that he saw 'no temple in the city, for its temple is the Lord God the Almighty and the Lamb' (Rev 21:22).

§ 5.3 God's Presence in Christ

Mention of the Lamb brings us to a dominant theme that runs throughout the New Testament, that of God's presence and its identification specifically with the man Jesus.[59] Affirmations of God's cultic presence persist throughout the New Testament, but they are expressed predominantly in terms that presuppose

---

[54] Middleton, *The Liberating Image*, 227.
[55] Beale, *The Temple and the Church's Mission*, 87.
[56] We will explore this further throughout § 6.
[57] Cf. Barker, *The Gate of Heaven*, 57.
[58] Beale, *The Temple and the Church's Mission*, 153. For Beale's discussion of eschatological and 'restoration' texts, scriptural or ótherwise, see 113–117, 123–167.
[59] See Beale's comprehensive survey of the New Testament texts in *The Temple and the Church's Mission*, 169–334, for further details. It is enough for our purposes simply to reference some of these passages and focus on two in particular, John 1:1-18 and 2:13-22.

the death of the now risen and ascended Christ. Matthew, for example, names Mary's child 'Emmanuel', 'God with us' (Mt 1:23), the one who is present 'where two or three are gathered in [his] name' (Mt 18:20) and 'always, to the end of the age' (Mt 28:20).[60] Paul argues that God put Jesus forward as the ἱλαστήριον (Rom 3:25), that is, the 'place of atonement' in the holy of holies (Ex 25:7); such imagery is drawn from the temple and employed to show that somehow Christ does that accomplished initially in the temple. Access to God, therefore, is now through Jesus (Eph 3:11-12), who, according to the author of the letter to the Hebrews, is 'a great high priest' (Heb 4:14), leading the way 'once for all' into the divine presence (Heb 9:11-12).[61] Already mentioned is John's vision of 'a new heaven and a new earth' (Rev 21:1), where there is 'no temple in the city, for its temple *is* the Lord God the Almighty and the Lamb' (Rev 21:22, emphasis mine). No longer, then, is the temple simply a building in which God resides; rather, it is the very presence of God himself that has embraced the entire world.

That God's presence is no longer identified with a specific, physical building is a crucial element of the christology of John's Gospel; and the Johannine Prologue (Jn 1:1-18) and the account of the temple action (Jn 2:13-22)[62] in particular demonstrate that the presence of God continues to be an elusive and sovereign presence, impossible to possess.[63] John shows this primarily by evoking a number of Old Testament passages that declare the divine creative power. The closest linguistic parallel to the opening text of the Prologue is Genesis 1:1-3.[64] Both passages, for example, commence with 'in the beginning' (Gen 1:1a; Jn 1:1a); both speak of God creating (Gen 1:1b; Jn 1:1c, 3); and both speak of the authority of light over darkness (Gen 1:2-3; Jn 1:5).[65] There is, however, an emphasis in John on God's Word or λόγος, who was 'with God' and 'was God' (Jn 1:1b). Where Genesis portrays God as speaking creation into being (Gen 1:3a), John claims that '[a]ll things came into being' through this Word, for 'in him was life' (Jn 1:3a, 4a). This focus is taken to new heights by John's announcement that this same Word 'became flesh and

---

[60] See D.D. Kupp, *Matthew's Emmanuel: Divine Presence and God's People in the First Gospel* (SNTSMS 90; Cambridge: Cambridge University Press, 1996), for an account of the concept of divine presence in Matthew's Gospel.

[61] We will explore issues of atonement, including Jesus's high priesthood, in § 7.

[62] Cf. N.T. Wright, *Jesus and the Victory of God* (London: SPCK, 1996), 413–414.

[63] Cf. P.S. Fiddes, 'The Quest for a Place which is "Not-a-Place": The Hiddenness of God and the Presence of God', in O. Davies and D. Turner (eds.), *Silence and the Word: Negative Theology and Incarnation* (Cambridge: Cambridge University Press, 2002), 35–60 (56).

[64] C.A. Evans, *Word and Glory: On the Exegetical and Theological Background of John's Prologue* (JSNTS 89; Sheffield: Sheffield Academic Press, 1993), 79; cf. N.T. Wright, *The New Testament and the People of God* (London: SPCK, 1992), 411: 'Jesus confronts his readers with a strange new Genesis.'

[65] Evans, *Word and Glory*, 78.

lived [ἐσκήνωσεν] among us' (Jn 1:14). Although his use of ἐσκήνωσεν recalls the tabernacle imagery of Exodus 33-34,[66] John's point is not so much to compare the incarnate Word with the places of God's presence in Israel as to demonstrate that the Word has fulfilled that which they anticipated.

We see this in a number of comparisons between Jesus (himself first identified as the incarnate Word in John 1:17b) and Moses.[67] The contrast between the law that came through Moses and the grace and truth that came through Jesus Christ (Jn 1:17) implies that 'the grace of the new covenant established through Jesus supersedes the grace of the covenant established through Moses.'[68] Certainly, the phrase χάριν ἀντὶ χάριτος – conventionally, 'grace upon grace' – in John 1:16 suggests such a contrast.[69] However much the law of Moses may be said to be a gracious provision of God,[70] it cannot fail to

---

[66] Evans, *Word and Glory*, 79; A.R. Kerr, *The Temple of Jesus' Body: The Temple Theme in the Gospel of John* (JSNTS 220; London: Sheffield Academic Press, 2002), 117–126; B. Salier, 'The Temple in the Gospel According to John', in T.D. Alexander and S. Gathercole (eds.), *Heaven on Earth: The Temple in Biblical Theology* (Carlisle: Paternoster, 2004), 121–134 (126–128). See also Wright, *The New Testament and the People of God*, 410–417, though he focuses upon John's retelling of Sirach 24:1-28.

[67] At this point, we follow Evans's structure in *Word and Glory*, 79–83.

[68] Evans, *Word and Glory*, 80.

[69] The precise meaning of ἀντὶ here is debated. Craig Evans argues that ἀντὶ should be translated 'in place of' (Evans, *Word and Glory*, 80), but Alan Kerr suggests it means 'after'. 'If ἀντὶ means "in place of",' Kerr reasons, 'then it follows that the grace and truth that come by Jesus Christ have replaced other grace, presumably the grace that was given by Moses, namely the law. But,' he continues, 'there is nothing in [John 1:17] that indicates that grace and truth have come via the law [and so] we cannot interpret this text as saying that grace and truth also come through the law, as they do through Jesus Christ.' (Kerr, *The Temple of Jesus' Body*, 115–116). Kerr concludes that the function of the law is 'to lead to Jesus and testify to him'; the law finds its fulfilment in Jesus and consequently is now 'redundant' and 'superseded'. (Kerr, *The Temple of Jesus' Body*, 130–131).

Certainly it is true that the text does not state that grace and truth come through the law; but if John means to identify χάριτος with the law, then it must be possible to describe the law as 'grace'. It matters little if grace and truth cannot be said to come *through* the law, because the law *itself* is a gift from God. (Cf. G.R. Beasley-Murray, *John*, 2nd ed. [WBC 36; Nashville: Thomas Nelson, 1999], 15). Indeed, if Kerr is right to assume that the law points to Jesus and is fulfilled somehow in him, then we see why John is able to portray the law as God's gift. Furthermore, an interpretation of ἀντὶ as 'in place of' may also connote the sense of 'after' that Kerr prefers: if one thing replaces another, that which is replaced must precede its successor. Indeed, a reading of ἀντὶ as 'in place of' more accurately reflects the force of John's (and Kerr's) point, as 'after' does not of necessity mean that that which precedes is in fact replaced. See also Salier, 'The Temple … According to John', 127.

[70] See § 6.2–§ 6.4 for our analysis of the Mosaic Law and its relation to Christ.

be secondary to the Word made flesh himself. Furthermore, John's comment about seeing God's glory in Christ (Jn 1:14b, 18) presupposes Moses's request to see God's glory (Ex 33:18); again, Jesus is shown to be superior to Moses, who could see only God's back and not his face (Ex 33:23).[71] Indeed, the 'Word existed "with (or *facing*: πρός) God" [Jn 1:1] and "in the bosom (that is, front) of the Father" [Jn 1:18b].'[72] Finally, the phrase πλήρης χάριτος καὶ ἀληθείας in John 1:14 – 'full of grace and truth', echoed in John 1:17 – recalls the description of God in Exodus 34:6 as 'abounding in steadfast love [*ḥesed*] and faithfulness', where χάριτος often translates *ḥesed*.[73] Taken individually, these comparisons suggest coincidence;[74] but cumulatively, they imply strongly that somehow the temple infrastructure has been overturned. Before, the tabernacle and the temples were the sites of God's presence among his people; but now, '[b]oth are supplanted by Jesus Christ. He is now the "place" where God's people meet with him';[75] indeed, he is 'the replacement and fulfilment of the Jewish Temple complex.'[76]

The story of the temple action makes this idea even more explicit. Jesus's reply to the Jews' request for a sign to justify his actions in the temple is pertinent: 'Destroy this temple, and in three days I will raise it up' (Jn 2:18-19). John explains that Jesus 'was speaking of the temple of his body' (Jn 2:21). This story bears similarities to the eschatological 'day of the Lord' concept as found in certain prophetic passages;[77] indeed, Jesus's action is 'a portent that the day of YHWH has come. Judgment has come to the house of YHWH and

---

[71] How should we balance Exodus 33:20 against the earlier comment that God would 'speak to Moses face to face, as one speaks to a friend' (Ex 33:11a)? James Palmer suggests that 'the intention [of the person(s) responsible for Exodus] was to point to the reality and intimacy of Moses' knowledge of God whilst at the same time stressing its limits and the fact that knowledge of God is not straightforward.' (Palmer, 'Exodus and the ... Tabernacle', 18; cf. Brueggemann, 'The Crisis and Promise of Presence in Israel', 152–169).

[72] Evans, *Word and Glory*, 81, emphasis original.

[73] Evans, *Word and Glory*, 81.

[74] Cf. Salier, 'The Temple ... According to John', 126–127.

[75] Kerr, *The Temple of Jesus' Body*, 112.

[76] Kerr, *The Temple of Jesus' Body*, 25. This reading assumes a post-70 CE dating for John; see, for example, M.M. Thompson, 'John, Gospel of', in *Dictionary of Jesus and the Gospels* (Leicester: IVP, 1992), 368–383 (371), and B. Lindars, *John* (NTG; Sheffield: Sheffield Academic Press, 1990), 19.

[77] For a survey of the 'day of the Lord' concept, see G. von Rad, 'The Origin of the Concept of the Day of Yahweh', *Journal of Semitic Studies* 4 (1959), 97–108, and *Old Testament Theology, Volume 2: The Theology of Israel's Prophetic Traditions* (London: SCM Press, 1975), 119–125. See also Kerr, *The Temple of Jesus' Body*, 73–77, for comparisons between John's account of Jesus's temple action and possible antecedents in Zechariah and Malachi.

the [t]emple is about to be destroyed and with it the sacrifices will end.'[78] By clearing the temple, Jesus, the lamb of God (Jn 1:29), makes room for his own sacrifice by which he stands in place of the sacrificial system;[79] but in doing so, Jesus, the Word of God made flesh, makes plain that this work is God's work, for it is supremely in him that we see God's active presence.

This conviction is echoed by Colossians 1:19: 'For in [God's beloved Son] all the fullness of God was pleased to dwell'. However, given the traditional claim that God is omnipresent, how can 'all the fullness of God' be pleased to dwell in a single human and still be said to be present to all things? There is no hesitation that Christ does relate to all things: the Son 'is the image of the invisible God'; in him 'all things on heaven and earth were created'; he 'is before all things, and in him all things hold together' (Col 1:15-17). The present tense (ἐστιν; Col 1:15, 17) that Paul uses indicates that it is Christ the *incarnate* Son – risen and exalted, but a man nonetheless – who does all these things normally attributed to divinity.[80] That Christ the *incarnate* Son is said to be the image of God, through whom all things were created and in whom all things hold together means that it is also Christ the *incarnate* Son in whom 'the whole fullness of deity dwells bodily' (Col 2:9; cf. 1:19). Furthermore, Christ is 'the head of the body, the church' (Col 1:18) that 'come[s] to fullness in him' (Col 2:10). Scripture's initial response to the question of divine omnipresence, then, is that somehow the Church, the body of Christ, is enabled to participate in God's presence. It is within this christological framework, shaped by Scripture, that ideas of God's omnipresence must be developed.[81]

A good example of how Scripture first inspires christological reflection upon matters of God's (omni)presence that in turn complements the scriptural witness is found in Karl Barth's account of the matter. When we think of the divine omnipresence, says Barth, we tend to do so 'as a whole in relation to all creation as such';[82] but even this 'does not form any obstacle to a whole series of special presences, of concrete cases of God being here or there, which rise like mountain peaks from the plain of God's general presence with His

---

[78] Kerr, *The Temple of Jesus' Body*, 81; cf. 77: '[I]f we allow the allusions to [Zech 14:21] and [Mal 3:1, 3], this would confirm an eschatological character to the narrative. That is to say, the dismissal of the traders from the [t]emple would signal the eschatological day of the LORD. With Jesus' action there are no longer any traders in the house of the LORD, the Father's house. The day of the LORD has come.'

[79] Cf. Salier, 'The Temple ... According to John', 129. As noted earlier, we will be looking at issues of atonement in § 7.

[80] N.T. Wright, *The Epistles of Paul to the Colossians and to Philemon: An Introduction and Commentary* (TNTC 12; Leicester: IVP, 1986), 68.

[81] Colossians makes no mention of the role of the Holy Spirit at this point.

[82] K. Barth, *Church Dogmatics* (13 vols.), edited by G.W. Bromiley and T.F. Torrance (Edinburgh: T&T Clark, 1957–1975), II/1, 476.

creation.'[83] Barth sees these 'special cases' occurring when God reveals himself, and he suggests that the real question of God's presence ought not to be discussed in abstraction from these as though God exists in all places at once for no other reason than he does so; omnipresence is simply not an issue of spatial occupation taken to the extreme. Rather, 'according to the order of biblical thinking and speech it is [the] special presence of God which always comes first and is estimated and valued as the real and decisive presence.'[84] If we do affirm God's omnipresence, we may do so only on the basis that we look first to his particular presence in order fully to appreciate it. '[A]s we look back and forwards from God's special presence,' Barth writes, 'His general presence in the world is recognised and attested.' The conventional understanding of God's omnipresence is not lessened, however, because its 'authenticity and efficacy ... consists always and exclusively in the identity of the God who is present generally with the God who is present in particular, and not *vice versa.*'[85] We see, then, that Barth does not deny God's omnipresence, but rather reorientates the perfection so that it cannot be discussed apart from the way that God reveals himself actively in history.

Barth's reason for arguing this reorientation is christological. The world is 'created, preserved and upheld' through God's Word, and God's Word is the one who is 'the essence and mystery of His revelation and so of His special presence in the world.'[86] Jesus Christ is 'the place to which every examination of the Old and New Testament witness to God's special presence must necessarily and subsequently point'.[87] For Barth, God's presence in Christ is not just another instance of God's 'special presence', but of 'His proper presence'; in this particular way, in his 'proper presence' in Christ, God is 'specially present to Israel and the Church, and as such generally present in the world as a whole and everywhere.'[88] If God's presence is properly to be found in Jesus Christ, then Barth surely is right to suggest that we do not look to a vague notion of omnipresence as though it is the first thing that must be said about the matter. Insofar as we must speak of God's general presence to all things, we can do so only on the basis that it is in Christ that God's 'proper presence' is discerned – this much Barth has already argued, albeit less explicitly; but insofar as it is only in Christ that we find this 'proper presence', we must therefore distinguish between this and every other form of God's presence, in much the same way as we distinguish between 'grace which

---

[83] Barth, *Church Dogmatics*, II/1, 477.
[84] Barth, *Church Dogmatics*, II/1, 477–478.
[85] Barth, *Church Dogmatics*, II/1, 478, emphasis original.
[86] Barth, *Church Dogmatics*, II/1, 478.
[87] Barth, *Church Dogmatics*, II/1, 478. It is not only Barth who holds this conviction, of course; we have already seen similar arguments in our discussion of the tabernacle imagery and John's Prologue.
[88] Barth, *Church Dogmatics*, II/1, 484.

bestows' and the 'grace which is bestowed', between 'the coming Messiah' and 'His people', between 'the coming Saviour' and 'His Church', and between 'the expectation and recollection of revelation and salvation' and 'its fulfilment and presence'.[89]

Barth sees this distinction as one of kind. Though God 'is really present to Israel and the Church as the body of humanity taken up into His covenant', he 'is present in Jesus Christ as the Head which constitutes and controls this body.'[90] Thus the difference 'is the distinction between *gratia adoptionis* and *gratia unionis*'; through his adoption of them, God is present to both Israel and the Church, 'adopted for the sake of Jesus Christ and not for their own sakes.' In their adoption, 'they are considered worthy and made partakers of a special divine presence', they are accepted in Jesus Christ. By adoption, 'everything which can be said of [Christ] ... can also be said of these His adopted children in the sense in which it can be theirs.' However, this '*adoptio* is different from *unio*. *Unio* is the basis of *adoptio*. *Adoptio* is based on *unio*. *Gratia unionis* is the bestowing grace of God, *gratia adoptionis* the divine grace bestowed. That,' says Barth, 'is the difference.'[91] It seems, then, that although God may be said to be present to all things, a fuller knowledge of God's presence is given to those who have been granted the opportunity to partake in his presence, namely, Israel and the Church. The crucial aspect, of course, is that this partaking is a matter of the grace God bestows upon them; his presence is not something to which they are privy by right or bribe. This body of humanity, Israel and the Church, may know God's special presence because graciously he has chosen to include them in his action to reconcile all things to himself; the very existence of Israel and the Church mediates God's presence in the world.

Yet Barth is keen to stress that such inclusion occurs only in Christ – hence the need to distinguish between *adoptio* and *unio*. God's proper presence in Christ is not some form of adoptionism, where of all the possibilities open to God, the man Jesus is the privileged single recipient of the divine presence. No, writes Barth, 'God is Himself this man Jesus Christ, very God and very man, both of them unconfused and unmixed, but also unseparated and undivided, in the one person of this Messiah and Saviour.... And it is on the basis of this *unio*, but clearly differentiated from it, that there is an *adoptio*.'[92] From this *unio*, Barth argues that 'God's most proper space is itself the space which this man occupies in the cradle and on the cross, and which He cannot therefore leave or lose again, for, as His resurrection and ascension reveal, it is now His permanent space.'[93] Barth concludes that 'the God who is everywhere present is so only if He is identical with the One who is present there and here, and

---

[89] Barth, *Church Dogmatics*, II/1, 484.
[90] Barth, *Church Dogmatics*, II/1, 485.
[91] Barth, *Church Dogmatics*, II/1, 485, emphasis original.
[92] Barth, *Church Dogmatics*, II/1, 486, emphasis original.
[93] Barth, *Church Dogmatics*, II/1, 486.

primarily here, in Jesus Christ, in the unity of the Word with what was created and is upheld by the Word.'[94]

According to Barth, then, the concept of God's presence needs to be understood first by looking at the place of his proper presence, namely, Jesus Christ, the Word made flesh; only in and from him may we see that God is present to all things. Secondly, God's presence is shown to the world through those whom God adopts on the basis of his reconciling work in Christ; this means that as Israel and the Church are present within the world, so, too, is God said to be present. However, only those who have been chosen in Christ can know the proper presence of God in Christ. Leaving aside the potentially thorny issue of whether Israel knows God's proper presence *in Christ*,[95] there are at least two matters that we now need to address. Given that God's proper presence is found only in Christ, what is the role played by the Holy Spirit?[96] Also, if God's general presence in the world is mediated by those adopted in

---

[94] Barth, *Church Dogmatics*, II/1, 486. I have reservations about the phrase 'everywhere present'. If we say that God is 'everywhere present', such as Barth says here and as Donald Baillie says elsewhere (D.M. Baillie, *The Theology of the Sacraments and Other Papers* [London: Faber & Faber, 1957], 97), we run the risk of affirming a receptacle notion of space that is absolute to the God who fills it. This is seen clearly in Jürgen Moltmann's view that 'only the concept of creation ... distinguishes the space of God from the space of the created world'. Creation 'does not exist in "the absolute space" of the divine Being', but 'exists in the space God yielded up for it through his creative resolve.' (J. Moltmann, *God in Creation: An Ecological Doctrine of Creation*, translated by M. Kohl [London: SCM Press, 1985], 156). Moltmann follows Isaac Luria's notion of *zimzum*, whereby God allows creation to have its own space by withdrawing himself to free the space for it to exist: 'Before God went out of himself in order to create a non-divine world, he withdrew into himself in order to make room for the world, and to concede it a space.... God gives space, God makes room, God withdraws in order to let a non-divine reality exist with himself and in himself.... Before the Almighty becomes "creator of heaven and earth" he has already made himself the receptive and sustaining *space* for those he had created.' (J. Moltmann, *Science and Wisdom*, translated by M. Kohl [London: SCM Press, 2003], 62, 119, 120, emphasis original).

The problem is that prior to God's act of creation, there is an act of vacation. (A.J. Torrance, '*Creatio ex Nihilo* and the Spatio-Temporal Dimensions, with Special Reference to Jürgen Moltmann and D C Williams', in C.E. Gunton [ed.], *The Doctrine of Creation: Essays in Dogmatics, History and Philosophy* [Edinburgh: T&T Clark, 1997], 83–103 [90]). Although God is said to withdraw *himself* in order to make room for creation, we cannot avoid the complication that in making space for creation, God is shown also to occupy a space that somehow contains even him.

[95] The complexity of the issue prohibits our discussion of this matter.

[96] For a useful overview of Karl Barth's pneumatology, see G. Hunsinger, 'The Mediator of Communion: Karl Barth's Doctrine of the Holy Spirit', in J. Webster (ed.), *The Cambridge Companion to Karl Barth* (Cambridge: Cambridge University Press, 2000), 177–194.

Christ, how closely is God's proper presence in Christ identified with God's general presence in the world through the Church – that is, how do we understand the concept of presence in connection with the relation of Christ to the Church as its head?

§ 5.4 Christ, the Holy Spirit and the Church

We noted earlier that humanity functions as an idol in the world-temple. However, unlike an idol conventionally understood, humanity represents the divine but is not equated with it; though humanity represents God, God remains distinct from humanity. Here we see that the basis for understanding the relationship between Christ and the Church stems from the type of distinction made in scriptural instances of 'image of God' language. Christ *is* the image of God (Col 1:15; cf. Heb 1:3); humanity is *made in* this image (Gen 1:27); and the Church is *being conformed to Christ's* image (Rom 8:29). Though we must not say that Christ is other than humanity, lest we imply that he is not fully human, neither must we make the opposite mistake of treating him as just another human. In Christ dwells the fullness of God, through whom God reconciles all things to himself (Col 1:19-20); this distinction belongs to no other.[97]

However, it is certainly an important distinction, for it shows that whatever we say about the Church's relationship with Christ must be shaped by the fact that Christ is constitutive for humanity in general and the Church in particular, and not *vice versa*. This distinction also helps us to understand better our theme of Christ as the temple of God. Both Christ (Jn 2:21; Rev 21:22) and the members of the Church (1 Cor 3:16-17; 6:19; 2 Cor 6:16; Eph 2:21-22; 1 Pet 2:5) are said to be God's temple. Christ *is* God's temple, that is, he is, to use Barth's phrasing, the proper presence of God, the Word made flesh recalling the tabernacle of the Old Testament. Yet the Church may also be called God's temple because it is Christ's body, because the Holy Spirit dwells within its corporate structures (1 Cor 6:19), because by the Spirit it participates in the presence of God (Eph 2:22; 3:19).

Consequently, God is present to the world because the Church both exists within that world and participates by the Spirit in the presence of God. In its witness, the Church proclaims God's presence and action within the world by speaking of his reconciling work in Christ.[98] This assumes, of course, that in its own participation in the presence of God, the Church knows the proper presence of God in Christ, who is its head (Col 1:18) and whose presence is mediated by the Spirit to the Church through the very same created structures into which he entered (cf. 1 Jn 1:1, 3). Thus it is no surprise that although we

---

[97] See also § 8.5.
[98] See, for example, the emphasis on being witnesses in Luke 24:45-49; Acts 1:8; 2:32-33, 36; 1 John 1:1-3.

may know God by the Spirit's testimony corporately in our hearts (Gal 4:6), the Spirit also presents Christ to us through Scripture (cf. Lk 24:27, 32) and draws us to the Father through Christ as we remember him in the sacrament of the Lord's Supper (1 Cor 11:26). As the Church remembers its Saviour, so the Saviour is present – not just as a memory of things past, but in expectation that he, the Word still incarnate, will one day return (cf. 1 Cor 11:26). Though Christ is physically absent, the Spirit presents him to the Church by enabling the latter to participate in Christ and therefore to enjoy his presence (cf. Eph 3:16-19).[99]

What is clear, then, is that the Church, under the guidance of the Spirit, plays a major role in the mediation of Christ's presence to the world. As the Church remembers Christ, it also proclaims him to the world (1 Cor 11:26). This eucharistic understanding of how Christ is present to the world may be easier to digest if we season it with a few thoughts from Colin Gunton. Starting with the observation that '[t]here is no Spirit without the Son', Gunton argues first that 'the incarnation represents among other things a particular use of the created order by the Father through the Spirit, in forming a body of flesh for his eternal Son.'[100] Gunton moves from this incarnational focus to the more explicitly soteriological one of Christ's various healings and exorcisms as depicted in the Gospels. Both Christ's redemptive actions in healing and exorcising, and his becoming a representative but true human person realising his dependence upon the Spirit's orientation, are eschatological in tone. '[T]hrough his Son and Spirit, his two hands,' writes Gunton, 'the Father both prevents the creation from slipping back into the nothingness from which it came and restores its teleology, its movement to perfection.'[101] Accordingly, this teleological restoration is given impetus and true direction by Christ's resurrection, again something fleshly and again by the Spirit:

> The one who breathed into Adam the breath of life now raises the second Adam to new life by the transformation of his body not to bodiliness but to a new form of bodily life. The Spirit is the Lord and giver of life, and this means both the everyday life of the mortal and the transformed life of the one whose mortality has put on immortality.[102]

Gunton argues, following Paul (2 Cor 5:4b-5), that the Spirit is a deposit guaranteeing to the Church that it will participate in this transformation itself; the Spirit affirms to the Church the promise made in and by Christ's resurrection. Thus Gunton takes us to an ecclesiological dimension:

---

[99] Cf. T. Smail, *The Giving Gift: The Holy Spirit in Person* (London: DLT, 1994), 194–195.

[100] Gunton, 'The Spirit Moved', 197. We will consider the relation of the Holy Spirit to Christ more fully throughout § 8.

[101] Gunton, 'The Spirit Moved', 197–198.

[102] Gunton, 'The Spirit Moved', 198.

[Christ's] death, resurrection and ascension, resulting in the sending of the eschatological Spirit, eventuated in the forming of a distinctive community gathered around him and dedicated to an – at least – fourfold form of life: 'the apostles' teaching and fellowship, ... the breaking of bread and the prayers' (Acts 2.42).[103]

The Lord's Supper in particular is a multi-faceted diamond reflecting the incarnational aspect that remembers Christ, 'represented by the bread'; the soteriological element of 'the covenant sealed in [Christ's] blood, the cup representing God's judgement'; and the eschatological 'until he comes' of 1 Corinthians 11:26.[104] That the Supper has this eschatological dimension is important, for it 'takes place in the bodily absence of the ascended Lord, between his resurrection and the end of time'; yet his 'bodily absence is the occasion of the sending of the "other παρακλητος" who is the means of the church's relation to the Father through the Son.'[105] Accordingly, it is 'the fact that [the Supper's bread and wine] set forth the incarnational, soteriological and eschatological realities as bread and wine that makes them able to represent the Lord's achievement as it takes up into itself both the human and with it the rest of the created order.'[106]

How should we understand the presence of Christ to us in the Lord's Supper if he is not present physically or, as Gunton prefers, bodily? Paul's discussion of the Supper in 1 Corinthians 11 certainly presupposes Christ's bodily absence.[107] It is this absence that means we cannot equate Christ with the Church. Christ has already been raised, whereas the Church is yet to be (1 Cor 15:23). Christ 'is one with the church only as also its transcendent Lord.'[108] Yet in his transcendence, Christ is still related to the Church by the Father's Spirit; Gunton qualifies this, insisting that 'the presence of Christ is not *as* but *through* the Spirit, who is the mediator of both Christ's presence and his (eschatological) otherness.'[109] Gunton continues, 'While being other than the Church even when that is understood as his body, he is present to and in it so far as the Spirit enables it from time to time to be that which it is elected to be.'[110] What, though, does all this have to do with the Lord's Supper? For Gunton, the church

---

[103] Gunton, 'The Spirit Moved', 198.
[104] Gunton, 'The Spirit Moved', 199.
[105] Gunton, 'The Spirit Moved', 199.
[106] Gunton, 'The Spirit Moved', 199.
[107] C. Gunton, '"Until He Comes": Towards an Eschatology of Church Membership', *International Journal of Systematic Theology* 3 (2001), 187–200 (193).
[108] Gunton, '"Until He Comes"', 193.
[109] Gunton, '"Until He Comes"', 197, emphasis original.
[110] Gunton, '"Until He Comes"', 198.

is enabled to [anticipate the age to come] by the Spirit who both makes present the life-giving death of Christ and will complete the eschatological perfecting on the last day. That is why worship, and especially what we call sacramental worship, cannot but be the focus of the church's life, for in both baptism ... and the Lord's Supper we are, so to speak, positioned in the realm of the eschatological kingdom while we live in created time and space.[111]

As currently we live in the time between Christ's resurrection and return,[112] 'Christ's presence in all its manifold forms is realised only through anticipation, and that means through the mediation of the eschatological Spirit, as anticipated eschatology.'[113]

Thus we see that both the notion of God's presence in Christ and the means by which Christ is made present to us are thoroughly pneumatological. Just as the presence of God in Christ is made flesh by the Spirit's action (cf. Lk 1:35), so, too, is the resurrected Christ made present to the Church as its head and Lord. The Spirit's particular action first towards Christ and then towards the Church means that although there is an intimate participation of each in the life of the other (cf. Jn 15:4-5), the two remain distinct but not separate; and this is something summed up in a series of 'tabernacling' images. Jesus is the new temple, in whom God is pleased to dwell; but by his Spirit, God also dwells in the Church, which is built upon Christ the cornerstone (Eph 2:19-22; 1 Cor 6:19). In the Lord's Supper, the Church is reminded of the Lord whom it serves even as it waits for him to return in fulfilment of the promise made to it by his resurrection. Importantly, it is the Spirit who relates Creator and created to one another, reminding us once more that it is only by the *gratia adoptionis* of which Barth spoke that we can enjoy God's presence, and therefore Christ's presence, in our midst.

Given our emphasis on Christ's presence as something mediated to the world through the Church, is there yet a possibility that Christ is present to the world outside this mediation? Certainly, this is what the panentheistic analogy seems to suggest, that because God is to the world as the mind or soul is to the body, there is definitely a sense in which it must be possible to say that indeed, God is present to the world in a general manner.[114] Herein lies the problem: Though God may be said to be present, is understanding this presence simply a matter of finding a fitting analogy by which to describe it? If Christ is God's proper presence shown to the world through the Church's own life as it looks forward to his return (cf. 1 Cor 11:26b), then surely we ought not to affirm any analogy that takes little if any account of God's specifically triune relation to the world. To speak of God's relation to the world is to speak of his presence to

---

[111] Gunton, '"Until He Comes"', 198.
[112] Cf. Gunton, '"Until He Comes"', 197.
[113] Gunton, '"Until He Comes"', 200.
[114] See § 4.5.

it ultimately in Christ, a presence that may be understood properly only by considering its pneumatological and, unavoidably, ecclesiological aspects. Furthermore, if we are speaking of God's presence in Christ, the one who went to the cross in obedience to his Father's call and command, we are not speaking of a presence of God that merely watches his creation act. No, Christ's presence reveals God's providence. Though the two concepts ought not to be identified, God's presence – properly in Christ, specifically in the Church and consequently more generally in the world – can be understood only in relation to his providence. God wishes to live amongst his people, and, as we have intimated, he does so by calling a people to himself amongst whom he will dwell, first in the tabernacle, then in the temple, and ultimately in Christ and, through him, the Church. As the Church witnesses to its head dwelling in its midst, so he is present and active within the world.[115] Eventually, God will dwell in the midst of his people on the new earth described in Revelation 21-22. Such eschatological direction surely indicates that God's presence is an *active* presence, defined by God's faithfulness to the promise he made to creation that his presence would extend throughout it. Providence and presence are inseparably linked as in Christ, God's providence is made flesh.

§ 5.5 Conclusion

We have argued that the conceptual framework of God's active presence in the world embodied in Jesus Christ and mediated by the Holy Spirit is a corrective to the conceptual framework of primary and secondary causation. This claim is demonstrated by the notion that the entire world is to be the temple of God, the place of his presence. According to the Old Testament, humanity is created in the image of God to mediate the divine presence to the world; this entails humanity's faithful obedience to its calling to 'fill the earth and subdue it' (Gen 1:28; cf. 2:15). God's intention is that through faithful human action, the place of his presence will extend from the garden of Eden and cover the entire world. Although the scriptural witness is that Adam, along with Eve, failed to discharge his responsibilities, God himself remains faithful and continues to act in the world to fulfil his promise. Ultimately, God's presence is embodied in the man Jesus and mediated to the world by the Church, which, through the power of the Spirit, is enabled faithfully to witness to God's action in Christ.

---

[115] We must be careful to stress that Christ's mediated presence to the world through the Church is not exclusive but elective. By the Spirit, Christ may be said to be present to all things; but it is specifically as Christ's body that the Church mediates him knowingly to the world as Christ and Lord of all. That the Church is and does so is God's sovereign choice, but this does not mean that the Church is an exclusive body, in Barth's words, 'a kind of institute of salvation'. (Barth, *Church Dogmatics*, IV/3.2, 567). God's election of the Church to mediate his presence in the world certainly is not cause for the Church to be smug.

Accordingly, it is in the Spirit-directed, obedient life of Christ, and in the Spirit-directed, obedient life of Christ's body, the Church, that God's providence is made flesh.

Our intention in this chapter was to summarise the notion of divine presence and explain more fully its appropriateness for the context in which the doctrine of providence is situated. As such, we have not attempted to exhaust the matter but have outlined the contours of the doctrine based upon this particular context. Throughout this chapter, then, we have spoken of God's faithfulness to his purposes for the world and of his desire that these should be fulfilled through faithful human action. The following three chapters explore the scriptural presentation of this dual faithfulness in order to demonstrate the legitimacy of the conceptual framework of God's presence for the foundation and context for the Christian doctrine of providence and the christological orientation of this foundation. We shall examine first the calling of Israel faithfully to mediate the divine presence to the surrounding nations; secondly, what Christ by his own faithfulness achieved as he struggled to obey his Father; and finally, the role of the Spirit in the life of Christ as unswervingly he remained faithful. These three chapters, based upon readings of Galatians 3, Hebrews and Matthew's Gospel respectively, should be understood as making explicit much of what has been sketched in this chapter concerning the christological orientation of the inseparable themes of divine presence and providence.[116]

At the heart, then, of the doctrine of providence is the notion that God gives *himself* to the world. Providence is not the pancausal execution of an eternal decree but the enabling of a fallen, sinful world to enter once more into relationship with God its creator. All this is focussed on God's action in Jesus Christ, whose faithfulness to his Father by the power of the Holy Spirit in turn demonstrates God's own faithfulness to the world.

---

[116] It is impossible, however expected or desirable, to comment further in any depth on the role of the Church in God's providential action; this is the neglected element of this study. A detailed discussion of the role of the Church and its relation to Israel as God's covenant people is properly a vital component of any doctrine of providence; however, our aim in this study, as we have noted elsewhere (see § 1.6, § 4.7 and § 5.1), is not to devise such a doctrine. Instead, we have sought to identify the problems with the conceptual framework of primary and secondary causation as the foundation for the Christian doctrine of providence and seek now, in the remaining chapters, to demonstrate the legitimacy of the conceptual framework of God's presence focussed in Christ as its most appropriate foundation and context.

CHAPTER 6

Providence and the Faithfulness of God

§ 6.1 Introduction

An explication of the doctrine of providence from within the conceptual framework of primary and secondary causation makes it difficult to affirm the action of the *triune* God within the world; at least, this is the implication of the teaching on providence that we have considered to this point. According to this conceptual framework, God wills to mediate his action through creaturely secondary causation; but in doing so, the mediation of the Son and the Holy Spirit is displaced, and the integrity of creaturely causal efficacy is severely jeopardised, if not denied. Against this, we have argued that the doctrine of providence understood from within the conceptual framework of God's presence safeguards the sovereign freedom of God's activity within a creation that retains its causal integrity. God is working to extend his presence throughout the world and does so by calling to himself a faithful people to mediate his presence. Fundamental to all this is the person of Jesus Christ, the Word made flesh (Jn 1:14) and the proper presence of God. Christ is both the focus of God's presence to the world and the locus of his presence within it, insofar as his presence is mediated by the Spirit to the Church and then, through the Church's witness, to the world. The concept of God's presence and the reality of God's activity in the world therefore converge definitively in this one man. Jesus Christ is God's providence made flesh, and a doctrine of providence that has no explicit role for him can only be deficient.

To understand Christ as the embodiment of God's presence in this way is also to appreciate the history of Israel. The Johannine expression of Christ as the incarnate Word of God assumes knowledge of and builds upon the historical reality of God's presence in Israel's midst, first in the tabernacle and then in Solomon's temple. For Israel, the God present in her midst is also the God whose laws and decrees she must strive to obey out of love for him and in response to his saving action. Israel was called out of Egypt to be 'a priestly kingdom and a holy nation' (Ex 19:6), but her being this nation is dependent on her faithful obedience (Ex 19:5). This history of Israel as a nation chosen by God with an identity forged by obedient response to that election is crucial as the context into which Jesus was born.

Permeating the New Testament is a conviction that somehow Jesus has fulfilled all that this context presupposed and anticipated. Christ and his body, the Church, have not superseded Israel as God's covenant people as such;

rather, Gentiles, along with Israel, are now members of the people called faithfully to mediate the divine presence.[1] We have seen already that John's Gospel depicts Jesus as the new temple (Jn 2:21);[2] but other passages mirror this attitude, indicating that the coming of Christ has effected a change in God's dealings with his creation. In Romans 10:4, for example, Paul claims that 'Christ is the end [τέλος] of the law', suggesting perhaps that the Mosaic Law is now invalid. Similarly, Hebrews 8:6 portrays Jesus as 'the mediator of a better covenant' (κρείττονός ἐστιν διαθήκης μεσίτης), intimating that all that came prior to Christ is now secondary and therefore redundant. Does this mean that God's giving of the law to his chosen people was a decision proved mistaken in hindsight? No; for though John establishes Jesus as superior to Moses (Jn 1:17). he speaks beforehand of the fullness of the grace that comes with Christ as grace upon *grace* (χάριν ἀντὶ χάριτος; Jn 1:16).[3] The provision of the law was an act of grace, the law itself divinely ordained and good (Rom 7:7, 12); but even as such, the law is but a stage – a temporary institution 'until Christ came' (Gal 3:24) – in God's plan to spread his presence across the world. These claims require elucidation and so we must now offer a more detailed account of the law and of Christ's relation to it.

§ 6.2 The Calling of Israel: Presence, Covenant and Law

In Exodus 19-20, we see the calling of Israel specifically to be God's 'treasured [or "special"] possession' (Ex 19:5) and the giving of the Decalogue three days later (Ex 19:16; 20:1-17). This passage features a sequence of themes scattered throughout the Pentateuch. First in this sequence is the theme of God's presence. Having left Egypt, the Israelites camp before Sinai-Horeb – 'the mountain' – and, 'on that very day', Moses goes up to God to hear from him (Ex 19:1-3). Moses seems somewhat enthusiastic about meeting God, in contrast to his earlier encounter there with God (Ex 3:1). At that time, God revealed that he was about to free his suffering people from their Egyptian oppressors and lead them 'to a good and broad land, a land flowing with milk and honey' (Ex 3:7-9); but his further announcement that Moses was to be his agent of deliverance was met with an incredulous response: 'Moses said, "Who am I that I should go to Pharaoh. and bring the Israelites out of Egypt?"' (Ex 3:11) However, the crucial emphasis falls not upon Moses inadequacy but upon God's response: '"I will be with you"' (Ex 3:12).[4] Although Moses is to be God's agent, he will not be alone; indeed, what Moses is called to do is possible

---

[1] See D.H. Knight, *The Eschatological Economy: Time and the Hospitality of God* (Grand Rapids: Eerdmans, 2006), 62–66, 93–95, 165, for some insightful comments about supersessionism.

[2] See § 5.3.

[3] See § 5.3, n. 69.

[4] J.I. Durham, *Exodus* (WBC 3; Nashville: Thomas Nelson, 1987), 33.

only because God is with him, as the rest of Exodus 3:12 suggests: '"[A]nd this shall be the sign for you that it is I who sent you: when you have brought the people out of Egypt, you shall worship God on this mountain."' The fact that the Israelites are now camped in front of the mountain (Ex 19:2) is the source of Moses's enthusiasm. God had remained faithful to his promise that he would be with Moses, and so it is towards this faithful God that a more confident Moses heads.

All this serves to emphasise that the mountain is God's abode (Ex 15:17), the place of his presence. Its portrayal in Exodus anticipates his later dwelling amongst Israel first in the tabernacle and then in the temple.[5] Here, though, it is the Israelites themselves who are called into God's presence; but this presence is not merely a communication of his existence, but a presence that sanctifies all that it touches.[6] Just as Sinai is transformed into 'holy ground' (Ex 3:5),[7] just as Moses's first Sinaitic encounter with God redirected his life as God demonstrated his desire to act and to liberate his people from Egyptian oppression, so now Israel herself is called to the mountain in order to be 'a holy

---

[5] The tabernacle (and later the temple) was divided into three main sections or 'zones of holiness' (P.P. Jenson, *Graded Holiness: A Key to the Priestly Conception of the World* [JSOTS 106; Sheffield: Sheffield Academic Press, 1992], 89–90): the court (Ex 27:9-19; Num 4:26, 32), the holy place (Ex 26:33; 29:30; Lev 6:30; Num 3:28; 28:7) and finally, the holy of holies (Ex 26:33; Num 4:4, 19). Each of these zones had a particular and increasing degree of holiness, from the least to the most holy. It is not difficult, then, to see why G.K. Beale suggests that 'Israel's encounter with God at Mount Sinai ... [is an] experience of worship at a sacred location that approximates a temple site.' (G.K. Beale, *The Temple and the Church's Mission: A Biblical Theology of the Dwelling Place of God* (NSBT 17; Leicester: Apollos, 2004), 105). 'Mount Sinai was divided into three sections of increasing sanctity: the majority of the Israelites were to remain at the foot of Sinai [Ex 19:12, 23], the priests and seventy elders ... were allowed to come some distance up the mountain [Ex 19:22; 24:1], but only Moses could ascend to the top and directly experience the presence of God [Ex 24:2].' (Beale, *The Temple and the Church's Mission*, 105). Thus Sinai's summit resembles the holy of holies insofar as God's presence was most keenly experienced there by Moses alone, Israel's 'high priest' (Ex 24:15-17; Beale, *The Temple and the Church's Mission*, 105–106). 'In this light,' Beale continues, 'Sinai was an appropriate place for God to show to Moses "the pattern of the tabernacle and the pattern of all its furniture" in order that they would construct it exactly as it was "shown" to Moses [Ex 25:9; cf. 25:40].' (Beale, *The Temple and the Church's Mission*, 107).

[6] Cf. G.A. Anderson, 'Mary in the Old Testament', *Pro Ecclesia* 16 (2007), 33–55 (54): 'any part of creation brought ... close to the presence of God is overwhelmed by his power and sanctity.'

[7] J.B. Wells, *God's Holy People: A Theme in Biblical Theology* (JSOTS 305; Sheffield: Sheffield Academic Press, 2000), 28; S. Terrien, *The Elusive Presence: The Heart of Biblical Theology* (RP 26; San Francisco: Harper & Row, 1978), 111.

nation' (Ex 19:6). Israel is camped before the mountain of God, consecrating herself in preparation for God's descent (Ex 19:10-11).

The dialogue that takes place between God and Moses on the mountain 'that very day' is therefore instrumental for understanding the second of our three themes, the covenant. Through Moses, God interprets the Israelites' recent experience as something that transpired from his own action on their behalf: '"You have seen what I did to the Egyptians, and how I bore you on eagles' wings and brought you to myself."' (Ex 19:4) This action then becomes an invitation for Israel to enter into a proper, responsive covenant relation with God:[8]

> Now therefore, if you obey my voice and keep my covenant, you shall be my treasured possession out of all the peoples. Indeed, the whole earth is mine, but you shall be for me a priestly kingdom and a holy nation. (Ex 19:5-6)

God has delivered the Israelites from oppression and 'is here offering [them] the means of appropriate response to what he has done for them, if they choose to make it.'[9] A positive response to God will mean the proper founding of Israel as God's own people.[10] In this respect, standing in the presence of God in turn gives rise to God's people;[11] but they can only truly be God's people as, in response to his presence, they choose 'to pay the most careful attention to his instruction concerning what is expected of them and then to "keep," that is, to abide by, the terms of his covenant.'[12] With this invitation, God calls to himself a corporate Adam,[13] 'a priestly kingdom and a holy nation' to serve in his

---

[8] According to W.J. Dumbrell, a 'covenant in the normal secular practice of the ancient world appears to have been a device whereby existing relationships which time, circumstances or other factors have brought into being, were given the semblance of legal backing in the form of a ceremony whose major thrust was that of solemn commitment. To this was given the added force of the self-imprecatory nature of the associated rites and language and associated with it was the further powerful and personally binding factor of oaths given and taken.' (W.J. Dumbrell, *Covenant and Creation: A Theology of the Old Testament Covenants* [BTCL 12; Carlisle: Paternoster, 1997], 19). Thus, 'God's covenant with individuals and with the human race is essentially a treaty. God the great king enters into a relationship with his servant people. It is thus a political–legal metaphor of God's relationship with his people. This covenant is not an agreement between two equal parties. Quite the contrary, it is a relationship initiated by a lord or suzerain with his vassal.' (L. Ryken, J.C. Wilhoit and T. Longman III [gen. eds.], *Dictionary of Biblical Imagery* [Leicester: IVP, 1998], 177).

[9] Durham, *Exodus*, 262.

[10] Durham, *Exodus*, 262.

[11] Cf. Terrien, *The Elusive Presence*, 124.

[12] Durham, *Exodus*, 262.

[13] Cf. Beale, *The Temple and the Church's Mission*, 120–121; N.T. Wright, *The New Testament and the People of God* (London: SPCK, 1992), 262; S.W. Hahn, 'Canon,

world-temple, through and by whom he will continue to extend his presence across the world. '"Indeed, the whole earth is mine,"' God says,[14] but he has brought the Israelites into his presence in order to make this covenant specifically with them. As God's 'holy nation', Israel is required to maintain relations with other nations so that she 'may represent [God's presence] and mediate it' to them.[15] Consequently, 'the goal of the Sinaitic covenant is the establishment of a special nation through whom Yahweh can make himself known to all the families of the earth';[16] and judging by the reaction of the elders of the people (Ex 19:7-8),[17] it seems that this mediating role was one Israel was pleased to accept (Ex 24:3).

Fundamental to Israel's election, then, is the idea that she is no different from the nations to whom she specifically is called to mediate God's presence. In Deuteronomy especially, we see that Israel's election does not grant her some soteriological advantage over other nations, as though her election benefits her alone. Rather, the emphasis is placed upon the fact that God loved Israel and rescued her in order to remain faithful to the promises he had made to her ancestors (Deut 7:8). This leads to the following assertion:

> Know therefore that the LORD your God is God, the faithful God who maintains covenant loyalty with those who love him and keep his commandments, to a thousand generations, and who repays in their own person those who reject him. He does not delay but repays in their own person those who reject him. Therefore, observe diligently the commandment – the statutes and the ordinances – that I am commanding you today. (Deut 7:9-11)

God requires Israel to remain faithful to the covenant and its nomistic framework because he first was faithful to the covenant he had established with

---

Cult and Covenant: The Promise of Liturgical Hermeneutics', in C. Bartholomew, S. Hahn, R. Parry, C. Seitz and A. Wolters (eds.), *Canon and Biblical Interpretation* (SHS 7; Milton Keynes: Paternoster, 2006), 207–235 (215).

[14] Cf. T.E. Fretheim, *God and World in the Old Testament: A Relational Theology of Creation* (Nashville: Abingdon Press, 2005), 100–109.

[15] Wells, *God's Holy People*, 50, 56–57; quote from 57; cf. Durham, *Exodus*, 263: 'Israel as the "special treasure" is Israel become uniquely Yahweh's prized possession by their commitment to him in covenant. Israel as a "kingdom of priests" is Israel committed to the extension throughout the world of the ministry of Yahweh's Presence.... Israel as a "holy people" then represents a third dimension of what it means to be committed in faith to Yahweh: they are to be a people set apart, different from all other people by what they are and are becoming – a display-people, a showcase to the world of how being in covenant with Yahweh changes a people.'

[16] P.R. Williamson, 'Covenant', in *Dictionary of the Old Testament: Pentateuch* (Leicester: IVP, 2003), 139–155 (150).

[17] The elders, as representatives of the people, responded positively on behalf of all Israel; see Durham, *Exodus*, 263–264.

Abraham;[18] indeed, the very basis of Israel's covenant with God is that earlier Abrahamic covenant. For Abraham, God's call was a simple command[19] that entailed a promise:

> 'Go from your country and your kindred and your father's house to the land that I will show you. I will make of you a great nation, and I will bless you, and make your name great, so that you will be a blessing. I will bless those who bless you, and the one who curses you I will curse; and in you all the families of the earth shall be blessed.' (Gen 12:1-3)

The promise itself is somewhat general, no doubt intentionally. 'It does not refer to any one specific blessing, such as the gift of a son, but to Abraham's entire life as blessed by God in all its aspects.'[20] Consequently, the promise lends itself to interpretation in terms of the original Adamic commission: just as creation would have been blessed through Adam's fruitfulness and keeping of the garden (Gen 1:28; 2:15), so the whole world will be blessed in Abraham (Gen 12:3).[21] God's faithfulness to his promise to Abraham, that all nations on earth will be blessed in him, demonstrates his faithfulness to his plan to extend his presence throughout the world. In calling Abraham, God shows his fidelity to creation itself: he does not want to leave it alone, but desires to transform its fortunes somehow through this man. Israel's election is therefore a demonstration of God's love for the entire world.[22]

---

[18] Though I have preferred to use 'Abraham' here to emphasise the continuity throughout the Pentateuch, the patriarch's name was, of course, 'Abram' at this stage in the Genesis narrative, remaining so until Genesis 17:5. At times, we shall use 'Abram' and 'Abraham' interchangeably.

[19] Colin Gunton phrases this memorably as the command 'to leave home and go somewhere else.' (C.E. Gunton, *The Christian Faith: An Introduction to Christian Doctrine* [Oxford: Blackwell, 2002], 30; cf. Wells, *God's Holy People*, 186).

[20] F. Watson, *Paul and the Hermeneutics of Faith* (London: T&T Clark, 2004), 188.

[21] N.T. Wright notes that the commands given to Adam in Genesis 1 are repeated to Abraham as '[he] and his progeny inherit the role of Adam and Eve.' (Wright, *The New Testament and the People of God*, 262–263; quote from 263). Beale links these commands explicitly with the temple theme. (Beale, *The Temple and the Church's Mission*, 94–99).

[22] This does not mean that Israel's own status before God is unimportant, for the other nations are blessed only because they themselves share in Israel's blessings. 'The point that God's people are the recipients of God's blessing in a way that will be determinative not only for themselves but for other nations too, is reiterated – indeed, augmented – in certain key places in the Hebrew canon ... Throughout, however, Israel's concern is not primarily with the place of *other* nations in God's plan, but with their *own* place in the plan, as recipients of the blessing.' (Wells, *God's Holy People*, 191–192, emphasis original). That God promises to bless or curse other nations in accordance with their relationship with Abraham indicates that any

The establishment of the covenant between God and Israel leads, then, to our third theme taken from Exodus 19-20, the *tôrāh* or law. God issues the Decalogue to the Israelites first by alluding to his action on their behalf: "'I am the LORD your God, who brought you out of the land of Egypt, out of the house of slavery'" (Ex 20:2). Similar words preceded God's earlier speech to Israel, his invitation to her to enter into a covenantal relationship with him (Ex 19:4). Having agreed to such a relationship, Israel now receives the law: not merely a set of commands to follow or an absolute moral code,[23] but rather the embodiment of God's standards and the revelation of his character.[24] This is given to Israel so that she may demonstrate her love for the God who called her out of slavery in Egypt to be his people.[25] Israel is to be holy as God himself is holy (Lev 11:44-45; 19:2); and by keeping the law, her character would mirror that of God and effectively mediate the divine presence throughout the world. Accordingly, Israel's identity is defined by the law she receives from God; of all the families of the earth, she alone is 'a priestly kingdom and a holy nation' (Ex 19:6). Through obedience to the law, Israel confirms her identity as such and so is distinguished from her neighbours:

> I am the LORD your God. You shall not do as they do in the land of Egypt, where you lived, and you shall not do as they do in the land of Canaan, to which I am bringing you. You shall not follow their statutes. My ordinances you shall observe and my statutes you shall keep, following them: I am the LORD your God. You shall keep my statutes and my ordinances; by doing so one shall live: I am the LORD. (Lev 18:2-5; cf. 20:8, 26)

Through her willing submission to God's commands, Israel accepts her place in the covenant and enters into a relationship of unparalleled depth with God; and through the law, God provides the means necessary for preserving this intimacy. These are instructions to build the tabernacle in which God will reside in her midst (Ex 25:8-9); exhortations to observe all God's statutes and

---

'benefit to others is a side-effect of God's primary commitment to bless Abram/Israel.' (Wells, *God's Holy People*, 201).

[23] Cf. G. von Rad, *Old Testament Theology, Volume 1: The History of Israel's Historical Traditions*, translated by D.M.G. Stalker (London: SCM Press, 1975), 193–194; Dumbrell, *Covenant and Creation*, 98.

[24] Cf. M.J. Selman, 'Law', in *Dictionary of the Old Testament: Pentateuch* (Leicester: IVP, 2003), 497–515 (509): 'Yahweh's character was the bedrock of *tôrâ*. It determined the nature of all the laws, commands and instructions as well as the motivation for Israel's response to the laws.'

[25] Cf. Wells, *God's Holy People*, 60; C.C. Newman, 'Covenant, New Covenant', in *Dictionary of the Later New Testament and its Developments* (Leicester: IVP, 1997), 245–250 (246); Dumbrell, *Covenant and Creation*, 98.

ordinances in acknowledgement of God's 'nearness' to her (Deut 4:5-8);[26] and, should she neglect the law at any point, directions for the sacrificial system by which Israel may approach God in spite of her failures and so maintain his presence among his people (Lev 1:1-6:7; 16:1-34). The provision of the law can be seen as nothing less than a gracious act of God towards Israel, his 'treasured possession' (Ex 19:5).[27]

All this suggests, then, that the law is a consequence of the covenant rather than its cause.[28] Furthermore, if the provision of the law is a gracious act of

---

[26] Concerning Deuteronomy 4:7-8 in particular, Peter Vogt notes the possibility that 'a deliberate parallelism is being drawn. If so, then the sense here is that the nearness of Yahweh and the *Torah* are closely related.... The logical inference to be drawn from this is that it is through *Torah* that Yahweh's nearness is experienced by Israel. Yahweh's immanence is somehow expressed and experienced through his word.' (P.T. Vogt, *Deuteronomic Theology and the Significance of Torah: A Reappraisal* [Winona Lake, Indiana: Eisenbrauns, 2006], 129, emphasis original).

[27] Fretheim, *God and World in the Old Testament*, 148.

[28] von Rad, *Old Testament Theology, Volume 1*, 194; *Old Testament Theology, Volume 2: The Theology of Israel's Prophetic Traditions*, translated by D.M.G. Stalker (London: SCM Press, 1975), 393; Selman, 'Law', 509.

The idea that covenant precedes law is famously E.P. Sanders's contention that *'obedience [to the law] maintains one's position in the covenant, but it does not earn God's grace as such.'* (E.P. Sanders, *Paul and Palestinian Judaism: A Comparison of Patterns of Religion* [London: SCM Press, 1977], 420, emphasis original). Accordingly, Second Temple Judaism exhibits a structure that may be described as 'covenantal nomism', that is, 'the view that one's place in God's plan is established on the basis of the covenant and that the covenant requires as the proper response of man his obedience to its commandments, while providing means of atonement for transgression.' (Sanders, *Paul and Palestinian Judaism*, 75; cf. 422). For Sanders, 'covenantal nomism was *pervasive* in Palestine before 70 [CE]. It was thus the basic *type* of religion known by Jews and presumably by Paul.' (Sanders, *Paul and Palestinian Judaism*, 426, emphasis original). An important feature of Sanders's work is his insistence that Judaism is not a religion that *'necessarily tends* towards petty legalism', as presumed historically by the majority of Protestant Christianity. (Sanders, *Paul and Palestinian Judaism*, 427, emphasis original).

Certainly, Sanders paints an attractive picture of the Judaism of Paul's time; but we should not forget that there was quite a gap – 430 years, according to Paul in Galatians 3:17 – between God's initial promises to Abraham and the actual giving of the law. This suggests that even though covenant and law are inseparable for Israel following her liberation from Egypt, the covenant promises themselves are prior to and so can stand independently from the law and need not imply, therefore, the rather mechanical and presumptuous relationship between Israel and God that Sanders himself seems to assume. (Cf. A.A. Das, *Paul, the Law, and the Covenant* [Massachusetts: Hendrickson, 2001], 72). Nor does Sanders suggest that the law is given to Israel as the means by which she is to mediate God's presence to other nations; a crucial aspect of the law is therefore omitted. Wright corrects this by offering a more nuanced view of Israel's understanding of her relation to other

God towards Israel, then, insofar as Israel is called to mediate God's presence to the other nations, the law is also God's gracious provision to the whole world. God calls Israel and provides her with the law to demonstrate his faithfulness to the promise he made to Abraham, that all nations would be blessed in him (Gen 12:3). Accordingly, we may say that the calling of Israel and her receipt of the law are crucial elements of God's providential action; but how does this relate to our central conviction that it is Christ himself who is the key element and therefore essential to a truly Christian doctrine of providence?

§ 6.3 The Law Opposed: Galatians 3:1-18[29]

Our response to this question will take the form of a theological reading of Galatians 3.[30] Here, Paul portrays the law as a disciplinarian or παιδαγωγός (Gal 3:24), an image that testifies indirectly both to God's providential activity in the world and the way in which this activity is defined by and centred in Christ. However, Paul's introduction of this image follows a tortuous argument in which he aims to convince his Galatian audience that the Mosaic Law ought to play no part in their lives. Essentially, a group of Christian-Jewish missionaries[31] had been presenting the Galatians with what Paul sees as 'a different gospel' (1:6); evidently, these missionaries 'believed Jesus to be the Messiah of Israel and saw themselves as summoning Gentiles in the name of Jesus to come under obedience to the Law revealed to Moses at Mount Sinai.

---

nations; see, for example, Wright, *The New Testament and the People of God*, 251–252.

[29] All scriptural references in § 6.3–§ 6.4 are from Galatians unless indicated otherwise.

[30] My restriction to this particular passage is deliberate. In my view, Galatians 3 makes the point I wish to make concerning Christ and the law far more effectively than any other Pauline writing. The reading itself splits Galatians 3 into two sections: the first, Galatians 3:1-18, emphasises the centrality of Christ in God's action; the second, Galatians 3:19-29 deals with the role of the law and Christ's relation to it. For a much condensed version of this reading in entirely a different context, along with its extension to include Galatians 4:1-7, see T.J. Wright, 'Collecting Memories: Identity, Nostalgia and the Objects of Childhood', in A. Shier-Jones (ed.), *Children of God: Towards a Theology of Childhood* (Peterborough: Epworth, 2007), 159–179 (170–172).

[31] Here we follow James Dunn's view that 'the letter [to the Galatians] makes clearest and fullest sense if we see it as a response to a challenge from *Christian–Jewish missionaries* who had come to Galatia to improve or correct Paul's gospel and to "complete" his converts by integrating them fully into the heirs of Abraham through circumcision and by thus bringing them "under the law".' (J.D.G. Dunn, *A Commentary on the Epistle to the Galatians* [BNTC; London: A&C Black, 1993], 11, emphasis original).

They probably regarded Jesus as the authoritative interpreter of the Law.'[32] The missionaries would thus have required the Galatians' circumcision and their total obedience to the law (as suggested by 3:10 and 5:2-4). Importantly, the missionaries assume that the law is a gracious provision of God, and Paul's ire is not directed against their theology on this particular point. Rather, he is concerned that they have misunderstood completely the centrality of Christ in God's new dealings with his creation – and this is Paul's crucial assumption throughout his letter to the Galatians. Indeed, the antithesis expressed famously in Galatians 2:16 – 'that a person is justified not by the works of the law [ἐξ ἔργων νόμου] but through the faith of Jesus Christ [διὰ πίστεως Ἰησοῦ Χριστοῦ]'[33] – is not a contrast between doing works of law and having faith in Christ but a contrast between the law itself and Christ himself: the law belongs to God's former way of dealing with his people, because now all who are counted as God's people are so because they are in Christ rather than under the

---

[32] R.B. Hays, *The Letter to the Galatians: Introduction, Commentary, and Reflections* (NIB XI; Nashville: Abingdon Press, 2000), 185.

[33] The phrase πίστεως Ἰησοῦ Χριστοῦ may be translated legitimately either as 'faith in Jesus Christ' (objective genitive) or 'the faith [or faithfulness] of Jesus Christ' (subjective genitive), as Roy Harrisville confirms (R.A. Harrisville III, 'Before ΠΙΣΤΙΣ ΧΡΙΣΤΟΥ: The Objective Genitive as Good Greek', *Novum Testamentum* 48 [2006], 353–358 [353–354, 356]); but each translation yields a different reading of Galatians. Douglas Campbell notes that an objective construal emphasises that activity performed by the Christian, that is, what the Christian must do to be saved. 'It consequently has nothing to do with the actual mechanics of that salvation as it is effected by God in relation to Christ' and, in short, devalues the place of Christ in Paul's argument to the Galatians. Against this, Campbell argues, the subjective reading makes full use of Christ: 'The story *already* contains an explicit element in terms of Jesus' obedience – the obedience and submission of the Son to the loving will of His Father – as well as a pronounced emphasis on the culmination of that process by his death by crucifixion.' (D.A. Campbell, *The Quest for Paul's Gospel: A Suggested Strategy* [London: T&T Clark, 2005], 91, emphasis original).

More clearly, Richard Hays believes that the traditional reading ('faith in Jesus Christ') does not explain why *now* we need to put our faith specifically *in Christ* rather than simply putting it in God, as did Abraham; instead, 'Paul's entire discussion makes much better sense if he is interpreted as presupposing that Jesus Christ, like Abraham, is justified ἐκ πίστεως ["from faith"] and that we, as a consequence, are justified in him ... as a result of his faith(fulness).' (R.B. Hays, *The Faith of Jesus Christ: The Narrative Substructure of Galatians 3:1–4:11*, 2nd ed. [BRS; Grand Rapids: Eerdmans, 2002], 151). Throughout our reading we will assume that πίστεως Χριστοῦ Ἰησοῦ refers to Christ's own faithfulness and therefore to divine action in contrast to human action.

For an alternative reading of πίστεως Χριστοῦ as 'Jesus-Christ-faith', that is, the faith that concerns Jesus Christ, see D.A. Brondos, *Paul on the Cross: Reconstruction the Apostle's Story of Redemption* (Minneapolis: Fortress Press, 2006), 89–90.

law. Thus any attempt to relate to God under the law effectively bypasses Christ and so is doomed to failure.

This contrast arises again in Galatians 3:1-5. In 3:2, Paul asks, 'Did you receive the Spirit by doing the works of the law [ἔργα νόμου] or by believing what you heard [ἀκοῆς πίστεως]?' Clearly, in setting one medium against the other, Paul assumes that the Spirit indeed came through the latter, through ἀκοῆ πίστεως. Conventionally, this phrase effectively is understood to mean something like 'hearing with faith' or, as we have said already, 'by believing what you heard' (3:2).[34] On this reading, Paul's antithesis in 3:2 essentially is a contrast between receiving the Spirit through performing works and receiving him through hearing and believing the gospel message.[35] However, the phrase ἀκοῆ πίστεως itself is somewhat ambiguous, for it may also be translated as 'the proclamation'[36] or 'the message that elicits faith'.[37] Despite the fact, therefore, that 'Paul sets up the two phrases as parallel and mutually exclusive alternatives',[38] the various renderings of ἀκοῆ πίστεως[39] mean that there is no *strict* parallelism. Alluding to the instances of ἀκοῆ in Romans 10:17,[40] Richard Hays notes that although 'faith comes ἐξ ἀκοῆς ... Law does not come ἐξ ἔργων; the relation is the reverse.'[41] Thus, 'the whole passage makes better sense if we suppose that Paul's primary intention is not at all to juxtapose one type of human activity ("works") to another ("believing-hearing") but rather to juxtapose human activity to God's activity, as revealed in the

---

[34] Both the NIV and the NRSV offer this translation.

[35] Cf. Hays, *The Faith of Jesus Christ*, 127.

[36] J.L. Martyn, *Galatians: A New Translation with Introduction and Commentary* (ABC 33A; New York: Doubleday, 1997), 281.

[37] Hays, *The Letter to the Galatians*, 251-252.

[38] Hays, *The Faith of Jesus Christ*, 129.

[39] Hays offers four possible interpretations: (a) 'by hearing [ἀκοῆ] with faith [πίστις]', that is, you heard and believed; (b) 'by hearing [ἀκοῆ] the gospel [πίστις]', that is, you heard the gospel; (c) 'from the message [ἀκοῆ] that enables faith [πίστις]', that is, the message itself produces faith; and (d) 'from the gospel-message [πίστις-ἀκοῆ]', that is, the emphasis falls upon the preaching of the gospel and not its hearing; see Hays, *The Faith of Jesus Christ*, 125-129, summarised in tabular form in Hays, *The Letter to the Galatians*, 252.

[40] In Romans 10:16, Paul quotes Isaiah 53:1: '"Lord, who has believed our ἀκοῇ?"' Paul concludes, 'So faith comes ἐξ ἀκοῆς' (Rom 10:17). Typically, Romans 10:17's ἐξ ἀκοῆς is translated 'from hearing', but a more consistent, contextual reading would favour 'from the message'. As J. Louis Martyn argues, 'In this exegesis of [Isaiah 53:1] Paul gives the Romans no hint that he intends the term *akoē* to bear a meaning other than the one it clearly bears in the text of Isaiah. It follows that in this instance he uses the word *akoē* to refer to the gospel message uttered by God through the apostle.' Martyn concludes, 'The same is surely his intention in [Galatians] 3:2.' (Martyn, *Galatians*, 288).

[41] Hays, *The Faith of Jesus Christ*, 130.

"proclamation."'[42] Crucial, then, to the opening of Galatians 3 is Paul's insistence that the Galatians' relationship with God is not through anything that they themselves have done, but because of what God himself has done for them. 'It was before [their] eyes that Jesus Christ was publicly exhibited as crucified' (3:1), and this led to their receipt of the Spirit (3:2). If the Galatians have experienced anything of the presence of God in their midst, it is because they received the Spirit of God through the gospel itself and not as some 'reward' for or 'effect' of prior action or belief. A turn to the law nullifies what God has already done for them in the crucified Christ. Paul's question carries all these connotations, certainly as it is repeated in 3:5: 'When God even now supplies the Spirit to you, and when he works wonders in the midst of your communities, is he doing those things because you observe the Law, or is he doing them through the proclamation that elicits your faith?'[43]

We must emphasise that the antithesis Paul posits is not between doing 'works of the law' (ἔργα νόμου) and the conventional 'hearing with faith' (ἀκοῆς πίστεως), for both essentially are human actions;[44] rather, Paul contrasts human action negatively with divine action – hence ἀκοὴ πίστεως is itself God's own action. If this is so, then how should we understand Paul's use of 'works of the law'? James Dunn argues that ἔργα νόμου should be interpreted to mean those things that 'the law required *of Israel as God's people*'.[45]

---

[42] Hays, *The Faith of Jesus Christ*, 130.

[43] Galatians 3:5, Martyn's translation (Martyn, *Galatians*, 281); cf. Hays, *The Faith of Jesus Christ*, 130–131: 'He who supplies the Spirit to you and works miracles among you – (does he do it) through works of the Law or through the proclamation of the gospel?'

[44] Moisés Silva argues that the equation of 'faith ... as a kind of (meritorious) work' is to misunderstand 'the nature of the act of believing'. (M. Silva, 'Faith Versus Works of Law in Galatians', in D.A. Carson, P.T. O'Brien and M.A. Seifrid [eds.], *Justification and Variegated Nomism, Volume 2: The Paradoxes of Paul* [Grand Rapids: Baker Academic, 2004], 217–248 [234]). 'Certainly,' he continues, 'the Protestant Reformers left no room for ambiguity that such faith was precisely the antithesis of "futile human activity." Indeed, *faith is by definition the abandonment of our works and efforts* so that we might rest solely on divine grace ... Thus to say that we are justified not by the works of the law but by faith *in* Christ is to acknowledge, in the most forceful terms possible, that we must renounce futile human activity and rely on gracious divine initiative.' (Silva, 'Faith Versus Works of Law in Galatians', 234, emphasis original). Silva is no doubt correct to emphasise that our faith arises through divine initiative, but the language he uses continues to focus on human action. If our faith is God's initiative, then we must dispose of any conceptuality that depicts our own faith as having its basis in our assent to belief. For this reason, Paul's contrast in Galatians between divine action and human action is entirely apposite.

[45] J.D.G. Dunn, *The Theology of Paul the Apostle* (London: T&T Clark, 1998), 355, emphasis original.

> Works of the law ... were what Israel's righteousness consisted of, Israel's part of the covenant which Yahweh had made with Israel in first choosing Israel as his special people. "Works of the law" were Israel's response to that grace, the obedience God called for in his people, the way Israel should live as the people of God [Lev 18:5].[46]

Dunn continues,

> As God's choice of Israel drew the corollary that God's saving righteousness was restricted to Israel, so the law's role in defining Israel's holiness to God became also its role in *separating Israel from the nations*. In this way the positive sense of "works of the law," ... became the more negative sense which we find in Paul – works of the law as not only maintaining Israel's covenant status, but as also protecting Israel's privileged status and restricted prerogative.[47]

For Dunn, although 'the phrase "the works of the law," ... refer[s] to all or whatever the law requires, ... in a context where the relationship of Israel with other nations is at issue, certain laws would naturally come more into focus than others.'[48] Hence, distinctively Jewish practices such as circumcision, sabbath observance and food laws[49] acted as 'identity markers'[50] to distinguish Jew from Gentile.[51] Thus in Galatians 2:16, Paul's 'denial that justification from works of law is, more precisely, a denial that justification depends on circumcision or on observation of the Jewish purity and food taboos.'[52] The implication is that the missionaries were encouraging the Galatians to keep the law so that they could be sure about their place in God's covenant people. Dunn

---

[46] Dunn, *The Theology of Paul the Apostle*, 355.
[47] Dunn, *The Theology of Paul the Apostle*, 355, emphasis original.
[48] Dunn, *The Theology of Paul the Apostle*, 358. Andrew Das notes that Dunn has modified his earlier position '[u]nder pressure from his critics'. (Das, *Paul, the Law, and the Covenant*, 155).
[49] Dunn, *The Theology of Paul the Apostle*, 356.
[50] J.D.G. Dunn, *Jesus, Paul and the Law: Studies in Mark and Galatians* (London: SPCK, 1990), 191.
[51] Cf. Wright, *The New Testament and the People of God*, 238: 'The "works of Torah" were not a legalist's ladder, up which one climbed to earn the divine favour, but were the badges that one wore as the marks of identity, of belonging to the chosen people in the present, and hence the all-important signs, to oneself and one's neighbours, that one belonged to the company who would be vindicated when the covenant god acted to redeem his people.'
[52] Dunn, *Jesus, Paul and the Law*, 191; cf. 220: 'In Galatians [2:16] ... ἔργα νόμου most obviously refers back to the issues at the centre of the preceding controversies – circumcision and food laws. That is what was at issue – whether to be justified by faith in Jesus Christ requires also observance of these "works", whether ... it is possible to conceive of a membership of the covenant people which is not characterised by precisely these works.'

argues that 'it would be virtually impossible [for a first century Jew] to conceive of participation in God's covenant ... apart from these observances, these works of the law.'[53] Effectively, the Galatians are encouraged to become Jews in order to ensure their participation in God's covenant blessings.

Dunn's suggestion seems plausible, not least because the discussion Paul recalls between Peter and himself (2:11-21) places food laws and possibly circumcision (2:12) at the heart of the issue. These were the laws that the Galatians initially would be expected to keep. However, by arguing that there were nationalistic 'works of the law' opposed to Christ, that these laws *specifically* were most significant, Dunn implies also that the rest of the law was somehow neutral. Yet the logic of Paul's argument itself in Galatians 3 does not convey such an impression. Moisés Silva writes,

> It seems futile to deny that the ceremonial question in Antioch affects the meaning of the phrase "law-works" in Galatians 2:16 and colours the subsequent discussion in chapter 3. It would be a mistake, however, to infer, without further evidence, that national identification is the specific issue that troubles Paul or even the principal factor he has in mind when speaks of "law-works."[54]

Furthermore,

> the point to appreciate is that in 2:15 to 3:29 Paul *does not once refer to the ceremonial regulations explicitly*. More important, the development of his argument is characterised by a much broader outlook, and his references to the law ... give no hint that he is referring narrowly to identity markers.[55]

Silva concludes,

> In short, then, we may readily agree that the phrase ἔργα νόμου *includes* those ceremonial elements of the Mosaic law that served to highlight the distinction between Jew and Gentile. But we have no good reason to infer that this phrase overshadows – much less that it excludes – the requirements of the Sinaitic covenant more generally.[56]

---

[53] Dunn, *Jesus, Paul and the Law*, 193, original emphasis removed.

[54] Silva, 'Faith Versus Works of Law in Galatians', 221. For Silva, 'law–works' is 'the least prejudicial way of representing [the phrase ἔργα νόμου] in English'. ('Faith Versus Works of Law in Galatians', 220).

[55] Silva, 'Faith Versus Works of Law in Galatians', 221–222, emphasis original.

[56] Silva, 'Faith Versus Works of Law in Galatians', 222, emphasis original; cf. Watson, *Paul and the Hermeneutics of Faith*, 334, emphasis original: '"Works of law", then, is a comprehensive expression that refers to the entirety of the actions and abstentions prescribed by the law. It does not refer only or primarily to so-called "identity markers" that differentiate Israel from the Gentiles, for the Pauline Israel is differentiated from the Gentiles not by individual observances such as circumcision

If Silva is correct, then ἔργα νόμου cannot refer merely to identity markers, whether in 2:16, 3:2 or later in 3:10; it must refer instead to the *entire* law. Any potential question regarding whether only certain laws need faithfully to be kept is not one that should intrude, therefore, into the logic of Paul's argument in the letter.[57] This is, of course, Paul's insistence that the Galatians received the Spirit not by doing works of the law but by the message that provoked their faith (3:5). For Paul, this message bears similarities to God's calling of Abraham. Initially, this involved a command: 'Go' (Gen 12:1). Yet in drawing attention to Abraham, Paul does not allude to this particular incident but to a later one that states simply that Abraham 'believed the LORD' (Gen 15:6). Abraham believes God when he promises that he shall have a true heir; indeed, with this promise comes the corollary: '"Look towards heaven and count the stars, if you are able to count them." Then [God] said to [Abraham], "So shall your descendants be"' (Gen 15:5). Importantly, it seems that Paul has chosen this particular text to emphasise that Abraham's faithful response was not an act of obedience; as Francis Watson comments,

> Unlike many of the divine utterances to Abraham, this one is not a command. When YHWH commands, Abraham habitually obeys – whether he is instructed to forsake his homeland or to sacrifice his son. But the statement, "... and he reckoned it to him as righteousness" is not attached to any of these acts of heroic obedience but to an act of consent to another's self-commitment.[58]

So although Abraham still acts, Watson argues that it 'is almost invisible as such, since it is oriented entirely to the divine promise that has evoked it and to which it responds.' Indeed, '[t]he speech-act of making a promise requires the addressee to acknowledge the promise as a promise and to regard it as dependable: when Abraham does this, his response simply marks the successful completion of the divine act of promise-making.'[59] Abraham's faith is secondary to the promise that produces it. If this is so, then Paul's allusion to this particular episode in the Abraham narrative follows naturally from Galatians 3:1-5, where he explains to the Galatians that they received the Spirit not ἐξ ἔργων νόμου but ἐξ ἀκοῆς πίστεως, from the message that elicits faith. There is a close connection between 3:5 and 3:6, indicated by 3:6's καθὼς,[60] which suggests that Paul is linking the Galatians' experience to

---

per se, but by the attempt to practise the law's requirements in their entirety.' See also Das, *Paul, the Law, and the Covenant*, 158.

[57] More pertinent is the question of whether the law *can* be kept in its entirety. We will address this issue in § 6.4.

[58] Watson, *Paul and the Hermeneutics of Faith*, 179.

[59] Watson, *Paul and the Hermeneutics of Faith*, 179.

[60] M. Silva, 'Abraham, Faith, and Works: Paul's Use of Scripture in Galatians 3:6-14', *Westminster Theological Journal* 63 (2001), 251–267 (253); Hays, *The Letter to the Galatians*, 255.

Abraham's own experience, where, effectively, he too responded to God ἐξ ἀκοῆς πίστεως.[61] No doubt, part of the attractiveness of the missionaries' message is that, by evoking the Abraham story, it shows the Galatians how they can enter into God's covenant people; they, like Abraham, can be circumcised (Gen 17:10)[62] and so participate in God's covenant. Paul's counterargument is simply that they are already members of God's covenant people because, like Abraham, their status has been affected positively by the ἀκοη πίστεως.

This means that for Paul, there are two groups of people whose identities are derived from different foundations:[63] 'those from faith' (οἱ ἐκ πίστεως; Gal 3:7)[64] and, by implication, those *not* from faith, that is, 'all who rely on the works of the law' (ὅσοι ἐξ ἔργων νόμου; 3:10).[65] The Galatians, Paul says, are the descendants of Abraham, for they, like him, are 'from faith'; if they were to submit to the law, they would, by default, become those *not* from faith. They would be required to do all that the law requires and, effectively, to become Jews. However, Paul points out that before there was a Jewish people as such, God had promised to bless all nations in Abraham (3:8, conflating Gen 12:3; 18:18; 22:18); indeed, before his circumcision, Abraham himself must have been a Gentile.[66] A person's ethnicity is not enough, then, to prevent God from calling him or her to his service, and so the Galatians ought not to be pressured into becoming Jews when it is not to their advantage to do so. It is enough that they are already 'those from faith', those who are Abraham's promised descendants because he, too, was one from faith.

Paul's contrast, then, is between οἱ ἐκ πίστεως, who are blessed, and ὅσοι ἐξ ἔργων νόμου, who are cursed; this is an allusion to the blessing-curse motif that stretches back to Genesis 12:3[67] but assumes classic form in Deuteronomy

---

[61] However, the Galatians do not share in God's blessing 'because their faith imitates Abraham's faith, but because they participate in Christ, who is Abraham's "seed."' (Hays, *The Faith of Jesus Christ*, 172). This suggests that the key focus of both the Galatians' and Abraham's experiences is God's own action. (Hays, *The Faith of Jesus Christ*, 170).

[62] Genesis 15:6 'provides Paul with crucial hermeneutical leverage against the Missionaries, who have almost certainly drawn the attention of the Galatians to Genesis 17, in which Abraham receives and obeys the commandment to circumcise himself and all the males of his household.' (Hays, *The Letter to the Galatians*, 255). Martyn provides a credible 'sermon' of the missionaries that suggests how vital the Abraham narrative was to their gospel and why Paul was thus required to counter them using the same narrative; see Martyn, *Galatians*, 303–306.

[63] Cf. Martyn, *Galatians*, 299.

[64] Both the NIV and the NRSV offer 'those who believe'.

[65] 'Scholars have not always appreciated that the meaning of ὅσοι ἐξ ἔργων νόμου εἰσίν is to a large extent determined by its semantic opposition to "the good guys", οἱ ἐκ πίστεως.' (Silva, 'Faith Versus Works of Law in Galatians', 224).

[66] Watson, *Paul and the Hermeneutics of Faith*, 213–214.

[67] Hays, *The Faith of Jesus Christ*, 177.

27-30. By quoting Deuteronomy 27:26, Paul suggests, curiously, that 'those who *do* the works of the law are cursed because Deuteronomy says that those who do *not* do the works of the law are cursed'.[68] Here, though, we must remember that Paul's problem is not with the simple doing of the law *per se* but rather 'with those who still live within the sphere of the deuteronomic covenant', that is, with those who are still living according to God's former means of relating to his covenant people. 'Thus Paul is simply informing the Galatians of a point repeatedly emphasised in Deuteronomy: Those who enter the covenant are subject to its sanctions and curses.'[69] However, Paul continues, 'no one is justified before God by the law; for "The one who is righteous [ὁ δίκαιος] will live by faith [ἐκ πίστεως]"' (Gal 3:11, quoting Hab 2:4). Indeed, it is futile for anyone to remain under the law given that God's people are οἱ ἐκ πίστεως, for 'the law does not rest on faith; on the contrary, "Whoever does the works of the law will live by them"' (Gal 3:12, quoting Lev 18:5).[70] The thrust of Paul's argument here essentially dichotomises faith and law (*not* faith and works) and so highlights the change in God's dealings with his people. Those who remain under the former scheme of God's law are cursed because God's people now comprise οἱ ἐκ πίστεως (Gal 3:10-11); the law cannot produce οἱ ἐκ πίστεως because, quite simply, it belongs to the former scheme (3:12).

Paul here associates οἱ ἐκ πίστεως with ὁ δίκαιος, the 'one who is righteous' who lives ἐκ πίστεως (3:11). His citation of Habakkuk 2:4 permits a messianic interpretation[71] – that is, Jesus Christ himself is ὁ δίκαιος – even

---

[68] Silva, 'Abraham, Faith, and Works', 263, emphasis original.

[69] Hays, *The Letter to the Galatians*, 258.

[70] Deuteronomy 27:26, Leviticus 18:5, possibly Deuteronomy 21:23, and, indeed, Genesis 12:3 and its parallels in Galatians 3:8, were favoured texts of the missionaries that Paul incorporated into his own counterargument; see, for example, R.N. Longenecker, *Galatians* (WBC 41; Nashville: Thomas Nelson, 1990), 116, 122–123, and Martyn, *Galatians*, 301, 309, 315, 319. Martyn is confident that Deuteronomy 21:23 is a quote of Paul's own choosing (Martyn, *Galatians*, 319) and suggests that the apostle cites Leviticus 18:5 in anticipation of the missionaries' response (Martyn, *Galatians*, 315).

[71] Hays, *The Faith of Jesus Christ*, 134–135. It is important not to understand this reference here *solely* as messianic. Dunn argues this on the basis that '"the righteous one" of verse 11b answers to the "no one" of verse 11a' (Dunn, *Epistle to the Galatians*, 174–175); there is a need for the plurality in 3:11a to be balanced by a similar plurality in 3:11b. However, as Paul later speaks more explicitly about a plurality in Christ (3:16), it may be that a christological reading of ὁ δίκαιος in 3:11 itself anticipates the christological reading of 'offspring' (σπέρματι) in 3:16. Thus we may see Paul's use of Habakkuk 2:4 as having a double reference, both to οἱ ἐκ πίστεως and to ὁ δίκαιος whereby the citation itself functions as a link between the early stages of his argument (3:1-12) and the explicit reintroduction of Christ into its logic (3:13-14).

though the text itself may be interpreted 'non-messianically, as an assertion that [it] provides the key to understanding how God has chosen to bring about rectification and life: through faith, not through the Law.'[72] Yet the possibility of a messianic interpretation of the Habakkuk text means that the reintroduction of the crucified Christ (Gal 3:13-14) into the discussion is not forced; the curse of the law – that is, the curse that holds for those who still live according to the law – somehow is removed for those who are associated with the crucified messiah, who himself lives 'through faith' (διὰ τῆς πίστεως, 3:14). Furthermore, a messianic interpretation of ὁ δίκαιος leads also to a possible messianic interpretation of the following citation from Leviticus 18:5,[73] that '[w]hoever does the works of the law will live by them'.[74] Accordingly, this 'whoever' is ὁ δίκαιος, Christ himself, who lives faithfully according to the law, performing its works so completely that he forges a new means by which God relates to his people. Certainly, this appears to be Paul's reasoning in Galatians 3:13-14, where his emphasis is not so much upon the fact that Christ became a curse (for the 'curse' terminology employed seems little more than a means of situating Christ within Israel's context in general under the law; see also 4:4-5)[75] but rather upon the fact that Christ is the agent in whom God blesses both Jews and Gentiles: 'Christ redeemed *us*' (3:13, emphasis mine). Indeed, Christ represents all Israel as her messiah and, as a man, all humanity;[76] thus his faithful action that led even to his hanging on a tree (3:13) impacts humanity *in toto*, first by freeing Israel from the curse of the law and then – as a

---

[72] Hays, *The Letter to the Galatians*, 259.

[73] Cf. K. Barth, *Church Dogmatics* (13 vols.), edited by G.W. Bromiley and T.F. Torrance (Edinburgh: T&T Clark, 1957–1975), II/2, 245.

[74] This does not mean that we should discontinue reading Paul's use of Leviticus 18:5 as an expression of the law's incompatibility with faith, for that indeed is his point. Yet if, as we have argued, the citation from Habakkuk 2:4 may be read as having a double reference that refers both to οἱ ἐκ πίστεως and to ὁ δίκαιος, then we should have few reservations about interpreting Leviticus 18:5's 'whoever' in turn as referring both to those 'who rely on the works of the law' (Gal 3:10) and to the Christ, ὁ δίκαιος, who lived ἐκ πίστεως whilst under the law (cf. 4:4).

[75] The quote from Deuteronomy 21:23, a text that had come to refer to crucifixion (cf. J.B. Green, 'Death of Jesus', in *Dictionary of Jesus and the Gospels* [Leicester: IVP, 1992], 146–163 [148]), appears simply to link Galatians 3:13 with 3:10's own citation from Deuteronomy. (Dunn, *Epistle to the Galatians*, 177–178). This assumes, of course, that Deuteronomy 27:26 was used by the missionaries to convince the Galatians of the need for the law's priority in their lives. As such, the precise nature of the curse does not matter; it is enough to know that there are serious consequences for those who do not fully obey the law. Paul's comment that Christ became a curse (Gal 3:13) is therefore an exploitation of the curse imagery within the law, whereby he finds a specific text that refers both to crucifixion and the curse eventually to show that Christ is superior to that which ostensibly condemns him.

[76] N.T. Wright, *The Climax of the Covenant: Christ and the Law in Pauline Theology* (Edinburgh: T&T Clark, 1991), 151–152; Dunn, *Epistle to the Galatians*, 176–177.

consequence of that redemptive action – by enabling the Gentiles' inclusion within God's covenant people (3:13-14). Thus the clear, efficacious portrayal of the gospel of the crucified Christ (the ἀκοη πίστεως) that led to the Galatians' receipt of the promised Spirit (3:1-2, 14) is itself enabled by Christ's prior, faithful action to God's commands in the law.[77]

To stress Christ's centrality further, Paul argues that 'the promises were made to Abraham and to his offspring ... who is Christ' (3:16). The purpose of this assertion is to accentuate the fact that the fulfilment of the promise does not come from the law but from the promise itself: God's promise to Abraham that 'in you all the families of the earth shall be blessed' (Gen 12:3) is a promise not to Abraham and Israel – or his 'offsprings' (σπέρμασιν) – as such, but to Abraham and the specific Israelite or 'offspring' (σπέρματι), Jesus Christ (3:16).[78] Christ dies both as one living under the law and as ὁ δίκαιος of God who lived ἐκ πίστεως in order to establish God's new dealings with humanity. Indeed, Christ's life is itself divine action,[79] God's continuing fulfilment of his promises to Abraham. Paul argues that, just as a human will (διαθήκη) cannot be changed once it has been set (3:15), so God's covenant (διαθήκη) with Abraham cannot be displaced on the basis of any later development, such as the arrival of the law.[80] As this came to Israel 430 years after the establishment of

---

[77] Cf. Martyn, *Galatians*, 323.

[78] Cf. Watson, *Paul and the Hermeneutics of Faith*, 190: 'According to Galatians [3:13-14] ... the promise of Genesis [12:3] has now been realised in the death and resurrection of Christ, the event in which the curse of the law gives way to the blessing of Abraham. Thus it can now be said ... that the blessing of Abraham comes to the Gentiles "in Christ Jesus". This is a further interpretative paraphrase of the scriptural statement that "in you all Gentiles shall be blessed", but on this occasion the statement is reinterpreted in the light of the event in which the blessing was actually bestowed on the Gentiles. Here, "in you" is no longer paraphrased simply as "with Abraham", although that interpretation is still valid, but rather as "in Christ Jesus". In the background here may be the exegetical observation that "the promises were spoken to Abraham and to his seed", which Paul takes as a reference to Christ [Gal 3:16]. If this observation is applied to Genesis [12:3], "in you" would apply not only to Abraham but also to Christ, Abraham's seed. In the light of the actuality of God's act to justify or bless the Gentiles, the scriptural promise must mean that "in Christ Jesus shall all Gentiles be blessed".'

[79] Cf. C.E. Gunton, *The Triune Creator: A Historical and Systematic Study* (ESCT; Edinburgh: Edinburgh University Press, 1998), 84: 'Here is the life of a man which, as a narrated whole, from beginning to end, is also, and without diminishing its character as human, also divine act. This is a divine act, an act of the eternal God, which is, so to speak, stretched out in time.'

[80] Martyn argues that for Paul, 'God played no part at all in the genesis of the Sinaitic Law.' (Martyn, *Galatians*, 366). This is too strong. Instead, we may argue, as does Hays, that Paul deliberately avoids the idea that the law was given by God to emphasise more strongly the dichotomy between the establishment of the covenant and the arrival of the law. (Hays, *The Letter to the Galatians*, 265, 268).

the Abrahamic covenant (3:17), Paul states that 'if the inheritance[81] comes from the law, it no longer comes from the promise; but God granted it to Abraham through the promise' (3:18).

§ 6.4 The Law Ousted: Galatians 3:19-29

Paul insists, therefore, that 'law and promise must be kept separate, for they operate on entirely different planes. To bring them together as equals ... is to destroy all that God has graciously established by promise.'[82] Nonetheless, the law *was* given to Israel; it must have had *some* purpose. Even Paul's question – 'Why then the law?' – presupposes that it *did* have a purpose: 'It was added because of transgressions [τῶν παραβάσεων χάριν προσετέθη], until the offspring [σπέρμα] would come to whom the promise had been made' (3:19). With this statement, Paul suggests that the law was always to be temporary, 'until the offspring would come'; clearly, 'offspring' here links back to 3:16's identification of 'offspring' with Christ, and so the law would be in place until *Christ* would come. The critical issue is what it means to say that the law 'was added because of transgressions'[83] – but to do this, we need to return to how the law functioned for Israel and to pick up on another matter suggested by Galatians 3:10.

As we have seen, the law was given to Israel to enable her to live as God's covenant people. By obeying the law's commands, Israel would demonstrate her love for the God who delivered her from Egyptian oppression. Her observance of the law would also distinguish her from the other nations: she

---

[81] The inheritance is the inclusion of Gentiles in God's covenant people (Hays, *The Letter to the Galatians*, 265; Martyn, *Galatians*, 343), confirmed by the receipt of the promised Spirit (R.A. Cole, *The Letter of Paul to the Galatians: An Introduction and Commentary*, 2nd ed. [TNTC 9; Leicester: IVP, 1989], 147–148; Dunn, *Epistle to the Galatians*, 186).

[82] Longenecker, *Galatians*, 134.

[83] Hays lists a number of interpretations of this phrase: the law was added (1) to produce or provoke transgressions; (2) to identify transgressions; (3) to restrain transgressions; (4) to provide a remedy for transgressions before Christ; (5) because of Israel's transgressions committed during the golden calf incident (Ex 32). For Hays, options (2) and (3) best fit the text. (Hays, *The Letter to the Galatians*, 266–267). Dunn argues that Paul was referring to 'the sacrificial system, whereby transgressions could be dealt with, whereby atonement was provided'. This, for Dunn, makes better sense of the temporariness of the law Paul implies. Thus 'the law was provided as an interim measure precisely to deal with the problem of transgression, until it could be dealt with definitively and finally in the cross of Christ'. (Dunn, *Epistle to the Galatians*, 190). Insofar as Christ's death certainly is the end of the law's cultic aspects, we may agree with Dunn; the problem is that the law comprised far more than those cultic aspects and so there is no reason for why *all* the law was given.

would be distinctive, separate, 'a priestly kingdom and a holy nation' (Ex 19:6), and this because God himself is holy (see, for example, Lev 11:44-45; 19:2). The law, then, was the given means by which Israel would be the holy nation of God, enabling her to mediate the presence of God to all those nations whom he had not chosen to be his people in this specific way.[84] Israel's obedience to the law allows her to participate in God's own holiness and so to mediate the divine presence to the world.

The problem is that despite her good intentions, Israel would be unable strictly to adhere to the law in its entirety.[85] This inability would not be due to some inherent difficulty posed by the law, that its requirements in and of themselves were too demanding. Taking Deuteronomy as his example, Gerhard von Rad comments that

> all the commandments are simply a grand explanation of the command to love Jahweh and to cling to him alone [Deut 6:4-5]. And this love is Israel's return of the divine love bestowed upon her. The many imperatives in Deuteronomy are therefore appeals, sometimes implicit and sometimes explicit, for gratitude to be shown in action, and Deuteronomy regards them as *easy* to fulfil.[86]

If Deuteronomy's imperatives are so easy to fulfil, it is no wonder that Paul quotes Deuteronomy 27:26 – "'Cursed is everyone who does not observe and obey all the things written in the book of the law'" – in Galatians 3:10. Those seeking to keep the law should have no excuse for failing to keep it. Yet there is possibly a missing premise here in 3:10, a premise that is often assumed to mean that the law requires perfect obedience of a people therefore cursed because of its inability to render such flawless devotion to a law whose commandments are *not* easy to fulfil.[87] On this view, the problem with the law is that it is too demanding and so impossible to uphold in its entirety; the law effectively provokes or causes its adherents to sin (3:19).[88] As we have seen, however, the law was given to enable Israel to live as God's covenant people, to distinguish her as God's holy nation; the possibility that the law was given deliberately to incite this holy nation to sin or to disrupt its attempts at covenantal living would militate against the reason for its election, particularly

---

[84] I say 'in this specific way' because Exodus 19:5 reminds us that 'the whole earth' belongs to God.

[85] As we have seen, Israel was required to keep the entire law and not just those things that, on Dunn's view, may have been designated 'works of the law'.

[86] von Rad, *Old Testament Theology, Volume 1*, 230, emphasis mine.

[87] See, for example, Dunn, *Epistle to the Galatians*, 171; Dunn, *The Theology of Paul the Apostle*, 361; Das, *Paul, the Law, and the Covenant*, 146; Longenecker, *Galatians*, 118; Cole, *The Letter of Paul to the Galatians*, 139; Hays, *The Letter to the Galatians*, 257.

[88] See, for example, Martyn, *Galatians*, 354–355.

if this was only to be 'until the offspring would come' (3:19).[89] The problem, then, is not so much with the impossibility of obeying the entire law because the law itself is an intolerable burden but with Israel's own inability to fulfil it because she is already sinful.[90] So although von Rad claims that the law's commands are easy to fulfil, there remains a danger that they will not be upheld; but this danger comes not from the law itself, but from Israel's possible refusal to obey its commands.[91] Certainly, Deuteronomy strongly indicates such a possibility;[92] this is seen particularly in Deuteronomy 27-30, where an interweaving of blessings and curses for Israel leads to an expectation that she will be exiled and eventually restored by God's action on her behalf (Deut 30:1-5). Crucial to Deuteronomy is the view that faithful obedience to the law entails a proper orientation of character towards God, an orientation described as the circumcision of the heart:

> So now, O Israel, what does the LORD your God require of you? Only to fear the LORD your God, to walk in all his ways, to love him, to serve the LORD your God with all your heart and with all your soul, and to keep the commandments of the LORD your God and his decrees that I am commanding you today, for your own well-being. Although heaven and the heaven of heavens belong to the LORD your God, the earth with all that is in it, yet the LORD set his heart in love on your ancestors alone and chose you, their descendants after them, out of all the peoples, as it is today. Circumcise, then, the foreskin of your heart, and do not be stubborn any longer. (Deut 10:12-16)

However, this circumcision of the heart will exist truly only when God himself performs the operation:

> Moreover, the LORD your God will circumcise your heart and the heart of your descendants, so that you will love the LORD your God with all your heart and with all your soul, in order that you may live. (Deut 30:6)

---

[89] Richard Longenecker comments, 'For although "because of transgressions" can be understood in a causal fashion, "to bring about or multiply sin" makes little sense of the following temporal clause "until the Seed to whom the promise was given should come." For why should God want an increase of sin building up to the coming of Christ?' (Longenecker, *Galatians*, 138).

[90] Essentially, the difference lies in the location of the problem: the law or the sinful person.

[91] von Rad, *Old Testament Theology, Volume 2*, 393.

[92] Paul Barker argues that Deuteronomy records 'three major accounts of Israel failing: the retelling of the spies incident (1:19-46), the retelling of the golden calf incident (9:1–10:11), and the future prediction of failure and exile in (29:15-27).' (P.A. Barker, *The Triumph of Grace in Deuteronomy: Faithless Israel, Faithful Yahweh in Deuteronomy* [PBM; Carlisle: Paternoster, 2004], 1-2). The effect of these accounts is to point beyond Israel's own (in)abilities to God's action on her behalf in faithfulness to his covenant with Abraham.

Paul Barker comments,

> In [Deuteronomy] 30:6, the reference to the circumcision of the heart is significantly transformed from 10:16. Rather than Israel being the subject, Yahweh is. Rather than a demand, it is an unconditional statement or promise. The implication of 30:6 is that Yahweh will now do what Israel is incapable of doing in her own strength or ability. Or, better, Yahweh will act on Israel's heart to enable it to do what it is otherwise unable to do, namely that which is required to keep the covenant. Israel's stubbornness and stiff-neckedness stem from the heart. To change the heart is too big a task, an impossible task, for Israel alone, for its sin is rooted there. Only Yahweh can change the heart. The circumcision of the heart by Yahweh in 30:6 is therefore the resolution to the problem of Israel's inability and infidelity to the covenant.[93]

This returns us to Paul's question in Galatians 3:19, 'Why then the law?' The law does not provoke or produce sin; but neither does it simply '*identify* humanity's inchoate sinfulness as conscious transgression, explicit violation of the revealed divine will', as Hays suggests.[94] Rather, the law *exposes* Israel's sin: as she struggles to live according to the law, she is shown to be fallen, sinful and therefore disobedient in a way that goes beyond mere cognition of the inappropriateness of her actions. Israel is called faithfully to observe the law that identifies her as God's holy people and so to represent God and mediate his presence to the world – yet through her infidelity to the law, her sinfulness is displayed for all to see. If Israel is truly to live as God's holy nation, she can do so only by God's own transformative action on her behalf; this action demonstrates to all that he is present within the world, that he has not abandoned it simply to follow its own course, and that, just as he acts to circumcise Israel's heart, so too he is acting to restore creation to its proper orientation towards him. Insofar as Israel herself is taken from humankind and thus represents the whole of humanity, God acts first within and towards her to reveal himself, secondly, to the whole world – that is, God acts within and towards Israel 'until the offspring would come' (3:19), when God's dealings with humanity will include both Jews and Gentiles. Again, Paul emphasises that Christ himself is crucial to God's action; he is the 'offspring' to whom the promises were made. It is in Christ that Jews and Gentiles together will be united as God's covenant people (3:19-20).[95]

---

[93] Barker, *The Triumph of Grace in Deuteronomy*, 164.
[94] Hays, *The Letter to the Galatians*, 266–267, emphasis original.
[95] Certainly, this is the thrust of Galatians 3:19-20, at least as Wright interprets it. The observation in 3:20 that 'God is one' entails the corollary that God desires 'one family, the single "seed", promised to Abraham and now fulfilled in Christ.' (Wright, *The Climax of the Covenant*, 169). Essentially, the Galatians are accused of seeking covenant membership through Moses, the mediator of 3:19, rather than Christ. Paul's point is 'that Moses is not the mediator through whom this promised "one seed" [that

Nonetheless, and despite appearances to the contrary, Paul can maintain that the law is not 'opposed to the promises of God'; it was not given to 'make alive' (3:21), for this is something only God himself can do – and this by his Spirit,[96] who was given as the result of Christ's own faithful obedience.[97] The law was not the means by which God sought to gather together one family from all peoples; it rather shows 'all things', that is, both Jews and Gentiles,[98] to be 'imprisoned ... under the power of sin' (3:22).[99] Indeed, the problem of sin cannot be restricted to a particular people: insofar as Israel represents the whole of humanity, the exposure of her sin must also reveal that of humanity *in toto*. However, with the coming of faith, the law no longer exposes sin, it no longer imprisons people under the power of sin, and so, effectively, it has been made redundant. Although 'the law was our disciplinarian [παιδαγωγός]', it was so only until faith came – and this faith has now come, Jesus Christ himself (3:24-25). Paul's description of the law as a 'disciplinarian' or a παιδαγωγός is telling,[100] as Richard Longenecker observes:

---

is, the single family of God] is brought into existence. He cannot be, since he (Moses) is mediator of a revelation to Israel only ... Moses is not the mediator of the "one family", *but God is one*, and therefore desires one family, as he promised to Abraham', a family comprising both Jews and Gentiles. (Wright, *The Climax of the Covenant*, 169, 170, emphasis original).

[96] Dunn, *Epistle to the Galatians*, 192–193. The life promised by texts such as Leviticus 18:5 'is life lived within the covenant'. (Dunn, *Epistle to the Galatians*, 193).

[97] This, of course, assumes that the 'what was promised' of Galatians 3:22 corresponds to 'the promise of the Spirit' and, through Christ's obedient action that prompted the arrival of the Spirit, the inclusion of Gentiles into the covenant people of God in 3:14; see Hays, *The Faith of Jesus Christ*, 153.

[98] Cole, *The Letter of Paul to the Galatians*, 151; Hays, *The Letter to the Galatians*, 268; Longenecker, *Galatians*, 144; Dunn, *Epistle to the Galatians*, 194.

[99] Galatians 3:22 actually reads, 'the scripture [ἡ γραφή] has imprisoned all things under the power of sin'. Commentators differ in their interpretations of ἡ γραφή here: is it a 'virtual synonym' for 'law' (Hays, *The Letter to the Galatians*, 268), or does it refer to the whole of Scripture (Dunn, *Epistle to the Galatians*, 194), to the Pentateuch (Cole, *The Letter of Paul to the Galatians*, 151), or to a specific passage (Longenecker, *Galatians*, 144)? Though this latter interpretation is tempting, our reading of Galatians 3 does not admit it quite so easily. The parallel between 'the scripture' as that which imprisons in 3:22 and 'the law' as that which imprisons in 3:23 suggests that Hays's interpretation is to be preferred.

[100] See A.T. Hanson, 'The Origin of Paul's Use of παιδαγωγός for the Law', *Journal for the Study of the New Testament* 34 (1988); reprinted in S.E. Porter and C.A. Evans (eds.), *New Testament Text and Language: A Sheffield Reader* (TBS 44; Sheffield: Sheffield Academic Press, 1997), 201–206, for an account of the Pentateuchal inspiration for Paul's παιδαγωγός metaphor. For a comprehensive account of the role of the παιδαγωγός as depicted by Greco–Roman literature, see D.J. Lull, '"The Law was our Pedagogue": A Study in Galatians 3:19-25', *Journal of Biblical Literature* 105 (1986), 481–498 (489–494).

> The παιδαγωγός, though usually a slave, was an important figure in ancient patrician households, being charged with the supervision and conduct of one or more sons in the family. He ... gave no formal instruction but administered the directives of the father in a custodial manner, though, of course, indirectly he taught by the supervision he gave and the discipline he administered.[101]

Accordingly, the role of a παιδαγωγός – 'to instruct in good manners, to correct as appropriate, to protect as necessary'[102] – was a positive one; indeed, the more negative depiction of a παιδαγωγός as someone cruel and nasty is 'a caricature' not to be 'imported into Paul's analogy'.[103] Of course, depending upon the maturity of his charge, the παιδαγωγός would guide and punish as necessary; but by embodying the father's standards, he would expose the shortcomings of the child and thus stimulate development in the appropriate, desired way. This would continue only until the child matured into adulthood, when wise decisions could be made and acted upon responsibly without custodial supervision; only then would the services of the παιδαγωγός be discontinued. For Paul, then, the παιδαγωγός metaphor 'affirm[s] that the Law once had a constructive role to play in God's overall plan, while at the same time insisting that its role is now at an end.'[104]

Although the law is temporary and limited in purpose, nonetheless, as we said earlier, it is the embodiment of God's standards and the revelation of his character; Israel would have become like God had she observed the law faithfully and fully. She would have embodied God in her own corporate flesh. Sadly, the Old Testament scriptures are a constant reminder of her failure to do so; the law remains a disembodied text other to her, continually calling her to account. Consequently, Paul's implicit judgment is that Israel herself is immature; but the abolition of the law does not mean that she has now reached maturity. Instead, Israel's messiah has come to offer to God the appropriate, mature response on her behalf. Thus the faith of which Paul has spoken consistently (2:16, 20; 3:14, 22-26)[105] is the faith or faithfulness of Christ himself: his faithfulness to the law, to the commandments of God, to God's calling that saw him crucified (3:13). This is the point of Paul's earlier citations from Habakkuk and Leviticus: ὁ δίκαιος will live ἐκ πίστεως (Hab 2:4), that is, 'the one who is righteous' will live by his faithfulness; and by doing the works of the law, he will live by them and so prove himself to be *the* faithful, *the* mature Israelite (Lev 18:5). Through Christ's faithfulness, through this

---

[101] Longenecker, *Galatians*, 148.

[102] Dunn, *The Theology of Paul the Apostle*, 142.

[103] Longenecker, *Galatians*, 148; cf. A.A. Das, *Paul and the Jews* (Massachusetts: Hendrickson, 2003), 154.

[104] Hays, *The Letter to the Galatians*, 260.

[105] At times, Paul seems to use 'faith' and 'Christ' (and, for that matter, 'offspring') as synonyms; each of these 'comes' and is antithetical to the law; cf. Campbell, *The Quest for Paul's Gospel*, 210.

divine action, the imprisoning grip of the law is loosened, its role as παιδαγωγός now at an end. All humanity – which Christ represents both as Israel's messiah and as a man – is now to relate to God not through the law that expects maturity but through Christ, the proper presence of God who embodies the law in his flesh and in whose maturity others share by the Spirit. Accordingly, Christ fulfils the law, or, as Paul phrases it, '[N]ow that faith has come, we are no longer subject to a disciplinarian, for in Christ Jesus you are children of God through faith' (Gal 3:25-26). If the Galatians have received the Spirit, if Jews and Gentiles together are members of God's one family, it is because they are now 'in Christ' (3:26), baptised into him and clothed with him (3:27). For Paul, the 'three binary oppositions that characterised all human existence in the old age' – that is, Jew and Greek, slave and free, male and female – 'have been dissolved' in Christ (3:28).[106] He concludes that the Galatians should not return to the law because they are members of God's one family already according to what was promised to Abraham (3:29), something that their receipt of the Spirit demonstrates (3:2, 5; 4:6-7); and, crucially, all this is not through the law but through God's action in Christ.[107]

---

[106] Hays, *The Letter to the Galatians*, 272.

[107] We may summarise our interpretation of Paul's tortuous argument in Galatians 3, then, as follows: The Galatians are seeking confirmation of their inclusion into God's covenant people by observing the Mosaic Law. However, Paul points out that their receipt of the Spirit already is this confirmation; their status before God is the result of the effective preaching of the gospel, the ἀκοη πίστεως (Gal 3:1-5). Furthermore, Abraham himself responded to God in this way while he was still a Gentile; the Galatians, then, are in good company as 'those from faith', οἱ ἐκ πίστεως (3:6-9). The negative corollary of this, however, is that there are those 'who rely on the works of the law' (3:10); in saying this, Paul builds upon his earlier distinction in 2:16 between those who derive their identity from the law and those who derive it through faith (not through *having* faith as such). He stresses that the two are incompatible, for one cannot have a true standing with God both through the law and through faith (3:11-12). Paul's subtle identification of Jesus Christ as ὁ δίκαιος who lives ἐκ πίστεως (3:11) whilst remaining obedient to the law (3:12) emphasises that this distinction is not between *doing* works of the law and *having* faith, but between the law itself and Christ himself: it is 'in Christ Jesus' that the blessing of Abraham comes to the Gentiles, 'in Christ Jesus' that 'we might receive the promise of the Spirit through faith' (3:14). There is no need, therefore, for the Galatians to observe the law, for it is not by doing its works that they are incorporated into God's people but by receiving the Spirit who does this in and through Christ (3:1-2, 14; cf. 4:6-7). Lest the Galatians consider the centrality of Christ to be a fiction, Paul argues that the fulfilment of God's promise to Abraham was always intended to focus on Christ, Abraham's 'offspring', a focus that would never have been jeopardised by the arrival of the law (3:15-18).

Despite Christ's centrality, the law was nonetheless a gracious provision of God, given to enable her to live as God's covenant people and the mediators of his presence to the whole world (3:19). However, the law exposed Israel's sinfulness –

§ 6.5 A Faithfulness Embodied

Throughout Galatians 3, Paul assumes a sequence of historical events to explain his antithesis between Christ and the law. God made certain promises to Abraham (Gal 3:8, 16-18); later, the law was given to Abraham's descendants, added to expose sin (Gal 3:17, 19); and eventually, the law was fulfilled by Christ's own faithfulness to its commandments and God's calling upon his life (Gal 1:3-4; 3:19, 22-25). That this is a sequence of historical events and not just a selection of random happenings arranged in a particular order is indicated by Paul's depiction of the law as temporary and subordinate to Christ: the law was given to Israel after God had made his promises to Abraham and would function only until the coming of Christ, in whom the promises to Abraham would be fulfilled. This sequence strongly suggests intentionality on God's part: the law would function in a particular way – that is, to expose Israel's sin as she attempts to live as God's holy nation – and thus form the context for his own action in Christ. Indeed, Christ's faithfulness to the covenant law is the means by which God remains faithful to his own covenant promises made to Abraham. Effectively, Paul's argument against the missionaries assumes that God is at work in Israel and, through her, in the world. The missionaries' stance denied the heart of God's action in the world because it did not consider the shift that had taken place through the coming of Christ, a shift Paul is extremely keen to declare.

We may see Galatians 3, then, as a portrayal of God's providential action within creation and therefore as an important text for a truly Christian doctrine of providence. It shows us that, essentially, God's providence is his faithfulness to his purposes for creation. For Paul, the promises God made to Abraham, that 'in [him] all the families of the earth shall be blessed' (Gen 12:3), cannot be annulled by any subsequent development such as the giving of the law. Only that which is promised by God himself commands faithfulness, for the promise to Abraham reflects God's original commission to Adam to serve in the garden of Eden and to expand its boundaries across the whole world (Gen 2:15; cf. 1:28). Similarly, God's calling of Israel, the descendants of Abraham, is a

---

and through Israel, that of the rest of humanity – as she proved incapable of living faithfully according to its commandments; but it was not given to remedy this situation by forming the one family of God (3:19-20). This would come only through faith, that is, through Christ (3:21-22). Paul likens the law to a παιδαγωγός, someone entrusted with the oversight and development of a child until it matures; but the maturity God seeks is manifested by one Jewish man alone, Jesus Christ (3:24). Christ abolishes the law as παιδαγωγός by his own faithfulness to God (3:25), and, as he represents both Israel and the whole of humanity, all those seeking to be members of God's one family must find their identity in him and not in the law. Thus Paul assures the Galatians that they are already members of God's covenant people and that they do not need to live according to the law because they are already in Christ – just as was promised to Abraham (3:26-29).

demonstration of his faithfulness to those promises made to him. Insofar as God acts to fulfil his promises, we may see this as his providential action.

Importantly, the fact that God remains faithful to Abraham means that even the giving of the law, which itself was not promised, is unable to prevent God from fulfilling his promises. God's providence is therefore his sovereign action within creation insofar as it is his freedom to fulfil his promises for the good of all things in the way that he so chooses. Thus Abraham's calling issued from God's sovereign decision to bless all nations of the earth through one man and his offspring (Gen 12:2-3), even though that man himself had done nothing to merit such attention. Israel, too, as Abraham's descendants, was chosen simply on the basis of God's love for her on account of his faithfulness to his promises (Deut 7:8). Indeed, although the whole world belonged to God, Israel in particular was chosen to serve him as his 'treasured possession', his 'priestly kingdom and ... holy nation' (Ex 19:5-6). However, despite the fact that the law was given to enable Israel to live as his covenant people, Paul's assertion that it 'was added because of transgressions' (Gal 3:19) perhaps suggests that God strongly anticipated its exposure of Israel's sin and thus her incapacity for holiness. The law's exposure of her sin discloses this to be a problem that she herself cannot resolve. God's specific interaction with Israel, therefore, is to overcome her sin and in doing so to remain faithful to the promises made to her father Abraham, that 'in [him] all the families of the earth shall be blessed' (Gen 12:3). Furthermore, God's decision to create Israel (cf. Isa 43:1) and to interact with her in this way is the context for the coming of her messiah, through whom he demonstrates his faithfulness to all creation. Sovereignly, God chooses Israel to be the nation by which he establishes a single family in Christ, comprising both Jews and Gentiles (Gal 3:26-29).

This means, then, that God's providence ultimately is defined by his action in Christ, who, by the Spirit, was faithful to God's law when Israel herself was not. The law was never intended or able to give life (Gal 3:21; cf. 2:21); this could come only through the Israelite whose total faithfulness to the law ensures the transformation of those who participate in his life by the Spirit (Gal 3:26-29; 5:22-25). Consequently, Christ alone was always intended to be the inaugurator of God's covenant people; it was always God's plan for his Son to act in this way on behalf of Israel and, through her, the whole of humanity. Christ's faithful action is therefore the supreme instance of God's own action to remain faithful to his intention to spread his presence across the world through a people in turn faithful to him. As the proper presence of God,[108] Christ is God's providence made flesh, that is, Christ himself is God providentially at work within creation, freeing humanity from the power of sin by his own faithfulness. We see in the coming of Christ a demonstration of God's sovereignty: it was the divine decision as to when 'the fulness of time had come', when God's Son would be 'born of a woman, born under the law, in

---

[108] Barth, *Church Dogmatics*, II/1, 484; cf. § 5.3.

order to redeem those who were under the law' and so herald the entrance of the Gentiles into God's covenant people (Gal 4:4-5).[109] Yet this demonstration is not simply the execution of a divine decision through secondary causation but the expression of God's faithfulness to the world in the human flesh of Christ, an expression implemented in creaturely space and time in order to assure creation of its creator's continual, loving involvement. For Paul, the coming of Christ into the world to act on our behalf is crucial to understanding God's providential dealings with the world. Providence is not, therefore, a matter of untethered divine omnipotence, but of God's sovereign action within creation to remain faithful to his ultimate promise that the world in its entirety will be the place of God's presence – a faithfulness embodied in the obedient action of the man Christ Jesus.

§ 6.6 Conclusion

Paul sought to assure the Galatians that they were part of God's covenant people and that they did not need to prove or guarantee their membership by observing the Mosaic Law; indeed, to do so would be to deny the efficacy of Christ's crucifixion. Crucial to Paul, then, is the faithfulness of Jesus Christ that demonstrates God's sovereign action in the world. The law could only instruct Israel on how to live and so, consequently, expose her sin; but Christ's faithfulness, whereby he 'gave himself for our sins to set us free from the present evil age' (Gal 1:4), was the means by which God freed humanity from the power of sin. By his total adherence to the law of God and its commandments, Christ would experience the trials and temptations that any person might encounter and emerge still with his love for God intact and undiminished. Such sinless devotion would lead him obediently to an ignominious death; yet through that death, God called to himself a people drawn from all nations of the earth.

Our reading of Galatians 3 serves to demonstrate the legitimacy of the conceptual framework of God's presence as the most appropriate foundation and context for the Christian doctrine of providence. Providence is God's sovereign action within creation to remain faithful to his promise that the world in its entirety shall be the place of his presence. The calling of Israel, the gracious provision but temporariness of the law, and the fulfilment of this law in Christ are all crucial examples of God's providence shaped by the conceptual framework of God's presence rather than by that of primary and secondary causation. Behind the divine providential activity that is Christ's death, then, lies the conceptuality apparent within the law's sacrificial system that enabled Israel to maintain her relationship with God in spite of her sin. To appreciate

---

[109] This assumes that the thrust of Paul's argument in Galatians 4:4-7 is that once Christ has liberated the Jews from the law, both Jews and Gentiles may be found in him, by the Spirit, as God's adopted sons.

Christ's faithful action as the supreme instance of God's own action, we must now explore this conceptuality a little further.

CHAPTER 7

Providence and the Faithfulness of Jesus Christ

§ 7.1 Introduction

Providence as we have defined it is God's sovereign action within creation to remain faithful to his promise that the world in its entirety shall be the place of God's presence. Humanity was created to 'fill the earth and subdue it' (Gen 1:28) and placed in the garden of Eden 'to till and keep it' (Gen 2:15). Through Adam's faithful service as priest in the garden-temple,[1] the place of God's presence would no longer be limited to Eden but would cover the whole world. The failure of Adam and Eve to remain faithful was countered by God's calling of a man, Abram, who was characterised by his belief in God's promise that in him 'all the families of the earth shall be blessed' (Gen 12:3; 15:6). To demonstrate fidelity to his promises, God later delivered Abram's descendants from slavery in Egypt and established them as 'a priestly kingdom and a holy nation' (Ex 19:6) – the people of Israel.

Despite her calling, Israel too was unable to remain faithful to God. The law that had been given to distinguish her as God's people and so to mediate his presence to the other nations instead exposed her own sinfulness (Gal 3:19). According to Paul's argument in his letter to the Galatians, the law was always intended to be a temporary institution 'until Christ came' (Gal 3:24). As the law exposed Israel's sin, it also – through Israel – exposed the sin of all humanity and thus humanity's inability to address it and live faithfully in relation to God. With the coming of Jesus Christ, God shows that the fallen condition of creation is transformed only by his own action on its behalf. Christ is the 'one who is righteous' (ὁ δίκαιος) who lives 'from faith' (ἐκ πίστεως; Gal 3:11), representing both Israel as her messiah and, through her, all the other families of the earth. What Christ does in faithfulness to God, he does on behalf of all humanity, Jew and Gentile alike.

This begs the question, however, as to what it is exactly that Christ has done on behalf of all humanity. Paul goes to great lengths to prove to the Galatians that their receipt of the Holy Spirit is the result of Christ's faithful action and not of their own obedience to the Mosaic Law. Clearly Paul affirms that it is the proclamation of Christ crucified that led to their receipt of the Spirit (Gal 3:1-2, 5); but because his main concern is to demonstrate the incorporation of Gentiles

---

[1] G.K. Beale, *The Temple and the Church's Mission: A Biblical Theology of the Dwelling Place of God* (NSBT 17; Leicester: Apollos, 2004), 66–70.

into God's one family, Paul does not discuss in any great depth – if at all – what it means to say that Christ remained faithful to God even at the cost of his own life (cf. Phil 2:8). It is enough for Paul here simply to affirm that Christ was crucified because in doing so he shows why the Galatians' identity is now found in Christ rather than in the law.

Of course, the variety of writings in the New Testament means that we are not expected to bleed every drop of insight from a single letter – even if that letter is written by Paul! Indeed, the decidedly non-Pauline letter to the Hebrews addresses similar concerns as that written to the Galatians.[2] Although relatively little is known about the circumstances for its writing,[3] the letter to the Hebrews was surely sent to a Jewish-Christian congregation tempted for whatever reason to place their hope primarily in the law and so to supplement or even bypass the need for Christ. The author of Hebrews connects Christ's faithfulness with his crucifixion in a way that Paul only implies when writing to the Galatians, and does so by interpreting Christ's death and his now exalted status in the light of the imagery of the sacrifices made on the Day of Atonement (Lev 16). To understand what Hebrews says about Christ's faithfulness, we need first to explore the place of sacrifice – and particularly the ḥaṭṭā't offering – within the Mosaic Law.

§ 7.2 The ḥaṭṭā't Offering: Leviticus 4[4]

From the mountain of Sinai-Horeb (Ex 19:3) to the newly completed tabernacle (Ex 40:34), God promises to be with Israel, his 'treasured [or "special"] possession' (Ex 19:5), and to remain faithful to her. Yet Israel's election 'cannot be viewed apart from obligation';[5] by entering into covenant relationship with God, she is expected to live faithfully in accordance to the terms of the covenant as expressed in the requirements of the law. The law identifies Israel as God's covenant people and so distinguishes her from the other nations (Lev 20:22, 26). Israel is the nation who can say, 'For what other

---

[2] B. Witherington III, 'The Influence of Galatians on Hebrews', *New Testament Studies* 37 (1991), 146–152 (151): 'Could it be that Hebrews provides for us the earliest example of an interpretation of Paul for a later and perhaps different audience? ... It seems likely that [Hebrews] does reflect the influence of Paul and in particular Galatians at various key points in his argument.'

[3] Although his own position is that Hebrews was written to a house church congregation in or around Rome where apostasy was a very real option for its members (W.L. Lane, *Hebrews 1–8* [WBC 47A; Nashville: Thomas Nelson, 1991], liii–liv, lviii, lxii), William Lane concedes that '[a]ll that can be said with certainty is that Hebrews was composed by a creative theologian who was well trained in the exposition of the Greek Scriptures.' (Lane, *Hebrews 1–8*, xlix).

[4] All scriptural references in § 7.2–§ 7.3 are from Leviticus unless indicated otherwise.

[5] H.D. Preuss, *Old Testament Theology, Volume 1*, translated by L.G. Perdue (Edinburgh: T&T Clark, 1995), 92.

great nation has a god so near to it as the LORD our God is whenever we call to him? And what other great nation has statutes and ordinances as just as this entire law that I am setting before you today?' (Deut 4:7-8) At the heart of the law was the notion that God was present amongst his chosen people.[6]

Despite the people's willingness to follow the law (Ex 24:3), they are quick to forget their collective promise and desire other gods – a calf made from gold, it transpires – to replace the absent Moses; with him gone, there is nobody to mediate between them and God (Ex 32:1, 4).[7] In his anger at their unfaithfulness, God is prepared to 'consume' his people and to start afresh with Moses (Ex 32:10), but relents at Moses's intercession (Exodus 32:11-14). Nonetheless, there are consequences (Ex 32:20, 27-35); and although God remains faithful to the promises he made to Abraham, Isaac and Jacob, he threatens not to go with Israel as she heads towards the promised land, intending instead to send an angel (Ex 33:1-3). Covenant unfaithfulness is a very serious matter that God does not take lightly in view of his own covenant faithfulness. Yet Moses points out that if God's presence does not accompany them, then the Israelites are in no way distinct from the nations they are about to face (Ex 33:15-16) – and so the covenant is renewed (Ex 34:9-10, 27). It is clear, however, that, on the basis of the incident with the golden calf, that Israel is unruly, a 'stiff-necked' people (Ex 32:9) and liable to violate the covenant repeatedly through unfaithfulness.

Israel's unfaithfulness leads, then, to the establishment of the sacrificial system. After filling the newly constructed tabernacle with his glory (Ex 40:34), God calls Moses into his presence (Lev 1:1) and instructs him on how Israel should make sacrifices and offerings. Broadly speaking, there are five main types[8] that could be combined in any one ritual (see, for example, Numbers 6:16-17).[9] First mentioned is the burnt or whole offering (*'ôlâ*; Lev 1:3-17), arguably the most important and versatile sacrifice offered to secure divine favour – however that might be understood in practice.[10] Following this comes the cereal or grain offering (*minḥâ*; 2:1-16), given in thanksgiving and,

---

[6] P.T. Vogt, *Deuteronomic Theology and the Significance of Torah: A Reappraisal* (Winona Lake, Indiana: Eisenbrauns, 2006), 129; cf. § 6.2.

[7] J.I. Durham, *Exodus* (WBC 3; Nashville: Thomas Nelson, 1987), 419.

[8] Cf. R.E. Averbeck, 'Sacrifices and Offerings', in *Dictionary of the Old Testament: Pentateuch* (Leicester: IVP, 2003), 706–733 (706).

[9] P.P. Jenson, *Graded Holiness: A Key to the Priestly Conception of the World* (JSOTS 106; Sheffield: Sheffield Academic Press, 1992), 155.

[10] E.S. Gerstenberger, *Leviticus: A Commentary*, translated by D.W. Stott (OTL; Louisville: Westminster John Knox Press, 1996), 27; J. Milgrom, *Leviticus 1–16: A New Translation with Introduction and Commentary* (ABC 3; New York: Doubleday, 1991), 175–176; R.K. Harrison, *Leviticus: An Introduction and Commentary* (TOTC; Leicester: IVP, 1980), 38; P.P. Jenson, 'The Levitical Sacrificial System', in R.T. Beckwith and M.J. Selman (eds.), *Sacrifice in the Bible* (Carlisle: Paternoster Press, 1995), 25–40 (28).

again, acts as a way of securing divine good will;[11] the peace or well-being offering ($š^elāmîm$; 3:1-17), a sacrifice that provides meat for celebratory feasts;[12] the sin or purification offering ($ḥaṭṭā't$; 4:1-5:13) that cleanses from sin and defilement;[13] and, finally, the guilt or reparation offering ($'āšām$; 5:14-6:7), with its distinctive feature of financial compensation (5:14-26).[14] The sacrificial system thus facilitates Israel's celebration both of her relationship with God and of the Israelites' relationships with one another, whilst also functioning as the gracious provision of God for the resolution of the inevitable estrangement between the various parties.[15]

Of particular interest to us is the $ḥaṭṭā't$ or purification offering, made whenever somebody does unintentionally that which God has forbidden (4:2). A purification offering requires the one who sins – or in the case of the whole congregation of Israel, her elders – to place a hand on the head of the animal to be sacrificed: a bull without blemish for the anointed priest (4:3-4) and for all Israel (4:13-15), a male goat for a 'ruler' (4:22-24) and a female goat or ewe for any of the 'ordinary people' (4:27-29, 32-33). The animal is then 'slaughtered before the LORD' (4:4, 15, 24; cf. 29, 33). When making a sacrifice for his own sin or for that of the whole congregation of Israel, the priest takes some of the blood into the tent of meeting and sprinkles it seven times 'before the LORD in front of the curtain of the sanctuary' (4:5-6, 16-17);[16] otherwise, in each performance, the priest daubs the horns of the altar with blood and then pours away the remainder at the foot of the altar (4:7, 18, 25, 30, 34). Once the blood rituals have been completed, the priest then removes all the fat from the slaughtered animal and burns it (4:8-10, 19, 26, 31, 35). In the case of the

---

[11] Gerstenberger, *Leviticus*, 41–42; Milgrom, *Leviticus 1–16*, 195–196; Harrison, *Leviticus*, 38; J.E. Hartley, *Leviticus* (WBC 4; Dallas: Word Books, 1992), 29. Jacob Milgrom suggests that 'the cereal offering must be viewed as a discrete, independent sacrifice that functions to duplicate the manifold purposes of the burnt offering for the benefit of those who cannot afford a burnt offering of quadruped or bird.' (Milgrom, *Leviticus 1–16*, 196).

[12] Gerstenberger, *Leviticus*, 46; Milgrom, *Leviticus 1–16*, 221; Harrison, *Leviticus*, 38; Hartley, *Leviticus*, 38; Jenson, 'The Levitical Sacrificial System', 30–31.

[13] Milgrom, *Leviticus 1–16*, 253–254; Harrison, *Leviticus*, 38; Hartley, *Leviticus*, 55; Jenson, 'The Levitical Sacrificial System', 29.

[14] Milgrom, *Leviticus 1–16*, 339, 345; Harrison, *Leviticus*, 38; Hartley, *Leviticus*, 76–77; Jenson, 'The Levitical Sacrificial System', 30.

[15] D. Tidball, *The Message of the Cross: Wisdom Unsearchable, Love Indestructible* (BST; Leicester: IVP, 2001), 75.

[16] 'The rituals for the anointed priest and for the community are identical, and demonstrate [a] principle of hierarchy and representation ... The defilement of the anointed priest is so serious because he is the religious head of the community and represents the people ... The sin of the congregation requires the same high degree of purification.' (Jenson, *Graded Holiness*, 173; cf. Jenson, 'The Levitical Sacrificial System', 32).

sacrifices made for the priest (4:3-12) and the whole congregation (4:13-21), the rest of the corpse is disposed outside the camp and burnt (4:11-12, 21). For all Israel, the 'ruler' and the 'ordinary people', it is said that by following these procedures, 'the priest shall make atonement [wĕkipper] for them' (4:20b) or 'on his' (4:26b) or 'on your behalf' (4:31b, 35b), atonement that enables God to forgive them (4:20c, 26c, 31c, 35c).[17]

By these procedures, the priest atones (kippēr); but they do not reveal explicitly the theology underlying the sacrificial system, nor do they say what is meant by the verb kippēr ('to atone'). Indeed, it is commonplace to note that the Levitical texts simply assume the efficacy of sacrificial rituals and set out procedures for them without commenting on how they are efficacious.[18] Appeal to the word kippēr itself, then, is likely to yield 'no more than the exact meaning of "breaking bread" reveals about the Christian Eucharist.'[19] We must instead try to discern the logic of sacrifice as presented by the Levitical texts if we are to offer an interpretation of what it means to 'make atonement' (kippēr). Evidently, the ḥaṭṭā't offering enables God's forgiveness to be extended to the sinner upon recognition of the sin committed (4:14, 23, 28), but it is unclear as to whether it does this by appeasing God or removing sin, by propitiation or by expiation, as, pending its context, kippēr may be understood either way.[20]

Do sacrifices propitiate God? The question surely insinuates that God's relationship with the world is fundamentally negative, as the sacrificial system must, on this understanding, be given to Israel as the means of averting divine anger at her sin. Yet because God himself provides Israel with this means, it is also implied that God wants his wrath to be tempered. Thus in Christian tradition, the doctrine of penal substitution – that is, the view that 'Christ has borne the wrath of God upon the cross, being punished by the Father in place of sinful human beings'[21] – accepts both principles. As David Peterson acknowledges, 'the cross proceeds from God's grace and does not "make God gracious"' – salvation is indeed a divine initiative, motivated by love for fallen creation; yet, Peterson continues, 'God is wrathful against sinners' and 'his wrath somehow needs to be appeased and averted', even if 'God in his love

---

[17] Milgrom, Leviticus 1–16, 245.
[18] G.J. Wenham, 'The Theology of Old Testament Sacrifice', in R.T. Beckwith and M.J. Selman (eds.), *Sacrifice in the Bible* (Carlisle: Paternoster Press, 1995), 75–87 (77); H.D. Preuss, *Old Testament Theology, Volume 2*, translated by L.G. Perdue (Edinburgh: T&T Clark, 1996), 238; N. Kiuchi, *The Purification Offering in the Priestly Literature: Its Meaning and Function* (JSOTS 56; Sheffield: Sheffield Academic Press, 1987), 17–18.
[19] M. Barker, 'Atonement: The Rite of Healing', in *The Great High Priest: The Temple Roots of Christian Liturgy* (London: T&T Clark, 2003), 42–55 (43).
[20] Hartley, *Leviticus*, 64.
[21] N. Wright, *The Radical Evangelical: Seeking a Place to Stand* (London: SPCK, 1996), 59.

provides the way by which his own wrath is both expressed and satisfied'.[22] Here there is potentially a serious problem. Although this view of atonement – that the Father's wrath needs to be appeased by judging sin but that the Son takes this judgement upon himself so that those who should receive it do not – sounds gracious, it constantly risks 'presenting a loving Son appeasing a wrathful and angry Father.'[23] We cannot deny that God manifests wrath towards sinners – and in this respect, the theology of penal substitutionary atonement cannot be faulted; but its emphasis on this point certainly implies that God's wrath somehow is equal to his love, that somehow they compete against each other to determine the true nature of God. However, '[t]he wrath of God is fleeting in comparison with his love and the two are not to be seen as equally balanced attributes. God *is* love and it would be entirely wrong to claim that he *is* wrath.'[24] To suggest that the two *are* in competition is to 'end up with an arbitrary or even schizophrenic God in whom good and evil have positions of equal significance.'[25] Scripture indeed portrays God as displaying wrath, but this is because 'God's love requires that he become angry when his love is violated. For God not to get angry when he is rejected ... would demonstrate indifference, not love.'[26]

If wrath is not constitutive of God's character, then, it would be surprising if the sacrificial system was given to Israel solely to avert that wrath. This is perhaps too restricted a role for the system and does not seem to account for the fact that other sacrifices are offered in thanksgiving or celebration. Furthermore, the declarations 'be forgiven' (4:20c, 26c, 31c, 35c) or 'be clean' in other passages (12:8; 14:18-20, 53; 16:30) after atonement is made suggests a close link between the state of forgiveness and the state of being ritually clean.[27] So although the *ḥaṭṭā't* offering (4:1-5:13) atones for sin and enables forgiveness to be declared, we must further recognise that the verb *kippēr* is

---

[22] D. Peterson, 'Atonement in the New Testament', in D. Peterson (ed.), *Where Wrath and Mercy Meet: Proclaiming the Atonement Today* (Carlisle: Paternoster, 2001), 26–67 (44)

[23] Wright, *The Radical Evangelical*, 59. Furthermore, this presentation 'is not the intention of the New Testament which clearly asserts the origin of the cross in the love of the Father. Neither has it been the intention of the best proponents of the doctrine. But the caricature lies close to hand.' (Wright, *The Radical Evangelical*, 59).

[24] Wright, *The Radical Evangelical*, 65, emphasis original; cf. J.B. Green and M.D. Baker, *Recovering the Scandal of the Cross: Atonement in New Testament and Contemporary Contexts* (Downers Grove: IVP, 2000), 54–55.

[25] H. Boersma, *Violence, Hospitality, and the Cross: Reappropriating the Atonement Tradition* (Grand Rapids: Baker Academic, 2004), 48.

[26] Boersma, *Violence, Hospitality, and the Cross*, 49.

[27] The *ḥaṭṭā't* offering could be made both for an impure person, with that person declared 'clean', and for the person who sins inadvertently, who is 'forgiven'. (Milgrom, *Leviticus 1–16*, 256).

found in contexts of both moral wrongdoing and cultic or ritual impurity.[28] When the priest makes atonement, he pronounces either forgiveness or ritual purity as the situation warrants.[29] Accordingly, we may suggest that whilst *kippēr* can at times *connote* propitiation, it does not *entail* propitiation or *require* atonement to be understood *solely as* or *equal to* propitiation. Atonement deals with sin fundamentally *by purifying* that which has been defiled by sin.

The proper context for understanding the sacrificial system, then, is not as a means to avert God's anger – though that is not entirely foreign to the system – but as a way to maintain the divine presence in Israel's midst. Throughout Leviticus, God is shown primarily not as wrathful but as holy and whose holiness characterises all that he is and does and says (see, for example, 11:44-45; 19:2; 20:3, 8, 26; 22:32). It is in God's holy presence that Moses receives the instructions for making sacrifices and it is entirely apposite, therefore, to understand the sacrificial system within this context of divine holiness,[30] as a response to Israel's sin, her covenant unfaithfulness, which stains that which should be holy. Yet the *ḥaṭṭā't* offering is made not to purify Israel as such but the tabernacle or sanctuary in which God lives (though the blood of the *ḥaṭṭā't* offering goes no further than the curtain separating the holy of holies from the holy place). As the holy God declares Israel to be holy, he is able to live within her midst; but as she defiles herself through covenant unfaithfulness, so her sin spreads to pollute his residence. Impurity was considered demonic by Israel's neighbours; but her view that sinful humans were capable of the demonic shows that the issue of (im)purity was no less important and a person's sin could easily 'contaminate the sanctuary and force God out.'[31] According to Jacob Milgrom, 'both Israel and her neighbours [considered that] impurity was a physical substance, an aerial miasma that possessed magnetic attraction for the realm of the sacred.'[32] He argues that the blood of the *ḥaṭṭā't* offering acts as a 'ritual detergent' that decontaminates the sanctuary:[33]

> If not the offerer, what then is the object of the *ḥaṭṭā't* purgation? [It is] that which receives the purgative blood: the sanctuary and its sancta. By daubing the altar with the *ḥaṭṭā't* blood or by bringing it inside the sanctuary (e.g., 16:14-19), the priest purges the most sacred objects and areas of the sanctuary on behalf of the

---

[28] For a discussion of the semantic range of *kippēr*, see Milgrom, *Leviticus 1–16*, 1079–1084; cf. J. Sklar, *Sin, Impurity, Sacrifice, Atonement: The Priestly Conceptions* (HBM 2; Sheffield: Sheffield Phoenix Press, 2005), 44–79.
[29] Sklar, *Sin, Impurity, Sacrifice, Atonement*, 1, 159.
[30] Cf. J. Goldingay, 'Your Iniquities Have Made a Separation Between You and Your God', in J. Goldingay (ed.), *Atonement Today* (London: SPCK, 1995), 39–53 (51).
[31] Milgrom, *Leviticus 1–16*, 256, 260; quote from 260.
[32] Milgrom, *Leviticus 1–16*, 257.
[33] Milgrom, *Leviticus 1–16*, 254–255; quote from 254.

person who caused their contamination by his physical impurity or inadvertent offence.[34]

We should emphasise that it is human sin that pollutes God's holy things: Israel's covenant unfaithfulness, both corporate and individual, illegitimately enters the sacred space of God's dwelling and threatens to erect an idol in that place. The effect of the *ḥaṭṭā't* offering, then, is to purge that which has become polluted by Israel's sin and so to ensure the continuation of God's presence amongst his people. By making atonement, the people are indeed forgiven but on the basis that God is pleased to remain with them: just as the people's sin contaminates holy things, so the continued presence of the holy God in their midst is evidence that the people are forgiven. Such an understanding demonstrates God's own covenant faithfulness to Israel, because through the *ḥaṭṭā't* rituals he provides them with the way of perpetuating his presence; and the provision of the *ḥaṭṭā't* offering also reminds Israel that though she is sinful, she is called nonetheless to be holy like her God and needs continually to remember and live out her calling.

Granted, this is an unconventional interpretation of how sacrifices atone. Derek Tidball believes that Milgrom's interpretation of *ḥaṭṭā't* as a purification offering, which focuses exclusively, it seems, on the blood manipulation, 'is not wholly adequate' as it 'gives little consideration to other aspects' such as 'the laying on of hands, the killing of the victim, the burning of select parts of it and the subsequent removal of its body outside the camp'.[35] Tidball is right to draw attention to these, particularly the hand-laying aspect, but in doing so detracts from the implication that the sacrifice is efficacious *because of* the blood manipulation. The burning of the slaughtered animal, 'the only ritual element common to *all* five types of sacrifice',[36] does play an important role, but mostly insofar as it produces a 'pleasing aroma' (1:9b; 4:31). 'Transformed by the fire of the altar, the material offering given by a human individual or community is "transported" to heaven in the ascending smoke'[37] and 'conveys the idea that God smells the odour of the sacrifice and thus receives it.'[38] Once the *ḥaṭṭā't* blood has been applied, the incineration of the animal signifies the end of the sacrifice and welcomes the pronouncement of God's forgiveness in response to the smell.[39] It is not a 'pleasing aroma' because God's wrath has been

---

[34] Milgrom, *Leviticus 1–16*, 256, emphasis original.

[35] D. Tidball, *The Message of Leviticus: Free to Be Holy* (BST; Leicester: IVP, 2005), 80.

[36] C.A. Eberhart, 'Characteristics of Sacrificial Metaphors in Hebrews', in G. Gelardini (ed.), *Hebrews: Contemporary Methods – New Insights* (BIS 75; Leiden: Brill, 2005), 46, emphasis original.

[37] Eberhart, 'Characteristics of Sacrificial Metaphors in Hebrews', 47.

[38] Eberhart, 'Characteristics of Sacrificial Metaphors in Hebrews', 46.

[39] By 'in response to the smell', I should emphasise that this is a sequential response – that is, God declares the sinner forgiven when *temporally* he smells the 'pleasing

propitiated but because atonement has been effected, the impurity of sin dissolved and God is pleased to remain with his people.

§ 7.3 The Day of Atonement: Leviticus 16

Although the *ḥaṭṭā't* offerings are made to preserve God's presence and to cleanse people from inadvertent sins, the *ḥaṭṭā't* blood does not penetrate the holy of holies itself – the specific area in which God dwells – until the Day of Atonement arrives, when the high priest enters and sprinkles blood on the atonement slate (*kappōret*).[40] The Day of Atonement features a variation on the *ḥaṭṭā't* offering and the so-called scapegoat ritual:[41] through the *ḥaṭṭā't* offering, the holy of holies is decontaminated from Israel's sin; but through the scapegoat ritual, Israel's sin is removed and taken to the wilderness, the place of chaos where it belongs.[42]

On the tenth day of Tishri, the seventh month, the Israelites are to recognise the severity of their sin and the solemnity of the Day of Atonement by '"afflicting" themselves, perhaps by fasting or other forms of self-discipline' (22:27-30).[43] Although the Day of Atonement revolves around the action of the high priest, it does so because the high priest represents the whole congregation of Israel. Certainly, the ephod and breastplate worn by the high priest indicates

---

odour' – and not a conditional response, that is, God refuses to impart forgiveness *unless* he smells the burning sacrifice. The distinction is subtle but important.

[40] Here we follow John Hartley's translation of *kappōret* as 'atonement slate' rather than the more traditional 'mercy-seat'. Derived from *kippēr*, the *kappōret* is 'the place where the people of the covenant maintained fellowship with their God by means of the expiating blood rites performed here on the Day of Atonement.' (Hartley, *Leviticus*, 235). In the Septuagint, ἱλαστήριον translates *kappōret* and is used also in Romans 3:25 to portray Christ as the 'place of atonement': 'Jesus is the [*kappōret*] of the new temple, and by the blood of his death he fulfils [the Day of Atonement], far surpassing it in finality and scope.' (D.G. Reid, 'Sacrifice and Temple Service', in *Dictionary of New Testament Background* [Leicester: IVP, 2000], 1036–1050 [1043]; cf. J.M. Gundry-Volf, 'Expiation, Propitiation, Mercy Seat', in *Dictionary of Paul and his Letters* [Leicester: IVP, 1993], 279–284 [283]; S.J. Gathercole, 'Justified by Faith, Justified by his Blood: The Evidence of Romans 3:21–4:25', in D.A. Carson, P.T. O'Brien and M.A. Seifrid [eds.], *Justification and Variegated Nomism, Volume 2: The Paradoxes of Paul* [Grand Rapids: Baker Academic, 2004], 147–184 [168]; D.A. Carson, 'Atonement in Romans 3:21-26', in C.E. Hill and F.A. James III [eds.], *The Glory of the Atonement: Biblical, Historical and Practical Perspectives. Essays in Honour of Roger Nicole* [Downers Grove: IVP, 2004], 119–139 [129]). The implication, of course, is that the New Testament writings interpret Christ's death in cultic terms.

[41] Jenson, 'The Levitical Sacrificial System', 33–34.

[42] Cf. D. Rudman, 'A Note on the Azazel-goat Ritual', *Zeitschrift für die Alttestamentliche Wissenschaft* 116 (2004), 396–401 (400).

[43] Harrison, *Leviticus*, 219.

that whatever he did, he did on behalf of the people, representing them to God (Ex 28:12, 29); even now, in simple apparel (Lev 16:4), he continues to exercise his duties for their sake.[44] Without his action on their behalf, the people will pollute God's dwelling place to such an extent that he will be forced to abandon it and therefore Israel, too. The Day of Atonement, then, is the ultimate decontamination of Israel's tabernacle because its purgation also reaches into the holy of holies.

Although the high priest – here, Aaron – is to enter the holy of holies, he can do so only at God's invitation (16:2). He passes into a realm that no human can ever enter by his or her own volition and he does so simply because he has been invited there in order to make atonement on behalf of the people that he represents. Aaron is to bathe (16:3; cf. Ex 30:20) and then dress appropriately in the holy linen garments (Lev 16:3; cf. Ex 28:39, 42). Once he is clean, he is to slaughter a bull as a *ḥaṭṭā't* offering for himself and his household (Lev 16:3, 6); although the text does not specify it, the 'many elements of the [*ḥaṭṭā't*] ritual not specified here may be assumed to be the same as those in the [earlier] regulation[s]' (4:3-12).[45] Thus Aaron sprinkles blood seven times before the curtain of the sanctuary (4:6), daubs blood on the horns of the altar and pours the remainder of the blood away (4:7) – though presumably he also keeps some blood to take with him into the holy of holies (16:14), which the usual *ḥaṭṭā't* offering does not stipulate. The 'coals of fire' and 'two handfuls of crushed sweet incense' are taken into the holy of holies to shield the high priest from the atonement slate, from where God speaks but cannot be seen (16:12-13; cf. Ex 25:21-22; 33:20). With some of the blood now taken beyond the curtain into

---

[44] James Torrance implies that the high priest also wore the ephod and breastplate on the Day of Atonement (J.B. Torrance, 'The Vicarious Humanity of Christ', in T.F. Torrance [ed.], *The Incarnation: Ecumenical Studies in the Nicene–Constantinopolitan Creed A.D. 381* [Edinburgh: Handsel Press, 1981], 127–147 [138]), even though Leviticus 16 itself makes no mention of these and actually depicts the high priest as making atonement in comparatively plain garments (16:4). The absence of the ephod and breastplate here does not mean that the high priest ceases to represent the people on this day; rather, the symbolism suggests not only that he represents his people as high priest but that his simple clothing also demonstrates his affinity with the people of Israel. (Cf. Jenson, *Graded Holiness*, 200). Torrance is certainly correct to say that the high priest 'stood before the people as their divinely appointed representative, bone of their bone, flesh of their flesh, their brother, in solidarity with the people he represented' (Torrance, 'The Vicarious Humanity of Christ', 138), even if the reason for its correctness is slightly different from what he claims. An alternative to both these readings is Margaret Barker's suggestion that the 'vested high priest in the temple was the Glory of the LORD veiled in matter.' (M. Barker, *Temple Theology: An Introduction* [London: SPCK, 2004], 30).

[45] Hartley, *Leviticus*, 239.

the holy of holies, that is, into heaven and the very presence of God himself,[46] Aaron sprinkles the front of the atonement slate seven times and a further seven times before it (Lev 16:14).

Aaron is also to take from the congregation of Israel two male goats as a single *ḥaṭṭā't* offering[47] and a ram for a burnt offering (16:5). Placing the goats at the entrance to the tent of meeting (16:7), he casts lots to determine which goat is 'for the LORD' and which goat is 'for Azazel' (16:8).[48] The goat 'for the LORD' is a traditional *ḥaṭṭā't* offering (16:9; cf. 4:13-21), though, like the *ḥaṭṭā't* offering for the high priest and his household, some of the blood is also taken beyond the curtain into the holy of holies. This blood, 'given' to make atonement (17:11), is necessary to cleanse the holy of holies from the stains caused by his sin and that of the people; the blood manipulation of the high priest purifies that which has been infected and grants life to that which Israel's sin has denied. Through his obedient action, the high priest recognises the importance of maintaining the presence of God in Israel's midst: without that presence, Israel no longer has anything to mediate to her neighbours, thus rendering her indistinct. By making atonement, the high priest purifies the place of God's presence and announces Israel's desire that he should stay. Thus in sprinkling blood upon and before the atonement slate (16:15-16), Aaron 'shall make atonement for the sanctuary, because of the uncleannesses of the people of Israel, and because of their transgressions, all their sins' (16:6). Once Aaron has atoned for his own sin, the sin of his household and that of all Israel, he applies blood from both the bull and the slaughtered goat to the horns of the altar[49] to cleanse it from Israel's uncleannesses (16:18-19).

---

[46] The tabernacle was built to mirror creation and the holy of holies represented heaven itself; see § 5.2.

[47] Kiuchi, *The Purification Offering in the Priestly Literature*, 148.

[48] It is thought that Azazel was the name of a demon that lived in the wilderness where the goat was sent (Milgrom, *Leviticus 1–16*, 1021; Hartley, *Leviticus*, 238); but the goat 'for Azazel' was in no way a sacrifice to be offered to this demon in parallel to the goat 'for the LORD' (Tidball, *The Message of Leviticus*, 191). Notwithstanding the absence of any priestly slaughtering and blood manipulation, the mere fact that it was carrying Israel's sins made the goat unclean and so precluded its use as a sacrifice; instead, as Hartley comments, 'this rite means that the sins carried by the goat were returned to this demon for the purpose of removing them from the community and leaving them at their source in order that their power or effect in the community might be completely broken.' (Hartley, *Leviticus*, 238).

[49] This must be a second application of blood to the horns of the altar in each instance. The first occurs before the high priest enters the holy of holies to atone for his own sin and that of his household, and then on behalf of the people. Effectively, there are two 'dual-action' blood rituals: before entry into and upon leaving the holy of holies.

Once he has finished atoning for the sacred spaces (16:20),[50] Aaron places 'both his hands on the head of the live goat, and confess[es] over it all the iniquities of the people of Israel, and all their transgressions, all their sins, putting them on the head of the goat, and sending it away into the wilderness' (16:21). Typically, the hand-laying element in the *ḥaṭṭā't* offerings (4:4, 15, 24, 29, 33) signifies that the animal for sacrifice truly belongs to the person offering it and so, by this declaration of ownership, is to act for and in that person's place; there is little point in the blood of the animal being used to purify the sacred things if the person who has contributed to their contamination has not admitted responsibility for that act through this rite.[51] On the Day of Atonement, the high priest lays both his hands on the live goat, perhaps encompassing both the sins of the priestly household of which he himself is a part and the sins of the congregation of Israel.[52] By transferring all the iniquities, transgressions and sins of Israel to the goat,[53] the high priest rids his own person of those sins – with the implication, of course, that he himself had borne all the sin of Israel, however temporarily[54] – to the appointed vehicle for its despatch to the wilderness (16:22) and away from Israel and, therefore, away from the place of God's presence. In the person of the high priest, God hears the repentance of all the people and forgives them accordingly.

To complete the ritual, Aaron removes his priestly garments, bathes and re-dresses before slaughtering the two rams (16:3, 5, 23-24) as burnt offerings and disposing with the bodies of the *ḥaṭṭā't* offerings (16:25, 27), presumably all with the concomitant 'pleasing aroma' that signifies God's acceptance of the

---

[50] Although Leviticus 16:20 focuses on the atoning of sacred spaces, it remains that the *ḥaṭṭā't* offerings are said also to make atonement for people (4:20b, 26b, 31b, 35b; 16:33b). I have already suggested that people are forgiven on the basis that the decontamination of the tabernacle enables God's continued presence in their midst.

[51] Cf. Harrison, *Leviticus*, 45; Averbeck, 'Sacrifices and Offerings', 709; Wenham, 'The Theology of Old Testament Sacrifice', 79–80. For a range of views on the meaning of the hand-laying rite, see Milgrom, *Leviticus 1–16*, 151–153.

[52] This would correspond to the Day of Atonement's *ḥaṭṭā't* offering of a bull for the priests and a goat for the people.

[53] 'These three terms together encompass all dimensions of humans' breaking of God's law. Futhermore, all these terms are in the plural, indicative of the frequency and the totality of humans' sinning.' (Hartley, *Leviticus*, 241).

[54] Kiuchi, *The Purification Offering in the Priestly Literature*, 148: 'By purifying sancta from uncleanness Aaron bears the guilt of the Israelites. Then the guilt he has borne is devolved upon the Azazel goat when Aaron lays his hands on it and confesses the sins.' See also Margaret Barker, *Temple Theology*, 63: 'When he emerged from the temple, the high priest placed both his hands on the head of the scapegoat and thereby put all the sins onto the goat. The logic of the ritual requires that the high priest was himself carrying all the sins of Israel at that point. He was the sin bearer.'

sacrifices (cf. 1:9; 4:31).[55] Finally, God instructs Moses that the Day of Atonement rituals are now 'an everlasting statute for you, to make atonement for the people of Israel once in the year for all their sins' (16:34).

We see, then, that atonement is achieved because the high priest accepts his responsibilities as high priest and carries them out faithfully according to the law's directives. He represents the people of Israel to God in his person and performs the Day of Atonement rituals on their behalf to uphold the covenant and so to maintain God's presence amongst them. It is through his obedient action that Israel has access to God. This means that atonement fundamentally is made not to appease God but to enable this access through purifying those things that have become desecrated through Israel's sin. Blood cleanses the tabernacle from the stain of sin and in doing so enables Israel in the person of her high priest to enter into God's presence. By making atonement, the high priest clears space for Israel to fulfil her own calling in freedom, unburdened by sin, as God's 'priestly kingdom and a holy nation' (Ex 19:6).

§ 7.4 Jesus, Our High Priest: Hebrews 1–7[56]

These themes are taken up by the author of the letter to the Hebrews. The conceptual framework of the letter is that of the Jewish cult with its distinction between the profane and the holy, and its overarching aim is to stress the unrestricted access to God that people now have through Jesus, the 'great high priest' (Heb 4:14), whose faithful response to God forged that path.[57] It does this through a series of contrasts, each time presenting Jesus as somehow superior to that which preceded him. Thus, although '[l]ong ago God spoke to our ancestors in many and various ways by the prophets, ... in these last days he has spoken to us by a Son' (1:1-2). He is superior to angels (1:4), to Moses (3:5-6), even to the mysterious prophet Melchizedek, who, though he blessed Abraham (7:6), can only resemble the Son of God (ἀφωμοιωμένος δὲ τῷ τοῦ υἱῷ τοῦ θεοῦ; 7:3). Indeed, it is the fact that Jesus is faithful to God as a Son (3:6) that he surpasses all that came before. Jesus is simply 'the mediator of a better covenant' (κρείττονός ἐστιν διαθήκης μεσίτης; 8:6), and Hebrews seeks 'to move his readers away from an understanding of the sacrificial system as an essential part of maintaining contact with God, to an acceptance of the

---

[55] We should acknowledge that although the high priest enters the holy of holies alone, other persons involved in the drama of the day are mentioned: the person designated to set the goat free in the wilderness (Lev 16:21) and the one who takes the carcasses of the ḥaṭṭā't offerings outside the camp for burning (16:27-28). Both persons (assuming it is not one person performing two tasks) are required to bathe before re-entering the camp (16:26, 28).

[56] All scriptural references in § 7.4–§ 7.5 are from Hebrews unless indicated otherwise.

[57] Cf. M.E. Isaacs, *Sacred Space: An Approach to the Theology of the Epistle to the Hebrews* (JSNTS 73; Sheffield: Sheffield Academic Press, 1992), 61.

death and ascension of Christ as its replacement.'[58] In doing so, he builds upon the imagery of the Day of Atonement,[59] first affirming its prior efficacy before transforming it entirely.[60]

The opening verses of Hebrews certainly seem to suggest that the reason for the Son's superiority is due to his being the one 'through whom [God] created the worlds' (δι' οὗ καὶ ἐποίησεν τοὺς αἰῶνας; 1:2c), 'the radiance of God's glory and the exact imprint of God's very being' who 'sustains all things by his powerful word' (ὃς ὢν ἀπαύγασμα τῆς δόξης καὶ χαρακτὴρ τῆς ὑποστάσεως αὐτοῦ, φέρων τε τὰ πάντα τῷ ῥήματι τῆς δυνάμεως αὐτοῦ; 1:3a-c).[61] It is most likely that Hebrews's description of the Son as 'the radiance of God's glory' (1:3a) alludes to certain Jewish traditions to associate God's creative wisdom with the Son's own creative action (Prov 8:22-31; Wis 7:26);[62] yet we cannot avoid the suggestion that Hebrews is speaking of a *human who has been exalted* and now sits 'at the right hand of the Majesty on high' because he has made 'purification for sins' (καθαρισμὸν τῶν ἁμαρτιῶν ποιησάμενος ἐκάθισεν ἐν δεξιᾷ τῆς μεγαλωσύνης ἐν ὑψηλοῖς; Heb 1:3d-e). G.B. Caird argues that the earliest disciples would have encountered Jesus first as a man with no thought lodged in their minds that he was anything more than that; only after his crucifixion and resurrection would they have begun to wrestle with the implication that he was God's agent, the man with God's authority to act as God in the world.[63] Caird continues,

> The Epistle [to the Hebrews] does *not* begin with a reference to the eternal Son; it begins with a contrast between what God has said in the past through the prophets and what He has now, in these last days, said through Jesus. Here, as in Paul, 'the Son' is a title for the human Jesus.[64]

---

[58] Isaacs, *Sacred Space*, 92.
[59] Isaacs, *Sacred Space*, 65.
[60] Isaacs, *Sacred Space*, 92.
[61] Commentators echo this sentiment; see, for example, some commonplace observations in H.W. Montefiore, *A Commentary on the Epistle to the Hebrews* (BNTC; London: A&C Black, 1964), 35; F.F. Bruce, *The Epistle to the Hebrews*, rev. ed. (NICNT; Grand Rapids: Eerdmans, 1990), 46–50; D. Guthrie, *The Letter to the Hebrews: An Introduction and Commentary* (TNTC 15; Leicester: IVP, 1983), 67; R.P. Gordon, *Hebrews* (RANBC; Sheffield: Sheffield Academic Press, 2000), 39; S.J. Kistemaker, *Exposition of the Epistle to the Hebrews* (NTC; Grand Rapids: Baker Book House, 1984), 30; Lane, *Hebrews 1–8*, 14.
[62] Gordon, *Hebrews*, 39; Lane, *Hebrews 1–8*, cxxxix.
[63] G.B. Caird, *New Testament Theology*, completed and edited by L.D. Hurst (Oxford: Oxford University Press, 1995), 280, 303; cf. R.A. Harrisville, *The Concept of Newness in the New Testament* (Minneapolis: Augsburg Publishing House, 1960), 51.
[64] Caird, *New Testament Theology*, 320, emphasis original.

Elsewhere, Caird comments,

> Christ was "appointed heir to the whole universe" (1:2). Yet this rank is his, not in virtue of some precosmic divine existence, but as the pioneer of man's salvation, destined to lead God's many sons to glory. He has indeed his part in creation and providence, but as the goal to which the whole process is directed.[65]

Caird perhaps overstates his case. It is hard to read the opening verses of Hebrews without thinking of the Son as the pre-existent agent of the act of creation.[66] However, the overall point is sound: Hebrews is concerned to show that 'in these last days [God] has spoken to us by a Son' (1:2a), that is, the man Jesus (2:9), and that it is this man who has been 'appointed heir of all things' because he has 'made purification for sins' (1:3d) and now sits at God's right hand interceding for those who follow him into God's presence (1:3e; 7:24-25; 8:1-2). This means that we risk minimising the Son's role in the act of creation if we abstract from it his priestly work of purification and intercession that sustains creation in the cultic framework Hebrews adopts. The Son sustains all things (1:3c) not just because he is 'the radiance of God's glory and the exact imprint of God's very being' (1:3a-b) but also because he is the one who 'made purification for sins [and] sat down at the right hand of the Majesty on high' (1:3d-e). As Israel's high priest would enter the holy of holies with the blood of the ḥaṭṭā't offerings to make atonement for her, so Jesus the high priest acts similarly to purify the garden-temple of the world in which God desires to live by his Spirit.

Fundamentally, the Son is able to save those who approach God through him (7:25) because he himself is like them. He shares their flesh and blood (2:14, 17) and is able to sympathise with their weaknesses with regard to remaining faithful to God because he too was required to exercise such faithfulness (4:15).[67] The crucial difference between Jesus and any other person was that he alone was called to be 'the pioneer of their salvation' (2:10) and so required to obey God in this particular way. As the high priest was appointed by God to make atonement for Israel's sins by representing her before God in the holy of holies, so too does Jesus act on behalf and in place of the people. Jesus has been invited into the sacred space that no other person is called to penetrate; it is in this sense that he is a pioneer, leading the way for others eventually to follow.

---

[65] G.B. Caird, 'Son by Appointment', in W.C. Weinrich (ed.), *The New Testament Age: Essays in Honour of Bo Reicke, Volume 1* (Macon: Mercer University Press, 1984), 73–81 (77–78).

[66] Cf. P. Ellingworth, 'Hebrews and the Anticipation of Completion', *Themelios* 14, no. 1 (1988), 6–11 (9).

[67] F.B. Craddock, *The Letter to the Hebrews: Introduction, Commentary, and Reflections* (NIB XII; Nashville: Abingdon Press, 1998), 58.

The recipients of the letter are encouraged not to lose heart because Jesus, 'the Son of God', is 'a great high priest' who has 'passed through the heavens' (4:14) and entered the presence of God.[68] Jesus's own covenant faithfulness to God has been tested and he was found to be 'without sin' (4:15), thus qualifying him to pass beyond the curtain and into the holy of holies. Consequently, those who 'approach the throne of grace' through Christ do so 'with boldness' to 'receive mercy and find grace to help in time of need' (4:16) – and all because he was a faithful high priest (4:14-15). Israel's high priest was appointed by God (5:4) to represent her to God and to act on her behalf (5:1), but he, like the people he represented, stumbled to keep the law of God and so was required to make ḥaṭṭā't offerings to ensure his own passage into the divine presence; only then could he act for the people on their behalf (5:2-3). Similarly, Jesus was appointed by God to be high priest, though not in the order of Aaron but that of the mysterious Melchizedek (5:5-6; Gen 14:18-20; Ps 110:4). Accordingly, in his high priestly role, 'Jesus offered up prayers and supplications, with loud cries and tears, to the one who was able to save him from death' (Heb 5:7). It is likely that this is an allusion to Christ's struggles in Gethsemane,[69] as this mirrors the high priest's need to prepare for his work on the Day of Atonement.[70] To remain faithful to God's calling on his life, Jesus would need to wrestle with whatever that calling would entail, even if it meant his death. His position as God's Son would not preclude him from grappling with his own conflicting desires to serve God faithfully and to spurn them through disobedience and denial of his responsibilities as high priest. He was called to be the 'pioneer of salvation' but first had to be made 'perfect' himself 'through suffering' (τὼν ἀρχηγὸν τῆς σωτηρίας αὐτῶν διὰ παθημάτων τελειῶσαι; 2:10);[71] by learning obedience through suffering, Christ is made

---

[68] Craddock, *The Letter to the Hebrews*, 58. The imagery used in Hebrews 4:14 is that of the Day of Atonement.

[69] Here Lane (*Hebrews 1–8*, 120) and Fred Craddock (*The Letter to the Hebrews*, 62) are more cautious in their judgements.

[70] Cf. S.J. Kistemaker, 'Atonement in Hebrews', in C.E. Hill and F.A. James III (eds.), *The Glory of the Atonement: Biblical, Historical and Practical Perspectives. Essays in Honour of Roger Nicole* (Downers Grove: IVP, 2004), 163–175 (168).

[71] The claim that Jesus needs first to be made perfect (Heb 2:10; cf. 5:9) does not mean that he was once 'imperfect' – whatever that in itself might mean! In Hebrews, τελειόω and its cognates (2:10; 5:9; 7:19; 7:28; 9:9; 10:1, 14; 11:40; 12:23) should be understood primarily – though not exclusively – in terms of the cult. Perfection is 'that state of purity which makes contact between God and the worshipper possible, together with the processes by which that is achieved' (Isaacs, *Sacred Space*, 102); thus the τελείωσις of the high priest was his faithfulness to that which was required of him. Through overcoming the temptation to disobey God, Jesus is made perfect, that is, achieves the necessary state of cultic purity that enables him rightly to be the high priest who enters the holy of holies by his own blood. His own perfection is the condition for the perfecting of those who approach God through him. See also P.

perfect and has thus become 'the source of eternal salvation for all who obey him' (5:8-9), that is, he has fulfilled his responsibilities as high priest in the order of Melchizedek (5:10).

The claim that Jesus has been 'designated by God a high priest according to the order of Melchizedek' (5:10) is the first indication that his high priesthood differs significantly from that of the Aaronic order. God had promised to Abram that he will be made into 'a great nation' and that in him 'all the families of the earth shall be blessed' (Gen 12:2-3). Thus when Abram later meets Melchizedek, we are surprised that the latter also blesses him, seemingly on God's behalf, and that Abram offers this man a tenth of everything he owned in response (Gen 14:18-20). For Hebrews, this story emphasises that the Levitical priesthood is inferior to that represented by Melchizedek, priest of God Most High (Gen 14:18; cf. Heb 7:1), who resembles the Son of God by remaining 'a priest for ever' on account of his unrecorded origin and destiny (7:3). Though usually dependent on the tithes of Abraham's other children (Num 18:21), the Levitical priesthood in fact pays its own unique tribute to Melchizedek in Abraham's offering (Heb 7:9-10). That another priesthood exists, apparently in competition with the Aaronic order, certainly suggests that there is some kind of flaw with the latter – otherwise there would be no reason for this second order to exist (7:11). A priest of the Levitical priesthood had to be a descendant of Levi; but Jesus is 'descended from Judah', from whom no priests came (7:13-14). Hebrews argues that because Jesus has been appointed high priest according to the order Melchizedek, the Levitical priesthood, being necessarily inferior to that order, has been fulfilled and superseded, therefore, by Christ's high priesthood (7:11-14).[72] Jesus is not high priest by descent but by appointment (7:15-16); accordingly, the change in priesthood that he established means that the requirement for Aaronic high priests to be descendants of Levi (7:16) has been annulled on the basis that the new high priesthood of Christ has shown it to be incapable of making perfect those who were dependent upon it for access to God (7:18-19). It 'symbolised access without genuinely providing it.'[73] Whilst Israel's high priest certainly represented her before God in the holy of holies on the Day of Atonement and that in him she truly stood before God,[74] the people of Israel also remained at a distance, waiting for the high priest to emerge from the tabernacle having

---

Ellingworth, *The Epistle to the Hebrews: A Commentary on the Greek Text* (NIGTC; Grand Rapids: Eerdmans, 1993), 161–163, and Craddock, *The Letter to the Hebrews*, 39.

[72] Isaacs, *Sacred Space*, 77.

[73] Caird, 'Son by Appointment', 80.

[74] We must not assume that Hebrews affirms the superiority of the new priesthood because the former was ineffective. His entire argument depends on the validity of the Mosaic Law and its sacrificial system; cf. Eberhart, 'Characteristics of Sacrificial Metaphors in Hebrews', 59.

completed his work. With the change in priesthood, Jesus enters the holy of holies as high priest and then throws back the curtain separating the people from God's presence and invites people to make their own approach towards God on the basis of what he has done for them in their place. From his position at the right hand of the Majesty on high (1:3e), which he occupies for all time, Jesus intercedes for those who are following him in his footsteps; although he has arrived at the destination, they are still en route and must go through similar trials and temptations to his own (7:23-25).[75] His intercession for them further demonstrates his ability to sympathise with them in their weaknesses and to furnish them with 'grace to help in time of need' (4:15-16).

§ 7.5 Jesus, Our Sacrifice: Hebrews 8–10

The priesthood of Jesus is permanent because he has 'been exalted above the heavens' (7:24-26).[76] He offers himself as a sacrifice 'once for all', thus negating the need to present further sacrifices for anyone (7:27). '[S]eated at the right hand of the throne of the Majesty in the heavens' (8:1), Jesus ministers in God's 'true tent' (8:2) of which the earthly versions are but a blueprint (ὑποδείγματι; 8:5). As the earthly tabernacle was constructed according to the pattern shown to Moses (Ex 25:9, 40), it could only have been based on something better – and so Jesus 'has now obtained a more excellent ministry, and to that degree he is the mediator of a better covenant, which has been enacted through better promises' (νυν δὲ διαφορωτέρας τέτυχεν λειτουργίας, ὅσῳ καὶ κρείττονός ἐστιν διαθήκης μεσίτης, ἥτις ἐπὶ κρείττοσιν ἐπαγγελίαις νενομοθέτηται; Heb 8:6). God had promised to establish a new covenant where his laws will be put in the minds and written on the hearts of his covenant people (8:8-12, quoting Jer 31:31-34); in so promising, he effectively renders the former covenant void.[77]

At this point, Hebrews engages specifically with the Day of Atonement rituals (Heb 9:1-14). Here, 'the Holy Spirit indicates' that as long as the sacrificial system remains in place – symbolised by the first tent – there can be

---

[75] Isaacs, *Sacred Space*, 184; cf. G.S. Dawson, *Jesus Ascended: The Meaning of Christ's Continuing Incarnation* (London: T&T Clark, 2004), 123–124: 'Now the Holy of Holies is opened to humanity. The way is clear. By the conveyance of the Holy Spirit, we may go into the presence of God and be accepted if we go under the cover of our priest, Jesus. In his name, that is, in union with Christ, we are, by the Spirit, carried on his back. Such a journey in the present is a spiritual one, but in our resurrection we will, glorified body and soul as one, be taken in Christ by the Spirit to the Father's presence.'

[76] The resurrection of Jesus is not a matter of concern for Hebrews (Ellingworth, *The Epistle to the Hebrews*, 316), though its occurrence is surely implied by the concept of exaltation.

[77] Cf. Lane, *Hebrews 1–8*, 210.

no full access to the presence of God (9:6-8).[78] Indeed, the tents are symbolic of the two covenants:[79] once the high priest enters into the holy of holies, the holy place is not in use. However, the high priest is bound to leave the holy of holies and return to the holy place. Christ's superiority lies in the fact that he entered the holy of holies and remains there to intercede for those making their own approach through him (cf. 9:11-12). Hebrews also makes a significant point that the sacrifices offered in the earthly tabernacle could not perfect the conscience of the worshipper (9:9). They succeeded in making purification for things pertaining to the body (9:9-10, 13), but could not do the same for the human interior.[80] 'In criticising the Levitical cult for not dealing with a continuing inner awareness of wrongdoing, our author is drawing attention to what he sees as an inherent weakness in the system. There was in fact no legislation within the cult which provided for a guilty conscience.'[81] Perhaps the reason for this is partly due to the fact that the blood of the $ḥaṭṭā't$ offerings was applied to the atonement slate and other physical objects in order to prevent God's presence from departing the holy of holies. If there was no legislation to purify a person's conscience, it was because that person's conscience was not the concern – or at least the main concern – of the sacrificial system.[82] Israel's relationship with God was maintained through decontaminating the place of his presence and not the people who had caused it to be defiled. The new covenant, with its promise that God's people will embody the law (8:10), introduces the matter of conscience and highlights the importance for those who live as God's people to be holy. This means that Hebrews can emphasise yet another benefit of Christ's high priesthood: his blood cleanses even the conscience (9:14)!

Significantly, Christ enters the presence of God by his own blood (9:12). Although the Aaronic high priest would remain faithful to his duties, the sacrifices he offered were animals selected from many for the purpose of being slaughtered. The blood was entirely adequate for the purpose of purifying the tabernacle, for God had 'given it ... for making atonement' (Lev 17:11); that said, it was unable to secure eternal redemption (Heb 9:12).[83] This suggests that

---

[78] W.L. Lane, *Hebrews 9–13* (WBC 47B; Nashville: Thomas Nelson, 1991), 223.
[79] Lane, *Hebrews 9–13*, 224.
[80] Isaacs, *Sacred Space*, 97–98.
[81] Isaacs, *Sacred Space*, 98–99.
[82] It is true that the reparation offering (*'āšām*; Lev 5:14–6:7) dealt with 'guilt', but this is concerned primarily with matters of economic or cultic indebtedness. See Jenson, 'The Levitical Sacrificial System', 30.
[83] At first glance, it seems that Hebrews 10:4 contradicts the idea that the blood of the sacrifices was sufficient, but, as Christian Eberhart observes, the sacrificial system assumed that 'human beings will always commit sins and become impure'; the 'elimination of sins is never intended in the sacrificial cult'. Furthermore, the metaphor of Christ's own sacrifice itself draws power from the actual effectiveness

the efficacy of a sacrifice lies not in its killing or even its blood but upon the promise of God who works through that which he had given for making atonement; the Levitical sacrifices 'were acts of liturgical obedience bearing witness to the fact that it is only God himself who can make atonement for sin and effect reconciliation.'[84] Christ's blood has this efficacy because the new covenant demands 'better sacrifices' (κρείττοσιν θυσίαις; 9:23) than those offered under the Levitical sacrificial system in tents based upon the superior, heavenly tabernacle (9:23). What makes his blood effective is that, unlike those of the former priestly order, Christ offered himself as a willing sacrifice, purposely shedding his own blood to enter God's presence and make atonement.[85] He entered heaven itself 'to appear in the presence of God on our behalf' (9:24), 'remov[ing] sin by the sacrifice of himself' (τῆς θυσίας αὐτοῦ πεφανέρωται; 9:26) that he offered obediently but after struggling with his calling. Indeed, in forging the new covenant, God himself phased out the sacrificial system through the obedience of the one appointed to do just that (10:5-9): 'it is by God's will that we have been sanctified through the offering of the body of Jesus Christ once for all' (10:10).

Crucial, then, to the metaphor of Christ as sacrifice is the fact of his obedience. The idea of Jesus wrestling with his calling to give his life absolutely to God, struggling with his natural desire for survival and the temptation to find another, less demanding way to please God or even reject his calling entirely,[86] runs throughout Hebrews (2:9-10, 14-18; 4:14-15; 5:7-8; 10:5-9; 12:2). Using cultic imagery, Hebrews argues that Jesus is 'the new and living way' (10:20) into the presence of God and that he is so because his death was the ordained sacrifice (9:26; 10:10) for this provision. Yet Jesus's obedience was not merely his simple compliance to the divine will. As God's high priest, Jesus shares the flesh and blood of humanity (2:14, 17) in order truly to act on behalf of his brothers and sisters and to take them into God's

---

of the cultic sacrifices. (Eberhart, 'Characteristics of Sacrificial Metaphors in Hebrews', 60).

[84] T.F. Torrance, *The Mediation of Christ*, rev. ed. (Edinburgh: T&T Clark, 1992), 108.

[85] T. Smail, *Once and For All: A Confession of the Cross* (London: DLT, 1998), 72-73, emphasis original: 'The value of [Christ's] sacrifice consists not in the *loss* of life but in the *offering* of the life in an act of free obedience.... The offering is not the suffering as such or the death as such, but the ultimacy of obedience that will endure that suffering and death in willing affirmation of the Father's saving purpose.'

[86] T.G. Weinandy, *In the Likeness of Sinful Flesh: An Essay on the Humanity of Christ* (Edinburgh: T&T Clark, 1993), 106: '[I]n the garden [of Gethsemane], Jesus encountered the ultimate and consummate trial (cf. Mt 26:36-46; Mk 14:32-42; Lk 22:39-46; Jn 12:27). He confronted the prospect of his imminent passion and death. As a man, living under the conditions of sin, such a prospect seemed overwhelming. His soul was "very sorrowful, even to death" (Mt 26:38; cf. Mk 14:34; Ps 42:6). While his humanity shrunk from the cross, yet the Spirit of Sonship strengthened his resolve.'

presence with him (2:13b, quoting Isa 8:18). By sacrificing himself to God in an act of high priestly faithfulness, Jesus re-presents to God those who had become estranged from him, doing so in his own humanity. Jesus provides the appropriate response of love and obedience to God expected of the ones created to spread his presence throughout the world. Thomas Torrance writes,

> We are to think of the whole life and activity of Jesus from the cradle to the grave as constituting the vicarious human response to himself which God has freely and unconditionally provided for us.... Jesus Christ *is* our human response to God.[87]

As truly human, Jesus is eminently qualified to make this response; but conceived as a sacrifice 'without blemish' (Heb 9:14), he is the *only* one who can make it. The Levitical sacrificial system was not, of course, established primarily to appease God but was the divinely ordained means given to Israel to maintain right relations with him. It was a gift from God. Within this cultic framework, the act of slaughtering an animal and the application of its blood to holy things suggests that the one who in the first place offers the sacrifice, indicated by the hand-laying rite, recognises that there is an estranged relationship between him- or herself and God that must be restored. That *ḥaṭṭā't* offerings are made means that sinful people cannot approach God without first sending a representative to act on their behalf – or a sacrifice, that is, in the words of Colin Gunton, 'something which or who is taken from the whole – the whole community, or indeed the whole world – and is offered to God in place of the others: *in place of* because apart from what the sacrifice is and does they cannot, by virtue of their bondage to evil, be made perfect.'[88] Gunton continues,

> But a sacrifice, to be acceptable, must be perfect. It follows that nothing that belongs to the fallen creation can become a *sacrifice*, a gift of the creation offered in praise to God, apart from cleansing.[89]

The implication is that

> only God can provide the sacrifice ... by taking on himself the consequences and weight of the accumulated evil. Therefore he *gives up*, sacrifices, his only Son [Rom 8:32]. The one who entrusted the world, as project,[90] to those made in his image, himself provides the means of its redirection.[91]

---

[87] Torrance, *The Mediation of Christ*, 80, emphasis original.
[88] C.E. Gunton, 'Atonement and the Project of Creation: An Interpretation of Colossians 1.15-23', in *The Promise of Trinitarian Theology*, 2nd ed. (Edinburgh: T&T Clark, 1997), 178–192 (188, emphasis original).
[89] Gunton, 'Atonement and the Project of Creation', 188–189, emphasis original.
[90] See § 5.2.
[91] Gunton, 'Atonement and the Project of Creation', 189, emphasis original.

Gunton adds that it is a properly human response that ultimately secures this redirection; hence Jesus,

> taking flesh from the polluted whole, must – through the Spirit – *become* perfect, because it is only as such that his gift is acceptable to God and so in turn is able to *become* the means of the perfecting of others ... The cleansing of one, particular, person becomes the means of the cleansing of the whole, though only at the end will this be complete.[92]

By affirming that Jesus is made perfect through his self-offering 'through the eternal Spirit' (Heb 9:14),[93] Gunton builds upon that which is implied throughout Hebrews: 'that the whole of Jesus' authentically human life is made what it uniquely is through the action of the Spirit.'[94] Indeed, Hebrews shows 'that the Son through whom God made and upheld the world, offers, triumphantly through testing and temptation and by the eternal Spirit, the sacrifice of praise and obedience that is the human calling.'[95] Jesus's temptations in the wilderness (Mt 4:1-11; Mk 1:12-13; Lk 4:1-13) and Gethsemane (Mt 26:36-46; Mk 14:32-42; Lk 22:39-46; cf. Jn 12:27; Heb 5:7) are both key moments by which his appointment as God's Son (Mt 3:13-17; Mk 1:9-11; Lk 3:21-22; cf. Jn 1:29-34; Heb 1:5) is tested, when his resolve to act faithfully is tested. Although these testings open Jesus to the various temptations put before him, they also open him to the possibility of drawing upon the Spirit's power to resist them. Unlike any other person, then, Jesus offers himself in submission to God to forge a new way to him through his own flesh (10:20) – and did so 'through the eternal Spirit' (9:14).

§ 7.6 A Faithfulness Emulated

God gave to Israel the law to be the means by which she should live as his covenant people (Ex 24:3; Lev 18:4-5; Deut 4:5-8). By observing the law, she would be distinguished from her neighbours, the holy people of a holy God (Lev 20:26), mediating his presence to them as she embodies his character and standards in her corporate flesh. The golden calf incident (Ex 32) shows, however, that Israel, like her neighbours, is sinful; the mere fact of her election as 'a priestly kingdom and a holy nation' (Ex 19:6) does not ensure that she will remain true to her calling. It is no guarantee of her faithfulness. Crucially,

---

[92] Gunton, 'Atonement and the Project of Creation', 189, emphasis original.

[93] The Holy Spirit is seldom mentioned in Hebrews, but this verse (Heb 9:14) in particular stresses that everything that Jesus the high priest does in making atonement is because of the Spirit's own action.

[94] C.E. Gunton, 'Martin Kähler Revisited. Variations on Hebrews 4.15', in *Father, Son and Holy Spirit: Essays Toward a Fully Trinitarian Theology* (London: T&T Clark, 2003), 144–163 (157).

[95] Gunton, 'Martin Kähler Revisited', 163.

God threatens to withdraw his presence, and it is only at Moses's intercession that he relents and assures Moses that he will indeed persevere with sinful Israel (Ex 33:1-3, 12-23). To deal with the matter of sin, God graciously institutes the Levitical sacrificial system (Lev 1:1-6:7), given not only to enable good relationship between both God and Israel and Israelite and Israelite, but also to maintain God's presence amongst his people in the tabernacle by purifying it from their sins. These sacrifices find ultimate expression on the Day of Atonement (Lev 16), when the high priest enters the holy of holies and purifies that most sacred of spaces, thus ensuring God's continued presence.

In Galatians 3, Paul contends that the law acted as a παιδαγωγός, exposing Israel's sin as she failed to embody its standards (Gal 3:19, 23-24). It was a temporary provision 'until Christ came' (Gal 3:24); but 'now that faith has come, we are no longer subject to a disciplinarian' (Gal 3:25).[96] This would suggest that, as part of the law, the sacrificial system is also temporary and that its procedures govern acts of atonement only whilst the law itself is operative. Therefore, just as the identity of God's covenant people is no longer determined by the law but by being in Christ, so the means of atonement must somehow be connected to him and not the law. The argument of the letter to the Hebrews is that Christ is the high priest who enters the very presence of God for us in our place, not by sacrificing animals according to the law but by shedding his own blood (Heb 9:12-14) according to God's promise that he will forge a new covenant people who will embody his law in their minds and hearts (Heb 8:10). Christ is the Son of God, the great high priest, whose faithfulness to God is the instrument by which God implements the new covenant (Heb 1:2; 2:17; 3:6; 4:14; 8:6).

We may see the letter to the Hebrews, then, like Galatians 3, as a portrayal of God's providential action within creation and therefore as another important text for a truly Christian doctrine of providence. It confirms that, essentially, God's providence is his faithfulness to his purposes for creation. However, whereas Paul argues in Galatians that God's covenant people are now defined by their relation to Christ, Hebrews demonstrates that, despite the impurity arising from human sin, God does not wish to withdraw his presence from his creation and, indeed, actively seeks the restoration of broken relationships first by providing the Levitical sacrificial system and, ultimately, in Christ. The *ḥaṭṭā't* offerings made purification for sins because God promised that they would; they were the divinely ordained means of maintaining God's presence amongst his people. In fact, the implementation of the sacrificial system indicates not only that God takes seriously the sinfulness of humanity but that he loves his creation so much that he takes appropriate steps to address the crisis sin incites.

Furthermore, we may affirm that God's providence is his sovereign action within creation, insofar as he acts freely to fulfil his promises to it first by

---

[96] Paul here seems to use 'faith' as a synonym for 'Christ'; see § 6.4.

implementing the law and its sacrificial system and then by acting definitively in Christ. As we have said, the temporality of the law implies the temporality of the Levitical sacrificial system. 'The entire cultic ministry of the tabernacle was only a temporary provision in the outworking of God's redemptive purpose for his people'.[97] Hebrews's claim that the earthly sanctuary was little more than 'a sketch and shadow of the heavenly one' (Heb 8:5) suggests that 'better sacrifices' (Heb 9:23) than those required by the sacrificial system were always a possibility and perhaps even intended.[98] Indeed, Hebrews's contention that the former sacrifices could not 'perfect the conscience of the worshipper, but [dealt] only with ... regulations for the body imposed until the time comes to set things right' (Heb 9:9-10) intimates that even though the law was given to deal with ritual impurity, there would one day come a time when more than just the flesh would be cleansed. In his high priestly representation of humanity, Jesus decontaminates both flesh and conscience (Heb 9:13-14) by offering them faithfully to God fully cleansed by 'the sacrifice of himself' (Heb 9:26) made through the Holy Spirit (Heb 9:14). With his repeated emphasis on that which is 'better' (Heb 7:19, 22; 8:6; 9:23; 10:34; 11:16, 35, 40; 12:24; cf. 11:4), Hebrews strongly implies that it was never God's plan for the sacrificial system – and thus the law in its entirety – to be absolutely definitive for access into the presence of God. This access is now, and was always intended to be, in and through his Son, Jesus Christ, 'the mediator of a new covenant' (Heb 12:24).

This means, then, that Christ's entrance into the holy of holies has opened it to all creation. God no longer segregates his presence from humanity but has revealed it to the world in Christ's faithful action. Jesus enables the extension of God's presence from the holy of holies to the world by himself being the means of its entry into that presence. The logic of Hebrews itself is not so much the expansion of God's presence into the world but the gathering and leading of the world into God's presence. Certainly, the ideas are not mutually exclusive, the chief difference being simply a matter of direction, and the essential content is identical: that God will be present to all. Thus we may say that Christ, the proper presence of God,[99] defines a people who, by the power of the Holy Spirit, mediate God's presence to the world through their own faithful action to God. Christ is the 'cause [$\alpha\ddot{\iota}\tau\iota\sigma\varsigma$] of eternal salvation for all who obey him' (Heb 5:9) and their intercessor (Heb 7:25) as they emulate 'the pioneer and perfecter of faith' (Heb 12:2). Here, then, we have confirmation that God's providence ultimately is defined by his action in Christ. By Christ's faithfulness, God demonstrates his own faithfulness to creation; and by his faithfulness, Christ accomplishes that which is necessary for God's presence to

---

[97] Lane, *Hebrews 9–13*, 225.
[98] Cf. Harrisville, *The Concept of Newness in the New Testament*, 49–50; G.B. Caird, 'The Exegetical Method of the Epistle to the Hebrews', *Canadian Journal of Theology* 5 (1959), 44–51 (47–49).
[99] Barth, *Church Dogmatics*, II/1, 484; cf. § 5.3.

spread from the holy of holies to all creation: the freedom to live in peace with God, in faithfulness to him.

§ 7.7 Conclusion

Our reading of Hebrews, as with that of Galatians 3 in the previous chapter, serves to demonstrate the legitimacy of the conceptual framework of God's presence as the most appropriate foundation and context for the Christian doctrine of providence. Starting from this context, Hebrews repeatedly emphasises the role of Jesus as high priest (Heb 2:17; 4:14; 9:11, 25; 10:21) entering the presence of God (Heb 9:12) to make a once for all atonement (Heb 7:27) that enables others likewise to have access to God as they follow his example (Heb 10:19-22; 12:2; cf. 2:10, 13). The Son's accomplishment as high priest to make atonement by his superior self-sacrifice (Heb 9:26) is given meaning by his unswerving obedience to God (Heb 2:17; 5:7-10) strengthened by the power of the Holy Spirit through whom Christ 'offered himself without blemish to God' (Heb 9:14). His death secures both his own entrance into the presence of God (Heb 9:12-14) and his subsequent exaltation whereby he continues to represent us before God in the holy of holies (Heb 7:25; 8:1-2). This priestly action in which the Son shares the flesh and blood of his brothers (cf. Heb 2:14, 17) demonstrates that God is unwilling to forego his fallen creation; indeed, the act of atonement is an affirmation of the goodness of creation even as the Son is himself the means by which it is restored. Consequently, we may build upon Hebrews's imagery of the Son as 'the radiance of God's glory' and his 'exact imprint' (Heb 1:3a-b) by suggesting that the one who both bears the stamp of God's nature[100] and shares flesh and blood is thus the Son's mediation of God to the world as a seal imprinting something valuable with the sovereign's insignia. By making 'purification for sins' (Heb 1:3d), then, the Son sustains all things and acts as the foundation for the preservation of the relationship between God and his creation.[101]

Providence is God's sovereign action within creation to remain faithful to his promise that the world in its entirety shall be the place of God's presence. Given the problem of sin, this promise can be fulfilled only if God acts to maintain the relationship between himself and the world. At the heart of Hebrews's understanding of atonement, then, is the providential activity of the triune God: The Father appoints the Son to be his agent in the world, the Son

---

[100] Cf. Guthrie, *The Letter to the Hebrews*, 66: 'The word used here for stamp (*charaktēr*) is the word for a die or an engraving. It is highly expressive since a stamp on a wax seal will bear the same image as the engraving on the seal.'

[101] Cf. T.J. Wright, 'The Seal of Approval: An Interpretation of the Son's Sustaining Action in Hebrews 1:3', in R.J. Bauckham, D.R. Driver, T.A. Hart and N. MacDonald (eds.), *The Epistle to the Hebrews and Christian Theology* (Grand Rapids: Eerdmans, forthcoming, 2009).

makes atonement by his own blood and the Spirit strengthens his resolve to remain faithful to his high priestly calling. We might wonder, however, why the Son of God needs the Holy Spirit to remain faithful – is not the fact that Jesus *is* the Son of God enough to prevent his covenant unfaithfulness? This question prompts us now to explore the issue of the Son's relationship to the Spirit.

CHAPTER 8

Providence and the Faithfulness of the Holy Spirit

§ 8.1 Introduction

In the previous two chapters, we sought to articulate the christological orientation of an understanding of God's providence that remains true to the fundamental notion that God wishes to spread his presence throughout the world he created through faithful, obedient human activity. God calls to himself a people – Israel, the children of Abraham – to be his 'treasured possession', a 'priestly kingdom and ... holy nation' (Ex 19:5-6). Israel received the Mosaic Law as a gift from God to enable her to live accordingly, to embody his character in her corporate flesh and so to mediate the divine presence to the other nations. Paul's argument in Galatians 3 is that this arrangement was temporary, that the law would remain in place only until the coming of Jesus Christ. Whereas Israel initially understood the law to be that which distinguished her as God's covenant people from her neighbours, 'in Christ' (Gal 3:26-28) the definition of this covenant people has been widened to include Gentiles, too. The author of the letter to the Hebrews has similar theological convictions: the sacrifices prescribed by the law that functioned to restore and maintain the relationship between God and sinful Israel have now been fulfilled by Christ's own sacrifice that he offered 'once and for all' (Heb 7:27; 10:10). Providence, then, is God's sovereign action within creation to remain faithful to his promise that the world in its entirety shall be the place of God's presence. This is a promise revealed and realised ultimately in Christ, God's providence made flesh.

Fundamental to this christological understanding of providence is the further conviction that Christ's obedience to his Father, the God of Israel, is that which demonstrates God's faithfulness to his creation. By sending his Son, God proves that he loves that which he has made – despite its fallenness – and provides the means for it to be reconciled to him (Gal 4:4-5). Similarly, by submitting willingly to his Father's commands, Christ, the Son of God, offers the appropriate response required of creation on its behalf and in doing so acts as God within the world's space and time. That Christ's obedience is central to this divine action is undeniable. The Synoptics, for example, emphasise Christ's struggle to remain faithful to his Father's will for him in Gethsemane (Mt 26:36-46; Mk 14:32-42; Lk 22:39-46; cf. Jn 12:27-28); Paul speaks of Christ being 'obedient to the point of death' (Phil 2:8), an obedience that somehow reverses the original Adamic act of disobedience (Rom 5:19); and

Hebrews draws attention to the fact that Christ 'learned obedience through what he suffered' (Heb 5:8). To be sure, Christ's obedience does not achieve salvation for humanity apart from his death on the cross;[1] but it does ensure that his crucifixion is not merely an execution, that his death is significant for the whole of creation, for Christ's life of obedience is the context in which the acceptability of his self-sacrifice to the Father is situated and from which it comes. It is why Hebrews can say that Christ 'offered himself without blemish to God' (Heb 9:14).[2]

Importantly, Hebrews also states that Christ's self-offering was 'through the eternal Spirit' (διὰ πνεύματος αἰωνίου; Heb 9:14). The phrase is ambiguous;[3] but we may understand it to mean, as we have suggested already,[4] that Christ is strengthened by the Holy Spirit to remain obedient to the will of God and willingly to offer himself as the ultimate sacrifice for sins. Accordingly, the Spirit's involvement in Christ's life is not limited to any one episode, however crucial, but rather throughout his entire life, from conception to resurrection, so that the whole course of Christ's obedience is established through dependence upon the Spirit.[5] Here, though, a series of related questions arises concerning Christ and the Spirit: Why does the Son of God need the Holy Spirit to remain faithful to God? If Jesus is both fully human and fully divine, as the traditional creeds and formulae proclaim, why, then, is it not enough simply to state that his obedience is achieved by his humanity but empowered by his divinity? Is mention of the Spirit's power at this point no more than tokenism, of forcing reference to the whole Trinity, and a concomitant diminishment of Christ's divinity? To address the concerns of these questions, we will return to the theology of John Calvin, which, despite affirming both Christ's humanity and his divinity, tends to prioritise the latter over and against the former. Consequently, we shall see not only that Calvin is ambivalent about the precise role of the Spirit in the life of Christ, but that his

---

[1] J.R.D. Kirk, 'The Sufficiency of the Cross (I): The Crucifixion as Jesus' Act of Obedience', *Scottish Bulletin of Evangelical Theology* 24 (2006), 36–64; J.R.D. Kirk, 'The Sufficiency of the Cross (II): The Law, the Cross, and Justification', *Scottish Bulletin of Evangelical Theology* 24 (2006), 133–154.

[2] Cf. W.L. Lane, *Hebrews 9–13* (WBC 47B; Nashville: Thomas Nelson, 1991), 240; D. Guthrie, *The Letter to the Hebrews: An Introduction and Commentary* (TNTC 15; Leicester: IVP, 1983), 189.

[3] For a discussion of the various ways of interpreting this phrase in Hebrews 9:14, see G.F. Hawthorne, *The Presence and the Power: The Significance of the Holy Spirit in the Life and Ministry of Jesus* (Eugene: Wipf and Stock, 1991), 180–184.

[4] See § 7.5.

[5] For accounts of the Spirit's action throughout Christ's life, see Hawthorne, *The Presence and the Power*; T. Smail, *The Giving Gift: The Holy Spirit in Person* (London: DLT, 1994), 89–115; and, more briefly, N.G. Wright, *God on the Inside: The Holy Spirit in Holy Scripture* (Oxford: BRF, 2006), 53–64.

depiction of Christ's obedience diminishes the importance of Christ's humanity and even threatens its reality.

§ 8.2 The Person of the Mediator in the Theology of John Calvin

Calvin frames his understanding of the constitution of the person of Christ soteriologically: since humanity's sin separates it from God, 'no man, unless he belonged to God, could serve as the intermediary to restore peace.'[6] Our proper knowledge of God and our reconciliation to him occur only through the action of the person of the Mediator.[7] Accordingly, 'it was of the greatest importance for us that he who was to be our Mediator be both true God and true man.'[8] The person of the Mediator is, of course, Christ, the Son of God who became the Son of man, taking 'what was ours as to impart what was his to us, and to make what was his by nature ours by grace'; by doing so, he restored us 'to God's grace as to make of the children of men, children of God; of the heirs of Gehenna, heirs of the Heavenly Kingdom.'[9] If it was important for the Son of God to assume human nature in order to restore us to God, it was equally important – 'imperative', says Calvin – that it was *only* the Son of God who could do so to restore us. Only the one who is both 'the Life' and 'very Righteousness' could 'swallow up death' and 'conquer sin'.[10] Thus Calvin affirms that the one person of the Mediator is both true God and true man; but he cautions,

> we ought not to understand the statement that "the Word was made flesh" [John 1:14] in the sense that the Word was turned into flesh or confusedly mingled with flesh. Rather, it means that ... he who was the Son of God became the Son of man – not by confusion of substance, but by unity of person. For we affirm his divinity so joined and united with his humanity that each retains its distinctive nature unimpaired, and yet these two natures constitute one Christ.[11]

To elucidate this claim, Calvin appeals to the anthropological parallel that each human person consists of soul and body: 'neither [soul nor body] is so mingled with the other as not to retain its own distinctive nature. For the soul is not the body, and the body is not the soul.' Importantly, though various distinctions may be made between the two substances, 'he who consists of these parts is one man, not many.'[12] Calvin continues,

---

[6] J. Calvin, *Institutes of the Christian Religion* (2 vols.), translated by F.L. Battles (LCC XX / XXI; Philadelphia: The Westminster Press, 1960), 2:12:1, 464.
[7] Calvin, *Institutes*, 2:6:1, 341. See § 2.4 for Calvin's theology of atonement.
[8] Calvin, *Institutes*, 2:12:1, 464.
[9] Calvin, *Institutes*, 2:12:2, 465.
[10] Calvin, *Institutes*, 2:12:2, 466.
[11] Calvin, *Institutes*, 2:14:1, 482.
[12] Calvin, *Institutes*, 2:14:1, 482.

Such expressions signify both that there is one person in man composed of two elements joined together, and that there are two diverse underlying natures that make up this person. Thus, also, the Scriptures speak of Christ: they sometimes attribute to him what must be referred solely to his humanity, sometimes what belongs uniquely to his divinity; and sometimes what embraces both natures but fits neither alone. And they so earnestly express this union of the two natures that is in Christ as sometimes to interchange them. This figure of speech is called by the ancient writers "the communicating of properties [*communicatio idiomatum*]."[13]

We should note that Calvin here does not seek to 'explain the mechanics of this relationship of union and distinction of the natures in Christ'; the body-soul simile is employed to show that 'such a union and distinction are not unreasonable.'[14] The so-called *communicatio idiomatum*, that is, the communication of properties that predicates the attributes of either the divine or the human nature to the whole person of Christ,[15] for Calvin is 'a hermeneutical

---

[13] Calvin, *Institutes*, 2:14:1, 482–483.

[14] S. Edmondson, *Calvin's Christology* (Cambridge: Cambridge University Press, 2004), 216.

[15] 'But what exactly is the *communicatio idiomatum*? Obviously, the expression refers to a transfer of attributes or properties. On the basis of the two-natures doctrine of Chalcedon, there are three logical possibilities for such a transfer: (1) The predicating of properties of the one or the other nature to the whole person of Christ. (2) The predicating of properties of the divine nature to the human nature of Christ. (3) The predicating of properties of the human nature to the divine nature of Christ.... The basic idea is that expressed in (1), that in view of the unity of Christ's person in the Incarnation both human and divine properties can be legitimately ascribed to him.' (P. Helm, *John Calvin's Ideas* [Oxford: Oxford University Press, 2004], 72; O.D. Crisp, *Divinity and Humanity: The Incarnation Reconsidered* [CIT 5; Cambridge: Cambridge University Press, 2007], 6–18).

Calvin himself was keen to distance himself from the notion that certain divine properties could be ascribed to Christ's humanity, seen especially in the Lutheran understanding of the Lord's Supper. According to Calvin, the Lutherans must hold to the 'monstrous notion of ubiquity' for their understanding of the Supper because '[u]nless the body of Christ can be everywhere at once, without limitation of place, it will not be credible that he lies hidden under the bread in the Supper.' (Calvin, *Institutes*, 4:17:30, 1401). Against this, Calvin argues that 'the one person of Christ so consists of two natures that each nevertheless retains unimpaired its own distinctive character.' (Calvin, *Institutes*, 4:17:30, 1402). Contained within the Lutheran teaching was for Calvin a threat to the proper distinction between Christ's humanity and divinity that would jeopardise the integrity of each nature; as Stephen Edmondson notes, 'a ubiquitous human nature is no human nature at all.' (Edmondson, *Calvin's Christology*, 211; cf. R.A. Muller, 'John Calvin and Later Calvinism: The Identity of the Reformed Tradition', in D. Bagchi and D.C. Steinmetz [eds.], *The Cambridge Companion to Reformation Theology* [Cambridge: Cambridge University Press, 2004], 130–149 [146]). For further comment, see, for example, D.

term that expresses Christ's unity without defining the mechanics of that unity or threatening the integrity of the natures in that unity.'[16] This permits Calvin to distinguish between those actions that Christ performs from his divinity and those accomplished by his humanity. Concerning Christ's divinity, Calvin writes,

> What Christ said about himself – "Before Abraham was, I am" [John 8:58] – was far removed from his humanity.... Paul declares him to be "the first-born of all creation ... who was before all things and in whom all things hold together" [Col. 1:15, 17]. Also, he says that he was "glorious in his Father's presence before the world was made" [John 17:5 p.]; and that he is working together with his Father [John 5:17]. These qualities are utterly alien to man. Therefore they and their like apply exclusively to his divinity.[17]

About Christ's humanity, Calvin observes,

> But he is called "the servant of the Father" [Isa. 42:1, and other passages]; he is said to have "increased in age and wisdom ... with God and men" [Luke 2:52], and not to "seek his own glory" [John 8:50]; "not to know the Last Day" [Mark 13:32; cf. Matt. 24:36]; not to "speak by himself" [John 14:10], and not to "do his own will" [John 6:38 p.]; he is said to have been "seen and handled" [Luke 24:39]. All these refer solely to Christ's humanity.[18]

For Calvin, none of the things that can be said of Christ's humanity may be ascribed to his divinity: Christ's divine nature, for example, 'cannot increase in anything ... and can be neither seen nor handled.' However, Christ 'does not ascribe these qualities solely to his human nature, but takes them upon himself as being in harmony with the person of the Mediator.'[19] Calvin distinguishes between the two natures but here emphasises their unity in the one person of Christ. Consequently,

> We therefore hold that Christ, as he is God and man, consisting of two natures united but not mingled, is our Lord and the true Son of God even according to, but not by reason of, his humanity.[20]

Farrow, *Ascension and Ecclesia: On the Significance of the Doctrine of the Ascension for Ecclesiology and Christian Cosmology* (Edinburgh: T&T Clark, 1999), 172–180, and J.E. Colwell, *Promise and Presence: An Exploration of Sacramental Theology* (Milton Keynes: Paternoster, 2005), 166–171.

[16] Edmondson, *Calvin's Christology*, 216–217; cf. Helm, *John Calvin's Ideas*, 76; B.L. McCormack, *For Us and Our Salvation: Incarnation and Atonement in the Reformed Tradition* (Princeton: Princeton Theological Seminary, 1993), 8–9.

[17] Calvin, *Institutes*, 2:14:2, 483.

[18] Calvin, *Institutes*, 2:14:2, 483–484.

[19] Calvin, *Institutes*, 2:14:2, 484.

[20] Calvin, *Institutes*, 2:14:4, 486.

If this is how we are to understand the constitution of the person of Christ, how, then, does Calvin conceive of the initiation of that constitution as the two natures in Christ are related to one another first at his conception and birth? Commenting on Luke 1:35, Calvin says that 'the angel shows that Christ must not be born by ordinary generation, that he may be *holy*, and that he may be *the Son of God*; that is, that in holiness and glory he may be high above all creatures, and may not hold an ordinary rank among men.'[21] This means that 'he who had been the Son of God in his eternal Godhead, appeared also as the Son of God in human flesh.' Calvin recognises that this passage 'not only expresses a unity of person in Christ, but at the same time points out that, in clothing himself with human flesh, Christ is the Son of God.'[22] Furthermore,

> As the name, *Son of God*, belonged to the divine essence of Christ from the beginning, so now it is applied unitedly to both natures, because the secret and heavenly manner of generation has separated him from the ordinary rank of men. In other passages, indeed, with the view of asserting that he is truly man, he calls himself *the Son of man*, (John v. 27;) but the truth of his human nature is not inconsistent with his deriving peculiar honour above all others from his divine generation, having been conceived out of the ordinary way of nature by the Holy Spirit.[23]

There is evidence here that Calvin portrays the Spirit in closest relation to the Son as he takes to himself human flesh, substantiated further by a conviction that the Spirit then ensures Christ's purity so that he 'contracted no defilement from a sinful nature'.[24] Importantly, this act of purification 'was done not merely that [Christ] might abound in personal holiness, but chiefly that he might sanctify his own people' as Mediator.[25] The soteriological intent is clear. In his discussion of the name 'Immanuel' in Matthew 1:23, Calvin urges that 'whenever we contemplate the one person of Christ as God-man, we ought to hold it for certain that, if we are united to Christ by faith, we possess God.'[26] This is a strong claim, but vital for humanity in its truth: Christ 'would

---

[21] J. Calvin, *Commentary on a Harmony of the Evangelists, Vol. 1* in *Calvin's Commentaries* XVI (CTS; Grand Rapids: Baker Books, 2003), 42–43, emphasis original.

[22] Calvin, *Comm. Evan. 1*, 43.

[23] Calvin, *Comm. Evan. 1*, 43, emphasis original.

[24] Calvin, *Comm. Evan. 1*, 43.

[25] Calvin, *Comm. Evan. 1*, 43–44.

[26] Calvin, *Comm. Evan. 1*, 106. Discussing the related Isaiah 7:14-15, Calvin notes that 'this name *Immanuel* could not be literally applied to a mere man; and, therefore, there can be no doubt that the Prophet referred to Christ.' (J. Calvin, *Commentary on the Prophet Isaiah, Vol. 1* in *Calvin's Commentaries* VII [CTS; Grand Rapids: Baker Books, 2003], 245, emphasis original). Christ is the Son of God clothed in flesh and united to humanity; thus the title 'Immanuel' indicates 'not only the power of God ...

not be a properly qualified Mediator, if he did not unite both natures in his person, and thus bring men into an alliance with God.'[27]

Calvin argues that each of Christ's two natures retains the properties appropriate to it; divinity and humanity are not conflated in any way. This conviction is seen in his discussion of the development of the boy Jesus in Luke 2:40. '[W]e infer,' writes Calvin, 'that this progress, or advancement, relates to his human nature: for the Divine nature could receive no increase.'[28] This may be so, but here we see the problems with Calvin's christology begin to emerge: surely it is unnecessary for Calvin to make this observation when clearly he is talking about the one person of the Mediator. It suggests that Calvin wishes to emphasise the distinction between the two natures and that this distinction somehow takes priority over their union in the one Son of God incarnate.

Accordingly, Calvin also introduces the idea that the Son's assumption of flesh and all its concomitant weaknesses was his willing decision: the divine maintains authority over that which is assumed. Here, the weaknesses are a seeming lack of spiritual gifts: as Calvin admits, 'it appears absurd to say, that the Son of God wanted any thing that was necessary to perfection.'[29] The conclusion, then, is that the Son '*chose* not only to grow in body, but to make progress in mind'[30] so that his receipt of the Spirit in his human nature may through him be given to all those who 'draw grace out of his grace.'[31] Ultimately, 'it was the decision of God to express in plain terms, how truly and completely Christ, in taking upon him our flesh, did all that was necessary to effect his brotherly union with men.'[32] In all this, Calvin does not attribute to the human nature what is divine, for, 'so far as was necessary for our salvation, the Son of God kept his divine power concealed'; nonetheless, he did

---

but a union of person, by which Christ became God-man.' (*Comm. Isa. 1*, 249). The fact that Christ here is depicted not only as Immanuel, 'God with us', but also as eating is a sure demonstration of his humanity; likewise, he is portrayed as growing in understanding, which 'relates to his human nature, for it cannot apply to his Divinity.' (*Comm. Isa. 1*, 249–250). Linking this text with its counterpart in Luke 2:52, Calvin says, 'Christ must therefore have been, for a time, like little children, so that, *so far as relates to his human nature*, he was deficient in understanding.' (*Comm. Isa. 1*, 250, emphasis mine). Although Calvin affirms the one person of the Mediator, he also strictly demarcates what is appropriate or inappropriate for humanity and divinity to do.

[27] Calvin, *Comm. Evan. 1*, 105.
[28] Calvin, *Comm. Evan. 1*, 166.
[29] Calvin, *Comm. Evan. 1*, 166.
[30] Calvin, *Comm. Evan. 1*, 166, emphasis mine.
[31] Calvin, *Comm. Evan. 1*, 166.
[32] Calvin, *Comm. Evan. 1*, 167.

voluntarily take upon himself 'everything that is inseparable from human nature.'[33]

This leads us to the accounts of Jesus's baptism. First to note is the opening of the heavens (Mt 3:16), which Calvin claims was mainly for John the Baptist's benefit; Christ, '*so far as he was man*, [merely] received from it additional certainty as to his heavenly calling.'[34] His comments on the parallel in Luke 3:21 suggest more than a simple distinction between two natures: '[though [Christ's] prayers were always directed towards the benefit of others, *yet as man*, when he commenced a warfare of so arduous a description, he needed to be armed with a remarkable power of the Spirit.'[35] We are not disturbed by the idea that Christ needed the Spirit – indeed, it is *because* Christ is a man that he needs such divine power to fulfil his calling – but we do note an insinuation that there *is* part of Christ that does *not* need the Spirit, that is, *Christ as God*. Such a suspicion is likely confirmed by Calvin's question, '[W]hy did the Spirit, who had *formerly* dwelt in Christ, descend upon him *at that time*?'[36] Does Calvin here imply that Christ has the Spirit by virtue of his divine nature?[37] To be fair, Calvin does say that the time has now come for Christ 'to discharge the office of the Redeemer' and so 'is clothed with a new power of the Spirit' – but *then* he adds that this is 'not so much for his own sake, as for the sake of others. It was done on purpose, that believers might learn to receive, and to contemplate with reverence, his divine power, and that the weakness of the flesh might not make him despised.'[38] For Calvin, it seems that Christ's receipt of the Spirit is more a demonstration of his divinity than because the Son of God made flesh must act by the power of the Spirit; and yet there is this latter notion also:

> When Christ was preparing to preach the Gospel, he was introduced by Baptism into his office; and at the same time was endued with the Holy Spirit. When John

---

[33] Calvin, *Comm. Evan. 1*, 167; cf. Calvin's comments on Hebrews 2:17 in J. Calvin, *Commentaries on the Epistle of Paul the Apostle to the Hebrews* in *Calvin's Commentaries* XXII (CTS; Grand Rapids: Baker Books, 2003), 74–75, emphasis original: 'In Christ's human nature there are two things to be considered, the real flesh and the affections or feelings. The Apostle then teaches us, that he had not only put on the real flesh of man, but also all those feelings which belong to man, and he also shews the benefit that hence proceeds; and it is the true teaching of faith when we in our case find the reason why the Son of God undertook our infirmities; for all knowledge without feeling the need of this benefit is cold and lifeless. But he teaches us that Christ was made subject to human affections, *that he might be a merciful and faithful high priest*'.
[34] Calvin, *Comm. Evan. 1*, 203, emphasis mine.
[35] Calvin, *Comm. Evan. 1*, 203, emphasis mine.
[36] Calvin, *Comm. Evan. 1*, 203, emphasis original.
[37] Cf. Smail, *The Giving Gift*, 94.
[38] Calvin, *Comm. Evan. 1*, 204.

beholds the Holy Spirit descending upon Christ, it is to remind him, that nothing carnal or earthly must be expected in Christ, but that he comes as a godlike man, descended from heaven, in whom the power of the Holy Spirit reigns. We know, indeed, that he is *God manifested in the flesh*, (1 Tim. iii. 16:) but even in his character as a servant, and in his human nature, there is a heavenly power to be considered.[39]

At times, then, Calvin does speak of Christ doing things in the power of the Spirit because he is a man, the Son of God made flesh, rather than because he, as God, naturally has divine power. This is seen in his account of Christ's temptations in the wilderness. Christ entered the wilderness, writes Calvin, for two reasons: to 'come forth as a new man, or rather a heavenly man, to the discharge of his office' and to 'be tried by temptation and undergo an apprenticeship, before he undertook an office so arduous, and so elevated.' To this end, Calvin observes that 'by the guidance of the Spirit, Christ withdrew from the crowd of men, in order that he might come forth as the highest teacher of the church, as the ambassador of God'.[40] It was the will of God that Christ be tempted – indeed, this is why the Spirit led him into the wilderness, that Satan's schemes against God's purposes to save people from their sins might be exposed and conquered.[41] The power by which Christ resisted Satan's attacks was that of the Spirit, who 'fortified' him so that he did not sin.[42] Commenting on Luke 4:18, Calvin also depicts this relation between Christ and the Spirit enduring into his public ministry: Christ 'does nothing by the suggestion or advice of men, but everything by the guidance of the Spirit of God'.[43] Nonetheless, Calvin continues to frustrate: whereas in these two examples he implies that Christ acts dependently on the power of the Spirit, elsewhere, for example, when considering the storm depicted in Matthew 14:22-24, he attributes what seems to be omniscience to Christ even while showing that this same, all-knowing Christ prays as a man: 'But in discharging all the parts of his office as Mediator,' Calvin writes, Christ 'showed himself to be God and man, and exhibited proofs of both natures, *as opportunities occurred*.'[44] Is there a suggestion here that the one Mediator would respond as God in one situation but as a man in another?

This tension persists in Calvin's interpretation of the Gethsemane temptation. Christ had to wrestle with his emotions to ensure that his Father's will would be accomplished. Although he desired to submit to his Father's will,

---

[39] Calvin, *Comm. Evan. 1*, 204, emphasis original.
[40] Calvin, *Comm. Evan. 1*, 207.
[41] Calvin, *Comm. Evan. 1*, 209–210.
[42] Calvin, *Comm. Evan. 1*, 212.
[43] Calvin, *Comm. Evan. 1*, 228.
[44] J. Calvin, *Commentary on a Harmony of the Evangelists, Vol. 2* in *Calvin's Commentaries* XVI (CTS; Grand Rapids: Baker Books, 2003), 237–238, emphasis mine.

Christ also asked for the cup of judgement to be taken from him (Mt 26:39). Calvin notes that in his purity and innocence, Christ 'was struck with fear and seized with anguish, so that, amidst the violent shocks of temptation, he vacillated – as it were – from one wish to another.'[45] At this point, however, Calvin asks an important question: 'How did [Christ] pray that the eternal decree of the Father, of which he was not ignorant, should be revoked?'[46] Here Calvin's concern is with the unchanging nature of the purpose of God, and he answers his question by saying that Christ, 'agreeably to the custom of the godly, leaving out of view the divine purpose, committed to the bosom of the Father his desire which troubled him.'[47] However, we may detect a different tension in what Calvin says. First, Christ asks for the cup to be taken from him, although, because he is 'not ignorant' of the Father's decree, he knows indeed that it is the Father's will that he should drink it. Against this, secondly, Christ prays that the cup be taken from him, 'agreeably to the custom of the godly', despite knowing it to be his Father's will – that is, he asks as one of those who seeks to discern God's will without knowing beforehand what is that will. Is Calvin here saying, then, that Christ, as a man, prayed to be delivered from something that he, as God, knew would happen?[48] To be sure, Calvin goes on to speak of how Christ brought his fearful, human will in line with the divine will,[49] but we cannot avoid the impression that at the heart of Calvin's christology is a disconnectedness between Christ's two natures – evidenced by his knowledge of God's will as God and ignorance of that same will as a man – rather than a firm union of them in his person.[50]

---

[45] J. Calvin, *Commentary on a Harmony of the Evangelists, Vol. 3* in *Calvin's Commentaries* XVII (CTS; Grand Rapids: Baker Books, 2003), 230.

[46] Calvin, *Comm. Evan. 3*, 230.

[47] Calvin, *Comm. Evan. 3*, 230.

[48] Edmondson notes that 'Calvin does at times attribute a certain independence of activity or feeling to Christ in his human nature' but claims nonetheless that 'this is an independence of will necessary to the integrity of his human nature and which in no way impinges on the unity of that nature with the divine.' (Edmondson, *Calvin's Christology*, 217).

[49] Calvin, *Comm. Evan. 3*, 232–233.

[50] Bruce McCormack says that Calvin 'rightly assigns fear and dread to Christ's human nature, rightly, because it is only through the addition of a human nature that the Logos can have this experience. Yet Calvin stops short of attributing this experience, on the basis of a real *communicatio*, to the Person of the Logos.' McCormack adds that Calvin 'senses that to make the eternal Son the Subject of the death in God-abandonment would seem to introduce a conflict or even rift between Father and Son. Calvin considered this impossible. The Father never ceased to love His eternal Son.' (McCormack, *For Us and Our Salvation*, 33, emphasis original).

§ 8.3 The Divided Mediator

Clearly, Calvin wishes to focus on the one person of the Mediator rather than the two natures that constitute him; but despite this intention, he has a tendency not only to distinguish between Christ's two natures but also to isolate them from one another.[51] In doing so, Calvin balances precariously over a trap that he thinks he avoids completely: he posits almost a Nestorian division within the person of Christ.[52] According to Roger Helland, such a near-Nestorian view 'attributes [Christ's] supernatural miracles, knowledge and power to his deity, while attributing his tiredness, temptations, trials, thirst, and emotions to his humanity', with the danger that Christ is presented as 'some sort of schizophrenic divine-man who functions back and forth between his two natures.'[53] This leads us to identify two problems with Calvin's christology. First, Calvin makes too sharp a distinction between Christ's two natures so that it is impossible to see how they actually relate; and secondly, Christ's divine nature is emphasised to such an extent that his human nature is rendered superficial. Both these problems are exacerbated by Calvin's use of the *communicatio idiomatum*, which ironically he employs to overcome these problems, and stem from his use of the body-soul simile.

As we saw earlier, Calvin thinks 'the most apposite parallel' of how Christ's two natures relate in his one person is that of the relation between body and

---

[51] Surely it is not enough to say, with Richard Muller, that Calvin's interest 'is not in the metaphysical problem of how such a union of natures is possible but the reality of the historical person of the mediator'. (R.A. Muller, *Christ and the Decree: Christology and Predestination in Reformed Theology from Calvin to Perkins* [Durham, North Carolina: The Labyrinth Press, 1986], 29). Were Calvin concerned solely with the reality of the person of the Mediator, he would not have needed to so stress the distinction between Christ's two natures.

[52] Calvin denies that his christology is Nestorian; see Calvin, *Institutes*, 2:14:4, 486; 2:14:7, 491. Properly speaking, the heresy of Nestorianism is the teaching that in the incarnate Christ, there are two separate persons, one divine, one human. For details of the circumstances surrounding the Nestorian heresy, both historical and theological, see J.N.D. Kelly, *Early Christian Doctrines*, 5th ed. (London: A&C Black, 1985), 310–343; T.G. Weinandy, *Does God Suffer?* (Edinburgh: T&T Clark, 2000), 172–213; and, more briefly, D. Macleod, *The Person of Christ* (Leicester: IVP, 1998), 181–183. My charge that Calvin's christology is near-Nestorian is not original; see, for example, the comments made in F. Wendel, *Calvin: The Origins and Development of his Religious Thought*, translated by P. Mairet (London: Collins, 1963), 225; McCormack, *For Us and Our Salvation*, 9; Weinandy, *Does God Suffer?*, 188, n. 32; and C. Gunton, 'Aspects of Salvation: Some Unscholastic Themes from Calvin's *Institutes*', *International Journal of Systematic Theology* 1 (1999), 253–265 (265).

[53] R. Helland, 'The Hypostatic Union: How Did Jesus Function?', *Evangelical Quarterly* 65 (1993), 311–327 (325–326). We prefer the term 'near-Nestorian' to Helland's own 'modern Nestorianism'. (Helland, 'The Hypostatic Union', 326).

soul in each human person.⁵⁴ Thomas Weinandy finds that Calvin's problems with Christ's two natures issue from his use of this body-soul simile. There are two ways in which this imagery may be employed, says Weinandy, one legitimate, one not so legitimate. The first, legitimate use is simply to say that '[a]s the soul and body formed the one ontological reality of a human being so, similarly, the divinity and humanity formed the one ontological reality of Jesus.' Against this, the second use of the simile is 'as an exact model for conceiving the type of relationship and for formulating the manner of the union which existed between the divinity and the humanity. It was used then not only to illustrate that the divinity and the humanity were ontologically united in the one Christ, but also as the model for designing how this ontological oneness was achieved.'⁵⁵ Essentially, the legitimate use compares the constitution of the human person as a union of body and soul 'giving rise to the one reality of a human being';⁵⁶ the emphasis is very much on the whole person rather than whatever may be said to constitute that person. However, the second employment of the simile encourages comparison of the relation between Christ's humanity and divinity with the body and soul. This comparison, for Weinandy, is 'patently false': although the union of body and soul constitutes a person and the union of divinity and humanity constitutes the person of Christ, 'the manner or mode of their respective ontological unions differs in kind.'⁵⁷

Why is this so? Weinandy argues that the soul-body relationship forms an ontological union that 'gives rise to a new and third reality called man.'⁵⁸ However, if this model were applied to the incarnation, this would make Christ a *tertium quid*, that is, something between divine and human. 'Jesus may be one, but he becomes a hybrid, for the divinity and the humanity, like the body and the soul, are seen as constitutive components whose ontological fusion gives rise to a new kind of being.'⁵⁹ This has the added complication that certain things are predicated to the apposite nature rather than to the Son of God as a person,⁶⁰ a complication that we find in Calvin. According to Weinandy, Calvin's use of the body-soul simile means that he employs the *communicatio idiomatum* to explain how Christ's divinity and humanity relate strictly to each other, whereas the *communicatio* should be used to show how the two natures relate together in the one person of Christ.⁶¹ Calvin's christology is, to use our term, near-Nestorian because he misunderstood the precise way in which the body-soul simile should influence a right

---

⁵⁴ Calvin, *Institutes*, 2:14:1, 482.
⁵⁵ Weinandy, *Does God Suffer?*, 182.
⁵⁶ Weinandy, *Does God Suffer?*, 183.
⁵⁷ Weinandy, *Does God Suffer?*, 183.
⁵⁸ Weinandy, *Does God Suffer?*, 184.
⁵⁹ Weinandy, *Does God Suffer?*, 184.
⁶⁰ Weinandy, *Does God Suffer?*, 184.
⁶¹ Weinandy, *Does God Suffer?*, 187–188.

conceptualisation of the relation between Christ's two natures. Any true relation between them is vastly overshadowed by the rhetorical or linguistic device of the *communicatio idiomatum*.[62]

Consequently, Calvin seems not to address the matter of how the two natures truly relate in Christ and so risks affirming a division in the Mediator. If the Mediator is divided, if his humanity and divinity are so distinct that there is no positive relation between them, then we have good cause to doubt the effectiveness of his work of atonement. Against the orthodox understanding of the Son suffering death as a man, we would instead have the Son suffering death in his humanity whilst his divinity lives on – and this raises the question of how truly he was united to his humanity at the start.[63] To compensate for his strong emphasis on the distinction between Christ's two natures, Calvin employs the *communicatio idiomatum*; but this does not resolve the matter, for 'the things that [Christ] carried out in his human nature are transferred *improperly, although not without reason,* to his divinity.'[64] The *communicatio* for Calvin effectively is a conceptual aid to affirm the relation between the two distinct natures rather than an attempt to clarify that relation.[65] There is, however, no actual *communicatio*, and no sense, as Bruce McCormack suggests, that a rhetorical understanding of the *communicatio* is possible precisely due to an actual *communicatio*,[66] that is, the incarnation of the Word. This situation arises due to a particular conception of the fundamental ontological distinction between God and the world: Calvin so emphasises the distinction between God and the world that, at times, this proper distinction – that God is God and the creature is not – becomes a sharp division affecting the way the two relate. Calvin's christology is near-Nestorian because his basic conception of the relationship between God and creation has dualistic leanings.[67] By frequently underscoring Christ's two natures over against his person, Calvin suggests that even though God and creation ostensibly enjoy a relationship with one another, this relation primarily is maintained by a Mediator who himself is divided precisely because divinity and humanity cannot easily interact. Crucially, then, the problem of the relation between God and creation in Calvin's theology finds its ultimate location in his christology.

---

[62] Weinandy, *Does God Suffer?*, 188. Against this, Paul Helm believes that Calvin 'seems to use the soul-body analogy ... simply to make the point that the two natures, the human and the divine, are not so mingled with each other as not to retain their distinctive natures.' (Helm, *John Calvin's Ideas*, 86). This may have been Calvin's intent, of course; but if Thomas Weinandy's identification of two uses of the simile is accurate, Calvin is not freed from the charge that he employed what was 'patently false' to aid his theology.

[63] We should note that Calvin does not appear to suggest this himself.

[64] Calvin, *Institutes*, 2:14:2, 484, emphasis mine.

[65] Helm, *John Calvin's Ideas*, 76.

[66] McCormack, *For Us and Our Salvation*, 8–9.

[67] See § 2.5.

This in turn impacts the genuineness of Christ's humanity. If the notion of a divided Mediator raises the possibility that the Son suffers death in his humanity whilst his divinity lives on, as we have said, then there is always a docetic suggestion that the Son's humanity is little more than a garment to be discarded upon death. Insofar as the Son of God assumes humanity to execute God's will in created space and time, Christ's flesh is the clothing in which the divine will is dressed and so impotent apart from the divinity that wears it. Calvin not only divides Christ's activity between what he does as a man and what he does as divine, but presents the former, human action as somewhat incidental for achieving salvation:

> our Lord came forth as true man and took the person and the name of Adam in order to take Adam's place in obeying the Father, to present our flesh as the price of satisfaction to God's righteous judgement, and, in the same flesh, to pay the penalty that we deserved. In short, since neither as God alone could he feel death, nor as man alone could he overcome it, he coupled human nature with divine that to atone for sin he might submit the weakness of the one to death; and that, *wrestling with death by the power of the other nature*, he might win victory for us.[68]

The problem is that this presents Christ as more than human, a *tertium quid*: he has a divine component from which to draw resources, something that no other human can claim. Whilst it is true that Jesus is the Son of God, the Word made flesh, this means neither that he has some intrinsic power to utilise to achieve God's purposes for the world, nor that somehow the Word causes the actions of the humanity he assumes.[69] To affirm the incarnation is to say no more than the Son of God took humanity to himself and now lives as a man. Although Jesus of Nazareth is unique insofar as no other human can claim truthfully to be the Word made flesh,[70] there is no ontological difference between him and any other human.[71] This means that when he was tempted to

---

[68] Calvin, *Institutes*, 2:12:3, 466, emphasis mine.

[69] Cf. I. McFarland, 'Christ, Spirit and Atonement', *International Journal of Systematic Theology* 3 (2001), 83–93 (87).

[70] Cf. McFarland, 'Christ, Spirit and Atonement', 86. Kelly Kapic notes that the Spirit's involvement in Jesus's conception introduces 'some element of discontinuity between Christ and the rest of humanity'. (K.M. Kapic, 'The Son's Assumption of a Human Nature: A Call for Clarity', *International Journal of Systematic Theology* 3 [2001], 154–166 [166]). Against Kapic, we may say that the Son's humanity certainly is continuous with our own and that the New Testament texts emphasise this to such an extent that we should have no reason to doubt the solidarity of the person of Christ with any other human person. To do so would be to affirm a near-Nestorian christology that wants always to keep the distinction between Christ's two natures in the foreground.

[71] Does this mean that the humanity assumed by the Son is *fallen* humanity, corrupted by the fall? If the Son assumes a humanity that is not corrupted by the fall, has he

disobey his Father and so to refuse his calling, Jesus resisted not because of some inner faculty but through the empowerment of the Holy Spirit.[72] Indeed, Jesus's faithfulness to God fundamentally is something prompted and enabled by the Spirit, who himself is the pledge of God's faithfulness to the whole of his creation through his action in Christ.[73] Calvin's pneumatology, so clearly present when he discusses the human relation to God through Christ,[74] is curiously absent from the constitution of the person of Christ.[75]

My suspicion, then, is that the *communicatio idiomatum* functions in Calvin's christology in place of the Holy Spirit or, at the very least, points away from a christology with a truly pneumatological accent. This is suggested by the idea that the *communicatio* is simply a rhetorical device: there is no account of genuine relation between the two natures in Christ save for a vague positing that there is such a relation, whereas surely the Spirit is the one who not only relates the two natures of the Mediator but does so whilst preserving them in

---

assumed *true* humanity – and if not, can he *really* save that which *is* corrupted? Conversely, can *corrupted* humanity be said to be *true* humanity? In assuming a *non-fallen* humanity, is Christ actually truly human whereas other persons are not? For a useful summary of the issues, see Kapic, 'The Son's Assumption of a Human Nature'. One further observation should be made: Hebrews 4:15 cannot be used to affirm either the sinlessness or fallenness of the Son's assumed humanity, for it refers to the fact that Jesus did not succumb to temptation: he was tested 'in every respect ... as we are, yet without sin.'

[72] Oliver Crisp suggests that this is 'not a conventional view', at least not when speaking about Christ performing miracles. (Crisp, *Divinity and Humanity*, 25). Maybe not; but it promises more than any view that depicts Christ drawing from his divine nature in order to power his human nature. Can a fully human person really do such a thing? Is it not better to say that it is the Holy Spirit who enables a human person to perform the works of God? This is why Ivor Davidson, whose stress falls on a slightly different accent, more appropriately observes that 'Jesus' humanity develops and functions as it does, in obedience and intimacy, *via* the personal work of the Spirit. If it were otherwise – that is to say, if the humanity of Jesus depended upon a direct or static relationship to the Father independently of the Spirit – the vital salvific link between Jesus' humanity and ours would be weakened, for his humanity would exist in a way that ours does not, and be capable of an equilibrium unavailable to us. That way, his humanity would not be prototypical in the way the Epistle to the Hebrews maintains it is'. (I. Davidson, 'Theologising the Human Jesus: An Ancient [and Modern] Approach to Christology Reassessed', *International Journal of Systematic Theology* 3 [2001], 129–153 [152, emphasis original]).

[73] See § 8.5.

[74] See, for example, Calvin, *Institutes*, 3:1:1, 537–538, and the comments in § 2.4.

[75] Cf. S.R. Holmes, 'Reformed Varieties of the *Communicatio Idiomatum*', in S.R. Holmes and M.A. Rae (eds.), *The Person of Christ* (London: T&T Clark, 2005), 70–86 (74).

their distinctiveness.[76] The matter is one of identification: *this* man *is this* God, acting by the power of the Spirit.[77] There are hints in Calvin's writings that he was drawn at times to this way of putting the matter: his observations on the relation of the Spirit to Jesus in Luke 4:18 or Mark 2:8 are but two interesting examples.[78] However, for the most part, Calvin depicts Christ doing divine things from his divinity and human things from his humanity, something that we may brand as near-Nestorianism. Without an adequate pneumatology, Calvin's position certainly invites comparison with its source heresy.

§ 8.4 The Spirit and Christ's Obedience: Matthew's Gospel[79]

For Calvin, the obedience of Christ is essential to the divine work of salvation.[80] Humanity is reconciled to God through Christ's abolition of sin, achieved 'by the whole course of his obedience.'[81] Christ's obedience is a lifelong manifestation of devotion to his Father that culminates in his voluntary self-offering in death.[82] However, the problems that we have identified with his christology – that there is too sharp a distinction between Christ's two natures and that the divine consequently has priority over the human – means that although Calvin wishes to say that Christ's death is truly an act of the Son of God *made* flesh, what he implies is that this death actually is performed by the Son of God *in* flesh, that is, it is the divine nature that enables Christ to obey whilst he is clothed in humanity.[83] We have said already that this notion presents Christ as more than human, a *tertium quid*, meaning that the Son of God's obedience was enacted not by a man but by a God-man. This suggests that Calvin's teaching on atonement – 'that man, who by his disobedience had become lost, should by way of remedy counter it with obedience, satisfy God's judgement, and pay the penalties for sin'[84] – is not in fact an account of an obedient human truly making atonement for fallen humanity or in its place. It

---

[76] This point arises from reflection upon conversations primarily with Lincoln Harvey and John Colwell; see also Smail, *The Giving Gift*, 94.

[77] Cf. R. Bauckham, *God Crucified: Monotheism and Christology in the New Testament* (Carlisle: Paternoster, 1998); R.W. Jenson, 'Christ in the Trinity: *Communicatio Idiomatum*', in S.R. Holmes and M.A. Rae (eds.), *The Person of Christ* (London: T&T Clark, 2005), 61–69 (67); McFarland, 'Christ, Spirit and Atonement', 87.

[78] Calvin, *Comm. Evan. 1*, 228, 395.

[79] All scriptural references in § 8.4 are from Matthew's Gospel unless indicated otherwise.

[80] See also § 2.4.

[81] Calvin, *Institutes*, 2:16:5, 507.

[82] Calvin, *Institutes*, 2:16:5, 507–508.

[83] Again, Calvin's contention that '[our Lord] ... wrestled with death by the power of the other [that is, the divine] nature' proves telling. (Calvin, *Institutes*, 2:12:3, 466).

[84] Calvin, *Institutes*, 2:12:3, 466.

concerns the execution of the divine will in creaturely space and time to bring the elect to eternal life and consign the remainder to eternal damnation.

Our contention, then, that in Calvin's theology the *communicatio idiomatum* supplants the role of the Holy Spirit in the life of Christ is an important observation, for we need to ensure a proper place for the former if we are to offer a correct analysis of Christ's obedience. For Hebrews, 'we do not have a high priest who is unable to sympathise with our weaknesses, but we have one who in every respect has been tested as we are, yet without sin' (Heb 4:15). Not only is the Son's true and full humanity affirmed, but also his life of sinlessness lived from that humanity – 'yet without sin'. The implication of Hebrews 9:14, in saying that Christ 'through the eternal Spirit offered himself without blemish to God', is that his work of atonement, achieved through his obedience and vindicated by his Father in his resurrection and exaltation (Heb 1:3), is guided and empowered by the Holy Spirit. It is the Spirit who enables Christ to live that faithful human life first required of humanity in the garden of Eden and then of Israel as God's covenant people, and so as representative of both Jew and Gentile as 'the pioneer and perfecter of faith' (τὸν τῆς πίστεως ἀρχηγὸν καὶ τελειωτήν; Heb 12:2). This theme of Christ's obedience, so central to Hebrews's argument, is especially clear in Matthew's Gospel;[85] indeed, Matthew explores the precise nature of the relation between the Spirit and Christ's obedience in a way that Hebrews largely assumes.[86] To demonstrate this, we shall now offer our own, brief analysis of the role of the Spirit as the one who enables Christ's obedience. We will focus on Matthew's pneumatology as found in his accounts of Jesus's birth (Mt 1:18-23), baptism (3:13-17) and temptations in the wilderness (4:1-11) and Gethsemane (26:36-46).[87]

It is clear from the opening words of his Gospel that Matthew acknowledges the activity of the Spirit in the life of Jesus. There was no human initiative to Jesus's birth, and no human agent, whether male or female, responsible for this particular pregnancy.[88] Mary is simply 'found to be with child from the Holy Spirit' (ἐκ πνεύματος ἁγίου; 1:18, 20), who 'sets the whole process of this

---

[85] R.N. Longenecker, 'The Foundational Conviction of New Testament Christology: The Obedience / Faithfulness / Sonship of Christ', in J.B. Green and M. Turner (eds.), *Jesus of Nazareth: Lord and Christ. Essays on the Historical Jesus and New Testament Christology* (Grand Rapids: Eerdmans, 1994), 473–488 (485).

[86] This is not to denigrate Hebrews's argument in any way, as his point is simply to show that Christ leads the way into God's presence by the death that crowns his obedience.

[87] See B. Charette, *Restoring Presence: The Spirit in Matthew's Gospel* (JPTS 18; Sheffield: Sheffield Academic Press, 2000) for a thorough account of Matthew's pneumatology, and Hawthorne, *The Presence and the Power* for a similarly thorough overview of the Spirit's role in the life of Jesus throughout the New Testament.

[88] Cf. F.V. Filson, *A Commentary on the Gospel According to St Matthew* (BNTC; London: A&C Black, 1960), 55.

special conception and gestation into motion.'[89] By witnessing to the Spirit's activity here, Matthew connotes that the birth of Jesus effectively is *ex nihilo* and so as much an act of the sovereign God as was the original act of creation in the beginning (Gen 1:1). Indeed, the Old Testament depicts the Spirit 'as the agent of God's activity, especially in creation and the giving of life' (Gen 1:2; Job 26:13; Ps 33:6; 104:30; Ezek 37:1-14);[90] it is no surprise, therefore, that Matthew's mention of the Spirit's involvement in Jesus's birth (γένεσις) is a deliberate allusion to the opening chapters of Genesis,[91] suggesting that this new, divine activity is the beginning (γένεσις) of a new creation.[92] 'Through the agency of the Holy Spirit, the divine creative power, Jesus the Messiah is conceived and with that conception the redemption associated with the Messiah is begun. When the Messiah is formed in Mary's womb the Spirit sets in motion the renewal of God's creation.'[93] Matthew's placement of the Spirit in the closest connection with Jesus at his birth thus indicates that God himself is manifest in this particular human graciously to implement this act of renewal.[94] Jesus's conception by the Spirit means that this anointed one (ὁ χριστός)[95] is 'Emmanuel', 'God with us' (Mt 1:23), God present within created time and space to 'save his people from their sins' (1:21). We have seen that Israel's sacrificial system was established to maintain God's presence within the holy of holies.[96] The function of the sacrifices made on the Day of Atonement was to

---

[89] Hawthorne, *The Presence and the Power*, 71.

[90] R.T. France, *The Gospel According to Matthew: An Introduction and Commentary* (TNTC 1; Leicester: IVP, 1985), 77; cf. W.F. Albright and C.S. Mann, *Matthew: A New Translation with Introduction and Commentary* (ABC 26; New York: Doubleday, 1971), 8; D.A. Hagner, *Matthew 1-13* (WBC 33A; Dallas: Word Books, 1993), 17-18; Charette, *Restoring Presence*, 38-39; D.D. Kupp, *Matthew's Emmanuel: Divine Presence and God's People in the First Gospel* (SNTSMS 90; Cambridge: Cambridge University Press, 1996), 55.

[91] Other allusions include Matthew's intention to provide an 'account of the genealogy [βίβλος γενέσεως] of Jesus the Messiah' (Mt 1:1), which deliberately echoes the 'generations' (γενέσεως) of Genesis 2:4 and 5:1 (G.K. Beale, *The Temple and the Church's Mission: A Biblical Theology of the Dwelling Place of God* [NSBT 17; Leicester: Apollos, 2004], 171; cf. Charette, *Restoring Presence*, 38; Hagner, *Matthew 1-13*, 9; France, *Matthew*, 73; Albright and Mann, *Matthew*, 2), and the parallels between the 'numerical' Matthew 1:1-17 and Genesis 1:1-2:3 and the 'narrative' Matthew 1:18-25 and Genesis 2:4-25. (Kupp, *Matthew's Emmanuel*, 160). Allusions such as these support the idea that for Matthew, Jesus's birth marks the beginning of a new creation.

[92] Beale, *The Temple and the Church's Mission*, 171-172.

[93] Charette, *Restoring Presence*, 39.

[94] Cf. Hagner, *Matthew 1-13*, 17-18.

[95] Matthew's recurring interest in Christ as ὁ χριστός (Mt 1:1, 16-18; 2:4; 11:2; 16:16, 20; 22:42; 23:10) itself surely acknowledges the anointing Spirit's continuous role in the life of Jesus.

[96] See § 7.2–§ 7.3.

decontaminate the sacred space polluted by Israel's sin and so to restore the divine presence within her midst and thus ensure the continuity of her identity as God's covenant people. Accordingly, the renewal of creation is actualised in the removal of sin that Jesus achieves as Israel's Messiah. He restores the presence of God to his people and, through them, to the world; but he does so only because the Spirit's own action first embodies him as the presence of God. For Matthew, then, the name 'Emmanuel ... underscores the notion that salvation from sin is intimately related to the renewal of God's presence.'[97]

The Spirit's formation of Jesus's humanity at his conception demonstrates that for Matthew, Jesus uniquely is the embodiment of God's presence in the midst of his people. That Jesus is this embodied presence does not mean, however, that somehow he is distinct from the rest of humanity: he is a man and as liable to the same temptations and failings as any human person. Accordingly, Jesus discerns that he must be baptised 'to fulfil all righteousness' (3:15); Matthew portrays Jesus as the Messiah of Israel in solidarity with his people who themselves have been baptised by John (3:5-6).[98] Jesus's deliberate and willing submission to John's baptism (3:13, 15) is a vital step of obedience that leads to his receipt of the Spirit (3:16) and the divine affirmation that he is God's Son (3:17).[99] This affirmation suggests both that Jesus is the true representative of his people and that he is the chosen servant of God who is called to remain faithful to his vocation. First, Jesus is described as 'my Son, the Beloved' (3:17); the allusion to Psalm 2:7 indicates that Jesus is the anointed king 'who is given rule over the nations' (cf. Mt 28:18-19).[100] He is Israel's messianic king; but as Emmanuel, God's embodied presence (1:23), Jesus also assumes Israel's responsibility for mediating God's presence to the other nations. Just as Israel was described to Moses – and through him, to Pharaoh – as God's son (Ex 4:22), so now is Jesus similarly announced to Israel.[101] Secondly, the divine affirmation echoes Isaiah 42:1, which speaks of God's 'servant ... in whom [God's] soul delights' and upon whom God has 'put [his] spirit'. Crucially, the references to Psalm 2:7 and Isaiah 42:1 suggest that although Matthew believes that Jesus is God's Son acting in the world to bring about divine justice and so the Father's sovereign rule, the Son must first subordinate himself to that very same sovereignty that he seeks to implement. Although Jesus would be enthroned as king over the whole world (Ps 2:7-8), he must first prove himself to be God's obedient servant, bringing justice to the

---

[97] Charette, *Restoring Presence*, 40.
[98] Hagner, *Matthew 1–13*, 57; France, *Matthew*, 94–95.
[99] Cf. Hawthorne, *The Presence and the Power*, 135.
[100] Charette, *Restoring Presence*, 48; cf. Hagner, *Matthew 1–13*, 58.
[101] Matthew's account of the heavenly voice differs from that of the other Synoptics, which suggest a more intimate, less public announcement from God to Jesus (Mk 1:11; Lk 3:22).

world (Isa 42:1).[102] For Matthew, then, Jesus must learn to be the Son of his Father through obedient suffering (cf. Isa 52:13-53:12; Heb 5:8): this is the vocation prepared for him, a vocation inaugurated by his anointing with the Spirit at his baptism.[103]

The anointed Jesus is 'led up by the Spirit into the wilderness to be tempted by the devil' (Mt 4:1). Again, Matthew portrays Jesus as the obedient Son of God by contrasting him with the Israelites, who were led around the wilderness for forty years so that God could test their hearts and know 'whether or not [they] would keep his commandments' (Deut 8:2).[104] Crucially, Matthew emphasises that the Spirit himself leads Jesus into the wilderness; that Jesus follows is a further demonstration, therefore, of his willing obedience to his calling. He is responsive to the Spirit's direction in and sovereignty over his life.[105] Furthermore, it is by the power of the Spirit that Jesus resists the three temptations dangled by the devil before him (Mt 4:3, 6, 9);[106] Gerald Hawthorne argues that Matthew juxtaposes the two phrases 'by the Spirit' and 'by the devil' to imply that 'the Saviour's victory over the tempter was due in large part to his being filled with the Spirit.' Indeed, Hawthorne continues, the Spirit 'enabled Jesus to see the subtle dangers that underlay the seemingly innocent appeals of Satan to exercise his messianic powers on his own authority.'[107] Succumbing to the temptations would have deviated Jesus from faithfulness to his Father; but Jesus emerged victorious from the temptations, not 'simply because of his own inner strength or because of the set determination of his will', but because he was 'fortified in his determination to obey the Father by the strengthening force of the Spirit within him.'[108] Though not explicit throughout the account of Jesus's temptations in the wilderness, the Spirit's leading of Jesus to that place (4:1), coupled with Matthew's ongoing comparison between Jesus's testing with that of Israel,[109] suggests that he understands the Spirit to be guiding Jesus ceaselessly, just as he also guided Israel (Neh 9:20; cf. Isa 63:7-10).[110] If Jesus was tested to see how he would

---

[102] Cf. T.G. Weinandy, *In the Likeness of Sinful Flesh: An Essay on the Humanity of Christ* (Edinburgh: T&T Clark, 1993), 96; Charette, *Restoring Presence*, 48.

[103] Cf. Weinandy, *In the Likeness of Sinful Flesh*, 97.

[104] Cf. Hagner, *Matthew 1-13*, 64; France, *Matthew*, 98; G.H. Twelftree, 'Temptation of Jesus', in *Dictionary of Jesus and the Gospels* (Leicester: IVP, 1992), 821-827 (823).

[105] Cf. Hawthorne, *The Presence and the Power*, 138.

[106] The precise character of the three temptations is not our concern; for analysis, see, for example, Twelftree, 'Temptation of Jesus', 823-824, and R.W.L. Moberly, *The Bible, Theology, and Faith: A Study of Abraham and Jesus* (CSCD; Cambridge: Cambridge University Press, 2000), 201-205.

[107] Hawthorne, *The Presence and the Power*, 140.

[108] Hawthorne, *The Presence and the Power*, 139.

[109] Longenecker, 'The Foundational Conviction of New Testament Christology', 485.

[110] Twelftree, 'Temptation of Jesus', 823.

respond to the responsibility entailed by his status as God's Son,[111] Matthew's conclusion, then, is that he resisted the temptation to abuse that position by the power of the Spirit of God.

We see the same dynamic at work – though presented more subtly – in Jesus's temptation in Gethsemane (Mt 26:36-46). 'Gethsemane is ... essentially about the obedience of Christ embodied in Christ's acceptance of his Father's will.'[112] Accordingly, Jesus is conscious that he is required to remain faithful to God, but increasingly he is aware that this faithfulness will result in death (16:21; 17:22-23; 20:18-19). There is a sense of inevitability that Jesus's betrayal, suffering and death will happen,[113] but Matthew does not suggest that they are predetermined events to which Jesus resigns himself. Instead, they will happen because Jesus believes and accepts them to be entailed by his calling and the consequence of his obedience. This is what makes his struggle with his calling in Gethsemane so anguished (26:38): Jesus is tempted to abandon his divinely appointed course, with the disquieting consequence that he will have failed in his mission, that Emmanuel (1:23) is actually Ichabod (1 Sam 4:21), signifying the absence of God from his people. Central to this temptation account are Jesus's prayers (Mt 26:39, 42, 44),[114] by which he seeks to orientate himself to God's will despite the fear that threatens to – and quite possibly does – overwhelm him. First, Jesus asks his Father that 'if it is possible, let this cup pass from me' (26:39); he knows what is coming but wonders if there is another way, that is, a way that does not involve his suffering and death.[115] Nonetheless, he indicates that he is still willing to obey: 'yet not what I want but what you want.' The second prayer is different in emphasis. Whereas before Jesus sought the possibility of an alternative way, this time he accepts that no such path exists: 'My Father, if this cannot pass unless I drink it, your will be done' (26:42, 44). Matthew shows Jesus wrestling with the implications of his Father's will and emerging from the contest firmly resolved to ensure that it happens. Crucially, the fact that Jesus addresses God as 'My Father' in his prayers implies – though very subtly – that the Spirit is active even in this most testing of trials. Without the anointing Spirit, Jesus has no confirmation of his status as God's Son and so no reason to call God 'My Father'. Furthermore, there is no reason to deny the probability that the Spirit who guided Jesus through his temptations in the wilderness also leads him through this temptation

---

[111] Twelftree, 'Temptation of Jesus', 827.

[112] M. Bonnington, 'The Obedient Son: Jesus in Gethsemane', *Anvil* 16 (1999), 41–48 (42).

[113] Cf. France, *Matthew*, 259, 267, 291; D.A. Hagner, *Matthew 14–28* (WBC 33B; Dallas: Word Books, 1995), 479–480, 507–508, 575–576; Albright and Mann, *Matthew*, 200.

[114] Moberly, *The Bible, Theology, and Faith*, 211.

[115] Cf. France, *Matthew*, 373.

in the garden.[116] So whilst the Spirit is not mentioned explicitly in Matthew's Gethsemane account, certainly his presence is implied, strengthening Jesus to enable him to fulfil his vocation.[117]

What, though, does it mean to say that the Spirit enabled Jesus to obey his Father? We must distinguish carefully between two senses of the verb 'to enable' that can be applied to the Spirit's role in the life of Jesus. To say that the Spirit enables Jesus to obey could mean either that he empowers Jesus to do so or, more forcefully, that he ensures Jesus's obedience. This latter sense is problematic: it invites a dangerous suggestion that Jesus's faithfulness could not have been otherwise, that is, although it was always possible for Jesus to disobey his Father, somehow the Spirit ensured that this would never happen. There is an echo here of Calvin's contention that Adam could have remained free from sin were it not God's design for him to fall: the integrity of Adam's ability to sin or not to sin is overruled by the divine will.[118] Similarly, to say that the Spirit enables Jesus not to sin could imply that the Spirit prevents Jesus from sinning; but if this is so, then it is legitimate to question the degree to which Jesus truly is obedient to God's will. Does Christ actually *learn* obedience, as Hebrews 5:8 contends, if the Spirit removes the need for him to *struggle* with temptation? Furthermore, we should not see the Spirit's enabling as somehow preserving Jesus from the effects of living in a fallen world, for that offers the latter a form of protection that other humans are not privileged to have; the implication would be that Jesus remains faithful to God because the temptations he faced would not have been real temptations at all.

Against both of these, it is preferable to see Jesus obeying his Father in the power and strength of the Spirit: the Spirit enables Jesus's obedience by prompting him to accept his vocation and then, by that same Spirit, consolidates that act of faithfulness by empowering his resolve to continue through to his crucifixion.[119] When the Son was tempted to turn away from the

---

[116] Gerald Hawthorne makes a similar case for the Spirit's involvement in Jesus's transfiguration (Mt 17:1-8) but seems not to extend it to the Gethsemane temptation. (Hawthorne, *The Presence and the Power*, 215–216).

[117] It is possible to read Matthew 27:50 – where Jesus 'gave up the spirit' (ἀφῆκεν τὸ πνεῦμα) – as indicating the Spirit's presence with Jesus up to his death. Blaine Charette argues that throughout Matthew, τὸ πνεῦμα 'regularly refers to the Holy Spirit' and that had he wanted to say nothing more than Jesus died, 'there would be no need for such an unusual turn of phrase.' (Charette, *Restoring Presence*, 93, 94). If Charette is right, then the fact that the Spirit is depicted as abiding with Jesus at least to the point of his death suggests that he must have been present with him through the whole of his life, including the Gethsemane temptation.

[118] See § 2.3.

[119] This does not mean that the Spirit leads Jesus to a point of decision only to abandon him for its duration. Jesus's acceptance of his vocation is a faithful response not only conditioned by the Spirit but also made in the Spirit's power. There is no time when Jesus must rely on his own strength, even if the decision to remain faithful is his

Father's will, 'the Spirit was present with him to enlighten his mind, to clarify the issues, to urge him toward the right choice, but not to make that choice for him.'[120] It is this conception of the Spirit's relation to Jesus that Matthew appears to endorse, and perhaps the absence of an explicit mention of the Spirit in his account of Gethsemane emphasises that ultimately it is Jesus who renders the obedience necessary, though not apart from the Spirit, to secure God's new beginning for creation by his death. 'The righteousness of the cross ... sprang from the human will of Jesus, fraught like ours with temptation yet counselled and empowered by the Holy Spirit.'[121] By the Spirit's power, Jesus remains faithful to God's will for him and in turn ensures that God's will for all things is done as his death renews the life of creation, the actuality of which is demonstrated supremely by his own resurrection (Mt 28:1-10).

§ 8.5 A Faithfulness Empowered

Although we must always be wary of imposing anachronistic categories onto texts, we may say that Matthew appears to have no interest in distinguishing between divine and human natures in Christ. His concern solely is in the one person of the Mediator, Jesus, Emmanuel, in whom God's presence is embodied through the agency of the Spirit. Where Calvin could not avoid speaking at times about Christ doing something as a man or as God, Matthew writes simply about a human person called by God to a specific vocation to which he submits willingly and unswervingly, his resolve consolidated by the Spirit's empowerment.

There is still the matter, however, of how the two natures in Christ relate. We said earlier that Calvin's employment of the *communicatio idiomatum* to account for their relation effectively replaces the action of the Holy Spirit. The *communicatio* is a rhetorical device that simply affirms the relation; instead, against this, we may identify the man Jesus as God acting in the world by the power of the Spirit. Jesus is recognised to be such because the New Testament texts credit to this man certain functions that traditionally are ascribed to God alone. According to Richard Bauckham, Second Temple Judaism distinguished Yahweh from the gods of the nations by acknowledging him as the sole Creator and Ruler of all things.[122] 'God alone created all things; all other things, including beings worshipped as gods by Gentiles, are created by him. God alone rules supreme over all things; all other things, including beings worshipped as gods by Gentiles, are subject to him.'[123] Whilst God would

---

own; and all that he does in faithfulness to his Father is because he offers himself continuously through the Spirit.

[120] Hawthorne, *The Presence and the Power*, 230.
[121] Weinandy, *In the Likeness of Sinful Flesh*, 108.
[122] Bauckham, *God Crucified*, 10–11.
[123] Bauckham, *God Crucified*, 11.

sometimes employ servants to carry out his will throughout the universe, the New Testament writers portray Jesus not simply as another of these servants but as exercising the very functions of the Creator and Ruler himself. Bauckham argues that the New Testament writers

> include Jesus in the unique divine sovereignty over all things, they include him in the unique divine creation of all things, they identify him by the divine name which names the unique divine identity, and they portray him as accorded the worship which, for Jewish monotheists, is recognition of the unique divine identity. In this way they develop a kind of christological monotheism which is fully continuous with early Jewish monotheism but distinctive in the way it sees Jesus Christ himself as intrinsic to the identity of the unique God.[124]

The New Testament's frequent application of Psalm 110:1 – 'The LORD says to my Lord, "Sit at my right hand until I make your enemies your footstool"' – to the risen Jesus further emphasises that this particular human being – and this particular human being alone – is included in the unique divine identity.[125] Is there a suggestion here of an adoptionist christology, where the man Jesus becomes divine by God's grace or reward? No; Bauckham argues that if Jesus 'participates in the unique divine sovereignty and is therefore intrinsic to the unique divine identity, he must be so eternally.'[126] It is the eternal Son of God who takes flesh to himself, who surrenders himself to the will of the Father, who dies, is buried and is raised to life, and who now sits exalted on the throne of God, still incarnate. Bauckham's argument that the man Jesus is included in the unique divine identity allows us to say, therefore, that the man Jesus is God acting in the world. There is no need whatsoever to distinguish between his two natures by predicating certain actions to either one as Calvin does, for it is the one person of the Mediator who acts.

Nonetheless, this inclusion of Jesus in the divine identity cannot truly be understood apart from the action of the Spirit who sustains that identity by constituting the person of the incarnate Son. It is by the power of the Spirit that the eternal Son of God takes flesh to himself and becomes the man Christ Jesus.[127] The Spirit both unites the divine and human natures in the one person

---

[124] Bauckham, *God Crucified*, 26–27.

[125] Bauckham, *God Crucified*, 29–31. Psalm 110:1 is quoted or referenced in Matthew 22:44; 26:64; Mark 12:36; 14:62; 16:19; Luke 20:42-43; 22:69; Acts 2:33-35; 5:31; 7:55-56; Romans 8:34; 1 Corinthians 15:25; Ephesians 1:20; 2:6; Colossians 3:1; Hebrews 1:3, 13; 8:1; 10:12-13; 12:2; 1 Peter 3:22; and Revelation 3:21.

[126] Bauckham, *God Crucified*, 36.

[127] Despite John Owen's emphasis on the role of the Spirit in framing, forming and conceiving the body of Christ in the womb of the virgin, he also states that the Son assumes humanity through an immediate act. (J. Owen, *Pneumatologia: Or, A Discourse Concerning the Holy Spirit*, in W.H. Gould [ed.], *The Works of John Owen, Volume III* [London: Banner of Truth, 1966], 160–164). Against Owen, there

of Christ and preserves them in their distinctiveness. There is no conflation of divinity and humanity in Christ but also no need to so emphasise the distinctiveness of each nature that it becomes possible to speak of a divided Mediator. Fundamentally, the Spirit provides the Son with the humanity necessary for him to remain faithful to the Father as a human person and enables that obedience by prompting the incarnate Son willingly to submit to the Spirit's guidance and strength.[128]

Given this, we may see that the Spirit is the pledge or guarantee of God's providential action within creation. Our definition of providence as God's sovereign action within creation to remain faithful to his promise that the world in its entirety shall be the place of God's presence is given shape by the Spirit's activity in the life of Jesus by which we may know that God is present and active within the world. Jesus is 'Emmanuel', 'God with us' (Mt 1:23), God's embodied presence within creation who himself makes possible its own entrance into God's presence. As Israel's Messiah and the representative of all humanity, Jesus offers to God that faithful response originally sought from that humanity to extend God's presence across the whole world. Although he struggles with numerous temptations to reject his vocation and instead to follow his own path, Jesus overcomes these not because his humanity is nourished by his divinity but because he consistently is attentive and responsive to the direction and empowerment of the Spirit. Consequently, to say that Jesus 'through the eternal Spirit offered himself without blemish to God' (Heb 9:14) is also to say that the Spirit prompted and strengthened the incarnate Son in his resolve to remain faithful to his vocation and in doing so demonstrated God's own faithfulness to his purposes for creation. God has not abandoned the world and reconciles it to himself through Christ's Spirit-enabled obedience.

Furthermore, the Spirit's involvement in the life of Jesus suggests that God displays his sovereignty by freely electing the Son to become a man in the person of Christ to act on behalf and in place of fallen humanity. The Spirit transcends the fundamental ontological distinction between God and the world, ensuring that God does not simply act *through* the man Jesus but *is* the man Jesus, God acting within the world. This means that the obedience Christ renders to God truly is the action of a human person struggling to remain

---

is no reason to see why the Son should not also assume humanity by the power of the Spirit; indeed, is there a significant difference between the Son's assuming humanity and the Spirit forming a body for Christ in Mary's womb? For comment on Owen's christology, see A. Spence, 'Christ's Humanity and Ours: John Owen', in C. Schwöbel and C.E. Gunton (eds.), *Persons, Divine and Human: King's College Essays in Theological Anthropology* (Edinburgh: T&T Clark, 1991), 74–97, and Holmes, 'Reformed Varieties of the *Communicatio Idiomatum*', 78–82, 85.

[128] We must affirm once more that the Spirit's enabling of the Son's obedience is not to say either that in some way the Spirit guaranteed the Son's obedience or that he preserved the Son from the effects of living in a fallen world.

faithful to his calling and not merely the execution of the divine will through secondary causation, as Calvin's theology of atonement can imply.[129] We may affirm, therefore, that the Spirit preserves both the integrity of Christ's obedience as genuinely *human* action and the integrity of that human action as authentic *divine* action.

Accordingly, we have confirmation once more that God's providence ultimately is defined by his action in Christ. However, if providence is God's faithfulness to his purposes for creation, then we see that this action in Christ must be understood as the faithful action of the triune God. Jesus's faithfulness to the Father is the supreme manifestation of the Father's own faithfulness to the world insofar as in Christ, God acts within the world to reconcile to himself that which is fallen and transform it; but without the Spirit's act of faithfulness that communicates the Father's will to the Son, strengthens the Son in his resolve to remain faithful to that will, and mediates the Son to the world through the people called to be his body, the Church, the world itself has no pledge or assurance that God in Christ is at work within it. Just as the Spirit upholds the integrity of Christ's obedience as genuinely human action, so he maintains the reality of the reconciliation of the world to God.

§ 8.6 Conclusion

Providence is God's sovereign action within creation to remain faithful to his promise that the world in its entirety shall be the place of God's presence; and this providential action is that of the triune God. As with Galatians 3 and Hebrews, our reading of Matthew's Gospel serves to demonstrate the legitimacy of the conceptual framework of God's presence as the most appropriate foundation and context for the Christian doctrine of providence. Within this context, the Father sends the Son to become incarnate and to act as God in the world, the Son obeys this calling within the freely accepted limitations that creaturely existence imposes, and the Spirit enables him continually to offer himself to the Father despite the temptation to reject his vocation. It is important to recognise the directing and empowering role of the Spirit in the life of Jesus, for the genuine humanity of the latter is severely jeopardised if there is any hint that he can draw from some inherent, divine resource to help him obey the Father. This would make Jesus more than human, a *tertium quid*, particularly if conceived in a near-Nestorian manner such as that found in Calvin's interpretation of some of the events in the life of Christ.

Jesus successfully mediates between God and the world. By the Spirit's power, Jesus is the embodied presence of God in the midst of his people, the Church, and, as we suggested earlier, through the Church, his body, the world;[130] and by faithfully offering humanity back to the Father in his own

---

[129] See § 2.4.
[130] See § 5.4.

flesh, again, by the Spirit, the world has access into the presence of God. We see, then, that divine providence, that is, the actualisation of God's intention to extend his presence throughout the world, is not a matter of God's will to mediate his active presence through creaturely secondary causation but something that happens through creaturely faithfulness made possible and guaranteed by his own, faithful action. By the will of the Father, by the empowerment of the Holy Spirit, the life of the man Jesus Christ is God's providence made flesh.

CHAPTER 9

Shaping a Theology of Providence

§ 9.1 Introduction

The aim of this final chapter is to summarise the argument of this study; to anticipate potential objections to our suggested foundation and context for the Christian doctrine of providence; to clear the ground for a theology of providence; and to indicate how a theology of providence could take shape from within the conceptual framework of God's active presence.

§ 9.2 Summary of the Argument

Given the Reformed tradition's emphasis on God's pancausal relation to the world, our initial concern was to discern its safeguarding of the integrity of creaturely causal efficacy. The Reformed tradition is clear that God's determination of all things is no obstacle to affirming the goodness and genuine causal efficacy of creaturely action. We explored the concept of creaturely secondary causation and its relation to divine primary causation in the theology of John Calvin; but we concluded that Calvin cannot avoid setting divine primary causation in opposition to secondary causation. This is because of his emphasis upon God's *will* to accommodate his action to secondary causation, which means either that creaturely activity is reduced merely to instrumentality or that it is opposed and subsequently overwhelmed by primary causation. Furthermore, an exploration of the reaction in sixteenth- and seventeenth-century England to the Reformed teaching on providence and predestination showed that it provided encouragement not only to those engaged in the development of the natural sciences but also to those who sought to distance God from direct involvement in creaturely affairs. It is the ambiguity of the concept of secondary causation that led to these differing responses, and we queried whether the conceptual framework of primary and secondary causation was the most adequate way of conceiving God's providence.

We sought to determine if this ambiguity is inherent in the concept of causation, but, following Aristotle, decided that it was possible to speak of a range of non-contradictory causes. Ostensibly, primary and secondary causation do not contradict: primary causation differs from secondary causation insofar as God founds, upholds and empowers the action of the creature. However, we noted that both primary and secondary causation are said to be *the* cause of any given creaturely action or effect. This is seen clearly in

Thomas Aquinas's teaching on providence; but Aquinas, like Calvin, cannot truly affirm the integrity of creaturely causal efficacy in relation to God's primary causation. More recent studies of divine action, including causal joint theories and the panentheistic analogy, also fail to avoid certain problems in their accounts of divine action. Either the problem of the relation or interaction between the two causal orders, divine and creaturely, is continued, or the analogies employed to describe divine action approximate neither necessarily nor sufficiently to the reality they aim to render.

The consistent and fundamental critique was that neither primary and secondary causation, nor analogies for divine action, has a place for the action of the *triune* God. Consequently, we argued that the conceptual framework of God's active presence in the world embodied in Jesus Christ and mediated by the Holy Spirit is a corrective to the conceptual framework of primary and secondary causation. This led to an account of the concept of divine presence as portrayed in Scripture, focussing first on God's decision to dwell within Israel's tabernacle and temple, then on the embodiment of this divine presence in Jesus Christ, and finally on the role of the Church, the body of Christ, and its participation in the divine presence by means of the power of the Holy Spirit. Throughout our discussion, we maintained that God has promised that the world in its entirety shall be the place of his presence and that this would happen through faithful human action. On this account, providence is defined as God's sovereign action within creation to remain faithful to the promise he made to it.

Having summarised the notion of divine presence, we sought to demonstrate its legitimacy for the foundation and context in which providence is situated by exploring the scriptural presentation of God's faithfulness to his purposes for the world and of his desire that these should be fulfilled through faithful human action. Accordingly, we offered a reading of Israel's receipt of the Mosaic Law and Paul's understanding of its place in God's purposes. The law was a temporary institution 'until Christ came' (Gal 3:24); and Christ himself is *the* faithful, *the* mature Israelite who offers the appropriate response to God that he desired originally from Adam and then from Israel. From this, we explored what Christ achieved through his faithfulness by considering the depiction of Christ as a high priest in the letter to the Hebrews and that letter's interpretation of Christ's self-offering the light of the law's sacrificial system. Focussing further on this self-offering, we argued that although Christ is the eternal Son of God made flesh, he is a man who needs the power of the Holy Spirit to enable and consolidate his faithfulness to God.

Overall, the doctrine of providence is demonstrated to concern the action of the triune God: The Father sends the Son to become incarnate and to act as God in the world; the Son obeys this calling within the freely accepted limitations that creaturely existence imposes; and the Spirit enables him continually to offer himself to the Father despite the temptation to reject his vocation. Furthermore, by the Spirit's power, Christ is the embodied presence of God in the midst of his people, the Church, and, through the Church, his body, the world; and by faithfully offering humanity back to the Father in his own flesh, again, by the Spirit, the world has access into – or becomes in its entirety the place of – the presence of God.

§ 9.3 Potential Objections

The conceptual framework of God's presence attends more specifically to the scriptural presentation of the providential activity of the triune God. Its central claim – that God promises to extend his presence from the garden of Eden across the entire world through faithful human action – is a declaration of God's providence focussed ultimately upon God's action in Christ. Conceiving of providence in this way is a significant departure from a claim such as that of the Westminster Confession that sees providence as God's *pancausal* upholding, directing, disposing and governing of all creatures.[1] Arguably the two central emphases of any traditional Reformed account of providence – that God orders all things for a particular end and this in the closest connection with the divine decree – appear to be diminished or missing altogether. However, it is quite clear that our presentation of providence *does* have a place for God's decree; but it is a decree that reveals God's desire to live within the world amongst his people and not the foreordination of certain individuals to eternal life and the remainder to everlasting condemnation. Similarly, it is also clear that God's action is his *sovereign* action; the scriptural witness is that the world in its entirety *will* be the place of God's presence, though the fulfilment of this promise depends not upon God's pancausal execution of the divine decree but upon faithful human obedience enabled first by Christ's own Spirit-empowered faithfulness to God's commands. Although our definition of God's providence bears little surface resemblance to most traditional Reformed confessions and doctrinal statements, it does continue to share those statements' concern for God's sovereignty over all things. Furthermore, we must be clear precisely what has been attempted in this study. Our contention that providence is best explicated from within the conceptual framework of God's presence is no more than the *foundation* for a truly Christian doctrine of providence; as such, the precise content requires further development.

Before we clear the ground for a theology of providence and indicate the shape it could take, we shall anticipate four potential objections to the claims we have made.[2] As we have acknowledged throughout, the conceptual framework of God's presence does not resolve the issues for which the

---

[1] 'Chapter 5: Of Providence, Article 1', *The Westminster Confession of Faith, 1647*, in J. Pelikan and V. Hotchkiss (eds.), *Creeds and Confessions of Faith in the Christian Tradition, Volume 2. Part Four: Creeds and Confessions of the Reformation Era* (New Haven: Yale University Press, 2003), 612.

[2] This does not mean, of course, that further objections cannot be made!

concepts of primary and secondary causation were developed. There are a number of scriptural texts – Genesis 45:7-8, Proverbs 21:1, Isaiah 45:1-7 and Acts 2:23, to name but a few – ostensibly illuminated only by the distinction between primary and secondary causation. Indeed, these are crucial texts that any thorough doctrine of providence needs to address. Does our neglect to discuss these texts, then, coupled with our attempt to demonstrate the legitimacy of depicting providence predominantly in terms of divine presence and faithfulness, indicate a reticence to grapple with the more traditional issues associated with the doctrine? Perhaps; but perhaps the texts mentioned need situating within a wider context that pays appropriate attention to the proper eschatological goal of God's action in the world. The dominant emphasis changes from how God and Joseph's brothers, for example, are all said to be the cause of Joseph's plight (Gen 45:7-8) to how God remains faithful to his promise to the world in spite of humanity's most conscientious attempts to refuse it. Admittedly, talk of primary and secondary causation may help to illuminate these passages; but the point is that they cannot *determine* their interpretation – and this is precisely the tendency of the conceptual framework of primary and secondary causation.

From this emerges a second concern. To what extent is an explication of providence in terms of divine presence simply an attempt to *force* a particular set of scriptural texts to apply to God's providential action in the world? This is an important point. Is the notion of divine presence in Scripture not as dominant a theme as has been suggested? Are we thoroughly misguided to claim it as the foundation for a doctrine of providence? Against this, we may note simply the pervasiveness of the concept of the presence of God both in Israel's cult and in the New Testament's reinterpretation of the cult's apparatus and rituals in christological terms. It is not the case, then, that a particular set of texts is being manipulated to yield a more palatable account of providence to counteract the apparent severity of the traditional Reformed stance on the matter.

A third objection relates specifically to our understanding of God's omnipresence. How is God to extend his presence across the world when surely he is present to all things? Texts such as 1 Kings 8:27 already wrestle with the implications of this question and acknowledge that God cannot be constrained by any place of dwelling. Yet God is said nonetheless to reside in certain places. The holy of holies, for example, was, according to the cult, the place of God's presence, the intersection of heaven and earth. Similarly, the New Testament describes Jesus using temple imagery, suggesting that he is the new temple and somehow the embodiment of the divine presence; but the New Testament also depicts the Church as the temple of God and so the place of his presence. Do we claim that God is present in Jesus but not in the Church, or suggest, as we have already,[3] that the intensity or fullness of God's presence

---

[3] See § 5.4.

differs according to the place of dwelling? If so, then we may say that any apparent inconsistency in the scriptural presentation of the precise location of the divine presence is mitigated by the pervasiveness of the concept and the stability of its logic. God's intention is that the whole world should become the equivalent to the cult's holy of holies; and God is faithful to ensure that this will happen, by dwelling first amongst Israel in the tabernacle and temple, and then, by the Spirit, properly in Christ and through his body, the Church, which mediates the divine presence to the world through its faithful witness. John's insistence that the temple of the heavenly city is in fact 'the Lord God the Almighty and the Lamb' (Rev 21:22) indicates that God will one day grace the entire world with the richness of his presence, as the risen and incarnate Son, in whom 'the whole fullness of deity dwells bodily' (Col 2:9), returns to live amongst his people.

God's provision to the world, then, ultimately is his provision of *himself*. How, though – and this is our fourth and final anticipated objection – how does this relate to the pancausal understanding of divine providence that has no problem in affirming God's involvement in everything that happens, however apparently insignificant? Calvin states the traditional conviction clearly when he observes that God 'sustains, nourishes, and cares for, everything he has made, even to the least sparrow'.[4] This is the element that we must confess not to have addressed. We have focussed on excavating a foundation for a doctrine of providence and so have not attempted to develop the meaning of God's providence for every particular creature; to use Allan Coppedge's distinctions, we have focussed more on *historical* providence and very little indeed on *special* or *personal* providence.[5] Eventually we must face questions of how God provides in specific situations, of why he fails to provide in others, and of what these two possibilities actually mean in practice. Whatever responses are offered, an explication of providence in terms of the conceptual framework of divine presence requires the shape of special or personal providence to be christological in orientation.

§ 9.4 Clearing the Ground for a Theology of Providence

The aim of this study has not been to develop a doctrine of providence but to suggest that the conceptual framework of God's presence is the most appropriate foundation and context for such development. Before indicating the shape that a theology of providence could take from within this conceptual framework, we should clear the ground for such a theology by weaving

---

[4] J. Calvin, *Institutes of the Christian Religion* (2 vols.), translated by F.L. Battles (LCC XX / XXI; Philadelphia: The Westminster Press, 1960), 1:16:1, 197–198.

[5] A. Coppedge, *The God Who is Triune: Revisioning the Christian Doctrine of God* (Downers Grove: IVP, 2007), 300–301. These distinctions are made within the context of God's redemption of humanity.

together four threads from the foregoing discussion that should lead to the crafting of a tapestry that details the history of God's dealings with the world.

The first of these threads is entailed by our definition of providence, which emphasises the notion of faithfulness: God's faithfulness to the world is fulfilled through faithful human action, a contention supported first by appeal to the Old Testament's depiction of humanity's role within the world as God's representative; next by reference to the New Testament's portrayal of Christ as the embodiment of the divine presence, who offers himself willingly to his Father to reverse the covenant unfaithfulness of the people of God; and finally, by pointing to the conviction that God's presence is mediated to the whole world through the Church, which is Christ's body as established by the action of the Spirit. These elements constitute our second thread: the contours of a Christian doctrine of providence based upon the conceptual framework of God's presence;[6] and these contours prompt certain interpretations of each aspect of the threefold scheme of providence: *conservatio*, *concursus* and *gubernatio*.[7] We shall consider each of these briefly in turn.

Gubernatio refers to God's government of the world, his sovereign action to ensure that that his intentions for all things will be realised. Given the conceptual framework of God's presence, the crucial task perhaps will be to develop *gubernatio* in terms of the Son's submission to the Father and response to the sovereign leading of the Holy Spirit. Related studies might concern the relation of God's will or eternal decree to its providential outworking, how God's will might be understood as the will of the triune God, or how we explain the divine attributes or perfections in the light of God's triune identity. More could be said to develop the idea of creation as God's project.[8] Issues of eschatology may also be important within the scope of divine government (or important even for divine preservation), as we seek to understand what it means for God to *guarantee* that the whole world shall be the place of his presence. The issue of theological determinism and its threat to the integrity of creaturely action will seldom stray far from this aspect of the threefold scheme.

To avoid a purely deterministic account of *gubernatio*, it is important to express God's concurrence with the creature as primarily an issue of pneumatology.[9] We have already claimed that the Holy Spirit accompanies the incarnate Son as he offers himself to his Father in faithful obedience. Studies of divine *concursus* may well reap the benefits of sustained engagement with the role of the Spirit in creaturely life, as it is the Spirit who maintains the integrity of creaturely action *as* genuine creaturely action.

---

[6] Discussion of these contours formed the basis of § 5.
[7] See § 1.3.
[8] See § 5.2.
[9] Cf. C.M. Wood, 'How Does God Act?', *International Journal of Systematic Theology* 1 (1999), 138–152 (147).

Christology provides the necessary support to this claim. The man Jesus is the eternal Son and Word of God made flesh; but this entails that, like any other human or creature, he, too, is subject to the Father's providential activity.[10] Indeed, this is demonstrated by the fact that Jesus submitted himself to his Father's will and, by the power of the Spirit, remained faithful to him at all times. There are two important things to be discerned here if we are eventually to speak of God's special or personal providence. First, the validity of Jesus's action as the Mediator who reconciles the world to God depends upon the integrity of that action as genuinely his own; and secondly, that Jesus differs ontologically from other humans only insofar as he is the Word made flesh[11] means that it is not inappropriate to claim that just as the Spirit safeguards the integrity of his action, so, too, does the Spirit uphold the integrity of the action of all other humans and, indeed, creatures. This means that we must be prepared to say that the Spirit safeguards the integrity of all creaturely action, whether meaningful or frivolous, good or evil.

Furthermore, it is possible to reconsider *concursus* not as God's accompaniment of the creature in its activity but of his invitation to the creature that allows it to accompany God in his activity.[12] Again, we have already suggested something like this with our claim that the Son *first* offers himself to the Father and thus prepares the way for anyone who would follow in response to the prompting of the Spirit. There is no reason why future accounts of *concursus* should not focus on scriptural accounts of creatures as God's co-workers (συνεργοί; 1 Cor 3:9) and to see how this imagery relates to the more general concern of God's presence and action within the world.[13]

This leads to *conservatio*. We suggested earlier that it is God's presence within creation that preserves it.[14] God grants to the world its own causal integrity but secures it by his own presence within the world. It is God's continuous presence in the world that prevents it from collapsing into chaos precisely *because* God has made the world into the place of his presence. Such a claim is defined more sharply by the New Testament conviction that Christ is both the one in whom 'all things hold together' (Col 1:17) and the one who

---

[10] Cf. T.J. Wright, 'Reconsidering *Concursus*', *International Journal of Systematic Theology* 4 (2002), 205–215 (211).

[11] See § 8.3.

[12] Cf. Wright, 'Reconsidering *Concursus*', 210–214.

[13] K. Barth, *Church Dogmatics* (13 vols.), edited by G.W. Bromiley and T.F. Torrance (Edinburgh: T&T Clark, 1957–1975), IV/3.2, 599–602; cf. T.J. Wright, 'Witnessing Christians from Karl Barth's Perspective', *Evangelical Quarterly* 75 (2003), 239–255. This emphasis on creatures as συνεργοί would also form part of an attempt to address those concerns about providence and ecclesiology raised in § 5.5, n. 116.

[14] See § 5.2; cf. Wright, 'Reconsidering *Concursus*', 211, 214. John Webster seems also to be pursuing this idea in his Kantzer Lectures of September 2007, entitled *Perfection and Presence: God With Us, According to the Christian Confession*. (http://henrycenter.org/kantzerlectures.php, accessed 11 September 2007).

'sustains all things by his powerful word' (Heb 1:3). The cultic imagery that the author to the letter of the Hebrews uses to describe the Son's sustaining activity strongly affirms the role of the Son in maintaining the presence of the holy God in a world polluted by its sin. For Hebrews, the Son makes atonement and thus ensures the continuance of God's presence within the world.[15] Accordingly, it would not be impossible or inappropriate to further discussion of the *conservatio Dei* by elucidating it on the basis of the temple cult and its portrayal of God's own action in the cult's ritual practices.

The conceptual framework of God's presence impacts not only our understanding of the threefold scheme but also our interpretation of Scripture; this is the third thread to weave into a theology of providence. A doctrine of providence attending to God's sovereign faithfulness will need to assess the scriptural accounts of God's action far more than we have in this study, and particularly those accounts that do appear to depict divine and creaturely action in terms of primary and secondary causation. If the heart of our argument is sound, this will also mean exploring more thoroughly the imagery and status of the temple cult in Israel so that the concept of God's presence is never portrayed as sedentary, impotent or, perhaps most importantly, disconnected from the providential relation between God and his covenant people. Christology and pneumatology are vital components in this process, particularly as the Son is presented as the new temple and the embodiment of God's presence, and as an awareness of the incarnate Son's dependence upon the Holy Spirit continues to emerge. We must ensure that our accounts of divine action testify to the action of the Son and the Spirit, lest God's relation to the world be articulated solely by using voluntaristic, causal or mechanistic conceptuality.

Our fourth and final thread is the need for appropriate engagement with Christian tradition and contemporary thought. This study's constraints precluded thorough engagement with the doctrine of providence as it has been expressed in the writings of various theologians through the centuries. For example, we have not examined in any detail Karl Barth's account of providence, an omission that some may deem totally inadequate. It would not be inappropriate to consider panentheism, quantum mechanics and other similar concepts in more depth, particularly if we wish to offer a description of God's action in a world increasingly explained by the natural sciences. We have also neglected to explore any issues concerning God's relation to time, including his foreknowledge of future events and the debate about open theism.[16] Some may

---

[15] See § 7.4 and T.J. Wright, 'The Seal of Approval: An Interpretation of the Son's Sustaining Action in Hebrews 1:3', in R.J. Bauckham, D.R. Driver, T.A. Hart and N. MacDonald (eds.), *The Epistle to the Hebrews and Christian Theology* (Grand Rapids: Eerdmans, forthcoming, 2009).

[16] Open theism is the view that God chooses not to foreknow the future, which means that God in part is conditioned by the world and takes risks in his dealings with it.

have wished for further interaction at these points, but in many respects they could only have been beyond the scope of this particular study. The point is that any theology of providence that neglects tradition or contemporary thought is likely to be deficient; any attempt to shape such a theology from within the conceptual framework of God's presence must engage with other accounts of providence.

§ 9.5 Providence and the Intensity of God's Presence

Despite these observations, we have not suggested abandoning the more traditional concerns of providence; rather, we have insisted that they take shape within the conceptual framework of God's presence and not be determined by issues of primary and secondary causation. The sovereign and faithful action of the triune God must constitute the heart of any truly Christian doctrine of providence. With this condition in mind, it is now appropriate to indicate the shape that a theology of providence could take from within this conceptual framework.

God is omnipresent; that is, he is present to all created space and time. Yet the intensity of God's presence varies from place to place and time to time.[17] There are some places that are considered holier than others on the basis that God's presence is more intense there: the very structure of Israel's tabernacle and temple point to this conviction. The ramifications here are significant, for the promise of God is that he intends the whole world to become equivalent to the temple's holy of holies. As we have argued, the presence of God that is found properly embodied in Jesus Christ graciously is given to the entire world

---

See, for example, J. Sanders, *The God Who Risks: A Theology of Providence* (Downers Grove: IVP, 1998), for arguably the most articulate and cogent expression of open theism. Sanders writes, 'There are many different views of divine providence [and] all of them may be placed under one of two basic models: the "no-risk" view and the "risk" view. Either God does take risks or does not take risks in providentially creating and governing the world. Either God is in some respects conditioned by the creatures he created or he is not conditioned by them. If God is completely unconditioned by anything external to himself, then God does not take any risks. According to the no-risk understanding, no event ever happens without God's specifically selecting it to happen. Nothing is too insignificant for God's meticulous and exhaustive control.... But if God is in some respects conditioned by his creatures, then God takes risks in bringing about this particular type of world. According to the risk model of providence, God has established certain boundaries within which creatures operate. But God sovereignly decides not to control each and every event, and some things go contrary to what God intends and may not turn out completely as God desires. Hence, God takes risks in creating this sort of world.' (*The God Who Risks*, 10–11).

[17] Cf. T.E. Fretheim, *God and World in the Old Testament: A Relational Theology of Creation* (Nashville: Abingdon Press, 2005), 25

as God brings his project to completion in Christ and through the Holy Spirit. At some eschatological point, the whole world will receive the full intensity of the presence of God in such a way that it will be irreversibly transformed and perfected. That this transformation and perfection will be accomplished is already confirmed by the resurrection of the man Jesus, ascended and exalted Lord of all, and the Spirit's activity in the world through his body, the Church.

Until the eschatological point at which created time and space is home to the full intensity of God's presence, there is still variation in the way that this presence is manifest. The claim that Jesus is the proper presence of God and that the Church participates in the divine presence through him and by the Spirit is but one indication of how the intensity of God's presence varies from place to place, even when those places are closely related. It is this variation in the intensity of God's presence that indicates a potential shape for a theology of providence based upon the conceptual framework of God's presence.

Here is my proposal: *Just as the intensity of God's presence is greatest in the holy of holies and lesser in, for example, the temple's outer court, so we may argue that the intensity of God's presence is greater in certain events and actions than in others, even while God continues to sustain all things by being present to them.* This has already been argued to some degree: Jesus Christ is God's providence made flesh, a man acting as God in the world. His actions testify to God's continual presence in the world and reveal the sovereign action of the Holy Spirit, who leads the world through Christ's faithfulness to its promised transformation and perfection. Similarly, the Church acts as God in the world; but as the Church's participation in the divine presence is not by nature but rather by its gracious incorporation into Christ by the Spirit, there is always potential for the Church to obscure God's presence in the world through its unfaithfulness to his commands.

Pancausal accounts of God's providence posit God as the first cause of creaturely actions and events, which are said to be secondary causes. On this account, talk of intensities of divine presence is meaningless: everything that happens is the result of God's direct involvement and influence. A person's lottery win; the terrorist destruction of a national symbol; Christ's willing self-sacrifice; a woodlouse falling off a log; a woman's rape; a thrilling (or not so thrilling) football match; all these events are specifically determined by God to happen in accordance with his eternal decree. God's presence in these actions and events does not differ in intensity, for he is present as the first cause of each. The advantage of my proposal is that although God is claimed to be present to all that happens, the intensity of that presence in all that happens varies. Although God sustains all that happens and safeguards the integrity of a creature's action as genuine creaturely action, there are some actions and events that more legitimately can be claimed to be God's action than others.

A scriptural example we could employ to illustrate this contention is God's anointing of Cyrus in Isaiah 45:1-7, one of the four texts supposedly supporting the case for secondary causation to which we have alluded on occasion. Isaiah

45:1 portrays God as holding the right hand of Cyrus, King of Persia, so that judgement may be levelled against the monarchs of various other nations. Though an exposition of this passage cannot be offered here, it appears that Deutero-Isaiah believed God to be present in the expansion of the Persian Empire across the ancient Near East, a result of which was the liberation of the Jewish exiles from Babylonian captivity. The intensity of the divine presence in this event was manifested as a demonstration of God's continuing faithfulness to his covenant people, despite their plight. Whereas the exile to Babylon was God's presence in judgement of his unfaithful covenant people, now this presence is an act of liberation for them and judgement on the nations.

My proposal of the shape a theology of providence could take from within the conceptual framework of God's presence immediately raises at least two problems. First, there is the problem of how we can know that God is intensely (or more intensely) present in one event than in another. To offer some illustrations: Was the destruction of the World Trade Center on 11 September 2001 something in which God was intensely present, perhaps in judgement, or an event in which, apart from his sustaining of its integrity as a genuine creaturely occurrence, he was completely absent? Is God intensely present equally in the execution of despot and the rape of a minor? Does God wish to be intensely present during my morning shave but not in my commute to work? These questions suggest a parallel between the problem of knowing the extent of God's presence in an event, and Calvin's claim that the 'eye of faith' recognises God working through the instruments that constitute secondary causation.[18] The difference between Calvin's stance and my proposal lies in the fact that either the eye of faith must recognise that *everything* is somehow God's action (as for Calvin); or it must discern with wisdom those things that are God's action, and those whose integrity is simply safeguarded as a creaturely action by the Holy Spirit (as per my proposal).

Secondly, my proposal still offers no account of *how* God acts. Indeed, there is even a vague suggestion that it is the intensity of God's presence at a certain time and place that brings about a particular action or event. Can this lead be followed in a direction that does not entail (pan)causal categories? At this point, we must remember that at no point has a claim been made that the conceptual framework of God's presence resolves the issue of how God acts in a world that is totally unlike him. What has been claimed is that this particular conceptual framework is the most appropriate place to discuss the matter of God's providence.[19] On this account, it is the scriptural presentation of the extension of God's presence across the world through faithful human action

---

[18] J. Calvin, *A Defence of the Secret Providence of God*, in *Calvin's Calvinism: Treatises on the Eternal Predestination of God and the Secret Providence of God*, translated by H. Cole (Grand Rapids: Reformed Free Publishing Association, 1987), 223–350 (231).

[19] See § 4.6.

that must govern any model of how God acts. To express the matter even more simply: God acts in the world through the incarnate Son and by the Holy Spirit. The *how?* question need not arise.

This triune divine action suggests two important aspects that should be included in the shaping of a theology of providence. The intensity of God's presence in any given action or event is an act of the Spirit. It is the Spirit who embodies God's presence in the particular body of flesh that is the man Jesus; it is the Spirit who establishes the Church as the body of Christ, transforming it into a faithful community capable of mediating God's presence to the world; it is the Spirit who guides the project of creation to its promised goal as the glad recipient of the full intensity of God's presence. Yet the Spirit does none of these things apart from Jesus Christ; for although the Spirit is the one who mediates and regulates the intensity of God's presence in any given action or event, the incarnate Son is the one through whom the Spirit acts to mould people into the image of the resurrected Jesus and transform the whole world into the place of God's most intense presence. Furthermore, the role of Jesus in God's providence points to a crucial question, perhaps *the* most crucial question that any theology of providence needs to address: *What does it mean to say that it is a particular human being, indeed, a particular man, who exercises God's sovereign providence over the whole of creation?*

My proposal here is no more than what it is claimed to be: it is simply an indication of how a theology of providence could take shape from within the conceptual framework of God's presence. These specific suggestions may not prove viable upon further reflection. As our concern has been to argue that this conceptual framework is a corrective to that of primary and secondary causation, it would be beyond the scope of this study to attempt the development of my proposal even further. That is a different task that must be conducted elsewhere, weaving the four threads identified above into a larger, more elegant tapestry.

The strength of explicating the doctrine of providence from within the conceptual framework of God's presence is not dependent upon our attempts to steer its heart in certain directions. Its strength lies instead in its consistent affirmation that divine providence is the activity of the triune God; that the man Jesus Christ is God's providence made flesh; that in Christ's Spirit-empowered obedience, the Father has demonstrated that he will never abandon that which he has made through the eternal Son; and that one eschatological day, God will bless it with his intensely abiding presence.

BIBLIOGRAPHY

Albright, W.F. and Mann, C.S., *Matthew: A New Translation with Introduction and Commentary* (ABC 26; New York: Doubleday, 1971)

Alexander, D., *Rebuilding the Matrix: Science and Faith in the 21st Century* (Oxford: Lion Publishing, 2002)

Alexander, T.D., 'Authorship of the Pentateuch', in *Dictionary of the Old Testament: Pentateuch* (Leicester: IVP, 2003), 61–72

Anderson, G.A., 'Mary in the Old Testament', *Pro Ecclesia* 16 (2007), 33–55

Aquinas, T., *Summa Contra Gentiles, Book One: God*, translated, with an introduction and notes, by Pegis, A.C. (Notre Dame: University of Nature Dame Press, 1975); *Book Two: Creation*, translated, with an introduction and notes, by Anderson, J.F. (Notre Dame: University of Nature Dame Press, 1975); *Book Three: Providence* (2 vols.), translated, with an introduction and notes, by Bourke, V.J. (Notre Dame: University of Nature Dame Press, 1975); *Book Four: Salvation*, translated, with an introduction and notes, by O' Neil, C.J. (Notre Dame: University of Nature Dame Press, 1975)

Aquinas, T., *Summa Theologica*, translated by Fathers of the English Dominican Province (Notre Dame: Christian Classics, 1981)

Aristotle, *Physics*, translated by Hardie, R.P. and Gaye, R.K., in *The Basic Works of Aristotle*, edited by McKeon, R. (New York: Modern Library, 2001), 213–394

Aristotle, *Metaphysics*, translated by Ross, W.D., in *The Basic Works of Aristotle*, edited by McKeon, R. (New York: Modern Library, 2001), 681–926

Aulén, G., *Christus Victor: An Historical Study of the Three Main Types of the Idea of Atonement*, translated by Hebert, A.G. (Eugene: Wipf and Stock, 1931)

Averbeck, R.E., 'Sacrifices and Offerings', in *Dictionary of the Old Testament: Pentateuch* (Leicester: IVP, 2003), 706–733

Averbeck, R.E., 'Tabernacle', in *Dictionary of the Old Testament: Pentateuch* (Leicester: IVP, 2003), 807–827

Baillie, D.M., *The Theology of the Sacraments and Other Papers* (London: Faber & Faber, 1957)

Balserak, J., '"The Accommodating Act Par Excellence?": An Inquiry into the Incarnation and Calvin's Understanding of Accommodation', *Scottish Journal of Theology* 55 (2002), 408–423

Barker, M., *The Gate of Heaven: The History and Symbolism of the Temple in Jerusalem* (London: SPCK, 1991)

Barker, M., *On Earth as it is in Heaven: Temple Symbolism in the New Testament* (Edinburgh: T&T Clark, 1995)

Barker, M., *The Risen Lord: The Jesus of History as the Christ of Faith* (SJT / CIT; Edinburgh: T&T Clark, 1996)

Barker, M., 'Atonement: The Rite of Healing', in *The Great High Priest: The Temple Roots of Christian Liturgy* (London: T&T Clark, 2003), 42–55

Barker, M., 'The Holy of Holies', in *The Great High Priest: The Temple Roots of Christian Liturgy* (London: T&T Clark, 2003), 146–187

Barker, M., *Temple Theology: An Introduction* (London: SPCK, 2004)

Barker, M., 'Creation Theology' (unpublished paper, 2004, downloaded from www.margaretbarker.com, early 2007)

Barker, M., 'Temple, Time and Space' (unpublished paper, 2005, downloaded from www.margaretbarker.com, early 2007)

Barker, M., *The Hidden Tradition of the Kingdom of God* (London: SPCK, 2007)

Barker, P.A., *The Triumph of Grace in Deuteronomy: Faithless Israel, Faithful Yahweh in Deuteronomy* (PBM; Carlisle: Paternoster, 2004)

Barrow, S. and Bartley, J. (eds.), *Consuming Passion: Why the Killing of Jesus Really Matters* (London: DLT, 2005)

Barth, K., *Dogmatics in Outline*, translated by Thomson, G.T. (London: SCM Press, 1949)

Barth, K., *Church Dogmatics* (13 vols.), edited by Bromiley, G.W. and Torrance, T.F. (Edinburgh: T&T Clark, 1957–1975)

Bauckham, R., *God Crucified: Monotheism and Christology in the New Testament* (Carlisle: Paternoster, 1998)

Bauckham, R., 'Monotheism and Christology in Hebrews 1', in Stuckenbruck, L.T. and North, W.E.S. (eds.), *Early Jewish and Christian Monotheism* (JSNTS 263; London: T&T Clark, 2004), 167–185

Bauer, D.R., 'Son of God', in *Dictionary of Jesus and the Gospels* (Leicester: IVP, 1992), 769–775

Bavinck, H., *Reformed Dogmatics, Volume 2: God and Creation*, translated by Vriend, J. (Grand Rapids: Baker Academic, 2004)

Baxter, C.A., 'The Cursed Beloved: A Reconsideration of Penal Substitution', in Goldingay, J. (ed.), *Atonement Today* (London: SPCK, 1995), 54–72

Beale, G.K., *The Temple and the Church's Mission: A Biblical Theology of the Dwelling Place of God* (NSBT 17; Leicester: Apollos, 2004)

Beale, G., 'The Final Vision of the Apocalypse and its Implications for a Biblical Theology of the Temple', in Alexander, T.D. and Gathercole, S. (eds.), *Heaven on Earth: The Temple in Biblical Theology* (Carlisle: Paternoster, 2004), 191–209

Beasley-Murray, G.R., *John*, 2nd ed. (WBC 36; Nashville: Thomas Nelson, 1999)

Beckwith, R.T., 'The Death of Christ as a Sacrifice in the Teaching of Paul and Hebrews', in Beckwith, R.T. and Selman, M.J. (eds.), *Sacrifice in the Bible* (Carlisle: Paternoster Press, 1995), 130–135

Bedford, R.D., *The Defence of Truth: Herbert of Cherbury and the Seventeenth Century* (Manchester: Manchester University Press, 1979)

Beeke, J.R., 'Calvin on Piety', in McKim, D.K. (ed.), *The Cambridge Companion to John Calvin* (Cambridge: Cambridge University Press, 2004), 125–152

Benedict, P., *Christ's Churches Purely Reformed: A Social History of Calvinism* (New Haven: Yale University Press, 2002)

Berkhof, L., *Systematic Theology* (London: Banner of Truth, 1958)

Berkouwer, G.C., *The Triumph of Grace in the Theology of Karl Barth*, translated by Boer, H.R. (London: Paternoster Press, 1956)

Berkouwer, G.C., *The Providence of God*, translated by Smedes, L.B. (Grand Rapids: Eerdmans, 1952)

Berofsky, B., 'Determinism', in *The Cambridge Dictionary of Philosophy*, 2nd ed. (Cambridge: Cambridge University Press, 1999), 228–229

Berry, R.J., 'Divine Action: Expected and Unexpected', *Zygon* 37 (2002), 717–728

Beza, T., *The Treasure of Truth*, translated by Stockwood, J. (London: Thomas Woodcocke, 1581)

Blocher, H., 'The Atonement in John Calvin's Theology', in Hill, C.E. and James III, F.A. (eds.), *The Glory of the Atonement: Biblical, Historical and Practical Perspectives. Essays in Honour of Roger Nicole* (Downers Grove: IVP, 2004), 279–303

Boersma, H., 'Penal Substitution and the Possibility of Unconditional Hospitality', *Scottish Journal of Theology* 57 (2004), 80–94

Boersma, H., *Violence, Hospitality, and the Cross: Reappropriating the Atonement Tradition* (Grand Rapids: Baker Academic, 2004)

Bonnington, M., 'The Obedient Son: Jesus in Gethsemane', *Anvil* 16 (1999), 41–48

Bouteneff, P.C., 'Sacraments as the Mystery of Union: Elements in an Orthodox Sacramental Theology', in Rowell, G. and Hall, C. (eds.), *The Gestures of God: Explorations in Sacramentality* (London: Continuum, 2004), 91–107

Bradley, I., *The Power of Sacrifice* (London: DLT, 1995)

Bray, G. (ed.), *Documents of the English Reformation* (Cambridge: James Clarke, 1994)

Breck, J., 'Reflections on the "Problem" of Chalcedonian Christology', *St Vladimir's Theological Quarterly* 33 (1989), 147–157

Brierley, M.W., 'Naming a Quiet Revolution: The Panentheistic Turn in Modern Theology', in Clayton, P. and Peacocke, A. (eds.), *In Whom We Live and Move and Have Our Being: Panentheistic Reflections on God's Presence in a Scientific World* (Grand Rapids: Eerdmans, 2004), 1–15

Brock, S.L., *Action and Conduct: Thomas Aquinas and the Theory of Action* (Edinburgh: T&T Clark, 1998)

Bromiley, G.W., *Historical Theology: An Introduction* (Edinburgh: T&T Clark, 1978)

Brondos, D., 'Why Was Jesus Crucified? Theology, History and the Story of Redemption', *Scottish Journal of Theology* 54 (2001), 484–503

Brondos, D.A., *Paul on the Cross: Reconstruction the Apostle's Story of Redemption* (Minneapolis: Fortress Press, 2006)

Brooke, J.H., *Science and Religion: Some Historical Perspectives* (Cambridge: Cambridge University Press, 1991)

Brown, C., *Philosophy and the Christian Faith: A Historical Sketch from the Middle Ages to the Present Day* (London: Tyndale Press, 1969)

Brown, C., *Christianity and Western Thought: A History of Philosophers, Ideas and Movements, Volume One: From the Ancient World to the Age of Enlightenment* (Leicester: Apollos, 1990)

Brown, D., 'Re-conceiving the Sacramental', in Rowell, G. and Hall, C. (eds.), *The Gestures of God: Explorations in Sacramentality* (London: Continuum, 2004), 21–36

Brown, D.A., 'Christianity and Mystery', *Theology* 72 (1969), 347–352

Bruce, F.F., *The Epistle to the Hebrews*, rev. ed. (NICNT; Grand Rapids: Eerdmans, 1990)

Brueggemann, W., 'The Crisis and Promise of Presence in Israel', in *Old Testament Theology: Essays on Structure, Theme, and Text*, edited by Miller, P.D. (Minneapolis: Fortress Press, 1992), 150–182

Brueggemann, W., *Theology of the Old Testament: Testimony, Dispute, Advocacy* (Minneapolis: Fortress Press, 1997)

Brueggemann, W., *The Covenanted Self: Explorations in Law and Covenant*, edited by Miller, P.D. (Minneapolis: Fortress Press, 1999)

Brueggemann, W., *Worship in Ancient Israel: An Essential Guide* (Nashville: Abingdon Press, 2005)

Brümmer, V., *Speaking of a Personal God: An Essay in Philosophical Theology* (Cambridge: Cambridge University Press, 1992)

Brun, R.B., 'Does God Play Dice? A Response to Niels H Gregersen, "The Idea of Creation and the Theory of Autopoietic Processes"', *Zygon* 34 (1999), 93–100

Buckley, M.J., *At the Origins of Modern Atheism* (New Haven: Yale University Press, 1987)

Burrell, D.B., *Freedom and Creation in Three Traditions* (Notre Dame: University of Notre Dame Press, 1993)

Butin, P.W., *Revelation, Redemption, and Response: Calvin's Trinitarian Understanding of the Divine–Human Relationship* (Oxford: Oxford University Press, 1995)

Byl, J., 'Indeterminacy, Divine Action and Human Freedom', *Science and Christian Belief* 15 (2003), 101–116

Byrne, J., *Glory, Jest and Riddle: Religious Thought in the Enlightenment* (London: SCM Press, 1996)

Byrne, P., *Natural Religion and the Nature of Religion: The Legacy of Deism* (RRSS; London: Routledge, 1989)

Caird, G.B., 'The Exegetical Method of the Epistle to the Hebrews', *Canadian Journal of Theology* 5 (1959), 44–51

Caird, G.B., *The Language and Imagery of the Bible* (London: Duckworth, 1980)

Caird, G.B., 'Son by Appointment', in Weinrich, W.C. (ed.), *The New Testament Age: Essays in Honour of Bo Reicke, Volume 1* (Macon: Mercer University Press, 1984), 73–81

Caird, G.B., *New Testament Theology*, completed and edited by Hurst, L.D. (Oxford: Oxford University Press, 1995)

Calvin, J., *The Bondage and Liberation of the Will: A Defence of the Orthodox Doctrine of Human Choice Against Pighius*, edited by Lane, A.N.S. and translated by Davies, G.I. (Grand Rapids: Baker Books, 1996)

Calvin, J., *Concerning the Eternal Predestination of God*, translated with an introduction by Reid, J.K.S. (Cambridge: James Clarke, 1982)

Calvin, J., *A Treatise on the Eternal Predestination of God*, in *Calvin's Calvinism: Treatises on the Eternal Predestination of God and the Secret Providence of God*, translated by Cole, H. (Grand Rapids: Reformed Free Publishing Association, 1987), 13–186

Calvin, J., *Brief Instruction for Arming All the Good Faithful Against the Errors of the Common Sect of the Anabaptists*, in *Treatises Against the Anabaptists and Against the Libertines*, translated and edited by Farley, B.W. (Grand Rapids: Baker Books, 1982), 36–158

Calvin, J., *Against the Fantastic and Furious Sect of the Libertines who are Called 'Spirituals'*, in *Treatises Against the Anabaptists and Against the Libertines*, translated and edited by Farley, B.W. (Grand Rapids: Baker Books, 1982), 187–326

Calvin, J., *Brief Reply in Refutation of the Calumnies of a Certain Worthless Person in which he Attempted to Pollute the Doctrine of the Eternal Predestination of God*, in *Calvin: Theological Treatises*, translated with introductions and notes by Reid, J.K.S. (LCC XXII; Philadelphia: The Westminster Press, 1954), 333–343

Calvin, J., *A Brief Reply, Intended to Refute the Calumnies of a Certain Worthless Person, by which he Endeavoured to Pollute the Doctrine of the Eternal Predestination of God*, in *Calvin's Calvinism: Treatises on the Eternal Predestination of God and the Secret Providence of God*, translated by Cole, H. (Grand Rapids: Reformed Free Publishing Association, 1987), 189–206

Calvin, J., *Articles Concerning Predestination*, in *Calvin: Theological Treatises*, translated with introductions and notes by Reid, J.K.S. (LCC XXII; Philadelphia: The Westminster Press, 1954), 179–180

Calvin, J., *A Defence of the Secret Providence of God*, in *Calvin's Calvinism: Treatises on the Eternal Predestination of God and the Secret Providence of God*, translated by Cole, H. (Grand Rapids: Reformed Free Publishing Association, 1987), 223–350

Calvin, J., *Institutes of the Christian Religion* (2 vols.), translated by Battles, F.L. (LCC XX / XXI; Philadelphia: The Westminster Press, 1960)

Calvin, J., *Calvin's Commentaries* (22 vols.), various translators (CTS; Grand Rapids: Baker Books, 2003)

Calvin, J., *Letters of John Calvin Selected from the Bonnet Edition with an Introductory Biographical Sketch* (Edinburgh: Banner of Truth, 1980)

Campbell, D.A., *The Quest for Paul's Gospel: A Suggested Strategy* (London: T&T Clark, 2005)

Campbell, W.S., 'Covenant and New Covenant', in *Dictionary of Paul and his Letters* (Leicester: IVP, 1993), 179–183

Canlis, J., 'Calvin, Osiander and Participation in God', *International Journal of Systematic Theology* 6 (2004), 169–184

Carmichael, C., 'The Origin of the Scapegoat Ritual', *Vetus Testamentum* 50 (2000), 167–182

Carson, D.A., 'Summaries and Conclusions', in Carson, D.A., O'Brien, P.T. and Seifrid, M.A. (eds.), *Justification and Variegated Nomism, Volume 1: The Complexities of Second Temple Judaism* (Grand Rapids: Baker Academic, 2001), 505–548

Carson, D.A., 'Atonement in Romans 3:21-26', in Hill, C.E. and James III, F.A. (eds.), *The Glory of the Atonement: Biblical, Historical and Practical Perspectives. Essays in Honour of Roger Nicole* (Downers Grove: IVP, 2004), 119–139

Chadwick, H., *The Early Church*, rev. ed. (PHC 1; London: Penguin Books, 1993)

Chadwick, O., *The Reformation* (PHC 3; London: Penguin Books, 1972)

Charette, B., *Restoring Presence: The Spirit in Matthew's Gospel* (JPTS 18; Sheffield: Sheffield Academic Press, 2000)

Chester, A.N., 'Hebrews: The Final Sacrifice', in Sykes, S.W. (ed.), *Sacrifice and Redemption: Durham Essays in Theology* (Cambridge: Cambridge University Press, 1991), 57–72

Chester, T., 'Justification, Ecclesiology and the New Perspective', *Themelios* 30, no. 2 (2005), 5–20

Christensen, D.L., *Deuteronomy 1:1–21:9* (WBC 6A, revised; Nashville: Thomas Nelson, 2001); *Deuteronomy 21:10–34:12* (WBC 6B; Nashville: Thomas Nelson, 2002)

Clarke, F.S., 'Christocentric Developments in the Reformed Doctrine of Predestination', *Churchman* 98 (1984), 229–245

Clayton, P.D., *God and Contemporary Science* (ESCT; Edinburgh: Edinburgh University Press, 1997)

Clayton, P., 'Panentheism in Metaphysical and Scientific Perspective', in Clayton, P. and Peacocke, A. (eds.), *In Whom We Live and Move and Have Our Being: Panentheistic Reflections on God's Presence in a Scientific World* (Grand Rapids: Eerdmans, 2004), 73–91

Clifton, R., 'Determinism, Scientific', in Honderich, T. (ed.), *The Oxford Companion to Philosophy*, 2nd ed. (Oxford: Oxford University Press, 2005), 210–211

Coffey, D., 'The "Incarnation" of the Holy Spirit in Christ', *Theological Studies* 45 (1984), 466–480

Cole, R.A., *The Letter of Paul to the Galatians: An Introduction and Commentary*, 2nd ed. (TNTC 9; Leicester: IVP, 1989)

Colwell, J.E., *Promise and Presence: An Exploration of Sacramental Theology* (Milton Keynes: Paternoster, 2005)

Copan, P. and Craig, W.L., *Creation Out of Nothing: A Biblical, Philosophical, and Scientific Exploration* (Grand Rapids: Baker Academic, 2004)

Coppedge, A., *The God Who is Triune: Revisioning the Christian Doctrine of God* (Downers Grove: IVP, 2007)

Craddock, F.B., *The Letter to the Hebrews: Introduction, Commentary, and Reflections* (NIB XII; Nashville: Abingdon Press, 1998)

Cragg, G.R., *The Church and the Age of Reason 1648–1789* (PHC 4; London: Penguin Books, 1970)

Cranfield, C.E.B., 'John 1:14: "Became"', *The Expository Times* 93 (1982), 215

Crisp, O.D., *Divinity and Humanity: The Incarnation Reconsidered* (CIT 5; Cambridge: Cambridge University Press, 2007)

Cumin, P.B., *Christ at the Crux: The Mediation of Creator and Creation in Systematic Christological Perspective* (unpublished PhD thesis, King's College London, 2007)

Dalferth, I.U., 'Christ Died for Us: Reflections on the Sacrificial Language of Salvation', in Sykes, S.W. (ed.), *Sacrifice and Redemption: Durham Essays in Theology* (Cambridge: Cambridge University Press, 1991), 299–325

Dalferth, I.U., 'Creation – Style of the World', translated by Knight, D., *International Journal of Systematic Theology* 1 (1999), 119–137

Dalferth, I.U., 'Representing God's Presence', *International Journal of Systematic Theology* 3 (2001), 237–256

Das, A.A., *Paul, the Law, and the Covenant* (Massachusetts: Hendrickson, 2001)

Das, A.A., 'Beyond Covenantal Nomism: Paul, Judaism, and Perfect Obedience', *Concordia Journal* 27 (2001), 234–252

Das, A.A., *Paul and the Jews* (Massachusetts: Hendrickson, 2003)

Davidson, I., 'Theologising the Human Jesus: An Ancient (and Modern) Approach to Christology Reassessed', *International Journal of Systematic Theology* 3 (2001), 129–153

Davidson, I.J., '"Not My Will but Yours be Done": The Ontological Dynamics of Incarnational Intention', *International Journal of Systematic Theology* 7 (2005), 178–204

Davies, B., *The Thought of Thomas Aquinas* (Oxford: Clarendon Press, 1992)

Davies, B., 'Aquinas on What God is Not', in Davies, B. (ed.), *Thomas Aquinas: Contemporary Philosophical Perspectives* (Oxford: Oxford University Press, 2002), 227–242

Davies, B., *Aquinas* (OCT; London: Continuum, 2002)

Davies, G.N., 'Sacrifice, Offerings, Gifts', in *Dictionary of the Later New Testament and its Developments* (Leicester: IVP, 1997), 1069–1072

Davies, H., *The Vigilant God: Providence in the Thought of Augustine, Aquinas, Calvin and Barth* (New York: Peter Lang, 1992)

Davis, T.J., 'Not "Hidden and Far Off": The Bodily Aspect of Salvation and its Implications for Understanding the Body in Calvin's Theology', *Calvin Theological Journal* 29 (1994), 406–418

Dawson, G.S., *Jesus Ascended: The Meaning of Christ's Continuing Incarnation* (London: T&T Clark, 2004)

Deane-Drummond, C.E., *Creation Through Wisdom: Theology and the New Biology* (Edinburgh: T&T Clark, 2000)

Deane-Drummond, C.E., 'The Logos as Wisdom: A Starting Point for a Sophianic Theology of Creation', in Clayton, P. and Peacocke, A. (eds.), *In Whom We Live and Move and Have Our Being: Panentheistic Reflections on God's Presence in a Scientific World* (Grand Rapids: Eerdmans, 2004), 233–245

Dearman, J.A., 'Theophany, Anthropomorphism, and the *Imago Dei*: Some Observations in the Light of the Old Testament', in Davis, S.T., Kendall, D. and O'Collins, G. (eds.), *The Incarnation: An Interdisciplinary Symposium on the Incarnation of the Son of God* (Oxford: Oxford University Press, 2002), 31–46

Deason, G.B., 'Reformation Theology and the Mechanistic Conception of Nature', in Lindberg, D.C. and Numbers, R.L. (eds.), *God and Nature: Historical Essays on the Encounter Between Christianity and Science* (Berkeley: University of California Press, 1986), 167–191

Deibert, R.I., 'The Justification of Covenantal Nomism: Reflections on *Justification and Variegated Nomism*, its Editorial Conclusions, and Pauline Theology' (PhD seminar paper presented June 2002, downloaded from www.tyndale.cam.ac.uk, September 2007)

Descartes, R., 'The Passions of the Soul, Part 1 (Selections)', in Wilson, M.D., (ed.), *The Essential Descartes* (New York: Meridian, 1983), 353–368

Di Noia, J.A., 'By Whom All Things were Made: Trinitarian Theology of Creation as the Basis for a Person-Friendly Cosmology', in Seitz, C.R. (ed.), *Nicene Christianity: The Future for a New Ecumenism* (Grand Rapids: Brazos Press, 2001), 63–73

Drane, J., 'Contemporary Culture and the Reinvention of Sacramental Spirituality', in Rowell, G. and Hall, C. (eds.), *The Gestures of God: Explorations in Sacramentality* (London: Continuum, 2004), 37–55

Dumbrell, W.J., *Covenant and Creation: A Theology of the Old Testament Covenants* (BTCL 12; Carlisle: Paternoster, 1997)

Dunn, J.D.G., *Jesus, Paul and the Law: Studies in Mark and Galatians* (London: SPCK, 1990)

Dunn, J.D.G., 'Paul's Understanding of the Death of Jesus as Sacrifice', in Sykes, S.W. (ed.), *Sacrifice and Redemption: Durham Essays in Theology* (Cambridge: Cambridge University Press, 1991), 35–56

Dunn, J.D.G. and Suggate, A.M., *The Justice of God: A Fresh Look at the Old Doctrine of Justification by Faith* (Carlisle: Paternoster, 1993)

Dunn, J.D.G., *A Commentary on the Epistle to the Galatians* (BNTC; London: A&C Black, 1993)

Dunn, J.D.G., *The Theology of Paul's Letter to the Galatians*, (NTT; Cambridge: Cambridge University Press, 1993)

Dunn, J.D.G., *The Theology of Paul the Apostle* (London: T&T Clark, 1998)
Durham, J.I., *Exodus* (WBC 3; Nashville: Thomas Nelson, 1987)
Eberhart, C.A., 'Characteristics of Sacrificial Metaphors in Hebrews', in Gelardini, G. (ed.), *Hebrews: Contemporary Methods – New Insights* (BIS 75; Leiden: Brill, 2005)
Edmondson, S., *Calvin's Christology* (Cambridge: Cambridge University Press, 2004)
Edmondson, S., 'Christ and History: Hermeneutical Convergence in Calvin and its Challenge to Biblical Theology', *Modern Theology* 21 (2005), 3–35
Edwards, D., 'A Relational and Evolving Universe Unfolding within the Dynamism of the Divine Communion', in Clayton, P. and Peacocke, A. (eds.), *In Whom We Live and Move and Have Our Being: Panentheistic Reflections on God's Presence in a Scientific World* (Grand Rapids: Eerdmans, 2004), 199–210
Ellingworth, P., 'Jesus and the Universe in Hebrews', *Evangelical Quarterly* 58 (1986), 337–350
Ellingworth, P., 'Hebrews and the Anticipation of Completion', *Themelios* 14, no. 1 (1988), 6–11
Ellingworth, P., *The Epistle to the Hebrews: A Commentary on the Greek Text* (NIGTC; Grand Rapids: Eerdmans, 1993)
Evans, C.A., *Word and Glory: On the Exegetical and Theological Background of John's Prologue* (JSNTS 89; Sheffield: Sheffield Academic Press, 1993)
Farrer, A., *Faith and Speculation: An Essay in Philosophical Theology* (London: Adam & Charles Black, 1967)
Farrow, D., *Ascension and Ecclesia: On the Significance of the Doctrine of the Ascension for Ecclesiology and Christian Cosmology* (Edinburgh: T&T Clark, 1999)
Farrow, D., 'Ascension and Atonement', in Gunton, C.E. (ed.), *The Theology of Reconciliation* (London: T&T Clark, 2003), 67–91
Fergusson, D., 'Divine Providence and Action', in Volf, M. and Welker, M. (eds.), *God's Life in Trinity* (Minneapolis: Fortress Press, 2006), 153–165
Fiddes, P.S., *Past Event and Present Salvation: The Christian Idea of Atonement* (London: DLT, 1989)
Fiddes, P.S., *Participating in God: A Pastoral Doctrine of the Trinity* (London: DLT, 2000)
Fiddes, P.S., 'The Quest for a Place which is "Not-a-Place": The Hiddenness of God and the Presence of God', in Davies, O. and Turner, D. (eds.), *Silence and the Word: Negative Theology and Incarnation* (Cambridge: Cambridge University Press, 2002), 35–60
Filson, F.V., *A Commentary on the Gospel According to St Matthew* (BNTC; London: A&C Black, 1960)
Finlan, S., *Problems with Atonement: The Origins of, and Controversy about, the Atonement Doctrine* (Collegeville, Minnesota: The Liturgical Press, 2005)
Fletcher-Louis, C.H.T., 'The Image of God and the Biblical Roots of Christian Sacramentality', in Rowell, G. and Hall, C. (eds.), *The Gestures of God: Explorations in Sacramentality* (London: Continuum, 2004), 73–89
Fletcher-Louis, C.H.T., 'God's Image, his Cosmic Temple and the High Priest: Towards an Historical and Theological Account of the Incarnation', in Alexander, T.D. and Gathercole, S. (eds.), *Heaven on Earth: The Temple in Biblical Theology* (Carlisle: Paternoster, 2004), 81–99
Fletcher-Louis, C.H.T., 'Jesus as the High Priestly Messiah: Part 1', *Journal for the Study of the Historical Jesus* 4 (2006), 155–175

Fletcher-Louis, C.H.T., 'Jesus as the High Priestly Messiah: Part 2', *Journal for the Study of the Historical Jesus* 5 (2007), 57–79

Foster, R.L., '"A Temple in the Lord Filled to the Fullness of God": Context and Intertextuality (Eph. 3:19)', *Novum Testamentum* 49 (2007), 85–96

France, R.T., *The Gospel According to Matthew: An Introduction and Commentary* (TNTC 1; Leicester: IVP, 1985)

Freeman, T., 'Dissenters from a Dissenting Church: The Challenge of the Freewillers, 1550–1558', in Marshall, P. and Ryrie, A., *The Beginnings of English Protestantism* (Cambridge: Cambridge University Press, 2002), 129–156

Fretheim, T.E., *God and World in the Old Testament: A Relational Theology of Creation* (Nashville: Abingdon Press, 2005)

Gamble, R.C., 'Switzerland: Triumph and Decline', in Reid, W.S. (ed.), *John Calvin: His Influence in the Western World* (Grand Rapids: Zondervan, 1982), 55–71

Gamble, R.C., 'Calvin's Controversies', in McKim, D.K. (ed.), *The Cambridge Companion to John Calvin* (Cambridge: Cambridge University Press, 2004), 188–203

Gathercole, S.J., 'Justified by Faith, Justified by his Blood: The Evidence of Romans 3:21–4:25', in Carson, D.A., O'Brien, P.T. and Seifrid, M.A. (eds.), *Justification and Variegated Nomism, Volume 2: The Paradoxes of Paul* (Grand Rapids: Baker Academic, 2004), 147–184

Gay, P., *The Enlightenment, An Interpretation: The Science of Freedom* (London: Norton Library, 1977)

George, T., *Theology of the Reformers* (Nashville: Broadman Press, 1988)

Gerstenberger, E.S., *Leviticus: A Commentary*, translated by Stott, D.W. (OTL; Louisville: Westminster John Knox Press, 1996)

Gilkey, L., 'Gregersen's Vision of a Theonomous Universe', *Zygon* 34 (1999), 111–115

Goldingay, J., 'Old Testament Sacrifice and the Death of Christ', in Goldingay, J. (ed.), *Atonement Today* (London: SPCK, 1995), 3–20

Goldingay, J., 'Your Iniquities Have Made a Separation Between You and Your God', in Goldingay, J. (ed.), *Atonement Today* (London: SPCK, 1995), 39–53

Gombis, T.G., 'The "Transgressor" and the "Curse of the Law": The Logic of Paul's Argument in Galatians 2–3', *New Testament Studies* 53 (2007), 81–93

Gordon, R.P., *Hebrews* (RANBC; Sheffield: Sheffield Academic Press, 2000)

Gorringe, T.J., *God's Theatre: A Theology of Providence* (London: SCM Press, 1991)

Gorringe, T.J., *The Education of Desire: Towards a Theology of the Senses* (London: SCM Press, 2001)

Gräb, W., 'Creation or Nature? About Dialogue Between Theology and Natural Sciences', in Reventlow, H.G. and Hoffman, Y. (eds.), *Creation in Jewish and Christian Tradition* (JSOTS 319; London: Sheffield Academic Press, 2002), 277–290

Grabbe, L.L., *Leviticus* (OTG; Sheffield: Sheffield Academic Press, 1993)

Grant, W.M., 'Must a Cause Be Really Related to its Effect? The Analogy Between Divine and Libertarian Agent Causality', *Religious Studies* 43 (2007), 1–23

de Greef, W., 'Calvin's Writings', in McKim, D.K. (ed.), *The Cambridge Companion to John Calvin* (Cambridge: Cambridge University Press, 2004), 41–57

Green, J.B., 'Death of Jesus', in *Dictionary of Jesus and the Gospels* (Leicester: IVP, 1992), 146–163

Green, J.B., 'Gethsemane', in *Dictionary of Jesus and the Gospels* (Leicester: IVP, 1992), 265–268

Green, J.B., 'Death of Christ', in *Dictionary of Paul and his Letters* (Leicester: IVP, 1993), 201–209

Green, J.B. and Baker, M.D., *Recovering the Scandal of the Cross: Atonement in New Testament and Contemporary Contexts* (Downers Grove: IVP, 2000)

Greenbury, J., 'Calvin's Understanding of Predestination with Special Reference to the Institutes', *The Reformed Theological Review* 54 (1995), 121–134

Gregersen, N.H., 'The Idea of Creation and the Theory of Autopoietic Processes', *Zygon* 33 (1998), 333–367

Gregersen, N.H., 'Autopoiesis: Less than Self-Constitution, More than Self-Organisation: Reply to Gilkey, McClelland and Deltete, and Brun', *Zygon* 34 (1999), 117–138

Gregersen, N.H., 'Three Varieties of Panentheism', in Clayton, P. and Peacocke, A. (eds.), *In Whom We Live and Move and Have Our Being: Panentheistic Reflections on God's Presence in a Scientific World* (Grand Rapids: Eerdmans, 2004), 19–35

Gregersen, N.H., 'Critical Realism and Other Realisms', in Russell, R.J. (ed.), *Fifty Years in Science and Religion: Ian G Barbour and his Legacy* (Aldershot: Ashgate, 2004), 77–95

Grudem, W., *Systematic Theology: An Introduction to Biblical Doctrine* (Leicester: IVP, 1994)

Gundry-Volf, J.M., 'Expiation, Propitiation, Mercy Seat', in *Dictionary of Paul and his Letters* (Leicester: IVP, 1993), 279–284

Gunton, C.E., *Yesterday and Today: A Study of Continuities in Christology* (London: DLT, 1983)

Gunton, C., 'Christ the Sacrifice: Aspects of the Language and Imagery of the Bible', in Hurst, L.D. and Wright, N.T. (eds.), *The Glory of Christ in the New Testament: Studies in Christology in Memory of George Bradford Caird* (Oxford: Oxford University Press, 1987), 229–238

Gunton, C.E., *The Actuality of Atonement: A Study of Metaphor, Rationality and the Christian Tradition* (London: T&T Clark, 1988)

Gunton, C.E., *Christ and Creation* (Carlisle: Paternoster Press, 1992)

Gunton, C.E., *The One, the Three and the Many: God, Creation and the Culture of Modernity* (Cambridge: Cambridge University Press, 1993)

Gunton, C.E., 'God, Grace and Freedom', in Gunton, C.E. (ed.), *God and Freedom: Essays in Historical and Systematic Theology* (Edinburgh: T&T Clark, 1995), 119–133

Gunton, C.E., 'Relation and Relativity: The Trinity and the Created World', in *The Promise of Trinitarian Theology*, 2nd ed. (Edinburgh: T&T Clark, 1997), 137–157

Gunton, C.E., 'Atonement and the Project of Creation: An Interpretation of Colossians 1.15-23', in *The Promise of Trinitarian Theology*, 2nd ed. (Edinburgh: T&T Clark, 1997), 178–192

Gunton, C.E., 'The End of Causality? The Reformers and their Predecessors', in Gunton, C.E. (ed.), *The Doctrine of Creation: Essays in Dogmatics, History and Philosophy* (Edinburgh: T&T Clark, 1997), 63–82

Gunton, C.E., *The Triune Creator: A Historical and Systematic Study* (ESCT; Edinburgh: Edinburgh University Press, 1998)

Gunton, C., 'Aspects of Salvation: Some Unscholastic Themes from Calvin's *Institutes*', *International Journal of Systematic Theology* 1 (1999), 253–265

Gunton, C.E., 'Holiness, Difference and the Order of Creation', in *Intellect and Action: Elucidations on Christian Theology and the Life of Faith* (Edinburgh: T&T Clark, 2000), 83–100

Gunton, C.E., '*Soli Deo Gloria*? Divine Sovereignty and Christian Freedom in the "Age of Autonomy"', in *Intellect and Action: Elucidations on Christian Theology and the Life of Faith* (Edinburgh: T&T Clark, 2000), 156–173

Gunton, C., 'And in One Lord, Jesus Christ ... Begotten, Not Made', in Seitz, C.R. (ed.), *Nicene Christianity: The Future for a New Ecumenism* (Grand Rapids: Brazos Press, 2001), 35–48

Gunton, C., '"Until He Comes": Towards an Eschatology of Church Membership', *International Journal of Systematic Theology* 3 (2001), 187–200

Gunton, C.E., *The Christian Faith: An Introduction to Christian Doctrine* (Oxford: Blackwell, 2002)

Gunton, C., 'The Spirit Moved Over the Face of the Waters: The Holy Spirit and the Created Order', *International Journal of Systematic Theology* 4 (2002), 190–204

Gunton, C.E., *Act and Being: Towards a Theology of the Divine Attributes* (London: SCM Press, 2002)

Gunton, C.E., 'Towards a Theology of Reconciliation', in Gunton, C.E. (ed.), *The Theology of Reconciliation* (London: T&T Clark, 2003), 167–174

Gunton, C.E., 'The Holy Spirit who with the Father and the Son together is Worshipped and Glorified', in *Father, Son and Holy Spirit: Essays Toward a Fully Trinitarian Theology* (London: T&T Clark, 2003), 75–90

Gunton, C.E., 'Christ the Wisdom of God. A Study in Divine and Human Action', in *Father, Son and Holy Spirit: Essays Toward a Fully Trinitarian Theology* (London: T&T Clark, 2003), 127–143

Gunton, C.E., 'Martin Kähler Revisited. Variations on Hebrews 4.15', in *Father, Son and Holy Spirit: Essays Toward a Fully Trinitarian Theology* (London: T&T Clark, 2003), 144–163

Gunton, C.E., '"One Mediator ... the Man Jesus Christ". Reconciliation, Mediation and Life in Community', in *Father, Son and Holy Spirit: Essays Toward a Fully Trinitarian Theology* (London: T&T Clark, 2003), 164–180

Gunton, C.E., 'The Sacrifice and the Sacrifices. From Metaphor to Transcendental?', in *Father, Son and Holy Spirit: Essays Toward a Fully Trinitarian Theology* (London: T&T Clark, 2003), 181–200

Guthrie, D., *The Letter to the Hebrews: An Introduction and Commentary* (TNTC 15; Leicester: IVP, 1983)

Haber, S., 'From Priestly Torah to Christ Cultus: The Re-Vision of Covenant and Cult in Hebrews', *Journal for the Study of the New Testament* 28 (2005), 105–124

Habgood, J., 'The Sacramentality of the Natural World', in Brown, D. and Loades, A. (eds.), *The Sense of the Sacramental: Movement and Measure in Art and Music, Place and Time* (London: SPCK, 1995), 19–30

Habgood, J., *The Concept of Nature* (London: DLT, 2002)

Hagner, D.A., *Matthew 1–13* (WBC 33A; Dallas: Word Books, 1993); *Matthew 14–28* (WBC 33B; Dallas: Word Books, 1995)

Hahn, S.W., 'Canon, Cult and Covenant: The Promise of Liturgical Hermeneutics', in Bartholomew, C., Hahn, S., Parry, R., Seitz, C. and Wolters, A. (eds.), *Canon and Biblical Interpretation* (SHS 7; Milton Keynes: Paternoster, 2006), 207–235

Hamilton, J., 'Were Old Covenant Believers Indwelt by the Holy Spirit?', *Themelios* 30, no. 1 (2004), 12–22

Hamilton, J., 'God with Men in the Prophets and the Writings: An Examination of the Nature of God's Presence', *Scottish Bulletin of Evangelical Theology* 23 (2005), 166–193

Hanson, A.T., 'The Origin of Paul's Use of παιδαγωγός for the Law', *Journal for the Study of the New Testament* 34 (1988); reprinted in Porter, S.E. and Evans, C.A. (eds.), *New Testament Text and Language: A Sheffield Reader* (TBS 44; Sheffield: Sheffield Academic Press, 1997), 201–206

Harper, G.W., '*Calvin and English Calvinism to 1649*: A Review Article', *Calvin Theological Journal* 20 (1985), 255–262

Harrison, P., *'Religion' and the Religions in the English Enlightenment* (Cambridge: Cambridge University Press, 1990)

Harrison, P., 'The Bible and the Emergence of Modern Science', *Science and Christian Belief* 18 (2006), 115–132

Harrison, R.K., *Leviticus: An Introduction and Commentary* (TOTC; Leicester: IVP, 1980)

Harrisville, R.A., *The Concept of Newness in the New Testament* (Minneapolis: Augsburg Publishing House, 1960)

Harrisville III, R.A., 'Before ΠΙΣΤΙΣ ΧΡΙΣΤΟΥ: The Objective Genitive as Good Greek', *Novum Testamentum* 48 (2006), 353–358

Hart, D.B., *The Doors of the Sea: Where Was God in the Tsunami?* (Grand Rapids: Eerdmans, 2005)

Hart, T., 'Humankind in Christ and Christ in Humankind: Salvation as Participation in our Substitute in the Theology of John Calvin', *Scottish Journal of Theology* 42 (1989), 67–84

Hartley, J.E., *Leviticus* (WBC 4; Dallas: Word Books, 1992)

Hartley, J.E., 'Atonement, Day of', in *Dictionary of the Old Testament: Pentateuch* (Leicester: IVP, 2003), 54–61

Harvey, A.E., 'Christ as Agent', in Hurst, L.D. and Wright, N.T. (eds.), *The Glory of Christ in the New Testament: Studies in Christology in Memory of George Bradford Caird* (Oxford: Oxford University Press, 1987), 239–250

Havrilak, G., 'Chalcedon and Orthodox Christology Today', *St Vladimir's Theological Quarterly* 33 (1989), 127–145

Hawthorne, G.F., *The Presence and the Power: The Significance of the Holy Spirit in the Life and Ministry of Jesus* (Eugene: Wipf and Stock, 1991)

Hays, R.B., *The Letter to the Galatians: Introduction, Commentary, and Reflections* (NIB XI; Nashville: Abingdon Press, 2000)

Hays, R.B., *The Faith of Jesus Christ: The Narrative Substructure of Galatians 3:1–4:11*, 2nd ed. (BRS; Grand Rapids: Eerdmans, 2002)

Heath, E.A., 'Grace', in *Dictionary of the Old Testament: Pentateuch* (Leicester: IVP, 2003), 371–375

Helland, R., 'The Hypostatic Union: How Did Jesus Function?', *Evangelical Quarterly* 65 (1993), 311–327

Helm, P., 'Grace and Causation', *Scottish Journal of Theology* 32 (1979), 101–112

Helm, P., *Calvin and the Calvinists* (Edinburgh: Banner of Truth, 1982)

Helm, P., *The Providence of God* (CCT; Leicester: IVP, 1993)

Helm, P., 'Calvin (and Zwingli) on Divine Providence', *Calvin Theological Journal* 29 (1994), 388–405

Helm, P., *Faith and Understanding* (Reason and Religion Series; Edinburgh: Edinburgh University Press, 1997)

Helm, P., *John Calvin's Ideas* (Oxford: Oxford University Press, 2004)

Heppe, H., *Reformed Dogmatics: A Compendium of Reformed Theology*, revised and edited by Bizer, E.; translated by Thomson, G.T. (London: Wakeman Great Reprints, 1950)

Edward, Lord Herbert of Cherbury, *De Veritate*, translated by Carré, M.H. (Bristol: J.W. Arrowsmith, 1937)

Herrmann, R.L., 'Emergence of Humans and the Neurobiology of Consciousness', in Clayton, P. and Peacocke, A. (eds.), *In Whom We Live and Move and Have Our Being: Panentheistic Reflections on God's Presence in a Scientific World* (Grand Rapids: Eerdmans, 2004), 121–130

Hesselink, I.J., 'Calvin's Theology', in McKim, D.K. (ed.), *The Cambridge Companion to John Calvin* (Cambridge: Cambridge University Press, 2004), 74–92

Hodge, C., *Systematic Theology* (3 vols.), (London: James Clarke, 1960)

Hoeksema, H., *Reformed Dogmatics* (Grand Rapids: Reformed Free Publishing Association, 1966)

Hoitenga, Jr., D.J., *John Calvin and the Will: A Critique and Corrective* (Grand Rapids: Baker Books, 1997)

Holder, R.W., 'Calvin's Heritage', in McKim, D.K. (ed.), *The Cambridge Companion to John Calvin* (Cambridge: Cambridge University Press, 2004), 245–273

Holmes, S.R., *God of Grace and God of Glory: An Account of the Theology of Jonathan Edwards* (Edinburgh: T&T Clark, 2000)

Holmes, S.R., 'Calvin Against the Calvinists?', in *Listening to the Past: The Place of Tradition in Theology* (Carlisle: Paternoster, 2002), 68–85

Holmes, S., 'Can Punishment Bring Peace? Penal Substitution Revisited', *Scottish Journal of Theology* 58 (2005), 104–123

Holmes, S.R., 'Reformed Varieties of the *Communicatio Idiomatum*', in Holmes, S.R. and Rae, M.A. (eds.), *The Person of Christ* (London: T&T Clark, 2005), 70–86

Hoonhout, M.A., 'Grounding Providence in the Theology of the Creator: The Exemplarity of Thomas Aquinas', *The Heythrop Journal* 43 (2002), 1–19

Horrell, D.G., 'Recent Pauline Studies', *Epworth Review* 32, no. 3 (2005), 65–74

Hughes, P.E., 'Calvin and the Church of England', in Reid, W.S. (ed.), *John Calvin: His Influence in the Western World* (Grand Rapids: Zondervan, 1982), 173–196

Hume, D., *An Enquiry Concerning Human Understanding and Other Writings*, edited by Buckle, S. (CTHP; Cambridge: Cambridge University Press, 2007)

Hunn, D., 'ΠΙΣΤΙΣ ΧΡΙΣΤΟΥ in Galatians 2:16: Clarification from 3:1-6', *Tyndale Bulletin* 57 (2006), 23–33

Hunsinger, G., 'The Mediator of Communion: Karl Barth's Doctrine of the Holy Spirit', in Webster, J. (ed.), *The Cambridge Companion to Karl Barth* (Cambridge: Cambridge University Press, 2000), 177–194

Hurst, L.D., 'The Christology of Hebrews 1 and 2', in Hurst, L.D. and Wright, N.T. (eds.), *The Glory of Christ in the New Testament: Studies in Christology in Memory of George Bradford Caird* (Oxford: Oxford University Press, 1987), 151–164

Isaacs, M.E., *Sacred Space: An Approach to the Theology of the Epistle to the Hebrews* (JSNTS 73; Sheffield: Sheffield Academic Press, 1992)

Isaacs, M.E., 'Priesthood and the Epistle to the Hebrews', *The Heythrop Journal* 38 (1997), 51–62

Isaacs, M.E., 'Why Bother with Hebrews?', *The Heythrop Journal* 43 (2002), 60–72

Jacob, M.C., 'Christianity and the Newtonian Worldview', in Lindberg, D.C. and Numbers, R.L. (eds.), *God and Nature: Historical Essays on the Encounter Between Christianity and Science* (Berkeley: University of California Press, 1986), 238–255

Jammer, M., *Concepts of Space: The History of Theories of Space in Physics* (New York: Harper Torchbooks, 1960)

Janz, D.R., 'Late Medieval Theology', in Bagchi, D. and Steinmetz, D.C. (eds.), *The Cambridge Companion to Reformation Theology* (Cambridge: Cambridge University Press, 2004), 5–14

Jenson, P.P., *Graded Holiness: A Key to the Priestly Conception of the World* (JSOTS 106; Sheffield: Sheffield Academic Press, 1992)

Jenson, P.P., 'The Levitical Sacrificial System', in Beckwith, R.T. and Selman, M.J. (eds.), *Sacrifice in the Bible* (Carlisle: Paternoster Press, 1995), 25–40

Jenson, R.W., 'The Body of God's Presence: A Trinitarian Theory', in McKinney, R.W.A. (ed.), *Creation, Christ and Culture: Studies in Honour of T. F. Torrance* (Edinburgh: T&T Clark, 1976), 82–91

Jenson, R.W., *Systematic Theology, Volume 1: The Triune God* (Oxford: Oxford University Press, 2001); *Volume 2: The Works of God* (Oxford: Oxford University Press, 2001)

Jenson, R.W., 'Reconciliation in God', in Gunton, C.E. (ed.), *The Theology of Reconciliation* (London: T&T Clark, 2003), 159–166

Jenson, R.W., 'Christ in the Trinity: *Communicatio Idiomatum*', in Holmes, S.R. and Rae, M.A. (eds.), *The Person of Christ* (London: T&T Clark, 2005), 61–69

Johnson, L.T., *The Writings of the New Testament: An Interpretation* (London: SCM Press, 1999)

Johnstone, W., *Exodus* (OTG; Sheffield: Sheffield Academic Press, 1990)

Kaiser, C.B., *Creation and the History of Science* (HCT 3; London: Marshall Pickering, 1991)

Kapic, K.M., 'The Son's Assumption of a Human Nature: A Call for Clarity', *International Journal of Systematic Theology* 3 (2001), 154–166

Kapitan, T. 'Free Will Problem', in *The Cambridge Dictionary of Philosophy*, 2nd ed. (Cambridge: Cambridge University Press, 1999), 326–328

Kelly, J.N.D., *Early Christian Doctrines*, 5th ed. (London: A&C Black, 1985)

Kendall, R.T., *Calvin and English Calvinism to 1649* (OTM; Oxford: Oxford University Press, 1981); new ed. (PBTM / SEHT; Carlisle: Paternoster Press, 1997)

Kendall, R.T., 'The Puritan Modification of Calvin's Theology', in Reid, W.S. (ed.), *John Calvin: His Influence in the Western World* (Grand Rapids: Zondervan, 1982), 199–214

Kerr, A.R., *The Temple of Jesus' Body: The Temple Theme in the Gospel of John* (JSNTS 220; London: Sheffield Academic Press, 2002)

Kesich, V., 'Hypostatic and Prosopic Union in the Exegesis of Christ's Temptation', *St Vladimir's Seminary Quarterly* 9 (1965), 118–137

Kettler, C.D., 'He Takes Back the Ticket ... For Us: Providence, Evil, Suffering, and the Vicarious Humanity of Christ', *Journal for Christian Theological Research* 8 (2003), 37–57

Kim, J., 'Causation', in *The Cambridge Dictionary of Philosophy*, 2nd ed. (Cambridge: Cambridge University Press, 1999), 125–127
Kirby, W.J.T., 'Stoic *and* Epicurean? Calvin's Dialectical Account of Providence in the *Institute*', *International Journal of Systematic Theology* 5 (2003), 309–322
Kirk, J.R.D., 'The Sufficiency of the Cross (I): The Crucifixion as Jesus' Act of Obedience', *Scottish Bulletin of Evangelical Theology* 24 (2006), 36–64
Kirk, J.R.D., 'The Sufficiency of the Cross (II): The Law, the Cross, and Justification', *Scottish Bulletin of Evangelical Theology* 24 (2006), 133–154
Kistemaker, S.J., *Exposition of the Epistle to the Hebrews* (NTC; Grand Rapids: Baker Book House, 1984)
Kistemaker, S.J., 'Atonement in Hebrews', in Hill, C.E. and James III, F.A. (eds.), *The Glory of the Atonement: Biblical, Historical and Practical Perspectives. Essays in Honour of Roger Nicole* (Downers Grove: IVP, 2004), 163–175
Kiuchi, N., *The Purification Offering in the Priestly Literature: Its Meaning and Function* (JSOTS 56; Sheffield: Sheffield Academic Press, 1987)
Knight, C.C., 'Theistic Naturalism and the Word Made Flesh: Complementary Approaches to the Debate on Panentheism', in Clayton, P. and Peacocke, A. (eds.), *In Whom We Live and Move and Have Our Being: Panentheistic Reflections on God's Presence in a Scientific World* (Grand Rapids: Eerdmans, 2004), 48–61
Knight, D.H., *The Eschatological Economy: Time and the Hospitality of God* (Grand Rapids: Eerdmans, 2006)
Knudsen, R.D., 'Calvinism as a Cultural Force', in Reid, W.S. (ed.), *John Calvin: His Influence in the Western World* (Grand Rapids: Zondervan, 1982), 13–29
Konkel, A., 'The Sacrifice of Obedience', *Didaskalia* 2 (1991), 2–11
van der Kooi, C., *As in a Mirror: John Calvin and Karl Barth on Knowing God. A Diptych*, translated by Mader, D. (SHCT 120; Leiden: Brill, 2005)
de Kroon, M., *The Honour of God and Human Salvation: A Contribution to an Understanding of Calvin's Theology According to his Institutes*, translated by Vriend, J. and Bierma, L.D. (Edinburgh: T&T Clark, 2001)
Kupp, D.D., *Matthew's Emmanuel: Divine Presence and God's People in the First Gospel* (SNTSMS 90; Cambridge: Cambridge University Press, 1996)
Kvanvig, J.L. and McCann, H.J., 'Divine Conservation and the Persistence of the World', in Morris, T.V. (ed.), *Divine and Human Action: Essays in the Metaphysics of Theism* (Ithaca: Cornell University Press, 1988), 13–49
Lam, W., 'Tensions in Calvin's Idea of Predestination', *Themelios* 6, no. 1 (1980), 14–18
Lamont, J., 'The Nature of the Hypostatic Union', *The Heythrop Journal* 47 (2006), 16–25
Lane, A.N.S., *John Calvin: Student of the Church Fathers* (Edinburgh: T&T Clark, 1999)
Lane, W.L., *Hebrews 1–8* (WBC 47A; Nashville: Thomas Nelson, 1991); *Hebrews 9–13* (WBC 47B; Nashville: Thomas Nelson, 1991)
Lane, W.L., 'Hebrews', in *Dictionary of the Later New Testament and its Developments* (Leicester: IVP, 1997), 443–458
Langford, M.J., *Providence* (London: SCM Press, 1981)
Lehne, S., *The New Covenant in Hebrews* (JSNTS 44; Sheffield: Sheffield Academic Press, 1990)

Lincoln, A.T., 'Hebrews and Biblical Theology', in Bartholomew, C., Healy, M., Möller, K. and Parry, R. (eds.), *Out of Egypt: Biblical Theology and Biblical Interpretation* (SHS 5; Milton Keynes: Paternoster, 2004), 313-338

Lindars, B., *The Theology of the Letter to the Hebrews* (NTT; Cambridge: Cambridge University Press, 1991)

Lindars, B., *John* (NTG; Sheffield: Sheffield Academic Press, 1990)

Link, C., 'Providence: An Unsolved Problem of the Doctrine of Creation', in Reventlow, H.G. and Hoffman, Y. (eds.), *Creation in Jewish and Christian Tradition* (JSOTS 319; London: Sheffield Academic Press, 2002), 266-276

Loades, A., 'Finding New Sense in the "Sacramental"', in Rowell, G. and Hall, C. (eds.), *The Gestures of God: Explorations in Sacramentality* (London: Continuum, 2004), 161-172

Locke, J., *An Essay Concerning Human Understanding*, edited by Woolhouse, R. (London: Penguin Books, 1997)

Longenecker, B.W., *The Triumph of Abraham's God: The Transformation of Identity in Galatians* (Edinburgh: T&T Clark, 1998)

Longenecker, R.N., 'The Pedagogical Nature of the Law in Galatians 3:19-4:7', *Journal of the Evangelical Theological Society* 25 (1982), 53-61

Longenecker, R.N., *Galatians* (WBC 41; Nashville: Thomas Nelson, 1990)

Longenecker, R.N., 'The Foundational Conviction of New Testament Christology: The Obedience / Faithfulness / Sonship of Christ', in Green, J.B. and Turner, M. (eds.), *Jesus of Nazareth: Lord and Christ. Essays on the Historical Jesus and New Testament Christology* (Grand Rapids: Eerdmans, 1994), 473-488

Lucas, E.C., 'Cosmology', in *Dictionary of the Old Testament: Pentateuch* (Leicester: IVP, 2003), 130-139

Lull, D.J., '"The Law was our Pedagogue": A Study in Galatians 3:19-25', *Journal of Biblical Literature* 105 (1986), 481-498

Lumley, W., 'The Logos in Early Christianity', *Theology* 102 (1999), 424-430

Luz, U., *The Theology of the Gospel of Matthew*, translated by J Bradford Robinson (NTT; Cambridge: Cambridge University Press, 1995)

McClelland, R.T. and Deltete, R.K., 'Creation, Co-Operation, and Causality: A Reply to Gregersen', *Zygon* 34 (1999), 101-109

McCormack, B.L., *For Us and Our Salvation: Incarnation and Atonement in the Reformed Tradition* (Princeton: Princeton Theological Seminary, 1993)

MacDonald, N.B., *Metaphysics and the God of Israel: Systematic Theology of the Old and New Testaments* (Milton Keynes: Paternoster, 2006)

McDonald, H.D., *The God Who Responds* (Cambridge: James Clarke, 1986)

McFague, S., 'Is God in Charge? Creation and Providence', in Placher, W.C. (ed.), *Essentials of Christian Theology* (Louisville: Westminster John Knox Press, 2003), 101-116

McFarland, I., 'Christ, Spirit and Atonement', *International Journal of Systematic Theology* 3 (2001), 83-93

McGrath, A.E., *Reformation Thought: An Introduction*, 3rd ed. (Oxford: Blackwell, 1999)

McGrath, A.E., *A Scientific Theology, Volume One: Nature* (Edinburgh: T&T Clark, 2001); *Volume Two: Reality* (Edinburgh: T&T Clark, 2002); *Volume Three: Theory* (Edinburgh: T&T Clark, 2003)

Mackie, P.J., 'Causality', in Honderich, T. (ed.), *The Oxford Companion to Philosophy*, 2nd ed. (Oxford: Oxford University Press, 2005), 131–133

McKnight, S., 'Matthew, Gospel of', in *Dictionary of Jesus and the Gospels* (Leicester: IVP, 1992), 526–541

Macleod, D., *The Person of Christ* (CCT; Leicester: IVP, 1998)

McNeill, J.T., *The History and Character of Calvinism* (Oxford: Oxford University Press, 1967)

Martyn, J.L., *Galatians: A New Translation with Introduction and Commentary* (ABC 33A; New York: Doubleday, 1997)

Mellor, D.H., *The Facts of Causation* (ILP; London: Routledge, 1995)

Metzger, P.L., 'The Migration of Monism and the Matrix of Trinitarian Mediation', *Scottish Journal of Theology* 58 (2005), 302–318

Middleton, J.R. and Walsh, B.J., *Truth is Stranger than it Used to Be: Biblical Faith in a Postmodern Age* (London: SPCK, 1995)

Middleton, J.R., *The Liberating Image: The* Imago Dei *in Genesis 1* (Grand Rapids: Brazos Press, 2005)

Milgrom, J., *Leviticus 1–16: A New Translation with Introduction and Commentary* (ABC 3; New York: Doubleday, 1991)

Moberly, R.W.L., *The Bible, Theology, and Faith: A Study of Abraham and Jesus* (CSCD; Cambridge: Cambridge University Press, 2000)

Moltmann, J., *God in Creation: An Ecological Doctrine of Creation*, translated by Kohl, M. (London: SCM Press, 1985)

Moltmann, J., *Science and Wisdom*, translated by Kohl, M. (London: SCM Press, 2003)

Montefiore, H.W., *A Commentary on the Epistle to the Hebrews* (BNTC; London: A&C Black, 1964)

Moo, D.J., 'Law', in *Dictionary of Jesus and the Gospels* (Leicester: IVP, 1992), 450–461

Morris, L., 'Sacrifice, Offering', in *Dictionary of Paul and his Letters* (Leicester: IVP, 1993), 856–858

Mosser, C., 'The Greatest Possible Blessing: Calvin and Deification', *Scottish Journal of Theology* 55 (2002), 36–57

Mowvley, H., 'John 1:14-18 in the Light of Exodus 33:7–34:35', *The Expository Times* 95 (1984), 135–137

Mühling-Schlapkohl, M., 'Why Does the Risen Christ Have Scars? Why God Did Not Immediately Create the Eschaton: Goodness, Truth and Beauty', *International Journal of Systematic Theology* 6 (2004), 185–193

Muller, R.A., *Dictionary of Latin and Greek Theological Terms Drawn Principally from Protestant Scholastic Theology* (Grand Rapids: Baker Book House, 1985)

Muller, R.A., *Christ and the Decree: Christology and Predestination in Reformed Theology from Calvin to Perkins* (SHT 2; Durham, North Carolina: The Labyrinth Press, 1986)

Muller, R.A., 'The Myth of "Decretal Theology"', *Calvin Theological Journal* 30 (1995), 159–167

Muller, R.A., *The Unaccommodated Calvin: Studies in the Foundation of a Theological Tradition* (OSHT; Oxford: Oxford University Press, 2000)

Muller, R.A., *Post-Reformation Reformed Dogmatics: The Rise and Development of Reformed Orthodoxy, ca. 1520 to ca. 1725. Volume Three: The Divine Essence and*

Attributes (Grand Rapids: Baker Academic, 2003); *Volume Four: The Triunity of God* (Grand Rapids: Baker Academic, 2003)

Muller, R.A., 'John Calvin and Later Calvinism: The Identity of the Reformed Tradition', in Bagchi, D. and Steinmetz, D.C. (eds.), *The Cambridge Companion to Reformation Theology* (Cambridge: Cambridge University Press, 2004), 130–149

Muller, R.A., 'The Placement of Predestination in Reformed Theology: Issue or Non-Issue?', *Calvin Theological Journal* 40 (2005), 184–210

Murphy, N., *Beyond Liberalism and Fundamentalism: How Modern and Postmodern Philosophy Set the Theological Agenda* (Pennsylvania: Trinity Press International, 1996)

Nadler, S., 'Occasionalism', in *The Cambridge Dictionary of Philosophy*, 2nd ed. (Cambridge: Cambridge University Press, 1999), 626–627

Need, S.W., 'Re-Reading the Prologue: Incarnation and Creation in John 1.1-18', *Theology* 106 (2003), 397–404

Nevin, M., 'Analogy: Aquinas and Pannenberg', in Porter, S.E. (ed.), *The Nature of Religious Language: A Colloquium* (RILP 1; Sheffield: Sheffield Academic Press, 1996), 201–211

Newman, C.C., 'Covenant, New Covenant', in *Dictionary of the Later New Testament and its Developments* (Leicester: IVP, 1997), 245–250

Newton, I., *The* Principia*: Mathematical Principles of Natural Philosophy*, translated by Cohen, I.B. and Whitman, A., assisted by Budenz, J. (Berkeley: University of California Press, 1999)

Nichols, T.L., *The Sacred Cosmos: Christian Faith and the Challenge of Naturalism* (CPEL; Grand Rapids: Brazos Press, 2003)

Nicholson, E.W., *God and his People: Covenant and Theology in the Old Testament* (Oxford: Clarendon Press, 1986)

Nicole, E., 'Atonement in the Pentateuch', in Hill, C.E. and James III, F.A. (eds.), *The Glory of the Atonement: Biblical, Historical and Practical Perspectives. Essays in Honour of Roger Nicole* (Downers Grove: IVP, 2004), 35–50

Norris, C., 'Critical Realism and Quantum Mechanics: Some Introductory Bearings', in López, J. and Potter, G. (eds.), *After Postmodernism: An Introduction to Critical Realism* (London: Athlone Press, 2001), 116–127

O'Brien, P.T., 'Was Paul a Covenantal Nomist?', in Carson, D.A., O'Brien, P.T. and Seifrid, M.A. (eds.), *Justification and Variegated Nomism, Volume 2: The Paradoxes of Paul* (Grand Rapids: Baker Academic, 2004), 249–296

Oakley, F., 'The Absolute and Ordained Power of God in Sixteenth- and Seventeenth-Century Theology', *Journal of the History of Ideas* 59 (1998), 437–461

Ong, M.-C., *John Calvin on Providence: The* Locus Classicus *in Context* (unpublished PhD thesis, King's College London, 2003)

Owen, J., *Christologia: Or, A Declaration of the Glorious Mystery of the Person of Christ*, in Gould, W.H. (ed.), *The Works of John Owen, Volume I* (London: Banner of Truth, 1965)

Owen, J., *Pneumatologia: Or, A Discourse Concerning the Holy Spirit*, in Gould, W.H. (ed.), *The Works of John Owen, Volume III* (London: Banner of Truth, 1966)

Page, R., *Ambiguity and the Presence of God* (London: SCM Press, 1985)

Page, R., 'Panentheism and Pansyntheism: God in Relation', in Clayton, P. and Peacocke, A. (eds.), *In Whom We Live and Move and Have Our Being: Panentheistic*

Reflections on God's Presence in a Scientific World (Grand Rapids: Eerdmans, 2004), 222–232

Pailin, D.A., 'Herbert of Cherbury and the Deists', *The Expository Times* 94 (1983), 196–200

Pailin, D.A., 'Should Herbert of Cherbury be Regarded as a Deist?', *Journal of Theological Studies, NS* 51 (2000), 113–149

Pailin, D.A., 'Truth in a Heresy? Deism', *The Expository Times* 112 (2001), 112–116

Palmer, J., 'Exodus and the Biblical Theology of the Tabernacle', in Alexander, T.D. and Gathercole, S. (eds.), *Heaven on Earth: The Temple in Biblical Theology* (Carlisle: Paternoster, 2004), 11–22

Pannenberg, W., 'Analogy and Doxology', in *Basic Questions in Theology, Volume One* (LPT; London: SCM Press, 1970), 211–238

Pannenberg, W., *Systematic Theology* (3 vols.), translated by Bromiley, G.W. (Edinburgh: T&T Clark, 1991–1998)

Pannenberg, W., *An Introduction to Systematic Theology* (Grand Rapids: Eerdmans, 1991)

Parker, T.H.L., *Calvin's Old Testament Commentaries* (Edinburgh: T&T Clark, 1986)

Parker, T.H.L., *Calvin's New Testament Commentaries*, 2nd ed. (Edinburgh: T&T Clark, 1993)

Parker, T.H.L., *Calvin: An Introduction to his Thought* (OCT; London: Geoffrey Chapman, 1995)

Parker, T.H.L., *John Calvin: A Biography* (Oxford: Lion, 2006)

Partee, C., *Calvin and Classical Philosophy* (Louisville: Westminster John Knox Press, 2005)

Partee, C., 'Predestination in Aquinas and Calvin', *Reformed Review* 32 (1978), 14–22

Peacocke, A., 'Articulating God's Presence in and to the World Unveiled by the Sciences', in Clayton, P. and Peacocke, A. (eds.), *In Whom We Live and Move and Have Our Being: Panentheistic Reflections on God's Presence in a Scientific World* (Grand Rapids: Eerdmans, 2004), 137–154

Peacocke, A., 'Emergent Realities with Causal Efficacy – Some Philosophical and Theological Applications', in Peters, T. and Hallanger, N. (eds.), *God's Action in Nature's World: Essays in Honour of Robert John Russell* (Aldershot: Ashgate, 2006), 189–204

Pelikan, J., 'Creation and Causality in the History of Christian Thought', *Journal of Religion* 40 (1960), 246–255

Pelikan, J. and Hotchkiss, V. (eds.), *Creeds and Confessions of Faith in the Christian Tradition, Volume 2. Part Four: Creeds and Confessions of the Reformation Era* (New Haven: Yale University Press, 2003)

Peterson, D., 'Atonement in the Old Testament', in Peterson, D. (ed.), *Where Wrath and Mercy Meet: Proclaiming the Atonement Today* (Carlisle: Paternoster, 2001), 1–25

Peterson, D., 'Atonement in the New Testament', in Peterson, D. (ed.), *Where Wrath and Mercy Meet: Proclaiming the Atonement Today* (Carlisle: Paternoster, 2001), 26–67

Peterson, G.R., 'God, Determinism, and Action: Perspectives from Physics', *Zygon* 35 (2000), 881–890

Pettegree, A., 'The Spread of Calvin's Thought', in McKim, D.K. (ed.), *The Cambridge Companion to John Calvin* (Cambridge: Cambridge University Press, 2004), 207–224

Pitkänen, P., 'From Tent of Meeting to Temple: Presence, Rejection and Renewal of Divine Favour', in Alexander, T.D. and Gathercole, S. (eds.), *Heaven on Earth: The Temple in Biblical Theology* (Carlisle: Paternoster, 2004), 23-34

Placher, W.C., *The Domestication of Transcendence: How Modern Thinking About God Went Wrong* (Louisville: Westminster John Knox Press, 1996)

Placher, W.C., 'Introduction to Chapter 3: Is God in Charge? Creation and Providence', in Placher, W.C. (ed.), *Essentials of Christian Theology* (Louisville: Westminster John Knox Press, 2003), 93-101

Plato, *Timaeus*, translated by Zeyl, D.J., in *Plato: Complete Works*, edited, with introduction and notes, by Cooper, J.M. (Indianapolis: Hackett Publishing, 1997), 1224-1291

Polkinghorne, J., *Science and Providence: God's Interaction with the World* (London: SPCK, 1989)

Polkinghorne, J., *Science and Christian Belief: Theological Reflections of a Bottom-Up Thinker* (London: SPCK, 1994)

Polkinghorne, J., *Scientists as Theologians: A Comparison of the Writings of Ian Barbour, Arthur Peacocke and John Polkinghorne* (London: SPCK, 1996)

Polkinghorne, J., *Belief in God in an Age of Science* (New Haven: Yale University Press, 1998)

Polkinghorne, J., *Faith, Science and Understanding* London: SPCK, 2000)

Polkinghorne, J., 'The Nature of Physical Reality', *Zygon* 35 (2000), 927-940

Potter, G. and López, J., 'After Postmodernism: The New Millennium', in López, J. and Potter, G. (eds.), *After Postmodernism: An Introduction to Critical Realism* (London: Athlone Press, 2001), 3-16

Powell, S.M., *Participating in God: Creation and Trinity* (Minneapolis: Fortress Press, 2003)

Preuss, H.D., *Old Testament Theology, Volume 1*, translated by Perdue, L.G. (Edinburgh: T&T Clark, 1995); *Volume 2* (Edinburgh: T&T Clark, 1996)

Pugh, J.C., *Entertaining the Triune Mystery: God, Science, and the Space Between* (Harrisburg: Trinity Press International, 2003)

Quinn, P.L., 'Divine Conservation, Continuous Creation, and Human Action', in Freddoso, A.J. (ed.), *The Existence and Nature of God* (UNDSPR 3; Notre Dame: University of Notre Dame Press, 1983), 55-79

Quinn, P.L., 'Divine Conservation, Secondary Causes, and Occasionalism', in Morris, T.V. (ed.), *Divine and Human Action: Essays in the Metaphysics of Theism* (Ithaca: Cornell University Press, 1988), 50-73

von Rad, G., 'The Origin of the Concept of the Day of Yahweh', *Journal of Semitic Studies* 4 (1959), 97-108

von Rad, G., *Old Testament Theology, Volume 1: The History of Israel's Historical Traditions*, translated by Stalker, D.M.G. (London: SCM Press, 1975); *Volume 2: The Theology of Israel's Prophetic Traditions* (London: SCM Press, 1975)

Rae, M., 'The Travail of God', *International Journal of Systematic Theology* 5 (2003), 47-61

Rae, M.A., 'The Baptism of Christ', in Holmes, S.R. and Rae, M.A. (eds.), *The Person of Christ* (London: T&T Clark, 2005), 121-137

Reardon, P.H., 'Calvin on Providence: The Development of an Insight', *Scottish Journal of Theology* 28 (1975), 517-533

Reid, D.G., 'Sacrifice and Temple Service', in *Dictionary of New Testament Background* (Leicester: IVP, 2000), 1036–1050

Reid, W.S., 'The Transmission of Calvinism in the Sixteenth Century', in Reid, W.S. (ed.), *John Calvin: His Influence in the Western World* (Grand Rapids: Zondervan, 1982), 33–52

Riches, J., *Matthew* (NTG; Sheffield: Sheffield Academic Press, 1996)

Ritschl, D., *Memory and Hope: An Inquiry Concerning the Presence of Christ* (New York: Macmillan, 1967)

Robinson, N.H.G., 'Is Providence Credible Today?', *Scottish Journal of Theology* 30 (1977), 215–231

Roche, J.J., 'The Scientific Theology Project of Alister E McGrath', in Chung, S.W. (ed.), *Alister E McGrath and Evangelical Theology: A Dynamic Engagement* (Carlisle: Paternoster, 2003), 33–89

Rogerson, J., 'Can a Doctrine of Providence be Based on the Old Testament?', in Eslinger, L. and Taylor, G. (eds.), *Ascribe to the Lord: Biblical and Other Studies in Memory of Peter C Craigie* (JSOTS 67, Sheffield: Sheffield Academic Press, 1988), 529–543

Ross, J.F., 'Creation II', in Freddoso, A.J. (ed.), *The Existence and Nature of God* (UNDSPR 3; Notre Dame: University of Notre Dame Press, 1983), 115–141

Rowell, G., 'The Significance of Sacramentality', in Rowell, G. and Hall, C. (eds.), *The Gestures of God: Explorations in Sacramentality* (London: Continuum, 2004), 1–20

Rudman, D., 'A Note on the Azazel-goat Ritual', *Zeitschrift für die Alttestamentliche Wissenschaft* 116 (2004), 396–401

Ryken, L., Wilhoit, J.C. and Longman III, T. (gen. eds.), *Dictionary of Biblical Imagery* (Leicester: IVP, 1998)

Salier, B., 'The Temple in the Gospel According to John', in Alexander, T.D. and Gathercole, S. (eds.), *Heaven on Earth: The Temple in Biblical Theology* (Carlisle: Paternoster, 2004), 121–134

Sanders, E.P., *Paul and Palestinian Judaism: A Comparison of Patterns of Religion* (London: SCM Press, 1977)

Sanders, E.P., *Judaism: Practice and Belief, 63 BCE – 66 CE* (London: SCM Press, 1992)

Sanders, J., *The God Who Risks: A Theology of Providence* (Downers Grove: IVP, 1998)

Sandnes, K.O., 'The Death of Jesus for Human Sins: The Historical Basis for a Theological Concept', *Themelios* 20, no. 1 (1994), 20–23

Sansbury, T., 'The False Promise of Quantum Mechanics', *Zygon* 42 (2007), 111–121

Saunders, N., *Divine Action and Modern Science* (Cambridge: Cambridge University Press, 2002)

Scheffczyk, L., *Creation and Providence*, translated by Strachan, R. (London: Burns & Oates, 1970)

Schmemann, A., *The World as Sacrament* (London: DLT, 1966)

Schreiner, S.E., *The Theater of His Glory: Nature and the Natural Order in the Thought of John Calvin* (Grand Rapids: Baker Academic, 1995)

Schreiner, T.R., 'Law', in *Dictionary of the Later New Testament and its Developments* (Leicester: IVP, 1997), 644–649

Schwöbel, C., 'Divine Agency and Providence', *Modern Theology* 3 (1987), 225–244

Schwöbel, C., 'God, Creation and the Christian Community: The Dogmatic Basis of a Christian Ethic of Createdness', in Gunton, C.E. (ed.), *The Doctrine of Creation: Essays in Dogmatics, History and Philosophy* (Edinburgh: T&T Clark, 1997), 149–176

Schwöbel, C., 'Reconciliation: From Biblical Observations to Dogmatic Reconstruction', in Gunton, C.E. (ed.), *The Theology of Reconciliation* (London: T&T Clark, 2003), 13–38

Segal, A.F., 'The Incarnation: The Jewish Milieu', in Davis, S.T., Kendall, D. and O'Collins, G. (eds.), *The Incarnation: An Interdisciplinary Symposium on the Incarnation of the Son of God* (Oxford: Oxford University Press, 2002), 116–139

Seifrid, M.A., 'Death of Christ', in *Dictionary of the Later New Testament and its Developments* (Leicester: IVP, 1997), 267–287

Selman, M.J., 'Law', in *Dictionary of the Old Testament: Pentateuch* (Leicester: IVP, 2003), 497–515

Sherman, R.J., 'Toward a Trinitarian Theology of the Atonement', *Scottish Journal of Theology* 52 (1999), 346–374

Sherman, R., *King, Priest, and Prophet: A Trinitarian Theology of Atonement* (London: T&T Clark, 2004)

Shults, F.L., *Reforming the Doctrine of God* (Grand Rapids: Eerdmans, 2005)

Silva, M., 'Abraham, Faith, and Works: Paul's Use of Scripture in Galatians 3:6-14', *Westminster Theological Journal* 63 (2001), 251–267

Silva, M., *Interpreting Galatians: Explorations in Exegetical Method*, 2nd. ed. (Grand Rapids: Baker Academic, 2001)

Silva, M., 'Faith Versus Works of Law in Galatians', in Carson, D.A., O'Brien, P.T. and Seifrid, M.A. (eds.), *Justification and Variegated Nomism, Volume 2: The Paradoxes of Paul* (Grand Rapids: Baker Academic, 2004), 217–248

Sklar, J., *Sin, Impurity, Sacrifice, Atonement: The Priestly Conceptions* (HBM 2; Sheffield: Sheffield Phoenix Press, 2005)

Slater, J., 'Salvation as Participation in the Humanity of the Mediator in Calvin's *Institutes of the Christian Religion*: A Reply to Carl Mosser', *Scottish Journal of Theology* 58 (2005), 39–58

Smail, T., *The Giving Gift: The Holy Spirit in Person* (London: DLT, 1994)

Smail, T., 'Can One Man Die for the People?', in Goldingay, J. (ed.), *Atonement Today* (London: SPCK, 1995), 73–92

Smail, T., *Once and For All: A Confession of the Cross* (London: DLT, 1998)

Smedes, T.A., 'Is Our Universe Deterministic? Some Philosophical and Theological Reflections on an Elusive Topic', *Zygon* 38 (2003), 955–979

Sonderegger, K., 'The Character of Christian Realism', *Scottish Journal of Theology* 57 (2004), 451–465

Sosa, E. and Tooley, M., 'Introduction', in Sosa, E. and Tooley, M. (eds.), *Causation* (ORP; Oxford: Oxford University Press, 1993), 1–32

Spence, A., 'Christ's Humanity and Ours: John Owen', in Schwöbel, C. and Gunton, C.E. (eds.), *Persons, Divine and Human: King's College Essays in Theological Anthropology* (Edinburgh: T&T Clark, 1991), 74–97

Spence, A., 'A Unified Theory of the Atonement', *International Journal of Systematic Theology* 6 (2004), 404–420

Stegemann, E.W. and Stegemann, W., 'Does the Cultic Language in Hebrews Represent Sacrificial Metaphors? Reflections on Some Basic Problems', in Gelardini, G. (ed.), *Hebrews: Contemporary Methods – New Insights* (BIS 75; Leiden: Brill, 2005)

Steinmetz, D.C., 'The Theology of John Calvin', in Bagchi, D. and Steinmetz, D.C. (eds.), *The Cambridge Companion to Reformation Theology* (Cambridge: Cambridge University Press, 2004), 113–129

Stewart, R.A., 'Creation and Matter in the Epistle to the Hebrews', *New Testament Studies* 12 (1966), 284–293

Stiver, D.R., *The Philosophy of Religious Language: Sign, Symbol, and Story* (Oxford: Blackwell, 1996)

Strange, D., 'A Little Dwelling on the Divine Presence: Towards a "Whereness" of the Triune God', in Alexander, T.D. and Gathercole, S. (eds.), *Heaven on Earth: The Temple in Biblical Theology* (Carlisle: Paternoster, 2004), 211–229

Sykes, S.W., 'Outline of a Theology of Sacrifice', in Sykes, S.W. (ed.), *Sacrifice and Redemption: Durham Essays in Theology* (Cambridge: Cambridge University Press, 1991), 282–298

Sykes, S., *The Story of Atonement* (London: DLT, 1997)

Tanner, K., *God and Creation in Christian Theology: Tyranny or Empowerment?* (Minneapolis: Fortress Press, 1988)

Tanner, K., 'Creation and Providence', in Webster, J. (ed.), *The Cambridge Companion to Karl Barth* (Cambridge: Cambridge University Press, 2000), 111–126

Tanner, K., *Jesus, Humanity and the Trinity: A Brief Systematic Theology* (SJT / CIT; Edinburgh: T&T Clark, 2001)

Tanner, K., 'Is God in Charge? Creation and Providence', in Placher, W.C. (ed.), *Essentials of Christian Theology* (Louisville: Westminster John Knox Press, 2003), 116–131

Tasker, R.V.G., *The Gospel According to St John: An Introduction and Commentary* (TNTC 4; Leicester: IVP, 1960)

Terrien, S., *The Elusive Presence: The Heart of Biblical Theology* (RP 26; San Francisco: Harper & Row, 1978)

Thatcher, T., 'The Plot of Gal 3:1-18', *Journal of the Evangelical Theological Society* 40 (1997), 401–410

Thielman, F., 'Law', in *Dictionary of Paul and his Letters* (Leicester: IVP, 1993), 529–542

Thompson, A.J., 'Blameless Before God? Philippians 3:6 in Context', *Themelios* 28, no. 1 (2002), 5–12

Thompson, J.L., 'Calvin as a Biblical Interpreter', in McKim, D.K. (ed.), *The Cambridge Companion to John Calvin* (Cambridge: Cambridge University Press, 2004), 58–73

Thompson, M.B., *The New Perspective on Paul* (Cambridge: Grove Books, 2002)

Thompson, M.M., 'John, Gospel of', in *Dictionary of Jesus and the Gospels* (Leicester: IVP, 1992), 368–383

Thompson, R., *Holy Ground: The Spirituality of Matter* (London: SPCK, 1990)

Tidball, D., *The Message of the Cross: Wisdom Unsearchable, Love Indestructible* (BST; Leicester: IVP, 2001)

Tidball, D., *The Message of Leviticus: Free to Be Holy* (BST; Leicester: IVP, 2005)

Tindal, M., *Christianity as Old as the Creation* (London: Garland Publishing, 1978)

Toland, J., *Christianity Not Mysterious* (London: Garland Publishing, 1978)

Torrance, A.J., '*Creatio ex Nihilo* and the Spatio-Temporal Dimensions, with Special Reference to Jürgen Moltmann and D C Williams', in Gunton, C.E. (ed.), *The Doctrine of Creation: Essays in Dogmatics, History and Philosophy* (Edinburgh: T&T Clark, 1997), 83–103

Torrance, J.B., 'The Vicarious Humanity of Christ', in Torrance, T.F. (ed.), *The Incarnation: Ecumenical Studies in the Nicene–Constantinopolitan Creed A.D. 381* (Edinburgh: Handsel Press, 1981), 127–147

Torrance, J.B., *Worship, Community, and the Triune God of Grace* (Carlisle: Paternoster, 1996)

Torrance, T.F., *The Mediation of Christ*, rev. ed. (Edinburgh: T&T Clark, 1992)

Torrance, T.F., 'The Greek Conception of Space in the Background of Early Christian Theology', in *Divine Meaning: Studies in Patristic Hermeneutics* (Edinburgh: T&T Clark, 1995), 289–342

Torrance, T.F., 'The Relation of the Incarnation to Space in Nicene Theology', in *Divine Meaning: Studies in Patristic Hermeneutics* (Edinburgh: T&T Clark, 1995), 343–373

Torrance, T.F., *Space, Time and Incarnation* (Edinburgh: T&T Clark, 1997)

Torrance, T.F., *Divine and Contingent Order* (Edinburgh: T&T Clark, 1998)

Towne, E.A., 'The Variety of Panentheisms', *Zygon* 40 (2005), 779–786

Trost, L.A., 'Non-Interventionist Divine Action: Robert Russell, Wolfhart Pannenberg, and the Freedom of the (Natural) World', in Peters, T. and Hallanger, N. (eds.), *God's Action in Nature's World: Essays in Honour of Robert John Russell* (Aldershot: Ashgate, 2006), 205–216

Trueman, C.R., 'The Theology of the English Reformers', in Bagchi, D. and Steinmetz, D.C. (eds.), *The Cambridge Companion to Reformation Theology* (Cambridge: Cambridge University Press, 2004), 161–173

Trueman, C.R., 'Calvin and Calvinism', in McKim, D.K. (ed.), *The Cambridge Companion to John Calvin* (Cambridge: Cambridge University Press, 2004), 225–244

Travis, S.H., 'Christ as Bearer of Divine Judgement in Paul's Thought about the Atonement', in Goldingay, J. (ed.), *Atonement Today* (London: SPCK, 1995), 21–38

Tuckett, C., 'Christology and the New Testament', *Scottish Journal of Theology* 33 (1980), 401–416

Twelftree, G.H., 'Temptation of Jesus', in *Dictionary of Jesus and the Gospels* (Leicester: IVP, 1992), 821–827

Tyacke, N., *Anti-Calvinists: The Rise of English Arminianism c. 1590–1640* (OHM; Oxford: Oxford University Press, 1990)

Vander Laan, D., 'Persistence and Divine Conservation', *Religious Studies* 42 (2006), 159–176

Vanhoozer, K.J., 'Effectual Call or Causal Effect? Summons, Sovereignty and Supervenient Grace', *Tyndale Bulletin* 49 (1998), 213–251

Vanhoozer, K.J., 'Providence', in *Dictionary for Theological Interpretation of the Bible* (Grand Rapids: Baker Academic, 2005), 641–645

Van Till, H.J., 'Basil, Augustine, and the Doctrine of Creation's Functional Integrity', *Science and Christian Belief* 8 (1996), 21–38

te Velde, R.A., *Aquinas on God: The 'Divine Science' of the Summa Theologiae* (ASHPT; Aldershot: Ashgate, 2006)

Verhey, A., 'Calvin's Treatise "Against the Libertines"', *Calvin Theological Journal* 15 (1980), 190–219

Via, D.O., 'Revelation, Atonement and the Scope of Faith in the Epistle to the Hebrews: A Deconstructive and Reader-Response Interpretation', *Biblical Interpretation* 11 (2003), 515–530

Vogt, P.T., *Deuteronomic Theology and the Significance of Torah: A Reappraisal* (Winona Lake, Indiana: Eisenbrauns, 2006)

Wallis, I.G., *The Faith of Jesus Christ in Early Christian Traditions* (SNTSMS 84; Cambridge: Cambridge University Press, 1995)

Walsham, A., *Providence in Early Modern England* (Oxford: Oxford University Press, 1999)

Watson, F., *Text, Church and world: Biblical Interpretation in Theological Perspective* (Edinburgh: T&T Clark, 1994)

Watson, F., 'Christ, Law and Freedom: A Study in Theological Hermeneutics', in Gunton, C.E. (ed.), *God and Freedom: Essays in Historical and Systematic Theology* (Edinburgh: T&T Clark, 1995), 82–102

Watson, F., *Text and Truth: Redefining Biblical Theology* (Edinburgh: T&T Clark, 1997)

Watson, F., *Paul and the Hermeneutics of Faith* (London: T&T Clark, 2004)

Weatherford, R.C., 'Determinism', in Honderich, T. (ed.), *The Oxford Companion to Philosophy*, 2nd ed. (Oxford: Oxford University Press, 2005), 208–209

Weatherford, R.C., 'Determinism, Logical', in Honderich, T. (ed.), *The Oxford Companion to Philosophy*, 2nd ed. (Oxford: Oxford University Press, 2005), 209–210

Weatherford, R.C., 'Freedom and Determinism', in Honderich, T. (ed.), *The Oxford Companion to Philosophy*, 2nd ed. (Oxford: Oxford University Press, 2005), 313–315

Wedin, M.V., 'Aristotle', in *The Cambridge Dictionary of Philosophy*, 2nd ed. (Cambridge: Cambridge University Press, 1999), 44–51

Weinandy, T.G., *In the Likeness of Sinful Flesh: An Essay on the Humanity of Christ* (Edinburgh: T&T Clark, 1993)

Weinandy, T.G., *Does God Suffer?* (Edinburgh: T&T Clark, 2000)

Wells, J.B., *God's Holy People: A Theme in Biblical Theology* (JSOTS 305; Sheffield: Sheffield Academic Press, 2000)

Wells, P., 'A Free Lunch at the End of the Universe? Sacrifice, Substitution and Penal Liability', *Themelios* 29, no. 1 (2003), 38–51

Wendel, F., *Calvin: The Origins and Development of his Religious Thought*, translated by Mairet, P. (London: Collins, 1963)

Wenham, G.J., *Genesis 1–15* (WBC 1; Nashville: Thomas Nelson, 1987)

Wenham, G.J., 'The Theology of Old Testament Sacrifice', in Beckwith, R.T. and Selman, M.J. (eds.), *Sacrifice in the Bible* (Carlisle: Paternoster Press, 1995), 75–87

Westfall, R.S., 'The Rise of Science and the Decline of Orthodox Christianity: A Study of Kepler, Descartes and Newton', in Lindberg, D.C. and Numbers, R.L. (eds.), *God and Nature: Historical Essays on the Encounter Between Christianity and Science* (Berkeley: University of California Press, 1986), 218–237

White, P., *Predestination, Policy and Polemic: Conflict and Consensus in the English Church from the Reformation to the Civil War* (Cambridge: Cambridge University Press, 1992)

White, S., 'The Theology of Sacred Space', in Brown, D. and Loades, A. (eds.), *The Sense of the Sacramental: Movement and Measure in Art and Music, Place and Time* (London: SPCK, 1995), 31–43

Whitehouse, W.A., 'Providence: An Account of Karl Barth's Doctrine', *Scottish Journal of Theology* 4 (1951), 241–256

Williams, G., 'The Cross and the Punishment of Sin', in Peterson, D. (ed.), *Where Wrath and Mercy Meet: Proclaiming the Atonement Today* (Carlisle: Paternoster, 2001), 68–99

Williamson, P.R., 'Covenant', in *Dictionary of the Old Testament: Pentateuch* (Leicester: IVP, 2003), 139–155

Wilson, T.A., '"Under Law" in Galatians: A Pauline Theological Abbreviation', *Journal of Theological Studies, NS* 56 (2005), 362–392

Wisse, M., '*Habitus Fidei*: An Essay on the History of a Concept', *Scottish Journal of Theology* 56 (2003), 172–189

Witherington III. B., 'The Influence of Galatians on Hebrews', *New Testament Studies* 37 (1991), 146–152

Wood, C.M., 'The Events in which God Acts', *The Heythrop Journal* 22 (1981), 278–284

Wood, C.M., 'The Question of the Doctrine of Providence', *Theology Today* 49 (1992), 209–224

Wood, C.M., 'How Does God Act?', *International Journal of Systematic Theology* 1 (1999), 138–152

Wood, C.M., 'Providence and a New Creation', (unpublished paper presented to the Oxford Institute of Methodist Theological Studies, 2002, downloaded from www.oxford-institute.org)

Wright, N.T., *The Epistles of Paul to the Colossians and to Philemon: An Introduction and Commentary* (TNTC 12; Leicester: IVP, 1986)

Wright, N.T., *The Climax of the Covenant: Christ and the Law in Pauline Theology* (Edinburgh: T&T Clark, 1991)

Wright, N.T., *The New Testament and the People of God* (London: SPCK, 1992)

Wright, N.T., *What St Paul Really Said* (Oxford: Lion, 1997)

Wright, N.T., *Jesus and the Victory of God* (London: SPCK, 1996)

Wright, N.T., *Paul: Fresh Perspectives* (London: SPCK, 2005)

Wright, N., *The Radical Evangelical: Seeking a Place to Stand* (London: SPCK, 1996)

Wright, N.G., *God on the Inside: The Holy Spirit in Holy Scripture* (Oxford: BRF, 2006)

Wright, S.D., *Our Sovereign Refuge: The Pastoral Theology of Theodore Beza* (SCHT; Carlisle: Paternoster, 2004)

Wright, T.J., 'Reconsidering *Concursus*', *International Journal of Systematic Theology* 4 (2002), 205–215

Wright, T.J., 'Witnessing Christians from Karl Barth's Perspective', *Evangelical Quarterly* 75 (2003), 239–255

Wright, T.J., 'How is Christ Present to the World?', *International Journal of Systematic Theology* 7 (2005), 300–315

Wright, T.J., 'Collecting Memories: Identity, Nostalgia and the Objects of Childhood', in Shier-Jones, A. (ed.), *Children of God: Towards a Theology of Childhood* (Peterborough: Epworth, 2007), 159–179

Wright, T.J., 'The Seal of Approval: An Interpretation of the Son's Sustaining Action in Hebrews 1:3', in Bauckham, R.J., Driver, D.R., Hart, T.A. and MacDonald, N. (eds.), *The Epistle to the Hebrews and Christian Theology* (Grand Rapids: Eerdmans, forthcoming, 2009)

Yarborough, R.W., 'Paul and Salvation History', in Carson, D.A., O'Brien, P.T. and Seifrid, M.A. (eds.), *Justification and Variegated Nomism, Volume 2: The Paradoxes of Paul* (Grand Rapids: Baker Academic, 2004), 297–342

Zachman, R.C., 'Calvin as Analogical Theologian', *Scottish Journal of Theology* 51 (1998), 162–187

Zachman, R.C., *John Calvin as Teacher, Pastor, and Theologian: The Shape of His Writings and Thought* (Grand Rapids: Baker Academic, 2006)

Zahl, P.F.M., 'Mistakes of the New Perspective on Paul', *Themelios* 27, no. 1 (2001), 5–11

GENERAL INDEX

Aaron, 176–178, 182
Abram, Abraham, 20, 123, 142, 143, 144, 145, 146, 151–152, 155, 156, 158, 159, 160, 162, 163–164, 167, 169, 179, 183, 193, 197
Adam, 18, 25–26, 34–35, 37–39, 42, 43, 46, 51, 108, 121–123, 132, 135, 142, 163, 167, 206, 214, 222
analogy, 12, 18, 91–96, 106, 134, 222
    analogy of attribution, 93–94
    analogy of proportionality, 93–94
    panentheistic analogy, 18, 104–105, 106, 134, 222
Anderson, G.A., 139
anthropomorphism, 115
Aristotle, 69, 80–81, 82, 85, 221
atonement, 20, 42–46, 171–179, 181, 185, 188, 189, 191, 205, 208, 209, 228
atonement slate, 118, 124, 175, 176, 177, 185
Augustine, 5, 101
autopoiesis, 102, 106
Azazel, 177, 178

Bailey, W., 70
Baillie, D.M., 130
Barker, M., 118, 176, 178
Barker, P.A., 158, 159
Baro, P., 62–63
Barth, K., 2, 3, 4, 5, 7, 15, 107, 127–130, 131, 134, 135, 228
Bauckham, R., 215–216
Bavinck, H., 7, 8, 10–11
Beale, G.K., 117–119, 122, 123, 139, 142
Berkhof, L., 6, 7–8, 10
Berkouwer, G.C., 7, 13
Beza, T., 60–61, 63–64, 73
Book of Common Prayer, 58
Braun, J., 7
Brock, S.L., 84–85
Brondos, D.A., 146

Brooke, J.H., 73
Brümmer, V., 83
Bucer, M., 57–58, 60
Buckley, M.J., 72
Burrell, D.B., 84
Byl, J., 99

Caird, G.B., 180–181
Calovius, A., 6
Calvin, J., 1, 4–5, 9, 13, 18, 20, 23–53, 55–56, 57, 58, 59, 60, 61, 62, 63–64, 67–69, 70, 71, 72, 73, 74, 75, 76, 77, 78, 79–83, 85, 86, 88, 90, 91, 96, 99, 105, 106, 107, 108–109, 115, 194–208, 209, 214, 215, 216, 218, 221, 222, 225, 231
Cambridge, 58
Cambridge Platonists, 66, 72, 73
Campbell, D.A., 146, 161
cause, causation
    causa creata, 107
    causa creatrix, 107
    causa divina, 107
    causa efficiens, 60, 62, 80–84, 95
    causa finalis, 80–84, 86
    causa formalis, 80–84
    causa instrumentalis, 82, 84, 95
    causa materialis, 80–84
    causa non divina, 107
    causal distinctions, 80–84
    causal joints, 18, 96–98, 100–101, 102, 104, 106, 110, 222
    causal orders, 12, 13, 18, 83, 85, 88, 90, 91, 96, 102, 105, 106, 110, 222
    double agency, 97
    effective cause, 83, 95
    mental causation, 104
    primary causation, 1, 9–14, 16, 17, 18, 19, 24–25, 30, 34, 38–39, 41, 42, 46, 49, 50–52, 55, 56, 69, 70,

72, 74–76, 77, 78, 79, 80, 82–85, 87, 89–91, 95, 96, 102, 103, 105–107, 108, 109, 110, 113, 114, 135, 136, 137, 165, 221–222, 224, 228, 229, 230, 232
  secondary causation, 1, 9–14, 16, 17, 18, 19, 21, 23, 24–25, 26, 30, 31–33, 34, 38–39, 40, 41, 42, 46, 49, 50–52, 53, 55, 56, 68, 69, 70, 71, 72, 74–75, 77, 78, 79, 80, 82–85, 87, 89–91, 95, 96, 99, 101, 102, 103, 105–107, 108, 109, 110, 113, 114, 135, 136, 137, 165, 218, 219, 221–222, 224, 228, 229, 230, 231, 232
  structuring causes, 102
  triggering causes, 102
Cecil, W., 59
Chadwick, O., 60
chaos theory, 98–100
Charette, B., 209
Church, 14, 19, 32, 47, 110, 114, 127, 128, 129, 130, 131–135, 136, 137, 218, 222, 223, 224, 226, 230, 232
Clayton, P.D., 98, 103–104
Colwell, J.E., 208
Common Notions, 65–66, 67
communicatio idiomatum, 196, 202, 203–209, 215
Cooper, T., 70
Coppedge, A., 109, 225
covenant, 5, 125, 129, 133, 140–142, 143, 144, 149–150, 152, 153, 155–156, 158, 159, 163, 168–169, 179, 182, 184, 185, 186, 190
covenantal nomism, 144
Craddock, F.B., 182
creation as project, 119, 187, 226, 230, 232
Crisp, O.D., 207
Cudworth, R., 66
Culverwel, N., 66

Das, A.A., 149
Davidson, I., 207
Dawson, G.S., 184

Day of Atonement, 20, 118, 168, 175–179, 180, 182, 183, 184, 189, 210
Dearman, J.A., 115
deists, deism, 67, 72, 73, 75, 78, 91, 100, 101, 104
Descartes, R., 97
determinism, 11, 16, 23, 70, 71, 75, 88, 226
Di Noia, J.A., 77
divine faithfulness, 21, 114, 135, 136, 142, 163–165, 174, 189, 193, 207, 217, 218, 219, 222, 226, 228
divine presence, 16, 17, 19–20, 21, 30, 50, 53, 55, 56, 71, 72, 74, 79, 80, 90, 103, 108, 110, 113–136, 137, 138–141, 142, 143, 144, 145, 148, 157, 159, 162, 164, 165, 167, 169, 173, 174, 175, 177, 178, 179, 181, 182, 184, 185, 186, 187, 188, 189, 190, 191, 193, 210, 211, 215, 217, 218, 219, 222–223, 224–225, 226, 227–228, 229–232
  intensity of divine presence, 224, 229–232
  omnipresence, 7, 127–128, 224, 229
Dretske, F., 102
Dumbrell, W.J., 140
Dunn, J.D.G., 145, 148–150, 153, 156, 157
Durham, J.I., 141

Eberhart, C., 185–186
Eden, garden of, 19, 135, 142, 163, 167, 209, 223
Edmondson, S., 196, 202
Edward VI, 57–58
Edward, Lord Herbert of Cherbury, 64–66, 67, 72, 73
election, 5, 60, 63, 82, 109, 135, 137, 141, 142, 157, 168, 188
Elizabeth I, 58–59, 70
England, 56, 57–61, 62, 69, 70, 72, 73, 221
Epicureans, Epicureanism, 25, 30, 32, 33, 52

Index

eternal decree, 4, 5, 9, 17, 37, 38, 47, 49, 50, 56, 85–86, 88, 109, 114, 136, 202, 223, 226, 230
Evans, C.A., 125

Farel, G., 57
Farrer, A., 97, 106
Farrow, D., 196–197
fate, 32, 51, 75, 76
Fiddes, P.S., 14, 97, 107, 114
Fletcher-Louis, C.H.T., 120, 121
Forty-Two Articles of Religion, 58
free will, 36–37
functional integrity, 101
fundamental ontological distinction, 13, 31, 32, 50, 52, 75–76, 85, 87, 90, 91, 92, 96, 105, 106, 108, 205, 217

Galatians, 20, 110, 136, 144, 145–165, 167, 168, 189, 191, 193, 218
Geneva, 57, 58, 59, 60, 61
Geneva Bible, 59
Gethsemane, garden of, 182, 186, 188, 193, 201–202, 209, 213–215
God the Father, 3, 5, 14, 16, 20, 21, 28, 43, 44, 45, 46, 50, 82, 126, 127, 132, 133, 135, 136, 146, 171, 172, 184, 186, 191, 193, 194, 197, 201–202, 206, 207, 208, 209, 211–215, 216, 217, 218, 219, 222–223, 226, 227, 232
Gorringe, T.J., 101, 121
Gottschalk of Orbais, 4–5
gratia adoptionis, 129, 134
gratia unionis, 129
Gregersen, N.H., 102
Grudem, W., 7, 19
Gunton, C.E., 13–14, 77, 91, 96, 107–108, 119–120, 132–134, 142, 155, 187–188

Hanson, A.T., 160
Harrisville III, R.A., 146
Harsnett, S., 62
Hart, T., 43, 109
Hartley, J.E., 118, 175, 177, 178
Harvey, L., 108, 208

ḥaṭṭā't, 168–179, 181, 182, 185, 187, 189
Hawthorne, G.F., 194, 209, 212, 214
Hays, R.B., 146, 147–148, 152, 155, 156, 159, 160
Hebrews, 20, 110, 124, 136, 138, 168, 179–191, 193, 194, 200, 207, 209, 214, 218, 222, 228
Helland, R., 203
Helm, P., 1, 5–6, 9, 23, 24, 35, 36, 40, 42, 46, 83–84, 196
Heppe, H., 9
Hodge, C., 10
Hoeksema, H., 6
holy of holies, 20, 117, 118–119, 124, 139, 173, 175–179, 181, 182, 183, 185, 189, 190–191, 210, 224, 229, 230
Holy Spirit, 14, 16, 17, 19, 20, 21, 28, 29, 32, 45–46, 50, 55, 76, 77, 78, 79, 91, 95, 105, 107–108, 109, 110, 114, 121, 127, 130, 131, 132, 133, 134, 135–136, 137, 147, 148, 151, 155, 156, 160, 162, 164, 165, 167, 181, 184, 186, 188, 190, 191, 192, 194, 198, 199, 200–201, 206–219, 222–223, 225, 226, 227, 228, 230, 231, 232
Hooker, R., 70
Hoonhout, M.A., 87, 91

Isaacs, M.E., 182
Israel, 17, 19, 20, 110, 115–123, 125, 128, 129, 130, 136, 137–145, 148–150, 154, 155, 156–165, 167, 168–179, 181, 182, 183, 185, 187, 188–189, 193, 209, 210–211, 212, 217, 222, 224, 225, 228, 229

Jenson, P.P., 170, 185
Jesus Christ, Son, 3, 5, 14–15, 16–17, 18, 19, 20–21, 26, 28, 33, 42–46, 50, 51, 60, 61, 62, 63, 64, 65, 75–76, 77, 79, 81, 82, 91, 95, 105, 107–108, 109, 110, 113, 114, 115, 119, 123–136, 137–138, 145–166, 167–168, 171–172, 175, 179–192, 193–

219, 222–223, 224–225, 226, 227–228, 229–230, 232
  Christ as *tertium quid*, 204, 206, 208, 218
  divinity and humanity of, 195–208, 215, 216–217
  obedience of, 19–21, 42–46, 51, 82, 135–136, 160–165, 182, 186–188, 191, 193–194, 208–218
  temptations of, 165, 182, 184, 186, 188, 201–202, 203, 206–207, 209, 211–215, 217, 218, 222

Kapic, K.M., 206, 207
Kendall, R.T., 63–64
Kerr, A.R., 125, 126, 127
kippēr, 171, 172–173, 175
Kirby, W.J.T., 33
Kiuchi, N., 178
Knight, D.H., 138
Kupp, D.D., 124

Lambeth Articles, 60, 62–63
Lane, A.N.S., 85
Lane, W.L., 168, 182
Leviticus, 115, 116, 153, 154, 160, 161, 168–179
Libertines, Libertinism, 25, 30–32, 33, 51, 52
Locke, J., 66; 71
Lombard, P., 85
Longenecker, R.N., 158, 160–161
Lord's Supper, 132–134, 196
Lull, D.J., 160
Luria, I., 130
Luther, M., 4–5, 76

MacDonald, N.B., 119
Martyn, J.L., 147, 148, 152, 153, 155
Mary I, 58
Matthew, Gospel of, 20, 110, 124, 136, 198, 201, 208–215, 216, 218
McCormack, B.L., 202, 205
McGrath, A.E., 98, 100–101
mediation, 13–16, 19, 28, 33, 50, 75, 77, 91, 96, 105, 106, 107, 110, 132, 134, 137, 191

Melchizedek, 179, 182, 183
metacorporeality, 115
Middleton, J.R., 121, 122
Milgrom, J., 170, 173–174, 178
Moberly, R.W.L., 212
Moltmann, J., 130
More, H., 66
Mosaic Law, 20, 109, 125, 138, 143–165, 167, 168, 169, 178, 179, 182, 183, 185, 188, 189, 190, 193, 222
Moses, 116, 125–126, 138–140, 145, 159, 169, 173, 179, 184, 189, 211
Mount Sinai, 138–139, 145, 168
Muller, R.A., 47, 203
Murphy, N., 104

natural laws, 71–72, 73, 100, 104
natural occurrence, 34, 71, 72, 74
necessary and sufficient conditions, 84
Nestorianism, 203, 204, 205, 206, 208, 218
Newton, I., 71–72, 76–77

occasionalism, 11, 23, 51, 52
omnipresence, *see* divine presence
Ong, M.-C., 30
open theism, 228–229
original sin, 34–35, 37–38, 65
Owen, J., 216–217
Oxford, 58

Page, R., 113
παιδαγωγός, 145, 160–162, 163, 189
Pailin, D., 67
Palmer, J., 126
panentheism, 102–105, 228
Pannenberg, W., 6, 94
pansyntheism, 113
pantheism, 30, 32, 33, 103
Partee, C., 86
Paul's Cross, 62, 63
penal substitution, 171–173
Perkins, W., 60, 61, 62, 64, 73
Peterson, D., 171–172
Peterson, G.R., 98, 100
πίστεως Ἰησου Χριστου, 146
Placher, W., 17, 76, 108
Plato, 9

Index

Polkinghorne, J., 97, 98, 99, 106
potentia Dei absoluta, 49
potentia Dei ordinata, 49
predestination, 4–5, 18, 26, 47–49, 50, 56, 60–66, 67, 70, 72, 73, 74, 75, 76, 77, 85–86, 88, 221
presence, *see* divine presence
providence made flesh, 15, 21, 135, 136, 137, 164, 193, 219, 230, 232
providence, contours of, 17, 114, 136, 226
providence, definition of, 19–20, 21, 110, 165, 167, 191, 193, 217, 218, 219, 222
providence, threefold scheme of, 6–8, 110, 226, 228
    concursus, 6–8, 226–227
    conservatio, 6–8, 226, 227–228
    gubernatio, 6–8, 226

quantum mechanics, 98, 99, 100, 101, 102, 106, 228
Quenstedt, J.A., 6

von Rad, G., 157, 158
Reardon, P.H., 5, 30, 32
Reformed doctrinal statements
    Belgic Confession, 2–3, 64
    Canons of Dordt, 2, 64
    Consensus Tigurinus, 2, 64
    Heidelberg Catechism, 2, 3, 64
    Second Helvetic Confession, 2, 9, 64
    Westminster Confession of Faith, 3, 4, 5, 9–10, 64, 223
Reid, D.G., 175
reprobation, 64, 86

sacrificial system, 20, 127, 144, 156, 165, 169, 171, 172, 173, 179, 183, 184, 185, 186, 187, 189, 190, 210, 222
Sanders, E.P., 144
Sanders, J., 48, 115, 229
Sansbury, T., 100
scapegoat, 175, 178
Scheffczyk, L., 87

science, natural science, 18, 53, 55, 56, 57, 67–74, 78, 79, 97, 99, 101, 221, 228
Selman, M.J., 143
Seneca, 32
Shults, F.L., 16–17
Silva, M., 148, 150–151, 152
Smail, T., 186, 194
Smedes, T.A., 99
Smith, D., 122
Smith, J., 66
Somerset, 5th Duke of (Edward Seymour), 58
Son, *see* Jesus Christ, Son
space, 130
Spence, A., 217
Sterry, P., 66
Stoics, Stoicism, 4–5, 23, 25, 30, 32–33, 52
supersessionism, 138
supervenience, 104

tabernacle, 19, 114, 116, 117, 118, 120, 121, 125, 126, 128, 131, 135, 137, 139, 143, 168, 169, 173, 176, 177, 178, 179, 183, 184, 185, 189, 190, 222, 225, 229
Tabula praedestinationis, 60–61
Tanner, K., 12, 105–106
temple, 19, 114, 116, 117, 118, 120, 121, 122, 123, 124, 126, 131, 134, 135, 137, 138, 139, 167, 175, 176, 178, 222, 224, 228, 229, 230
temple imagery, 117–119, 124, 224
theomorphism, 115
Thirty-Nine Articles, 58, 60
Thomas Aquinas, 4–5, 12, 14, 18, 76, 85–96, 97, 99, 100, 105, 106, 107, 108, 109, 222
Tidball, D., 174
Toland, J., 67
Torrance, J.B., 176
Torrance, T.F., 187
Trinity, trinitarianism, triune God, 14, 15, 16, 19, 21, 28, 30, 46, 50, 75–78, 80, 91, 105, 107, 108, 109, 110, 111, 113, 114, 134, 137, 191, 194, 218, 222, 223, 226, 229, 232

Trueman, C.R., 64
Twelftree, G.H., 212
Tyacke, N., 63

unique divine identity, 216

Van Till, H.J., 101–102
Vanhoozer, K.J., 16–17, 104
te Velde, R., 92
Vermigli, P.M., 58
Vogt, P.T., 144

Watson, F., 120–121, 150–151, 155
Webster, J., 227
Weinandy, T.G., 186, 203, 204–205
Wells, J.B., 142–143
Whichcote, B., 66

Whitaker, W., 60
will of God, 1, 3, 10, 13–14, 16, 17, 25–26, 31, 33, 37–41, 46–49, 50–52, 56, 60, 62, 66, 69, 75–76, 77, 79, 81, 82, 85–91, 96, 101, 105, 107, 110, 121, 137, 159, 186, 194, 201–202, 206, 209, 213–215, 218, 219, 221, 226
Witherington III, B., 168
Wood, C.M., 6, 8, 75–76
Wright, N.G., 172, 194
Wright, N.T., 124, 125, 142, 144–145, 149, 159–160
Wright, T.J., 113, 145

zimzum, 130
Zwingli, H., 4–5

Paternoster Biblical Monographs

(All titles uniform with this volume)
Dates in bold are of projected publication

Joseph Abraham
Eve: Accused or Acquitted?
A Reconsideration of Feminist Readings of the Creation Narrative Texts in Genesis 1–3
Two contrary views dominate contemporary feminist biblical scholarship. One finds in the Bible an unequivocal equality between the sexes from the very creation of humanity, whilst the other sees the biblical text as irredeemably patriarchal and androcentric. Dr Abraham enters into dialogue with both camps as well as introducing his own method of approach. An invaluable tool for any one who is interested in this contemporary debate.
2002 / 0-85364-971-5 / xxiv + 272pp

Octavian D. Baban
Mimesis and Luke's on the Road Encounters in Luke-Acts
Luke's Theology of the Way and its Literary Representation
The book argues on theological and literary (mimetic) grounds that Luke's on-the-road encounters, especially those belonging to the post-Easter period, are part of his complex theology of the Way. Jesus' teaching and that of the apostles is presented by Luke as a challenging answer to the Hellenistic reader's thirst for adventure, good literature, and existential paradigms.
***2005** / 1-84227-253-5 / approx. 374pp*

Paul Barker
The Triumph of Grace in Deuteronomy
This book is a textual and theological analysis of the interaction between the sin and faithlessness of Israel and the grace of Yahweh in response, looking especially at Deuteronomy chapters 1–3, 8–10 and 29–30. The author argues that the grace of Yahweh is determinative for the ongoing relationship between Yahweh and Israel and that Deuteronomy anticipates and fully expects Israel to be faithless.
2004 / 1-84227-226-8 / xxii + 270pp

Jonathan F. Bayes
The Weakness of the Law
God's Law and the Christian in New Testament Perspective
A study of the four New Testament books which refer to the law as weak (Acts, Romans, Galatians, Hebrews) leads to a defence of the third use in the Reformed debate about the law in the life of the believer.
2000 / 0-85364-957-X / xii + 244pp

July 2005

Mark Bonnington
The Antioch Episode of Galatians 2:11-14 in Historical and Cultural Context

The Galatians 2 'incident' in Antioch over table-fellowship suggests significant disagreement between the leading apostles. This book analyses the background to the disagreement by locating the incident within the dynamics of social interaction between Jews and Gentiles. It proposes a new way of understanding the relationship between the individuals and issues involved.

2005 / 1-84227-050-8 / approx. 350pp

David Bostock
A Portrayal of Trust
The Theme of Faith in the Hezekiah Narratives

This study provides detailed and sensitive readings of the Hezekiah narratives (2 Kings 18–20 and Isaiah 36–39) from a theological perspective. It concentrates on the theme of faith, using narrative criticism as its methodology. Attention is paid especially to setting, plot, point of view and characterization within the narratives. A largely positive portrayal of Hezekiah emerges that underlines the importance and relevance of scripture.

2005 / 1-84227-314-0 / approx. 300pp

Mark Bredin
Jesus, Revolutionary of Peace
A Non-violent Christology in the Book of Revelation

This book aims to demonstrate that the figure of Jesus in the Book of Revelation can best be understood as an active non-violent revolutionary.

2003 / 1-84227-153-9 / xviii + 262pp

Robinson Butarbutar
Paul and Conflict Resolution
An Exegetical Study of Paul's Apostolic Paradigm in 1 Corinthians 9

The author sees the apostolic paradigm in 1 Corinthians 9 as part of Paul's unified arguments in 1 Corinthians 8–10 in which he seeks to mediate in the dispute over the issue of food offered to idols. The book also sees its relevance for dispute-resolution today, taking the conflict within the author's church as an example.

2006 / 1-84227-315-9 / approx. 280pp

Daniel J-S Chae
Paul as Apostle to the Gentiles
His Apostolic Self-awareness and its Influence on the Soteriological Argument in Romans

Opposing 'the post-Holocaust interpretation of Romans', Daniel Chae competently demonstrates that Paul argues for the equality of Jew and Gentile in Romans. Chae's fresh exegetical interpretation is academically outstanding and spiritually encouraging.

1997 / 0-85364-829-8 / xiv + 378pp

Luke L. Cheung
The Genre, Composition and Hermeneutics of the Epistle of James

The present work examines the employment of the wisdom genre with a certain compositional structure and the interpretation of the law through the Jesus tradition of the double love command by the author of the Epistle of James to serve his purpose in promoting perfection and warning against doubleness among the eschatologically renewed people of God in the Diaspora.

2003 / 1-84227-062-1 / xvi + 372pp

Youngmo Cho
Spirit and Kingdom in the Writings of Luke and Paul

The relationship between Spirit and Kingdom is a relatively unexplored area in Lukan and Pauline studies. This book offers a fresh perspective of two biblical writers on the subject. It explores the difference between Luke's and Paul's understanding of the Spirit by examining the specific question of the relationship of the concept of the Spirit to the concept of the Kingdom of God in each writer.

2005 / 1-84227-316-7 / approx. 270pp

Andrew C. Clark
Parallel Lives
The Relation of Paul to the Apostles in the Lucan Perspective

This study of the Peter-Paul parallels in Acts argues that their purpose was to emphasize the themes of continuity in salvation history and the unity of the Jewish and Gentile missions. New light is shed on Luke's literary techniques, partly through a comparison with Plutarch.

2001 / 1-84227-035-4 / xviii + 386pp

Andrew D. Clarke
Secular and Christian Leadership in Corinth
A Socio-Historical and Exegetical Study of 1 Corinthians 1–6
This volume is an investigation into the leadership structures and dynamics of first-century Roman Corinth. These are compared with the practice of leadership in the Corinthian Christian community which are reflected in 1 Corinthians 1–6, and contrasted with Paul's own principles of Christian leadership.
2005 / 1-84227-229-2 / 200pp

Stephen Finamore
God, Order and Chaos
René Girard and the Apocalypse
Readers are often disturbed by the images of destruction in the book of Revelation and unsure why they are unleashed after the exaltation of Jesus. This book examines past approaches to these texts and uses René Girard's theories to revive some old ideas and propose some new ones.
2005 / 1-84227-197-0 / approx. 344pp

David G. Firth
Surrendering Retribution in the Psalms
Responses to Violence in the Individual Complaints
In *Surrendering Retribution in the Psalms*, David Firth examines the ways in which the book of Psalms inculcates a model response to violence through the repetition of standard patterns of prayer. Rather than seeking justification for retributive violence, Psalms encourages not only a surrender of the right of retribution to Yahweh, but also sets limits on the retribution that can be sought in imprecations. Arising initially from the author's experience in South Africa, the possibilities of this model to a particular context of violence is then briefly explored.
2005 / 1-84227-337-X / xviii + 154pp

Scott J. Hafemann
Suffering and Ministry in the Spirit
Paul's Defence of His Ministry in II Corinthians 2:14–3:3
Shedding new light on the way Paul defended his apostleship, the author offers a careful, detailed study of 2 Corinthians 2:14–3:3 linked with other key passages throughout 1 and 2 Corinthians. Demonstrating the unity and coherence of Paul's argument in this passage, the author shows that Paul's suffering served as the vehicle for revealing God's power and glory through the Spirit.
2000 / 0-85364-967-7 / xiv + 262pp

Scott J. Hafemann
Paul, Moses and the History of Israel
The Letter/Spirit Contrast and the Argument from Scripture in 2 Corinthians 3
An exegetical study of the call of Moses, the second giving of the Law (Exodus 32–34), the new covenant, and the prophetic understanding of the history of Israel in 2 Corinthians 3. Hafemann's work demonstrates Paul's contextual use of the Old Testament and the essential unity between the Law and the Gospel within the context of the distinctive ministries of Moses and Paul.
2005 / 1-84227-317-5 / xii + 498pp

Douglas S. McComiskey
Lukan Theology in the Light of the Gospel's Literary Structure
Luke's Gospel was purposefully written with theology embedded in its patterned literary structure. A critical analysis of this cyclical structure provides new windows into Luke's interpretation of the individual pericopes comprising the Gospel and illuminates several of his theological interests.
2004 / 1-84227-148-2 / xviii + 388pp

Stephen Motyer
Your Father the Devil?
A New Approach to John and 'The Jews'
Who are 'the Jews' in John's Gospel? Defending John against the charge of antisemitism, Motyer argues that, far from demonising the Jews, the Gospel seeks to present Jesus as 'Good News for Jews' in a late first century setting.
1997 / 0-85364-832-8 / xiv + 260pp

Esther Ng.
Reconstructing Christian Origins?
The Feminist Theology of Elizabeth Schüssler Fiorenza: An Evaluation
In a detailed evaluation, the author challenges Elizabeth Schüssler Fiorenza's reconstruction of early Christian origins and her underlying presuppositions. The author also presents her own views on women's roles both then and now.
2002 / 1-84227-055-9 / xxiv + 468pp

July 2005

Robin Parry
Old Testament Story and Christian Ethics
The Rape of Dinah as a Case Study

What is the role of story in ethics and, more particularly, what is the role of Old Testament story in Christian ethics? This book, drawing on the work of contemporary philosophers, argues that narrative is crucial in the ethical shaping of people and, drawing on the work of contemporary Old Testament scholars, that story plays a key role in Old Testament ethics. Parry then argues that when situated in canonical context Old Testament stories can be reappropriated by Christian readers in their own ethical formation. The shocking story of the rape of Dinah and the massacre of the Shechemites provides a fascinating case study for exploring the parameters within which Christian ethical appropriations of Old Testament stories can live.

2004 / 1-84227-210-1 / xx + 350pp

Ian Paul
Power to See the World Anew
The Value of Paul Ricoeur's Hermeneutic of Metaphor in Interpreting the Symbolism of Revelation 12 and 13

This book is a study of the hermeneutics of metaphor of Paul Ricoeur, one of the most important writers on hermeneutics and metaphor of the last century. It sets out the key points of his theory, important criticisms of his work, and how his approach, modified in the light of these criticisms, offers a methodological framework for reading apocalyptic texts.

2006 / 1-84227-056-7 / approx. 350pp

Robert L. Plummer
Paul's Understanding of the Church's Mission
Did the Apostle Paul Expect the Early Christian Communities to Evangelize?

This book engages in a careful study of Paul's letters to determine if the apostle expected the communities to which he wrote to engage in missionary activity. It helpfully summarizes the discussion on this debated issue, judiciously handling contested texts, and provides a way forward in addressing this critical question. While admitting that Paul rarely explicitly commands the communities he founded to evangelize, Plummer amasses significant incidental data to provide a convincing case that Paul did indeed expect his churches to engage in mission activity. Throughout the study, Plummer progressively builds a theological basis for the church's mission that is both distinctively Pauline and compelling.

2006 / 1-84227-333-7 / approx. 324pp

David Powys
'Hell': A Hard Look at a Hard Question
The Fate of the Unrighteous in New Testament Thought

This comprehensive treatment seeks to unlock the original meaning of terms and phrases long thought to support the traditional doctrine of hell. It concludes that there is an alternative—one which is more biblical, and which can positively revive the rationale for Christian mission.

1997 / 0-85364-831-X / xxii + 478pp

Sorin Sabou
Between Horror and Hope
Paul's Metaphorical Language of Death in Romans 6.1-11

This book argues that Paul's metaphorical language of death in Romans 6.1-11 conveys two aspects: horror and hope. The 'horror' aspect is conveyed by the 'crucifixion' language, and the 'hope' aspect by 'burial' language. The life of the Christian believer is understood, as relationship with sin is concerned ('death to sin'), between these two realities: horror and hope.

2005 / 1-84227-322-1 / approx. 224pp

Rosalind Selby
The Comical Doctrine
The Epistemology of New Testament Hermeneutics

This book argues that the gospel breaks through postmodernity's critique of truth and the referential possibilities of textuality with its gift of grace. With a rigorous, philosophical challenge to modernist and postmodernist assumptions, Selby offers an alternative epistemology to all who would still read with faith *and* with academic credibility.

2005 / 1-84227-212-8 / approx. 350pp

Kiwoong Son
Zion Symbolism in Hebrews
Hebrews 12.18-24 as a Hermeneutical Key to the Epistle

This book challenges the general tendency of understanding the Epistle to the Hebrews against a Hellenistic background and suggests that the Epistle should be understood in the light of the Jewish apocalyptic tradition. The author especially argues for the importance of the theological symbolism of Sinai and Zion (Heb. 12:18-24) as it provides the Epistle's theological background as well as the rhetorical basis of the superiority motif of Jesus throughout the Epistle.

2005 / 1-84227-368-X / approx. 280pp

Kevin Walton
Thou Traveller Unknown
The Presence and Absence of God in the Jacob Narrative
The author offers a fresh reading of the story of Jacob in the book of Genesis through the paradox of divine presence and absence. The work also seeks to make a contribution to Pentateuchal studies by bringing together a close reading of the final text with historical critical insights, doing justice to the text's historical depth, final form and canonical status.
2003 / 1-84227-059-1 / xvi + 238pp

George M. Wieland
The Significance of Salvation
A Study of Salvation Language in the Pastoral Epistles
The language and ideas of salvation pervade the three Pastoral Epistles. This study offers a close examination of their soteriological statements. In all three letters the idea of salvation is found to play a vital paraenetic role, but each also exhibits distinctive soteriological emphases. The results challenge common assumptions about the Pastoral Epistles as a corpus.
2005 / 1-84227-257-8 / approx. 324pp

Alistair Wilson
When Will These Things Happen?
A Study of Jesus as Judge in Matthew 21–25
This study seeks to allow Matthew's carefully constructed presentation of Jesus to be given full weight in the modern evaluation of Jesus' eschatology. Careful analysis of the text of Matthew 21–25 reveals Jesus to be standing firmly in the Jewish prophetic and wisdom traditions as he proclaims and enacts imminent judgement on the Jewish authorities then boldly claims the central role in the final and universal judgement.
2004 / 1-84227-146-6 / xxii + 272pp

Lindsay Wilson
Joseph Wise and Otherwise
The Intersection of Covenant and Wisdom in Genesis 37–50
This book offers a careful literary reading of Genesis 37–50 that argues that the Joseph story contains both strong covenant themes and many wisdom-like elements. The connections between the two helps to explore how covenant and wisdom might intersect in an integrated biblical theology.
2004 / 1-84227-140-7 / xvi + 340pp

Stephen I. Wright
The Voice of Jesus
Studies in the Interpretation of Six Gospel Parables
This literary study considers how the 'voice' of Jesus has been heard in different periods of parable interpretation, and how the categories of figure and trope may help us towards a sensitive reading of the parables today.
2000 / 0-85364-975-8 / xiv + 280pp

Paternoster
9 Holdom Avenue,
Bletchley,
Milton Keynes MK1 1QR,
United Kingdom
Web: www.authenticmedia.co.uk/paternoster

Paternoster Theological Monographs

(All titles uniform with this volume)
Dates in bold are of projected publication

Emil Bartos
Deification in Eastern Orthodox Theology
An Evaluation and Critique of the Theology of Dumitru Staniloae

Bartos studies a fundamental yet neglected aspect of Orthodox theology: deification. By examining the doctrines of anthropology, christology, soteriology and ecclesiology as they relate to deification, he provides an important contribution to contemporary dialogue between Eastern and Western theologians.

1999 / 0-85364-956-1 / xii + 370pp

Graham Buxton
The Trinity, Creation and Pastoral Ministry
Imaging the Perichoretic God

In this book the author proposes a three-way conversation between theology, science and pastoral ministry. His approach draws on a Trinitarian understanding of God as a relational being of love, whose life 'spills over' into all created reality, human and non-human. By locating human meaning and purpose within God's 'creation-community' this book offers the possibility of a transforming engagement between those in pastoral ministry and the scientific community.

***2005** / 1-84227-369-8 / approx. 380 pp*

Iain D. Campbell
Fixing the Indemnity
The Life and Work of George Adam Smith

When Old Testament scholar George Adam Smith (1856–1942) delivered the Lyman Beecher lectures at Yale University in 1899, he confidently declared that 'modern criticism has won its war against traditional theories. It only remains to fix the amount of the indemnity.' In this biography, Iain D. Campbell assesses Smith's critical approach to the Old Testament and evaluates its consequences, showing that Smith's life and work still raises questions about the relationship between biblical scholarship and evangelical faith.

2004 / 1-84227-228-4 / xx + 256pp

Tim Chester
Mission and the Coming of God
Eschatology, the Trinity and Mission in the Theology of Jürgen Moltmann
This book explores the theology and missiology of the influential contemporary theologian, Jürgen Moltmann. It highlights the important contribution Moltmann has made while offering a critique of his thought from an evangelical perspective. In so doing, it touches on pertinent issues for evangelical missiology. The conclusion takes Calvin as a starting point, proposing 'an eschatology of the cross' which offers a critique of the over-realised eschatologies in liberation theology and certain forms of evangelicalism.
2006 / 1-84227-320-5 / approx. 224pp

Sylvia Wilkey Collinson
Making Disciples
The Significance of Jesus' Educational Strategy for Today's Church
This study examines the biblical practice of discipling, formulates a definition, and makes comparisons with modern models of education. A recommendation is made for greater attention to its practice today.
2004 / 1-84227-116-4 / xiv + 278pp

Darrell Cosden
A Theology of Work
Work and the New Creation
Through dialogue with Moltmann, Pope John Paul II and others, this book develops a genitive 'theology of work', presenting a theological definition of work and a model for a theological ethics of work that shows work's nature, value and meaning now and eschatologically. Work is shown to be a transformative activity consisting of three dynamically inter-related dimensions: the instrumental, relational and ontological.
2005 / 1-84227-332-9 / xvi + 208pp

Stephen M. Dunning
The Crisis and the Quest
A Kierkegaardian Reading of Charles Williams
Employing Kierkegaardian categories and analysis, this study investigates both the central crisis in Charles Williams's authorship between hermetism and Christianity (Kierkegaard's Religions A and B), and the quest to resolve this crisis, a quest that ultimately presses the bounds of orthodoxy.
2000 / 0-85364-985-5 / xxiv + 254pp

Keith Ferdinando
The Triumph of Christ in African Perspective
A Study of Demonology and Redemption in the African Context
The book explores the implications of the gospel for traditional African fears of occult aggression. It analyses such traditional approaches to suffering and biblical responses to fears of demonic evil, concluding with an evaluation of African beliefs from the perspective of the gospel.
1999 / 0-85364-830-1 / xviii + 450pp

Andrew Goddard
Living the Word, Resisting the World
The Life and Thought of Jacques Ellul
This work offers a definitive study of both the life and thought of the French Reformed thinker Jacques Ellul (1912-1994). It will prove an indispensable resource for those interested in this influential theologian and sociologist and for Christian ethics and political thought generally.
2002 / 1-84227-053-2 / xxiv + 378pp

David Hilborn
The Words of our Lips
Language-Use in Free Church Worship
Studies of liturgical language have tended to focus on the written canons of Roman Catholic and Anglican communities. By contrast David Hilborn analyses the more extemporary approach of English Nonconformity. Drawing on recent developments in linguistic pragmatics, he explores similarities and differences between 'fixed' and 'free' worship, and argues for the interdependence of each.
2006 / 0-85364-977-4 / approx. 350pp

Roger Hitching
The Church and Deaf People
A Study of Identity, Communication and Relationships with Special Reference to the Ecclesiology of Jürgen Moltmann
In *The Church and Deaf People* Roger Hitching sensitively examines the history and present experience of deaf people and finds similarities between aspects of sign language and Moltmann's theological method that 'open up' new ways of understanding theological concepts.
2003 / 1-84227-222-5 / xxii + 236pp

John G. Kelly
One God, One People
The Differentiated Unity of the People of God in the Theology of Jürgen Moltmann

The author expounds and critiques Moltmann's doctrine of God and highlights the systematic connections between it and Moltmann's influential discussion of Israel. He then proposes a fresh approach to Jewish–Christian relations building on Moltmann's work using insights from Habermas and Rawls.

2005 / 0-85346-969-3 / approx. 350pp

Mark F.W. Lovatt
Confronting the Will-to-Power
A Reconsideration of the Theology of Reinhold Niebuhr

Confronting the Will-to-Power is an analysis of the theology of Reinhold Niebuhr, arguing that his work is an attempt to identify, and provide a practical theological answer to, the existence and nature of human evil.

2001 / 1-84227-054-0 / xviii + 216pp

Neil B. MacDonald
Karl Barth and the Strange New World within the Bible
Barth, Wittgenstein, and the Metadilemmas of the Enlightenment

Barth's discovery of the strange new world within the Bible is examined in the context of Kant, Hume, Overbeck, and, most importantly, Wittgenstein. MacDonald covers some fundamental issues in theology today: epistemology, the final form of the text and biblical truth-claims.

2000 / 0-85364-970-7 / xxvi + 374pp

Keith A. Mascord
Alvin Plantinga and Christian Apologetics

This book draws together the contributions of the philosopher Alvin Plantinga to the major contemporary challenges to Christian belief, highlighting in particular his ground-breaking work in epistemology and the problem of evil. Plantinga's theory that both theistic and Christian belief is warrantedly basic is explored and critiqued, and an assessment offered as to the significance of his work for apologetic theory and practice.

2005 / 1-84227-256-X / approx. 304pp

Gillian McCulloch
The Deconstruction of Dualism in Theology
With Reference to Ecofeminist Theology and New Age Spirituality
This book challenges eco-theological anti-dualism in Christian theology, arguing that dualism has a twofold function in Christian religious discourse. Firstly, it enables us to express the discontinuities and divisions that are part of the process of reality. Secondly, dualistic language allows us to express the mysteries of divine transcendence/immanence and the survival of the soul without collapsing into monism and materialism, both of which are problematic for Christian epistemology.
2002 / 1-84227-044-3 / xii + 282pp

Leslie McCurdy
Attributes and Atonement
The Holy Love of God in the Theology of P.T. Forsyth
Attributes and Atonement is an intriguing full-length study of P.T. Forsyth's doctrine of the cross as it relates particularly to God's holy love. It includes an unparalleled bibliography of both primary and secondary material relating to Forsyth.
1999 / 0-85364-833-6 / xiv + 328pp

Nozomu Miyahira
Towards a Theology of the Concord of God
A Japanese Perspective on the Trinity
This book introduces a new Japanese theology and a unique Trinitarian formula based on the Japanese intellectual climate: three betweennesses and one concord. It also presents a new interpretation of the Trinity, a co-subordinationism, which is in line with orthodox Trinitarianism; each single person of the Trinity is eternally and equally subordinate (or serviceable) to the other persons, so that they retain the mutual dynamic equality.
2000 / 0-85364-863-8 / xiv + 256pp

Eddy José Muskus
The Origins and Early Development of Liberation Theology in Latin America
With Particular Reference to Gustavo Gutiérrez
This work challenges the fundamental premise of Liberation Theology, 'opting for the poor', and its claim that Christ is found in them. It also argues that Liberation Theology emerged as a direct result of the failure of the Roman Catholic Church in Latin America.
2002 / 0-85364-974-X / xiv + 296pp

Jim Purves
The Triune God and the Charismatic Movement
A Critical Appraisal from a Scottish Perspective

All emotion and no theology? Or a fundamental challenge to reappraise and realign our trinitarian theology in the light of Christian experience? This study of charismatic renewal as it found expression within Scotland at the end of the twentieth century evaluates the use of Patristic, Reformed and contemporary models of the Trinity in explaining the workings of the Holy Spirit.

2004 / 1-84227-321-3 / xxiv + 246pp

Anna Robbins
Methods in the Madness
Diversity in Twentieth-Century Christian Social Ethics

The author compares the ethical methods of Walter Rauschenbusch, Reinhold Niebuhr and others. She argues that unless Christians are clear about the ways that theology and philosophy are expressed practically they may lose the ability to discuss social ethics across contexts, let alone reach effective agreements.

2004 / 1-84227-211-X / xx + 294pp

Ed Rybarczyk
Beyond Salvation
Eastern Orthodoxy and Classical Pentecostalism on Becoming Like Christ

At first glance eastern Orthodoxy and classical Pentecostalism seem quite distinct. This ground-breaking study shows they share much in common, especially as it concerns the experiential elements of following Christ. Both traditions assert that authentic Christianity transcends the wooden categories of modernism.

2004 / 1-84227-144-X / xii + 356pp

Signe Sandsmark
Is World View Neutral Education Possible and Desirable?
A Christian Response to Liberal Arguments
(Published jointly with The Stapleford Centre)

This book discusses reasons for belief in world view neutrality, and argues that 'neutral' education will have a hidden, but strong world view influence. It discusses the place for Christian education in the common school.

2000 / 0-85364-973-1 / xiv + 182pp

Hazel Sherman
Reading Zechariah
The Allegorical Tradition of Biblical Interpretation through the Commentary of Didymus the Blind and Theodore of Mopsuestia

A close reading of the commentary on Zechariah by Didymus the Blind alongside that of Theodore of Mopsuestia suggests that popular categorising of Antiochene and Alexandrian biblical exegesis as 'historical' or 'allegorical' is inadequate and misleading.

2005 / 1-84227-213-6 / approx. 280pp

Andrew Sloane
On Being a Christian in the Academy
Nicholas Wolterstorff and the Practice of Christian Scholarship

An exposition and critical appraisal of Nicholas Wolterstorff's epistemology in the light of the philosophy of science, and an application of his thought to the practice of Christian scholarship.

2003 / 1-84227-058-3 / xvi + 274pp

Damon W.K. So
Jesus' Revelation of His Father
A Narrative-Conceptual Study of the Trinity with Special Reference to Karl Barth

This book explores the trinitarian dynamics in the context of Jesus' revelation of his Father in his earthly ministry with references to key passages in Matthew's Gospel. It develops from the exegeses of these passages a non-linear concept of revelation which links Jesus' communion with his Father to his revelatory words and actions through a nuanced understanding of the Holy Spirit, with references to K. Barth, G.W.H. Lampe, J.D.G. Dunn and E. Irving.

2005 / 1-84227-323-X / approx. 380pp

Daniel Strange
The Possibility of Salvation Among the Unevangelised
An Analysis of Inclusivism in Recent Evangelical Theology

For evangelical theologians the 'fate of the unevangelised' impinges upon fundamental tenets of evangelical identity. The position known as 'inclusivism', defined by the belief that the unevangelised can be ontologically saved by Christ whilst being epistemologically unaware of him, has been defended most vigorously by the Canadian evangelical Clark H. Pinnock. Through a detailed analysis and critique of Pinnock's work, this book examines a cluster of issues surrounding the unevangelised and its implications for christology, soteriology and the doctrine of revelation.

2002 / 1-84227-047-8 / xviii + 362pp

Scott Swain
God According to the Gospel
Biblical Narrative and the Identity of God in the Theology of Robert W. Jenson
Robert W. Jenson is one of the leading voices in contemporary Trinitarian theology. His boldest contribution in this area concerns his use of biblical narrative both to ground and explicate the Christian doctrine of God. *God According to the Gospel* critically examines Jenson's proposal and suggests an alternative way of reading the biblical portrayal of the triune God.
2006 / 1-84227-258-6 / approx. 180pp

Justyn Terry
The Justifying Judgement of God
A Reassessment of the Place of Judgement in the Saving Work of Christ
The argument of this book is that judgement, understood as the whole process of bringing justice, is the primary metaphor of atonement, with others, such as victory, redemption and sacrifice, subordinate to it. Judgement also provides the proper context for understanding penal substitution and the call to repentance, baptism, eucharist and holiness.
2005 / 1-84227-370-1 / approx. 274 pp

Graham Tomlin
The Power of the Cross
Theology and the Death of Christ in Paul, Luther and Pascal
This book explores the theology of the cross in St Paul, Luther and Pascal. It offers new perspectives on the theology of each, and some implications for the nature of power, apologetics, theology and church life in a postmodern context.
1999 / 0-85364-984-7 / xiv + 344pp

Adonis Vidu
Postliberal Theological Method
A Critical Study
The postliberal theology of Hans Frei, George Lindbeck, Ronald Thiemann, John Milbank and others is one of the more influential contemporary options. This book focuses on several aspects pertaining to its theological method, specifically its understanding of background, hermeneutics, epistemic justification, ontology, the nature of doctrine and, finally, Christological method.
2005 / 1-84227-395-7 / approx. 324pp

Graham J. Watts
Revelation and the Spirit
A Comparative Study of the Relationship between the Doctrine of Revelation and Pneumatology in the Theology of Eberhard Jüngel and of Wolfhart Pannenberg

The relationship between revelation and pneumatology is relatively unexplored. This approach offers a fresh angle on two important twentieth century theologians and raises pneumatological questions which are theologically crucial and relevant to mission in a postmodern culture.

2005 / 1-84227-104-0 / xxii + 232pp

Nigel G. Wright
Disavowing Constantine
Mission, Church and the Social Order in the Theologies of John Howard Yoder and Jürgen Moltmann

This book is a timely restatement of a radical theology of church and state in the Anabaptist and Baptist tradition. Dr Wright constructs his argument in dialogue and debate with Yoder and Moltmann, major contributors to a free church perspective.

2000 / 0-85364-978-2 / xvi + 252pp

Paternoster
9 Holdom Avenue,
Bletchley,
Milton Keynes MK1 1QR,
United Kingdom
Web: www.authenticmedia.co.uk/paternoster

July 2005

www.ingramcontent.com/pod-product-compliance
Lightning Source LLC
Chambersburg PA
CBHW070234230426
43664CB00014B/2301